A New History of the United States

OTHER BOOKS BY WILLIAM MILLER

THE AGE OF ENTERPRISE: A Social History of Industrial America (with T. C. Cochran) 1942

THE BOOK INDUSTRY 1949

MEN IN BUSINESS 1952

THE UNITED STATES: The History of a Republic (with Richard Hofstadter and Daniel Aaron) 1957

A NEW HISTORY
OF THE
UNITED STATES

By William Miller

GEORGE BRAZILLER, INC.
NEW YORK—1958

The author and publisher gratefully acknowledge permission to use selections
from the following books and poems:

The quotations on page 319 from "The White-Man's Burden" by Rudyard
Kipling in *The Five Nations* by Rudyard Kipling, published by Doubleday &
Company, Inc., in the United States, by the Macmillan Co. of Canada Ltd.
in Canada, and by Methuen & Co. Ltd. in the British Commonwealth and
Empire other than Canada. With the permission of Mrs. George Bambridge
and the publishers.

The quotations on pages 368-369 from "The Dispossessed," reprinted by
special permission from the February 1940 issue of *Fortune Magazine;*
Copyright 1940 by Time Inc.

The quotations on pages 189-190 from *The Mind of the South* by W. J.
Cash, published by Alfred A. Knopf, Inc., with the permission of Alfred A.
Knopf, Inc.

The quotations on page 287 from "Unguarded Gates," by Thomas Bailey
Aldrich in *American Issues* by Thomas Bailey Aldrich, published by J. B.
Lippincott Company.

The quotations on page 348 from "The Hill" by Edgar Lee Masters in
Spoon River Anthology by Edgar Lee Masters, published by The Macmillan
Company. With the permission of Mrs. Edgar Lee Masters.

The quotation on page 393 from *The Growth of the American Republic,*
Volume 2, by S. E. Morison and H. S. Commager, published by the Oxford
University Press, Inc., and with the permission of the publisher.

The quotations on pages 250-251 from *The Cowboy* by P. A. Rollins, pp.
253-255, published by Charles Scribner's Sons, and with the permission of
the publisher.

LIBRARY OF CONGRESS CATALOG CARD NUMBER: 58-11479

PRINTED IN THE UNITED STATES OF AMERICA BY
KINGSPORT PRESS, INC., KINGSPORT, TENNESSEE

For VIRGINIA, GREG *and* PAT

Contents

Maps

Prepared especially for this book by Theodore R. Miller

Acknowledgments

In writing this *New History of the United States* I have had counsel from my scholarly friends. I especially wish to acknowledge the enlightening criticism I received from Professors Frank Freidel of Harvard, Richard Hofstadter of Columbia, Robert R. Palmer of Princeton, and Frank Thistlethwaite of St. John's College, Cambridge (England), all of whom were generous enough to read much of this work in manuscript; and Professors Fred H. Harrington of Wisconsin and William E. Leuchtenburg of Columbia, who read the work in galleys. None, of course, is responsible for any errors that may remain or for interpretations in which I have persisted.

I also wish to express my appreciation to Howard Warrington and Prentice-Hall, Inc., for permission to adapt, especially in chapters five and nine of the present work, certain material I wrote originally for their publication, *The United States: The History of a Republic,* of which they own the copyright.

It is a pleasure for me to acknowledge the talented and willing service of my typist, Mrs. Christine G. Loring.

WILLIAM MILLER

Ridgefield, Conn.
April, 1958

Introduction

Amid the continuing flow of writings on American history, this is one of the few notable books to address itself to the mature general reader. Those who would like to explore the fascinating "why" of American history, cutting loose from much irrelevant detail and soaring beyond textbook accounts, will find William Miller's *A New History of the United States* exciting and enlightening. They will learn what I should think adults would like to know about their nation's development.

Far too many Americans by the time they leave school have learned and re-learned certain aspects of United States history to a point of bored indifference. In elementary grades they were exposed to the early explorers and the Founding Fathers; later they memorized lists of elections, tariffs, and treaties. At worst, they acquired a factual knowledge of the bare bones of history which enabled them to answer true-false examinations, and prepared them better to participate in quiz shows than to understand their nation's past. They studied not enough of the "why" and too much of the "what."

Some fortunate others have retained their excitement about American history because they took some of the truly excellent history courses in which they learned not only relevant facts but also their meaning. They became familiar with the flesh and sinew as well as the bones of history, and it had some value for them besides that of obtaining a passing grade. Even this happy minority will profit from Miller's reappraisal because it will direct their minds, now older and more sophisticated, in new directions.

The reading of good history is a continuing quest for those meaningful parts of our distinctive past that can help us understand the patterns of the present and the directions of the future. Each age in consequence has developed its own syntheses of American history.

The historians and chroniclers among the early settlers saw divine manifestations in many natural phenomena, and the shaping of American destiny through a wonder-working providence. Most of the generation of the Founding Fathers and their immediate successors turned to history and biography as eulogistic patriotic exercises to build fervid support for the young republic and its leaders. The founders became noble, veracious, and infallible—in every way Olympian.

Still later generations after the Civil War, seeking to be more scientific than their forebears, discarded the myth of the cherry tree, but continued to look with awe upon the gallery of national heroes from Washington through Abraham Lincoln and Robert E. Lee, as being almost superhuman in their perfection. The emphasis continued to be upon political and constitutional development—or in more scholarly works, on the origins and growth of governmental institutions. For the most part history seemed to reinforce reverence for existing institutions, to be a handmaiden of the defenders of the status quo. Its task was more to support than to explain the America of the Gilded Age.

Toward the end of the nineteenth century, as the forces of reform which precipitated the Progressive era began to gather strength, a search for new themes and a new iconoclasm wrought a revolution in historical writing. In 1893, Frederick Jackson Turner, speaking at the Chicago World's Fair, argued that the main influence on American history was not the development of political institutions from obscure Roman or Germanic origins, but the impact of the frontier upon American society. As historians explored and exaggerated Turner's thesis, they wrote a new and even more nationalistic America saga hailing western settlement, development of transportation and communication, and the exploits of the heroic, democratic frontiersman. Other Progressives, critical of the malfunctioning of some governmental institutions which had become sacred with time, began to challenge the Olympian position of the Founding Fathers. Charles A. Beard created an uproar in 1913 by suggesting that in part economic motives had led them to frame the Constitution.

As Turner introduced western expansion as a theme in American history, so Beard established economic factors. In the 1920s, social history received a new emphasis as Arthur M. Schlesinger and Dixon Ryan Fox began editing the *History of American Life* series. In 1927, Vernon L. Parrington published the first two volumes of *Main Currents in American Thought,* which in ardently Jeffersonian terms appraised American intellectual history. Out of this broadening of the horizons of the historians came new general studies of American history which did far more than any of their predecessors to explain the past and throw light on the present. Outstanding among these general works was *The Rise of American Civilization* by Charles and Mary Beard, published in 1927.

Not all of the new history was as wise and mellow as it might have been. Just as some of the most ardent of Turner's followers made all history revolve around the West, some who followed in Beard's footsteps saw it wholly in economic determinist terms or forced it into a crude Marxist mold. Others, fascinated by the ideas of Freud, tried to fit biography into a rigidly psychoanalytic pattern —thus trying to explain a spectacular political career in terms of a painful sibling relationship. Still others, caught up in the iconoclastic spirit of the twenties, tore from Washington and other heroes not only their pedestals, but most of their dignity, and all of their meaning.

William Miller's *A New History of the United States* succeeds in escaping entirely the pitfalls of the painfully modern "interpretations." At the same time it offers the reader a view of American history illuminated by the best modern work in the different fields of social thought.

In *A New History of the United States*, the reader will find a judicious interweaving in bright hues of many of the themes of American history. To Miller, the warp is not political development or a synthesis of Presidents, but the explosion out of Europe onto American soil of vigorous, ambitious people, bringing with them long-established institutions which underwent rapid modification in the New World. The central thread is economic not of a doctrinaire determinist sort, but complex and everchanging, interacting with social, intellectual, and political forces. The emphasis is upon people and events, and out of these grows the synthesis.

The viewpoint is necessarily different from that of earlier surveys of American history. William Miller has written from the vantage point of the middle of the twentieth century, in an age of growing organization of men and machines at home, and of frantic quest to maintain a precarious "balance of terror" in a thermonuclear world. He has stressed those factors which help explain how we have arrived at this era, and has sketched the traditions and institutions which are helping to shape our future. This is peculiarly American history for today.

FRANK FREIDEL

A New History of the United States

Chapter One

The Four Worlds of the Fifteenth Century

The very first map to show the New World was that drawn in 1500 by Juan de la Cosa, the best cartographer of the day, who had shipped with Columbus on his voyages of discovery in 1492 and 1493. Like his rivals, Cosa dressed up his map with ships, castles, Madonnas, kings, and other talismans and trumpery. But most conspicuous among his renderings, and most meaningful, was one of huge St. Christopher bearing Christ on his back through "that river without a bridge which can only be crossed at great peril of drowning." "Do thou who art so tall and strong," a holy hermit is said to have advised the pagan giant seeking Christ, "take up thine abode by the hither bank, and assist poor travelers to cross; that will be very agreeable to Our Lord, and mayhap He will show Himself to thee." Christopher did the hermit's bidding and one night a small Child cried out for help. He taxed the incredulous giant with the weight of "the whole world and Him Who created it," yet was deposited safely on the other side. Christopher means "bearer of Christ"; as Cosa knew, it was more than a name to Columbus.

Christopher Columbus, whose own unusual height and shock of red hair lent him greater distinction than his origins, was born in 1451 in the declining city of Genoa to an artisan's family that had seen its best days. In his boyhood, everyone was familiar with the legends of the Saints, not least with that of Columbus's Patron. In the troubled times of the waning Middle Ages faith itself had come to rest largely on the belief in saintly intercession, and the superstition had become common that "it sufficed to have looked

3

at a St. Christopher, painted or carved, to be protected for the rest of the day from a fatal end." This superstition Columbus may well have shared. In later years of bedevilment and frowning fortune, in any case, his Saint's connection with it helped sustain Columbus's faith in his own ever weightier project.

Mysticism and materialism were well mixed in the obsessed and ambitious discoverer. In the opening paragraphs of the journal of his first voyage, he laid out this program for his venture, his life, and his eternal reward:

"By the route of the Occident," the route "by which no one to this day knows for sure that anyone has gone," he would sail to the world of the Great Khan of the Indies, incidentally making "a new chart of navigation" as he went. On arrival he would seek out "the manner in which may be undertaken the conversion to our Holy Faith" of the "princes and peoples" there. This accomplished, he would enlist the converts in Christendom's life and death struggle with the world of Islam from which Spain herself, after seven hundred years, had only just won her freedom. And for all this, the King and Queen of Spain would provide "that henceforth I might call myself by a noble title and be Admiral-in-Chief of the Ocean Sea and Viceroy and Perpetual Governor of all the islands and mainlands that I should discover . . . and that my eldest son should succeed me, and thus from rank to rank for ever."

THE TROUBLED WORLD OF CHRISTENDOM

No age—unless it be our own—needed a "New World" more than the age of Columbus. During the century before his birth the whole of Christendom had been staggered by visitations that drove most men to the edge of sanity and many thousands mad. In the 1340s and 1350s epidemics of bubonic plague, of which the Black Death of 1348 was only the most severe, wiped out a third of the people of western Europe. A hundred years of almost continuous warfare then cut down the flower of the surviving families. The destruction of property and the breakdown of production became such that the land could no longer support even the remaining population, and starvation added hideously to the epoch's toll.

This was not all. The enduring calamity in feudal agriculture was matched by a century of faltering trade. Commodities of every sort became so scarce in Christendom that prices rose continually, mocking even the wealth of kings. Land-poor nobles struggling to keep face at court, to maintain soldiers in the field, and to offer respectable hospitality at home, faced an ever-worsening predicament. The boldest of them set up as robber barons and waylaid defenseless travelers for the gold they carried. Others, in place of the customary feudal services, increasingly demanded money rents and other money payments of their impoverished serfs. For some serfs this marked the beginning of freedom of contract and a step toward citizenship. But it only ground down most of those who clung to the old ways on the stricken soil, and transformed many of those who fled into beggars, scavengers, thieves, and convicts.

In the half-deserted villages and the stagnant commercial towns, the loss of opportunity and the loss of hope, as a fourteenth-century chronicler says, turned men of all classes into "brutes devoid of sense and reason." Insurrections against the rural aristocracy and against town businessmen who fiercely hugged their old commercial and industrial monopolies became commonplace. And eventually the popular uprisings grew so morbidly—so aimlessly —bloodthirsty that "men became disgusted with life."

Nor could they find solace in religion. In the thirteenth century the Roman Catholic Church had attained its greatest power. Economically, it owned the most land and had the largest income in Europe; spiritually, it engaged the profound allegiance of the people; politically, it dominated their worldly lords. But the Church, like society, had fallen upon evil days. The very Crusades, by which in the twelfth century it temporarily recaptured and held the Holy Land from the infidel, had tempted its soldiers and pilgrims with the vast and beguiling riches and the pagan learning of the East. This helped to secularize the faithful. As feudalism declined, moreover, national kings grew in power and pretense and a run of venal popes began to cater to them. Gradually this tarnished the spiritual charm of the Church, weakened its political grip, and reduced its wealth.

Corruption then fed upon itself. To maintain Church income,

Church offices, not excepting the Papacy, were with growing frequency auctioned off. To reimburse the purchasers and assuage their cravings, sins were ever more often remitted for a price, and business in relics boomed. The superstitious remained in awe and terror of the Church. But in the fifteenth century more and more cynics came to see it simply as a gilded engine of extortion, while the pure in heart and humble in spirit quaked before its offenses to Christ.

Strong-minded evangelists—or puritans, as they came to be called—from time to time had sought to reform the Church and rediscover the Saviour. They were abetted after 1450 by the circulation of the first printed Bibles, many editions of which were promptly translated from dead Latin into the common tongues of the day. These opened the message of Christ to the individual and at the same time sapped the authority of the shameless clergy. But the Popes responded to the alleged heresies that resulted by making the Inquisition all the more indiscriminate and heartless, while they themselves sank deeper into Babylonian plots and pleasures. The same churchmen who patronized the masterful artists, scientists, poets, and philosophers of the early Renaissance also openly sired families, maintained harems in the Vatican, and kidnaped and murdered for ransom.

There were half-decades of peace in Christendom in the fifteenth century which interrupted the downward tendency of trade, and islands of security and learning where men preserved the knowledge of the world that trade brought. Yet for most of the time and most of the people Europe remained an afflicted place. In it, as the poet Langland wrote as early as the 1370s, men "more or less mad according as the moon sits," walk "witless but with good will in many wide countries." Thereafter even this blank "good will" faded. Catholics deliriously embracing ghostly skeletons began performing the Dance of Death in cemeteries, while the Black Mass became as common as the Holy one, its furtive ceremonies parodying ritual in shocking ways to appease the Devil. Until this demented epoch, the execution of persons accused as witches had been deemed murder by the Church; but this did not save tens of thousands from zealots who tortured them into confessions anyway and burned them alive. After 1485 the Church openly sanctioned this means of dispatching the Devil's alleged collaborators and the toll of witches soared.

THE ENCROACHING WORLD OF ISLAM

But these evidences of mass hysteria did not persist simply because of the state of society and the sins of the Church. For ominously confronting the unhinged world of Christendom in the fifteenth century, and indeed conspiring within its gates, was the newly aggressive world of Islam, itself the brutally degenerate heir to a wealthier and more brilliant culture than most of Europe had yet seen. It is customary to think of the warm Mediterranean as the very womb and haven of western culture. But as late as 1492, even the rock of Gibraltar remained an Islamic—or Moslem—stronghold, while on every shore, except in Italy, France, and part of Spain, the mother sea laved only Mohammedan lands.

Mohammed of Mecca, the founder of Islam, had been anything but a "weaponless prophet." By waylaying Arab merchant caravans to feed his first few impoverished followers early in the seventh century, he proved his mettle to the warlike Bedouins of the desert. In the next hundred years, newly inspired by one God, Allah, these fighters overran much of Asia, Africa, and southwestern Europe. Most of the peoples of these lands they converted to the easy brotherhood of Islam. Those they failed to convert they usually tolerated for a price in tribute. Often they also enlisted their captives' assistance in governing and in acquiring the urban amenities of life. Thus from Persians, Jews, Hindus, Moors, Egyptians, Greeks, and others, Moslem culture in succeeding centuries absorbed the legends, lore, and learning of the world.

Within the borders of Islam at the start of the Crusades late in the eleventh century lay most of the great cities known to man: Cairo and Alexandria, Bagdad, Antioch, and Damascus, Tabriz and Samarkand, and of course Jerusalem. To such cities (known collectively as the Levant, or the land of the rising sun) the luxuries of the fabled and still farther East found their way, to be distributed more deeply into Islam and into poorer Christendom. Everything valued by the upper classes was available in the Levant.

Spices and herbs that turned pabulum into delicacies for the improving European palate; brilliant dyes for domestic cloth; delicate silks and cottons; artful tapestries; exquisite glassware; splendid rugs and robes; and above all precious metals wrought into breathtaking forms and figures, and precious stones of unheard-of size and brilliance—all these, their intrinsic wonders in no way diminished by the mysterious remoteness of their origins, were to be had there for a price.

Italian traders were visiting Levantine cities for such goods long before the first Crusade in 1095. It was in the following two hundred and fifty years, however, that merchants of Venice, Genoa, and Pisa, much enriched by carrying millions of European pilgrims to the Holy Land, established and enlarged their own Levantine headquarters. Often these were on land that Christians captured from Arabs while allegedly in quest of the Holy Sepulcher. As the Italians' trade grew, middlemen in the rest of Christendom also flourished, and this in turn gave an impetus to Europe's own industry, finance, and internal commerce. The resulting general prosperity lent a sheen of justification to Church exactions and a simulacrum of peace to Christian life.

But even in the expansive years of the twelfth and thirteenth centuries peace bred confidence and confidence aggression. The initial victories of the first Crusade prompted Christendom's general offensive against Islam. Islam's own victories transformed the Mediterranean into a virtual Mohammedan lake and sent Christian missionaries and explorers seeking aid and allies in the Orient.

Islam itself, however, had been victimized before her conquests in Christendom were won. Early in the thirteenth century the Mongols of deepest Asia, under the incredible Ghengis Khan, crashed the great wall of China, and after securing for themselves the immense wealth of Cathay, started to expand westward. This drive eventually pressed upon other peoples, among them the terrifying Turks. These particular infidels (an epithet they felt free to lavish upon Christians later) had come together as the well-mounted remnants of a once imposing Seljuk empire to the north and east of Allah's outposts in Asia. The Mongol hordes forced the Turks into Islam itself; whence about 1300 under the wary leader-

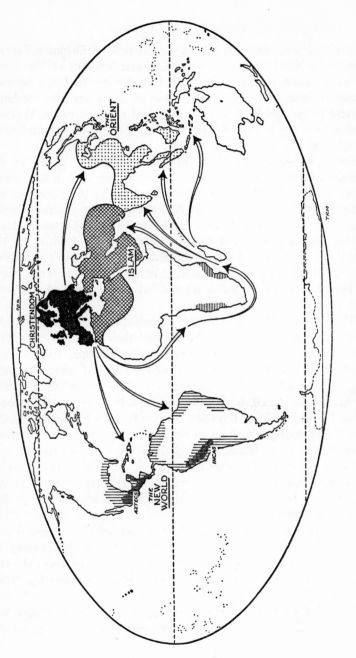

Expansions of European Cultures: Fifteenth and Sixteenth Centuries

ship of their chief Othman (hence the designation, Ottoman Turks), they began nibbling on the exposed Asiatic holdings of the supine Greek Catholic regime centered in Constantinople. Fired by easy successes here, Othman's heirs next eyed the richer Moslem lands around them, and by 1350 not only had subdued much Mohammedan territory in Asia Minor but had themselves succumbed to its religion.

By then warring Christian princes had long engaged in the practice of inviting Moslem troops to assist them in their feudal and imperial wars. In 1345, when the succession to the throne of the Greek Catholic Empire was in doubt, one of the aspirants again turned to Islam for aid. This fateful move brought the barbaric Turks, headlong ambition riding with them, into Europe for the first time. At the very juncture, indeed, when western Christendom was sent reeling by its own internal catastrophes, the Turks were on hand to take over the defense and indeed the renewed onslaught of Islam.

The Turks rode as well as any Comanche Indian ever did, and ahorse in the heat of battle brandished their scimitars with consummate and conclusive art. On entering Europe, their leaders augmented this irresistible cavalry with the most fanatical infantry corps Christendom had yet encountered. These were the renowned Janissaries, recruited, barbarously enough, from among the strongest and most intelligent boys of Christian families in captured lands. The Turks took these boys at the age of ten or twelve, forcibly converted them to Islam, isolated them for military training, and schooled them for six years to carry out only the more zealously the dying admonition of old Othman himself: "Rejoice my departed soul with a beautiful series of victories, and when thou art become conqueror of the world, propagate religion by thy arms." In the hundred years culminating in the sack of Constantinople in 1453, this professional army of Janissaries was the scourge of Europe. In the following half-century it not only reached the gates of Vienna and threatened dissolute and shivering Rome itself, but also moved outward in Asia and Africa.

Long before this the empire of the great Mongol Khans had started to fall apart and its own internal wars had disrupted the movement of far Eastern goods to Islam and injured the Arab and Italian trade. The Turks, who had no sense of Arabic culture and only contempt for commerce, next had made things much worse by preying upon Christian establishments in the Levant. The withdrawal of credit and the demand of payment in gold ruined many old Italian firms. Those allowed to continue were deprived of their privileges and exorbitantly taxed. The pressure thus placed upon Venice, Genoa, and Pisa even before the end of the fourteenth century drove them into suicidal warfare among themselves. Gradually the faltering trickle of goods from the Orient, especially the spices which had become virtual necessities in Europe, sought longer, costlier, but supposedly safer routes. Trade revived, but hazards to trade multiplied and hemmed it in.

THE FANTASY WORLD OF THE ORIENT

How deeply into Africa and Asia did Mohammedan lands extend? What peoples lived beyond their limits? How could encroaching Islam be outflanked and succor and sustenance brought to Christendom from the outside—from distant lands, real or hungrily imagined, to whose existence legend, hearsay, rumor, and invention testified? Such questions tugged at the hearts of certain Christian princes throughout the fifteenth century. For answers they gathered around them all the learned men they could find and all the books. "You who wish to learn of the coasts of countries," Henry VII of England was told, "must learn . . . what Strabo, Ptolemy, Pliny, and Isidore taught." But practical ends required more practical means than these promptings of the medieval spirit; action required better guides than the contradictions of ancient pundits, hope greater optimism than the crabbed cackling of the monasteries. "No man sailing south of [Africa's] Cape Bajodar returns alive," said one medieval monk. "God willed not that men should be able to sail over the whole world," advised another. But on what authority? The rising princes and sailors of the fifteenth century decided they had better find these things out for themselves. The guiding geniuses among them were Prince Dom Enrique of Portugal, better known as Henry the Navigator, and Christopher Columbus.

Somewhere in the distant East—or was it the distant South?—lay the land of Prester (that is, "Presbyter" or "Priest") John, a Christian potentate grown incredibly strong in the defense and propagation of the faith in a heathen world—or so rumor said. No reliable reports of him were to be had. Was not he the one to come to the aid of God's children in Europe? Dom Enrique meant to find him and inquire.

Somewhere more distant still lay the yet richer "lands of India, and . . . a prince who is called 'Grand Khan' which is to say . . . 'King of Kings.' I have given Your Highnesses full information," Columbus wrote to Ferdinand and Isabella, "how many times he and his ancestors had sent to Rome to seek doctors in our Holy Faith to instruct him therein, and that never had the Holy Father provided them, and thus were lost so many people through lapsing into idolatries and receiving doctrines of perdition." May he not yet be converted to the faith of Christ and conscripted in its defense against "the abominable sect of Mahomet?"

What did it matter that Prester John was to prove to be nothing more than an Abyssinian native chieftain, and that the entire dynasty of "Grand Khans" had collapsed back in 1368? No one in Europe was aware of this and Christendom's need was great.

Other motives also wove themselves into the Oriental pattern. Like many Italians, Giovanni Caboto, for example, had visited Mecca in the spice trade, and "when he asked those who brought them what was the place of origin of these spices, they answered that they did not know, but that other caravans came with this merchandise to their homes from distant countries, and these again said that the goods had been brought to them from other remote regions. He therefore reasons that if the easterners declare to the southerners that these things come from places far away from them and so on from one to the other . . . presupposing the rotundity of the earth . . . it follows as a matter of course that the last of all must take them in the north towards the west." Caboto arrived in England in the late 1480s aflame with this idea, and, as John Cabot, in 1496 got the backing of Henry VII to seek their mutual fortunes by testing its validity.

The overwhelming depression in fifteenth-century Christendom ruined many of the great families that had survived plague and famine and war; slowly new men of resolution and talent like Columbus and Cabot appeared who found paths to the mighty open, and opportunity ultimately to be had. To such men religion and its forms as often served to justify as to inspire action, and usually they did not scruple to decide which. If myth and legend and ancient saws—religious and pagan both—terrified or paralyzed most, a few found in them the hint, the goad, the lure, the massive compulsion to seek God and truth and gold all at once. In the fifteenth century the weakening of the faith helped to dissipate the prestige of its healers; the catastrophes at home to dissipate fear of venturing abroad; the scale of the reward to dissipate anxieties about dark and unknown risks. Indeed, little could be lost; the whole world might be won for God; and in it nobodies might rise and set up gilded dynasties of their own.

Not everyone looked at life this way; like the Galileos, Darwins, and Freuds of the future who would add whole worlds to the universe of knowledge, Henry the Navigator until "Gold made a recantation of former Murmurings" had to endure "what every barking tongue could allege against a Service so unserviceable and needless." Yet for the few determined to act there were plenty of exhilarating clues, and intriguing if shadowy suggestions. Here and there were also kindred souls working to improve ships, instruments, and knowledge of navigation; and yet others, desperate or forlorn or simply eager, with neither science nor faith to sustain them but ready to man the ships and let the Devil do his worst. To such men a knowledge of coasts, as had been dangled before Henry VII, was all very well for a start; but gradually they ventured ever deeper on *mare tenebrosum,* "the green sea of gloom," as the Moslems called the forbidding Atlantic, ever farther out of sight of dear, familiar shores, until they circumnavigated the globe.

Portugal, at land's end, led the way. By 1250 Portugal had become the first European nation occupied by Islam to throw off its yoke. Trade treaties with Venice and England followed and led to the development of her fleet, her sailors, and her knowledge of Atlantic navigation. After recovering from the Black Death she was eager to carry the fight against the Moslems right to Africa. And after spectacular successes in north Africa in 1415, Henry the Navigator, a prince of the ruling family, set up his famous Naval Arsenal at Sagres, "where two seas, the Mediterranean and the Great Ocean, fight together." From here he would explore the whole coast of Africa to discover the southern limits of Islam and a water route around them to Eastern allies.

Until his death in 1460 Dom Enrique sent expedition after expedition ever farther down the western coast of Africa and had his extraordinary staff of experts study every bit of information they brought back. He never did find the tip of Africa or the land of Prester John, but his accomplishments were significant. His men discovered the African gold and ivory coasts and opened new wealth to Christendom. Between 1439 and 1453 they found and settled the nine islands of the Azores, the farthest of which was but a thousand sea miles from Newfoundland; and sent many expeditions to seek out additional Atlantic lands. In carrying out these projects, they developed the small and handy caravel, a ship rugged enough to face up to the winds and waves of the turbulent ocean and yet maneuverable enough to "claw off" its most hazardous shore. This was but one of their contributions to scientific navigation and exploration; more important, their work proved the old authorities wrong on so many points that others leaped into the great game of discovery.

The works of Ptolemy, the imaginative philosopher of the second century, had been recovered by the Arabs in 1410 and had become the chief of the ancient authorities. The tropics, Ptolemy held, were "uninhabitable because of the great heat." "And we found quite the contrary!" exclaimed one of Dom Enrique's men. "The illustrious Ptolemy who wrote so well on many things, was quite mistaken here!"

Columbus had sailed as a youth in the service of the Dom's successors in caravels similar to his own *Niña, Pinta* and *Santa Maria* of the future. As early as 1477 he began dickering for his own venture to reach the East by sailing west, but his questionable arguments and exorbitant demands put the Portuguese rulers off. In 1485 he went to Spain, but there Ferdinand and Isabella were still wholly engaged in ridding their own lands of the Moslems. Back in Portugal in 1488, Columbus was present when the great news came that the year before Bartholomew Dias had at last found the southernmost tip of Africa and had sailed around the Cape of Good Hope.

Dias proved that there was a southern and eastern all-water route to the Orient, and Portgual soon profited immensely from this discovery. But Dias's accomplishment cost Columbus whatever interest Portugal's rulers might have entertained for his own more daring theories. Columbus then tried the kings of England and France and finally the rulers of Spain once more. By January, 1492, Ferdinand and Isabella had eliminated the remnants of Moslem resistance in Granada, and were ready at last to listen to a project for the gospel, for glory, and for gold. Vasco da Gamma had not yet sailed for the rulers of Portugal over Dias's route all the way to India and returned with immense wealth, which he did in 1499. But in any case Columbus promised a shorter route to the riches and regiments of the Grand Khan.

To Columbus and his fellow explorers there was never any doubt that the earth was round, though their faith in this ancient and well-established principle was sometimes shaken. On his third voyage in 1498, for example, the Admiral himself, desperate after two failures to reach the East, recorded in his journal: "I have come to another conclusion respecting the earth, namely that it is not round as they describe, but of the form of a pear . . . upon one part of which is a prominence like a woman's nipple . . . I believe it is impossible to ascend thither, because I am convinced that it is the spot of the terrestrial paradise, whither no one can go but by God's permission."

But such thoughts were only feverish maunderings; the real issue was the breadth of the Ocean Sea. How far and how long could ships sail without basic reconditioning, and men without new provisioning and the security of near-by harbors? How long would it take to get to friendly Oriental ports? In his zeal to get on with his destiny, to bear Christ to the "other bank," and to be well rewarded for it, Columbus underestimated the breadth of the ocean 75 per cent by modern reckonings, and 25 per cent on the basis of the most optimistic estimates of his own day; in the process, he persisted in calculating a degree at a smaller distance than anyone else. Perhaps by such means he sustained his own keen faith; in any case, his optimistic reckonings did not hurt him in seeking the support of his monarchs and the service of his crew.

Even so, on his first voyage Columbus dared to doctor the log to keep his men from forcing his return. On October 10, 1492, after they had been out thirty days and doubled all known records for ocean sailing, he was forced to quell a mutiny on his flagship, *Santa Maria,* before he could proceed. Then, in two more days, what did he find? Primitive San Salvador in the steaming Bahamas! The otherwise naked natives wore enough fool's gold trinkets to feed a fanatic's conviction that the great cities of the East must be near by; and when Columbus asked where the Grand Khan was to be found, they assured him that indeed he was not very far off—a discomfiting native way of getting rid of intruders, as all later explorers found.

For all his effort, Columbus, with worn men and worn ships, dared not linger long. He named one island Hispaniola (modern Haiti and the Dominican Republic) and left a few men to hold the claim. After two months of exploration, he himself hastened back to Spain to announce his success, collect his reward for himself and all future generations of Columbuses, and organize a massive second voyage. On this voyage he carried 1,500 settlers to "the Indies" to begin the real development of his Oriental island in the Ocean Sea.

These settlers arrived late in 1493, and soon after some of them found gold in Hispaniola streams. Columbus himself brought back this heady news to Spain in 1496; and while he could not yet claim that he had found the Grand Khan, his sponsors began to take sufficient interest in the intrinsic value of what he did discover to appoint a more able administrator than the Admiral had proved to be. Columbus and the other explorers, meanwhile, persisted in their search for the greater prize.

Marco Polo had traveled over much of China in the thirteenth century and served the Grand Khan of the Mongol dynasty for nearly thirty years. In 1298 after his return to Venice, he wrote the famous account of his experiences only to be laughed at by his contemporaries for the wonders he reported—"Marco's Millions," the Venetians jeered. It was from Marco Polo that the vague rumors of Prester John had begun to circulate in stricken Europe in the fourteenth century; and it was from him that Christendom had learned of Kublai Khan, the grandest of the Mongols, and his interest in missionaries from the Pope. Polo reserved his most inflammatory language for the vast riches of the islands of Zipangu (Japan), where he had not in fact visited himself.

Copies of Marco Polo's work had been virtually out of circulation for a century and a half when it was printed for the first time in 1477. Then the aspiring navigators devoured it, Columbus most eagerly of all. Modern scholarship has proved the accuracy and acumen of Marco Polo's observations and insights; Columbus was among the few to accept them in his own day. On his later voyages —he made four in all—it was very hard to convince Columbus that Cuba (after he had satisfied himself at last that it was not the mainland but an island) was not in fact Zipangu and that South America could be anything but the mainland of Asia.

Neither Columbus nor his immediate successors could locate the marvelous port of Canton, of which the great Polo had written: "The quantity of pepper imported there is so considerable, that what is carried to Alexandria, to supply the demand of the western parts of the world, is trifling in comparison, perhaps not more than the hundreth part." Nor did they find Kublai's capital, Hangchow, "a name that signifies 'The Celestial City,' which it merits from its pre-eminence to all others in the world, in point of grandeur and beauty, as well as from its abundant delights, which might lead an inhabitant to imagine himself in paradise." These places remained fantasies to a Christian world needing to believe in them.

THE NEW WORLD BARRIER

Though Portugal and Spain had driven the old Arabic Moslems from western Europe by the end of the fifteenth century, the Turks only redoubled their onslaughts on Christendom from the East, continuing their encroachments and their terror for another hundred and fifty years. From the Orient no help came; but Portugal established an immensely lucrative empire in India and used it as a base for further expeditions in search of Prester John. Once India was opened, others fought for footholds there; but since Portugal managed to control the waterway of Dias and da Gama, the others, sailing west, kept encountering the barrier of the New World. The search for a passage through this barrier, for a free, short route to the East, occupied Europeans until the eighteenth century; but it also led to the exploration and settlement of the New World Columbus had found.

The discovery of America was no accident. Ancient prophecies had suggested its existence; perhaps the most remarkable of them was that of the Alexandrian, Eratosthenes, in the third century B.C.: "If the extent of the Atlantic were not an obstacle, we might easily sail from Iberia to India, on the same parallel . . . it is quite possible that within the same temperate zone there may be two or even more inhabited earths." In the tenth and eleventh centuries the Northmen had confirmed this possibility by their efforts to colonize Vinland, somewhere on the North American coast between Cape Cod and Labrador. Moreover, until 1418, when Europe's own mounting catastrophes choked off commerce and thwarted learning, Scandinavia had maintained a steady trade with Greenland and Iceland; and there is every likelihood that the Greenland and Labrador currents carried some storm-tossed Vikings to the Canadian shore.

This record had dwindled to vague rumor and fuzzy legend in Columbus's time, but modern scholarship has confirmed it. No one knows how many other voyages may have been made, talked about, and forgotten. Before the spread of printed books, even the greatest scientists and scholars often failed to publish their findings. No more striking instance of this can be found than the amazing Leonardo da Vinci, Columbus's exact contemporary, who had the ear of the rich and great of his day and recorded his marvelous scientific insights and experiments only in a shorthand notebook which was not deciphered and published until our own time. It is fair to suppose that America, huge as it is, could hardly have failed of discovery often before Columbus, even by some seeking the East by sailing west; note that Columbus himself says of this route only that "no one to this day knows *for sure* that anyone" had tried it.

If America had not been discovered earlier, it would only have escaped discovery in Columbus's time by the grossest accident. As Columbus wrote, "That art [of navigation] inclines him who follows it to want to know the secrets of the world." Columbus was far from being the only one who considered the westward route; in 1493, four months after he had sailed under Spanish colors, a proposal virtually identical with his but made in ignorance of his departure, was presented to the King of Portugal on behalf of the German cartographer, Martin Behain. The East was most energetically sought for in this age in which for the first time the implacably inquiring spirit of modern science was added to other impulses. Columbus is the first known to us to have sailed westward to reach the East. But no one else taking this route and persisting on it could possibly have missed the New World. As has been said, three hundred years were spent later in trying to get around it.

This motive, in fact, spurred on the numerous expeditions following the Discoverer's epic find. In 1494, a papal bull had divided the heathen lands of the world between Portugal and Spain, with the latter's share mainly in the western hemisphere. This division did not prevent John Cabot, in 1497, from establishing England's claim to Labrador and any surrounding territory she could make her own; nor John Cabral, finding himself on the coast of Brazil in 1500, from claiming it for Portugal, his native land; nor French fishermen, after 1504, from taking an annual catch of cod off Newfoundland and drying it on those shores. Yet Spain did lead the way.

Under Spanish colors, Amerigo Vespucci in 1497 explored Puerto Rico, the coasts of Central America and Mexico, and later on much of the South American coast as well. He earned the fame his name acquired when in 1507 a German writer, "the fourth part of the world having been discovered by Americus," first called the New World after him. In 1508 Alonso de Ojeda began Spanish settlement of the New World mainland at Panama; and in 1513 Vasco Nuñez de Balboa, "a man of action rather than judgment," hacked his way across Panama's forty-five mile isthmus and sighted the Pacific. In the same year Ponce de Leon, who had subdued Puerto Rico in 1508, began exploring the Florida coast and the shores of the Gulf of Mexico—the first Spanish expedition to North America. And in 1524-25 Estevan Gómes, a Portuguese in the employ of Spain, made a comprehensive survey of the Atlantic coast from the Grand Banks off Newfoundland all the way to Florida—"to search," as he reported, "whether amongst the multitudes of windings and the vast diversities of our ocean any passage can be found leading to the Kingdom of him we commonly call the Grand Khan."

Gómes's work completed the earliest phase of exploration. For by then two events had taken place which put the New World in an exciting new perspective. In August 1519, the Portuguese Ferdinand Magellan, fresh from seven years in the Orient in the service of his now smug native land, sailed under Spanish colors to try his hand at finding the elusive westward route to the wealth he had seen with his own eyes. Fourteen dreary months later, having survived mutiny and shipwreck, he discovered those murderous straits at the tip of South America now named for him. Proceeding at last into the Pacific, Magellan found the Philippines, which he claimed for Spain. There, of all places, a Moslem chieftain, feigning conversion to Christ, won his assistance in a local war which cost Magellan his life. Preferring to return the way they had come but forced by the prevailing winds to venture ever farther on unknown seas, the last half-dead eighteen of Magellan's 239 men, in the last of his five foul ships, limped home to Spain in 1522. Despite themselves they had completed the first circumnavigation of the globe. And now the truth was known about how desperately long indeed was Columbus's favorite westward passage to the East—at least in the southern latitudes.

If this seemed a calamity, however, events in the southern latitudes of the New World itself softened the blow. For there in 1519, Hernando Cortés, risen like almost all his fellow adventurers from obscurity, in his case a meager clerkship, began his conquest of Aztec Mexico.

"Do you know, gentlemen," the stout *conquistador* addressed his men after a particularly vicious battle on the way to the heart of Montezuma's empire, "it seems to me that the Indians are terrified at the horses and may think they and the cannon make war on them by themselves." Cortés could not only make such imaginative calculations, but could act daringly upon them. Deception to take advantage of his miraculous equipment made it easier for his fanatical corps of a few hundred to overwhelm professional armies a hundred times as large. News of his awesome victories he then systematically sent ahead of his marches. As Cortés neared Mexico City itself, Montezuma tried bribery to head him off, and when this policy failed, he feigned submission to the white *conquistador*. But Cortés was interested in nothing short of total victory, and in the end his self-made reputation virtually hypnotized Montezuma into guiding the Spaniard into his palace stronghold and there becoming Cortés's prisoner and slave.

"We were amazed," one of Cortés's men recorded of their first sight of the civilization of the Aztecs, "and said that it was like the enchantments they tell of in the legend of Amadis on account of the great towers and temples and buildings rising from the water, and all built of masonry. And some of our soldiers even asked whether the things that we saw were not a dream. . . . We did not know what to say, or whether what appeared before us was real . . . in front of us stood the great city of Mexico, and we did not even number four hundred soldiers."

Cortés had been sent to Mexico from Cuba by the energetic governor there to trade with the mainland Indians, whose great wealth rumor naggingly reported and earlier tentative expeditions tended to confirm. But opportunity never had a sharper lookout. To trade for the governor of Cuba was picayune; tribute from Montezuma would be infinitely more lavish, but not enough. Cortés decided very early to make a Christian province of his incredible conquest and to notify his King direct, not failing to send with his message breathtaking evidence of Aztec wealth.

Actually, Cortés's conquest of Montezuma was to be his easiest. The Aztecs were themselves conquerors and oppressors of many peoples who believed in a great white god, Quetzalcoatl. Born, like Christ, of a virgin, he had ruled these peoples' ancestors in their golden day. Once Quetzalcoatl's satanic brother made him drunk, caused him to lose his chastity, and defeated him in battle. Quetzalcoatl slunk away, yet promised to return to rescue his peoples in the first year of one of the fifty-two-year cycles of the Mexican calendar. As Cortés's star would have it, 1519 was just such a year. His marvelous horses and cannon thus but furthered a welcome illusion. And this he nurtured by his inquisitory zeal in urging Christ on the people, liquidating the obdurate, and wrecking Aztec images and temples to cleanse the country of the blood of countless thousands of cannibalistic sacrifices.

When Cortés first confronted old Montezuma himself—who had been as great a voluptuary as any of the fifteenth-century rulers in Christendom—the full meaning of this coincidence was brought home to the Indian. "We have known for a long time," said the hopeless monarch, "that neither I, nor those who inhabit this country, are the descendants from the aborigines of it. . . . And we have always held that those who descended from . . . their lord . . . would come to subjugate this country and us; . . . and according to the direction from which you say you come, which is where the sun rises, and from what you tell us of your great lord, or king, who sent you here, we believe and hold for certain, that he is our rightful sovereign, especially as you tell us that since many days he had no news of us."

Though Montezuma thus consigned himself to the questionable mercies of his conqueror, the Aztec war lords stonily withstood Cortés's wiles and stubbornly fought his ever more expansive plans. In Cuba, moreover, his insubordination and his success both aroused hostility, and the governor's forces swarmed in to level Cortés's ambitions. With his usual genius, Cortés eventually subdued his enemies and his new land, but not before many years went by. In the meantime, the flow to Spain of New World gold had commenced, to further at once the development of modern capitalism and the secular art and learning it supported.

If the white man's coming worked on the imagination of the depressed denizens of the New World, the New World itself thus began to work on the imaginations of the depressed denizens of the Old. Years before Cortés, indeed, Thomas More had placed his Utopia in America. A little later Luther himself allowed his dreams to sail to the New World as a Christian haven. Poets and philosophers like Ariosto and Montaigne began to speculate on its wonders and the popular consciousness to be drawn to it. Nevertheless, much time passed before large numbers were ready to brave the New World's difficulties.

Chapter Two

El Dorado and a Place to Hide

"The Lorde hath admonished, threatened, corrected, & astonished us," wrote Puritan lawyer John Winthrop, of the English people, in the fateful spring of 1629, "yet we grow worse and worse. . . . He hath smitten all other Churches before our eyes. . . . We sawe this, & humbled not ourselves; . . . therefore he is turninge the Cuppe toward us also, & because we are the last, our portion must be, to drinke the verye dreggs which remaine: . . . but be of good comfort . . . my dear wife," the troubled man went on, "the hardest that can come shall . . . bring us into nearer comunion with our Lord Jesus Christ, & more assurance of his kingdom. If the Lord seeth it wilbe good for us, he will provide a shelter & a hidinge place . . . as a Zoar for Lott."

The following March, under Winthrop's direction, began that Great Migration from the tyranny of Charles I "to inhabit and continue in New England." In ten years 25,000 persons sailed for Massachusetts Bay and secured the permanent settlement of the more northerly latitudes of the New World.

The Pilgrims of Plymouth, "well weaned," as they said, "from the delicate milk of our mother land," had preceded the Saints of the Bay Colony by a decade; while thirteen years before the Pilgrims, in 1607, Captain John Smith had landed an almost hopeless medley of Englishmen at swampy and feverish James Towne. In 1608, moreover, Samuel de Champlain had set up the French in Quebec, and in 1624 the Dutch had established themselves in Albany. But as late as 1630 there was no assurance that these slender North American "plantations" would not go the way of numerous still earlier ones—their "mayne end," according to Winthrop, "Carnall & not Religious"—that had either quit or mysteriously dis-

23

appeared. And in the meantime, Spain held the vast new world practically to herself. True, the Portuguese had opened Brazil; but their
interest in America was secondary to their new hegemony in India
and Africa, and in any case, Portugal and all her possessions had
fallen to Spain in 1580, not to be freed before 1640.

THE SPANISH MAIN

Portuguese historians sometimes claim that da Gama's conquests
and those of his countrymen in the Orient, "having revealed two-
thirds of this world to the remaining third," dwarf Cortés's achievement in the Mexican highlands. Yet countries like India had been
invaded before and tribute levied from strategic footholds on the
whole of their production and wealth; indeed, the Portuguese in
effect simply supplanted the Turks in control of the waters around
the Indian Ocean and in a short time were supplanted themselves.
In the new world, the country was raw, wild, noxious, and alarmingly strange; yet the "all-devouring Spaniard" subdued much of it
in the span of one man's life and held it for centuries. Cortés said
he "wished in everything to copy Alexander of Macedon." He
didn't, quite; but the *conquistadores* he turned loose accomplished
more, and with a rapidity and permanence almost unknown to
history.

Spanish serfs were bound to the land at home: Cortés's followers
were chiefly landless *hidalgos* (disaffected *hijos de algo,* "sons of a
somebody") who had spent their lives in many strange parts of the
world in mortal combat with the infidel. With them came their re-
tainers, retinues, and hangers-on, and desperate gamblers and adventurers from city docks and jails. Such men brought to the new
world as among their headiest possessions all the gilded legends of
the Middle Ages. In the new world itself the myth-ridden natives
proved eager to confirm any and all of the white man's hopeful
suggestions as to the whereabouts of gold and embroider them with
lavish tales of their own.

"The Indians who went with them conducted them to a very
lofty mountain, and thence showing them the country all around,
as far as the eye could reach, told them there was gold in every
part." So Columbus's men had reported to him (and he, on their

say-so, reported home) about "Veragua, which was five-and-twenty leagues distant from the place where we then were." But exactly where were they? Columbus did not know—except that it was the magic "mainland." Veragua, Cibala, Apaleche, the "seven caves" and the "seven cities"—each danced before the *conquistadores'* eyes. Above all loomed the lands and lake of the Gilded Man— *El Dorado*—which "for the greatness, for the richness, for the excellent seate, . . . far ex-ceedeth any . . . Citie . . . of the world, at least so much of the world as is known to the Spanish nation." To find and take these treasured territories, to reign in them like kings or return home like princes, Cortés and his masterful company (priests and crown placemen sticking close for their share) explored and established an empire.

In the twenty-five years following Montezuma's fall, Cortés himself ranged as far south as Honduras; his second in command, Pedro de Alvarado, made a personal satrapy of Guatemala, the very fount of Mayan wealth and culture; while the bloody Montejos, Elder and Younger, subdued the Mayan stronghold of Yucatán. Meanwhile, ever since Balboa's epic push across Panama, rumors had wafted all the way to Europe of an empire to the south and west richer by far even than Aztec Mexico. Between 1520 and 1530 by land and sea from the new world and the old, adventurers with the covetous blessings of kings and rising capitalists, raced to find it. The victor, in 1528, was Francisco Pizarro, one-time subordinate in the new world to Ojeda and Balboa himself. The very soul of persistence, Pizarro had prowled the western shores of South America for three years before making his strike. Seven savage years later he at last subjugated the Incan rulers of the sun-worshipers of Peru and established his Spanish capital at Lima. By then the conquest of Venezuela, Colombia, and Ecuador was also under way; while down the coast Chile had come under siege, whence incredible explorers later scaled the Andes to help annex Argentina.

In these years other and far more luckless Spaniards were wandering about the future United States all the way from Cape Hatteras to New Mexico and "from the land of the cactus on the south to the ranges of the buffalo on the north." Starting west from Florida, Hernando de Soto discovered the Mississippi in 1541 and finding no gold beyond it returned to the river he had cursed as an obstacle and died there of fever. In 1541 and 1542, Francisco de Coronado, in search of fabled Quivira and Arache, explored west Texas, Colorado, and New Mexico before despairing of any future for the "limitless plains." Only the work of seventeenth-century Franciscan missionaries brought this vast northern domain under a semblance of Spanish rule. But by then the main struggle for the new world was no longer the uneven one between arabesques and arrows, armored white men and naked red; but one between crown and crown, Christian and Christian.

There was no question of the Spanish crown, like all others characteristically in debt, promoting the ventures of its empire builders. On the contrary, the *conquistadores* usually took the initiative themselves, arranged their own financing, and with their private backers managed their own affairs. Through their *capitulaciónes* with the crown they agreed to supply *it* with the "royal fifth" of their treasure, the crown assuring itself of a fair share or better by monopolizing the assay office. Some years passed before this treasure amounted to much on a regular basis. The *conquistadores* got rich on the hoards they captured, but otherwise were too busy fighting nature, Indians, and themselves to organize the systematic production of gold and silver. What they did produce, moreover, the freelance mariners of jealous powers (whose rulers often shared in the proceeds) pirated ever more boldly on the high seas. Injury and insult finally impelled the Spanish government, grown suspicious of the lording of its distant vassals, to take over the administration and defense of the "Indies." Since it also assigned its fighting fleet to convoy its treasure galleons, open piracy soon turned into open war.

By the 1540s the reign of the *conquistadores* was virtually over. In the next decade the great silver mines of Mexico and Peru began to add thirty million dollars a year to the currency of world commerce. But staple agriculture already challenged mining as the major Spanish-American occupation. Five million aborigines, unlike those of the later British colonies, had survived *conquistador* violence and taken the *conquistadores'* God; these aborigines made up the labor force, with much smaller numbers of Negro slaves, many of them smuggled in from Portuguese Africa by French, British, and Dutch freebooters. The Spanish elite, meanwhile, quickly imposed its cultural institutions on the natives. In 1544 the first new-world printing press, in Mexico City, produced its initial work, a *Compendium of Christian Doctrine, "en lengua Mexicana y Castellana."* In 1551 the first new-world universities were opened in Mexico City and Lima. Soon imposing new cathedrals dominated the landscape of the coastal ports, while all over the country hundreds of monasteries plied their business of saving souls. In time the established Church owned half the property and collected most of the income of the Spanish empire.

With the official and temporary exception of a few German creditors of the crown and the everlasting unofficial exception of smugglers, this empire's ports, ships, and business life were restricted not only to Spanish Catholics but to a few favorite monopolists among them. The latter's freedom of action, in turn, was short-tethered by the red tape of the court and its overweening bureaucracy. Liberty was unheard of; and gradually the dead hand of repression brutalized both the administration and its victims. Spain established her American empire a hundred years before the British and kept all of it almost twice as long as England could hold her own first colonies. Yet the development of New Spain never again attained the momentum of the *conquistadores'* unflagging half-century. Their exploits made the Spanish Main Europe's "focus of envy." Spain's decline set in soon after the *conquistadores'* own, when she herself became Europe's "focus of hate."

FOCUS OF ENVY, FOCUS OF HATE

In the middle of the sixteenth century Spain had scarcely six million people at home; but her rulers held temporal sway over many millions more in Europe alone and sought to control the high road to Eternity for everyone. Precious new-world metals both stimulated and supported their aspirations. Yet in the old world a new spirit was itself developing that would tap Spanish wealth near its source and use it to pave an independent road to God.

For a century before the organization of the Spanish (and Portuguese) empires, coin-starved European monarchs, by systematically debasing their currency, had been unsuspectingly reducing the exchange value of money and forcing up commodity prices. The flow of new-world gold and silver in the sixteenth century gave an irreversible impetus to this epic inflation. Men with aristocratic tastes and inelastic incomes suffered, as did the poor in town and country who were taxed ever more harshly to support their betters. Yet as prices rose, the prospect of buying cheap and selling dear opened the eyes of calculating merchants in many Atlantic lands. Some of them, to fill the needs of Europe's expanding population, ventured everything they owned and pledged their children's futures in financing the reorganization and expansion of domestic industry. Others, their hearts softened toward loans at 15 to 30 per cent or more secured by Mexican silver, turned merchant bankers and cautiously opened new long-term lines of credit to responsible businessmen.

Medieval ideas of profit, usury, and the "just price," were by now disappearing from the market place. The new entrepreneurs, more often than not supported by their capricious kings, proceeded to trample the surviving industrial and mercantile restrictions of the old medieval towns. Late in the sixteenth century, when the lesson had been dearly learned that "private purses are cold comforts to adventurers," corporations chartered by the crown and sometimes enjoying its participation in the shares, began to succeed individuals in the larger undertakings. Typical were the Dutch West India Company of 1621 which settled New Amsterdam, the series of Royal African Companies which exploited the Guinea slave marts, and the British East India Company of 1600 which much later lost a cargo in the Boston Tea Party. Such corporations were commonly given monopolies, as against their own countrymen, of certain lines and certain regions of trade. Like the old guilds, they also built up systems of restrictions which later provoked violent political as well as business uprisings. But their initial role was to complete the annihilation of the ancient bonds and bounds of trade.

The new capitalists and companies naturally had their enemies at home and abroad. But from redress through manorial or municipal justice, they were protected by the enforcement and rising popularity of the common or the crown law. As commerce gradually girdled the globe, the first slender shoots of international law and diplomacy also appeared. But these flowered only later. Commerce has often been the handmaiden of peace. No doubt Spanish and Portuguese commerce, when those nations claimed by papal decree to share the whole heathen world, would have thrived on peace. But Dutch, French, British, and Scandinavian commerce had to fight for territorial footholds on hostile shores and for cargoes of goods and treasure on hostile seas. Corporations engaged in distant trading (in Spain and Portgual the government controlled this itself) thus were encouraged to plant their national flags, build forts, enlist private soldiers, and arm their ships. They were commonly required, moreover, to win the local heathen to their cause by converting him to their national church.

Modern capitalism had roots deeper in European history than the sixteenth century. The new world itself was one of its discoveries. Yet it was on the anvil of sixteenth-century Spanish wealth and Spanish (and Portuguese) overseas empires that the new business spirit in Europe was lastingly hammered out. To all appearances, Spain had an irretrievable head start in shaping the new epoch. Seven hundred years under the whip of infidel invaders, however, had warped Spain's point of view.

Earlier than in any other European country a zealous national spirit and towering national ambitions burned in Spain of which, alas, the discoveries of Columbus and the conquest of the new world proved but incidental and undigested fruits. The apparent political unity imposed on the country by the marriage in 1469 of King Ferdinand of Aragon and Isabella, the future Queen of Castile, was itself directed toward the major goal: a last grand mobilization of the people against Islam. Defensibly enough, the new monarchs' policy included a campaign against Catholic "heretics" in their midst and questionable *conversos* of other faiths. To root them out, the Crown opened the fateful Inquisition in 1478, with Torquemada, Isabella's own confessor, as Inquisitor-General.

Ferdinand and Isabella's centralization of power was resented by the Catalans whose very language was foreign to Castile, and forcibly resisted in sometimes-French Navarre and elsewhere on the Spanish peninsula. It was not long, therefore, before the hand of the Holy Office—with its panoply of denouncers, informers, talebearers, and torturers; its morbid parades of victims and spectacular sacrificial pyres—was extended to political as well as religious dissidence. The final expulsion of the Moslems from Granada in 1492, far from satiating the Spanish soul, only fired the populace and the clergy to their own final craving: the utter antiseptic cleansing of their reclaimed land of every vestige of non-Catholic life.

With Torquemada himself the zealots' firebrand, the wavering Crown saw little choice but to yield to its Frankenstein. Least mercy was shown those who had financed and administered the whole long crusade against Islam but whose wealth was now coveted and who could themselves be spared. In the very age of Columbus and the *conquistadores,* Spain's inquisitors would burn or banish her most business-minded Moors and Jews, Moriscos and Maranos. Her new bureaucrats would then garrote what survived of Spain's commercial life, while her tax collectors proceeded to bankrupt her remaining manufacturers whom her untaxed crusading knights despised. Thus under the lash of the Cross was black-robed, black-visaged, quixotic Spain driven to dissolve in blood and misery the sources of her wealth and power at home.

Her American golden hoard, in turn, Spain would consume on her Catholic mission elsewhere in Europe, where her reach grew as long as it was merciless. Isabella died in 1504 and Ferdinand in 1516, when their grandson, Charles, ascended the Spanish throne. Charles's other grandparents were Archduchess Mary, daughter of Charles the Rash of Burgundy; and Maximilian, the Hapsburg Archduke of Austria, who was also Holy Roman Emperor. From Ferdinand and Isabella, Charles inherited, besides their rising new-world empire, most of Spain itself and the holdings of the Aragons in southern Italy. In 1519, the year in which Cortés began his conquest of Mexico and Magellan the voyage that would annex the Philippines, Maximilian died; and from him Charles inherited directly all of Austria, and Milan in northern Italy. Through his grandmother he also inherited the Duchy of Burgundy in eastern

France, and the Netherlands, comprising present Belgium and Holland, to the north.

Hapsburg Charles reigned in Spain and his immense possessions in two worlds as Charles I. After paving the way with money borrowed from the German banker, Jacob Fugger, he also succeeded Maximilian as Holy Roman Emperor, and as Charles V reigned over all the German states as well. In 1526, when the Turks killed the Hungarian king and threatened all central Europe, the princes of Hungary and Bohemia wooed Hapsburg aid by electing as their monarch Charles's brother, Ferdinand. Meanwhile, until her unsavory divorce from Henry VIII which hung fire from 1529 to 1533, and which started England's revolt against Catholicism, Charles's aunt, Catherine of Aragon, had been Queen of England. To make up for England's defection Charles in 1530 was named King of Italy by Pope Clement VII. Territorially this title was as empty as Charles's purse; but, along with that of Holy Roman Emperor, it tied him all the more securely to the interests of the Popes when they most needed a defender.

In 1517 on the door of the castle church in Wittenberg, Martin Luther had posted the ninety-five theses in which he asserted that men were saved by faith alone and that the Pope and the clergy could be dispensed with. Luther's act set the Catholic world afire only because it had for so long been ready for the torch. In 1521, after Pope Leo X had excommunicated Luther, Charles swore that he would not spare his "dominions, friends, body, blood, life, and soul" in crushing the monk, his heresy, and his followers. Toward this end in 1522 the Spanish Inquisition was exported to Charles's non-Spanish lands, and was later supplemented by Rome's own Inquisition in lands which Charles did not rule. In 1534, Charles sanctioned the establishment by the Spanish monk, Ignatius Loyola, of the Society of Jesus, to whose work the Pope gave his sanction in 1541. Superbly equipped in character and training to cajole the elite into retaining or returning to the ancient faith, the Jesuits also undertook its propagation among the masses in the shattered old world and the savage new. Beyond this, Charles fought endless and expensive wars against heretical princes of the Empire and, incidentally, against other enemies of the Hapsburgs.

And yet Charles failed. He was still Emperor and King when

in 1555 he was forced by the Peace of Augsburg to recognize the right of each German prince to decide whether he and his people (the latter themselves were not consulted) would be Lutheran or Catholic. By then half of Germany had defected to Lutheranism as had all the neighboring Scandinavian countries, while England in her own way had renounced the Pope and his religion. Elsewhere, especially among Charles's Dutch subjects, heretics were getting rich supplying Spain herself with the goods and commercial services she had forfeited by the Inquisition, and by making light of her paper domination of America.

In 1556, wearied of the thankless struggle, Charles divided his empire between his brother Ferdinand, who also became Holy Roman Emperor, and his son who as Philip II ruled most of the Hapsburg lands. Charles himself retired to a monastery.

Two years earlier Philip had married the daughter of Henry VIII and Catherine of Aragon, Mary Tudor, who was Queen of England until her death in 1558. He himself took the title King of England, and on Mary's death sought to marry Elizabeth, Mary's step-sister and successor, and thereby retain Spain's hold on the island. Mary had restored Catholicism to England, earning notoriety, under Philip's prompting, as "Bloody Mary" by burning some three hundred Protestants. After Elizabeth rejected Philip she made herself supreme head of the Anglican Church. Henceforth she was baited by Catholics as illegitimate; and Spain and England spoiled for war. But by then a new religious agitation had begun which was to divide the English more brutally even than the Catholic issue and which made for Philip himself warmer enemies outside England than Luther ever earned from Charles. The new religious agitation sprang from the work of John Calvin.

Luther early had made his peace with the German princes and near-by kings who established his Church as their own, collected taxes for its support, and persecuted nonconformists. Calvin, who had presented his ideas to the world in 1536 in his *Institutes of the Christian Religion,* written in Latin for the learned, yielded to no lay rulers whatever. Like Luther he believed that men were saved by the inner light of faith alone, kept steady and bright by daily study and contemplation of the Bible. Confessions, intercessions, mortifications, and reformations in themselves he held mere superstitious acts. But Calvin stressed much more than Luther the idea that if what a man did on earth could not save him, then, if men were actually saved, their eternal reward must be predestined. Calvin was more radical still: the slough of immorality in which men obviously wallowed on every side must mean that only a few choice spirits were preordained by God to participate in the "Covenant of Grace"—a few choice spirits, that is, and their children; for by the "Covenant of Baptism," a kind of inheritance by sacrament, they alone might grow into the "elect," the illuminated countenances, the vessels of Christ.

Calvin was as deep a believer in the divine right to rule as the Hapsburgs themselves, and no less intolerant than their Inquisition. In the old world and in the new his followers burned at the stake Baptists, Quakers, and heretics of more familiar stripe who might deny the Trinity, or indulge the carnal passions, or defy the rule of the self-appointed "Saints." Calvin's alone was the "true religion." Let Calvinists, then, direct Church *and* State. Let them rule life. And let the corrupt fail to profit from the example of the "elect"— and the "elect" from the example of their elders—at their peril.

Calvin did much more than write and preach. Harried from his native France to Switzerland in 1535, a year before he issued the powerful *Institutes,* he soon supplanted a hireling bishop of the Duke of Savoy as ruler of turbulent Geneva. There he promptly established a stern theocracy over which he presided without compromise. The spreading fame of his regime and his book brought reformers to Calvin from England, Scotland, France, Germany, the Netherlands, Poland, Hungary, even Spain. From him they returned uplifted and inspired, with a revolutionary mission and a revolutionary model—threats, unlike Luther's more docile converts, to monarchy and popery both. The failure of the Peace of Augsburg to give them the recognition shared by Lutherans and Catholics only heightened the Calvinists' intransigence and independence. Intolerant themselves, they found intolerance unbearable. Since, in fact, they often were among the elect in talent and energy as well as spirit, they had the means to make themselves heard.

As non-New Englanders in America later grew fond of pointing out, the "Saints" were prone to hypocrisy, cant, bigotry, and cunning; the elect could do no wrong. But they were also required to wear a mask of faith, probity, dignity, and honor that more often than among other groups of their time proved to be the outward sign of inward conscience, simplicity, and devotion. Their numbers everywhere included members of the landed classes: "a nobleman, a gentleman, a yeoman—that is a good interest," boasted Oliver Cromwell of his own heritage and allegiance; while in France the first Bourbon king himself, the redoubtable Henry IV, took up (to renounce later) the Genevan persuasion. Nevertheless, the Calvinists were more likely to be men of commerce and money capital, men of free cities and free trade, self-governing and ungovernable, practical and proud, taciturn in accounting for their silver, their slaving, and their souls. Calvinism confirmed and enlarged their character; it did not create it. Like them international in outlook and action, the new faith brought a mutuality of sympathy and respect to a mutuality of interest.

Outside of Scotland where John Knox by the 1560s had secured his "Congregation of the Lord," Calvinism waxed strongest among Philip's own seafaring Dutch subjects and among the Flemish capitalists in the great ports of modern Belgium. Scarcely a hundred sea miles from Belgium lay the maritime towns of East Anglia, and a little farther on, the Channel ports of the west country of England, where Philip ached to be King. Here, too, were centers of capitalism and Calvinism. Just across the Channel, meanwhile, in Bourbon France whose borders Hapsburg rulers had long menaced on three sides and whose own ambitions traditionally menaced the Hapsburgs, lay the inviting Gulf of St. Mâlo, overlooked by the austere port city of the same name. Here and in other French ports the populace generally held to the old Church, but the local capitalists and the neighboring nobles with capitalist aspirations turned Calvinist, or "Huguenot" as they were called, meaning "confederates" with the Swiss. To many of these cities had fled Jews and Moriscos banished from Spain, bringing their experience, talents, taste, and memories. Over these cities, should they fall afoul of Philip's might or the Pope's vengeance, hung the dread shadow of the Inquisition.

Philip II was the perfect enemy of Calvinism. Severe in dress, dour in demeanor, studious to a fault, busy always at his kingly "calling," he too was the "true believer." If the word of God were one, his followers and the hated Calvinists must clash. When they did, following the close of the Council of Trent in 1564, recognition of the spirit of Satan in one another set men on both sides slaying and pillaging without mercy.

The Council of Trent had been called by the chief Catholic monarchs of Europe in 1545 to plan the reformation and revitalization of their own Church and the reconquest of its lost lands. Until his death in 1598, Philip was the Council's chief executioner. His own strength, as the Protestants well knew, lay in his American treasure. But therein lay his fatal weakness too. "Money," Francis Bacon advised Queen Elizabeth, "is the principal part of the greatness of Spain; for by that they maintain their veteran army. But" it is also "the ticklish and brittle state of the greatness of Spain. Their greatness consisteth in their treasure, their treasure in the Indies, and their Indies (if it be well weighed) are indeed but an accession to such as are masters of the sea."

For decades Spain's maritime vassals, free neighbors, and seeming friends had probed and pirated her American treasure and laid the foundations of their own wealth. Covetousness had fed their capitalist spirit, envy their enterprise. Henceforth, hate and the company of Heaven would lend pride to piracy, passion to politics. "Almighty God," cried John Hawkins, the first of the great Elizabethan "sea dogges," when he survived a bit of trouble off the Spanish Main, "would not suffer His elect to perish."

THE PARTITION OF NORTH AMERICA

Actually the French were the first to tweak the Spaniard's nose in the new world. In 1523 Jean Fleury, a corsair in the employ of the merchant-pirate Jean D'Ango of Dieppe, caught some of Cortés's first treasure ships off the Azores and carried Montezuma's hoard home to his King, Francis I. When Charles V learned of Fleury's adventure, he protested mightily. Francis disdainfully replied, "Show me the clause in Adam's will by which he divided the world between my brothers of Spain and Portugal."

Considering that he had made his case, Francis the next year sent

Giovanni de Verrazano to explore the coast of North America for the elusive northwest passage to the Indies. Verrazano searched from Newfoundland to North Carolina, a region Dutch map makers henceforth popularized as "New France," to vent their own derision on Spain's comprehensive claims. Ten years after Verrazano, in 1534, Jacques Cartier of St. Mâlo began the series of voyages on which he explored the Gulf and River of St. Lawrence, southwest to what we still call the Lachine (that is, China) Rapids. His work strengthened French claims to the sites of Quebec and Montreal and the neighboring northern country.

Thereafter until 1603, when Henry IV sponsored the capitalists who employed the great Champlain, France bled with brothers' blood in the wars between Calvinist and Catholic, and official French exploration ceased. Free-lance Frenchmen, most of them Huguenots, nevertheless kept the pressure on Spain. It was French corsairs who forced Spain after 1543 to assign more and more warships to convoy her treasure fleets. In 1565, as a base of operations against French marauders, Spain established St. Augustine, the first permanent settlement on territory to become the United States. Far to the north, meanwhile, French fishermen continued to visit forbidden Newfoundland, where they eventually established the real foundations of French power and wealth in the new world.

From their first visits in 1504, these fishermen found that the Indians craved any old pieces of metal with which to improve their stone weapons and lord it over old-fashioned tribes. In exchange for metal, the Indians offered generous packs of fur. Europe's own supply of fur had long been running thin, and since Europeans valued the skins both as a means of warmth and a mark of worth, the fur trade with the Indians flourished. The less domesticated of the fishermen, indeed, forsook their ships to set up temporary new world trading posts. Their experiences eventually formed the basis of Champlain's calculations for a permanent colony, and work like theirs assured its ultimate success.

Champlain was as avid an explorer as Columbus. When he felt from time to time that he had secured a monopoly of the fur trade of the north, he would send expeditions from his base in Quebec in quest of the elusive northwest route to China. Before his death in

1635, Champlain's expeditions took his devoted young followers to territory beyond the "inland sea" we know as the Great Lakes. His Huron Indian allies, meanwhile, trapped the country ever farther west. In 1628, Cardinal Richelieu placed Canada under control of the Company of New France, and Jesuit missionaries became the chief instruments of French expansion. Most famous of the Jesuits was Père Jacques Marquette who, with Louis Joliet, paddled down the Mississippi in 1673. On learning that the river emptied into the Spanish Gulf of Mexico and not the Oriental sea, Marquette and Joliet turned back before reaching the Mississippi's mouth.

More enterprising even than Jesuit missionaries were the fabulous *coureurs de bois,* the first American backwoodsmen. Often well-born, these French youths came to America for adventure and quickly took on the Indians' nomadic habits, their women, and their work. "We weare Cesars, being nobody to contradict us," wrote Pierre Esprit Raddison. Actually the *coureurs de bois* more than paid their way by organizing the ever more distant Indian trading into an efficient operation. Raddison and his brother-in-law, Médard Chouart, Sieur des Groseilliers, explored the Hudson Bay country in the 1660s. When the autocratic Governor of New France punished them for this unauthorized venture, they promptly made a deal with England. In 1670 English capitalists chartered the Hudson's Bay Company to exploit and administer the region.

Coureurs de bois were also among the ablest lieutenants of that most imaginative of Frenchmen, Robert Cavelier de La Salle. In 1682, as a mere preliminary to his grandiose scheme for a comprehensive commercial system on the waters of the West, La Salle completed the exploration of the Mississippi to the Gulf and claimed for France "possession of that river, of all the rivers that enter it and of all the country watered by them." In 1718, like a thorn in the flesh of dying Spain, the French "planted" New Orleans to anchor this claim.

Louis XIV ruled France from 1643 to 1715 and hungered for colonies to glorify his reign. Yet even Louis preferred to concentrate more on his massive army and its employment in furthering his ambitions in Europe than on outposts in New France. French sea power in later years seldom attained the scope and spirit of the mid-sixteenth century, and the French settlements were enfeebled by this weakness. Thus it was left first to the Dutch and ultimately to the British, staunch seafaring Protestant nations both, to give the coup de grâce to Catholic Spain's pretensions to exclusive control of the old world, the new world, and the next world.

As the sixteenth century wore on and trade moved steadily from the Mediterranean to the Atlantic and neighboring northern waters, the urban Dutch, strategically situated and endowed with excellent harbors, became the equivalents of the fourteenth-century Italians. Their coasts and their ships dominated the North Sea, which itself commanded communication between booming Scandinavia, the newest source of lumber and naval stores, and ambitious England, France, and Spain. Dutch enterprise, moreover, improved on nature. By arranging early to meet Portuguese ships at sea, Dutch merchants became the distributors to the continent of the marvelous goods of the Orient. To these goods the Dutch merchants added, without noticeable scrupling, the booty landed by the notorious Dutch "water beggars," whose pirate keels furrowed every sea. Dutch manufactures, meanwhile, flourished under the guidance of religious refugees; while Dutch herring fisheries supplied the latter's Catholic persecutors abroad with their ritual food. And all the while the Dutch Calvinists grew more restive under Spanish taxation, corruption, and contempt.

When Philip II, after the Council of Trent, became the militant arm of the Counter-Reformation, his Dutch subjects faced double jeopardy. First, Philip wanted their wealth. After 1560 he greatly increased their taxes, and worse, sent his detested minions to insure collection. Having thus aroused the burghers to the defense of their precious purses, Philip next undertook their religious regeneration. It was only natural that he should try to get his own house in order before proceeding to reclaim the rest of Europe for Catholicism. And all the more so since, if he were to succeed with the Dutch, he would have the wherewithal for aggression elsewhere.

But Philip, like his father before him, failed. In 1566, the Dutch rebelled against Spain and succeeded in setting up an independent

Dutch Republic for which they won general recognition in 1609. Seven years earlier, having been deprived of their Portuguese connection when Spain took over Portugal and the Portuguese empire in 1580, Dutch capitalists had established their own East India Company to recapture the Oriental trade for themselves. Their success was immediate and immense. In their operations they not only discovered Australia and New Zealand, but developed an Oriental empire centered in modern Indonesia, which they retained until 1949. When the war with Spain was resumed in 1621 after a twelve-year truce, the Dutch chartered a West India Company to harass the Spanish Main. The fury of its attack so shattered Spanish power in the Caribbean that, along with the Dutch, English, French, and Scandinavian adventurers swarmed in. Virtually unmolested, except by one another, the newcomers occupied the Lesser Antilles and began the large-scale exploitation with slave labor of West Indian sugar and tobacco.

In 1609 the Dutch East India Company sent out the *Half Moon,* commanded by the Englishman, Henry Hudson, to make yet another attempt to find the Northwest Passage to the Orient. Naturally, neither the river nor the bay to which Hudson gave his name afforded him any more success than his many predecessors enjoyed. But certain of the mariners with Hudson grasped the possibilities in trading for fur with the Iroquois, and returned in 1614 to set up an armed fur-trading post near Albany. This venture failed; but the Indians were so impressed with the white man's weapons that, when the latter returned to stay in 1624, the Iroquois swore lasting friendship in exchange for a monopoly of firearms. This friendship the English inherited later on.

By 1624 the Dutch *West* India Company also became interested in the fur trade, and two years later, as a base of operations, purchased Manhattan Island from the local braves. At Manhattan's southernmost point the armed trading post of Fort Amsterdam had already been set up. The West India Company extended its claim to the Connecticut River with a fort near Hartford, and to the Delaware near Camden. In 1629, in an effort to stimulate settlement, the Dutch made their first lavish grants of land to the patroons who were expected to bring in permanent tenants. Ten years later, when Scandinavians sought to get into the colonial swim, the Dutch winked at a Swedish company occupying Delaware. These Swedes introduced the log cabin to America.

But the Dutch had spread themselves far too thin for their own tiny population. New Amsterdam, open after 1638 to ships of all comers, throve as a trading center. Otherwise the Dutch colonial venture languished. By 1664 the Dutch administration under choleric Peter Stuyvesant and similar second-raters had grown so harsh that even the Netherlanders, by then but a minority of the mixed population, welcomed the English conquest.

Long before they became enemies of the Dutch, the English had assisted them materially against Philip. England and Spain had started as friends. By the 1520s such an active trade had grown up between the two countries that numerous English commercial families settled permanently in Spanish ports. During the 1530s, the English sea captain, William Hawkins, father of the great Sir John and Mayor of Plymouth, established a regular transatlantic packet service with the *conquistadores*. In the 1560s John Hawkins himself engaged most actively in the illicit but locally welcomed business of supplying Spanish-America with African slaves. But by then the rift that had opened decades earlier, when Henry VIII divorced Catherine of Aragon, had widened and soon a chasm of hate divided the two nations.

After "Bloody Mary" and Philip, Elizabeth committed England not only to Protestantism at home but to aiding Protestants abroad. For this Pope Pius V excommunicated her in 1570. Thereafter, half of England being Catholic, Philip's English friends plotted unceasingly against Elizabeth's life. In the 1560s many English sailors caught in Spanish home ports were "questioned" and burned by the Inquisition. Those who escaped fled home to shout its terror through the island. In 1571 the Spanish Holy Office was extended to the new world where English ships as well as English sinners were numbered among its victims.

The division among her own people compelled Elizabeth to avoid open war. But she could urge on and honor her loyal subjects and would-be swains who, in the cause of Protestantism and property, hijacked Spanish treasure and humbled the Spanish flag. In this work John Hawkins and his cousin Francis Drake became heroes to their countrymen and their Queen. Their own heroes were the irrepressible Dutch "water beggars" and the Huguenot corsairs, all of whom proceeded now to work together to run the Spaniard down. Their crowning exploit was Drake's voyage around the world in the *Golden Hind*. Drake went out in 1577. After raiding Spanish shipping and the Atlantic and Pacific coasts of New Spain's lands, he returned in 1580 with £1,500,000 in Spanish silver and gold, equal to a profit of 4,700 per cent on the initial investment in which Elizabeth had a share. To Philip's consternation, Elizabeth publicly knighted the raider.

While British sailors became the scourge of the seas, British soldiers dreamed their own dreams of adventure and wealth and the hand of their Queen. The greatest of them was Walter Raleigh, impecunious courtier, philosopher, lyricist, and lover, who while awaiting the day his own ship would come in, journeyed to distant battlefields in France, Ireland, and the Netherlands to strike blows against Philip. But Raleigh's consuming passion was the conquest of the new world itself, of which he cried later, after many failures there: "I shall yet live to see it an Inglishe nation."

Though he did not scruple to talk of precious metals to gain backers for his projects and though later in life he made a desperate search for El Dorado to restore his personal fortune at the expense of Spain, Raleigh was no gold bug. While still in his twenties he won Elizabeth's favor and in 1577 got permission to send out his half-brother Humphrey Gilbert "to inhabit and possess all remote and Heathen lands not in the possession of any Christian prince." Raleigh's idea was to build up the economy of his plantation so that the "shipping, victual, munition, and transporting of five or six thousand soldiers may be defrayed." With these, he hoped, he would march from a grand New England to conquer New Spain. Between 1577 and 1587 Raleigh engineered the departure of at least six expeditions, one of which gave the name Virginia, for the Virgin Queen, to the region now so known. That proved to be Raleigh's only lasting monument in the new world, though all later English settlement profited from his work.

By land and by sea "Merrie England" had taken the lead in affronting Spain. The final insult came in 1587 when Elizabeth ordered the execution of her Catholic cousin and heir apparent, Mary, Queen of Scots. Twenty years before, Mary had fled from John Knox to Westminster. She repaid Elizabeth's own calculated hospitality by conspiring constantly with Philip's treasonous friends to grasp the English crown. For this Elizabeth was forced by her ministers, her Parliament and most of her people to cut off Mary's head. In 1588, his patience with England gone, Philip sent up the English Channel the grand Armada with which he hoped to demolish Britain, proceed to victory over the stubborn Dutch beyond the Straits of Dover, and aid the Catholic party in France to crush the Huguenots. England worried; but Drake and Hawkins rejoiced.

While England's little tubs cannonaded the giant Spanish galleons, the Dutch also swept down for the fray. But most decisive was the work of the good Lord Himself. "He blew and they were scattered," held the Lord's elect when a storm blew up in the North Sea to complete the Spanish rout. The Dutch Republic was saved; the Huguenots proceeded, if only for a decade, to hold the crown of France, and for a century more to enjoy tolerance under the Edict of Nantes; even the distant German Calvinists took heart. Soon after, England, the Netherlands, and France chartered East India companies to raid Spain's Oriental empire and planned to renew active exploration and settlement in suddenly wide-open America.

A PLACE TO HIDE

But England herself moved in a moment from this glorious peak of triumph onto the road toward civil war.

"Since the English had overthrown the Spanish Navy in the year 1588," a Roman Cardinal acknowledged a few years after the annihilation of the famous Armada, "there was no small hope of reducing England to Papistry." That menace removed, what, asked the English Calvinists who had led the fight on Spain, stood in the way of "completing" England's *religious* Reformation? To the English Calvinists Henry VIII's break with the Pope had been at best a political if not a personal act which Elizabeth's own "settlement" hardly did more than confirm. Attacking the Anglican clergy, in Milton's later words, as shepherds whose "Hungry sheep look up and are not fed," the Calvinists urged the end of compromise in the liturgy and creed of the English Church. Surviving Roman "works" could assure no one of Heaven, nor were "ignorant and unpreaching" ministers useful substitutes for practical piety in a troubled world. The surviving Roman hierarchy of archbishops, bishops, and priests only perpetuated a privileged and not a holy caste. Subordination of the Church to the power of the State was above all an affront to God and to the "privileges and immunities" of His elect.

Since she had become supreme head of the Church of England, Elizabeth took these attacks on the Anglican establishment as treason against the Crown itself. As early as 1583 Elizabeth had shown her claws by sending to the gallows three Separatists—or Congregationalists—who seemed to threaten to divide her kingdom by agitating for the establishment of Calvinist churches *independent* of the Anglican bishops. Two years after the defeat of the Armada, Elizabeth turned her attention to the more orthodox Calvinists of the Presbyterian persuasion who sought not to leave but to capture and purify the Anglican Church. In 1590 she opened a regular "Romish Inquisition" which hanged three Puritan "martyrs" and imprisoned others. Elizabeth's example stirred the populace in East Anglia in particular, where Puritanism had become most deeply seated, to take it upon themselves to burn several Saints for "diverse detestable heresies."

Nursing their wounds and nurturing their memories, the Puritans waited patiently for the aging Queen's death and the crowning of her heir, James Stuart of Scotland, who had been raised a Presbyterian in the school of John Knox. But when James became king in 1603 he showed how little this training meant to royalty. "If you aim at a Scottish presbytery," he told confident Puritans seeking a church council to "complete" the Reformation, "it agreeth as well with monarchy as God with the devil." Far from conceding anything to the agitators, James cried, "I shall make them conform themselves, or I shall harry them out of the land." It was with the hope that they would indeed go that he agreed in 1606 to charter two commercial companies to develop "that part of America, commonly called Virginia." And it was their depression over prospects at home that in 1609 sent the Pilgrims from their mother land to the hospitable Dutch as the first step on their hegira to New England.

James's political evil genius was George Villiers, "Britaine's . . . foe, Spaine's agent, Holland's bane, Rome's friend," whom he made Duke of Buckingham. Between them they sank the navy to so low a state that Turkish pirates enslaved English seamen in the Channel itself, while the Dutch captured London's trade and the French returned to the sea. Under Charles I, who became King in 1625, Buckingham engineered military and maritime adventures to regain mercantile support. But these proved such costly fiascoes that the Crown itself was brought into growing disrepute and Parliament into growing rebellion. Both Stuart kings sold peerages and trade monopolies for revenue, and this practice heightened the Puritans' contempt for the King's faction and their concern over competition from the King's commercial favorites. The Parliamentary Puritans' own refusal to vote funds for further adventures brought Charles, at the last, to the policy of "forced loans," refusal of which meant imprisonment without trial, and to the billeting of rough and ready soldiers in private homes and inns. "If this be law," cried Puritan leaders, "why do we talk of our liberties?"

In 1628 the Puritan party in Parliament, led by Sir John Eliot, demanded that the King sign the Petition of Right denying the divinity of his office and acknowledging that billeting, arbitrary taxation, and arbitrary imprisonment for refusal to pay were illegal. For small favors Charles signed, but he proceeded to ignore the Petition's restraints. A compliant clergy had attempted to aid Charles by declaring refusal of taxes a sin. This reminder of papal corruption completed the mortification of the Puritans who had already become alarmed by the alteration of the Anglican creed from an acceptance of Calvinist predestination to Arminian grace for "good works." In 1629, therefore, in one of his famous "Three Resolutions," Eliot demanded that the King declare "as a capital enemy to this kingdom and commonwealth," not only him who levies and him who pays taxes "not being granted by Parliament," but him who "shall bring in innovation in religion." Charles refused to do Eliot's bidding. When Parliament voted Eliot's resolutions anyway, Charles dissolved the body and did not recall it until 1640.

In 1628 Charles named William Laud, a leading Arminian and Buckingham's confessor, as Bishop of London. That year John Felton, a Puritan, assassinated the hated Duke. London rejoiced.

> Live ever Felton, thou hast turned to dust
> Treason, ambition, murther, pride, and lust.

But Laud needed no such extraneous motivation to shut Puritan chapels, close Puritan mouths, shrivel Puritan loyalty, and anguish Puritan consciences. Between him and Charles, after 1629 Puritans and Parliament were both driven into hiding, and the cause of Calvinists and Commons became one. That year, though the Puritan revolt itself was still more than a decade off, lawyer John Winthrop decided reluctantly that "he cannot live in the same place and calling (as before) and so, if he should refuse this opportunity [to go to the new world] that talent which God hath bestowed upon him for publick service were like to be buried." He then began serious preparations for the settlement of Massachusetts Bay.

The first of the two companies chartered by James I in 1606 to settle Virginia (the second never amounted to anything), drew its support mainly from London capitalists and was called the London Company. In December 1606, it was ready to embark its first 120 colonists in three ships, all in command of Captain Christopher Newport. Before the day in April 1607, that found the poorly led expedition accidentally washed up on the very shore it sought, sixteen had died. By 1625, when the Company's disastrous lack of progress moved Charles I to revoke its charter and make Virginia a royal colony, 5,500 persons had been sent out to the settlement, of whom 4,000 had perished on the voyage or in the new world. About three hundred had the good sense to return home. A mere 1,200 were yet to be found in America.

The first English settlers hoped in everything to emulate if not to outdo the Spanish. During the second spring in Virginia, when crops of corn should have been planted if settlers were to eat that winter, Captain John Smith complained that there was "no talke, no hope, no worke, but dig gold, wash gold, refine gold, loade gold." Captain Newport himself had been commanded by the Company "not to return without a lumpe of gold [or] a certaintie of the South Sea."

There was no gold in Virginia, but neither was there any incentive to leave off seeking it. Until 1617 all property in the colony was held communally, and officers of the Company doled out the land's scant produce as needed. Virginia's charter contained the famous clause that all Englishmen in the colonies and their children born there "shall have and enjoy all liberties, franchises, and immunities . . . as if they had been abiding and born, within this our realm of England." But not before 1618 did the Company permit the introduction of English common law and the establishment of a local parliament, known henceforth as the House of Burgesses. That year, also, the land was distributed to individuals as private property and ownership of land became the basis for the franchise. To augment the population, the system of "head rights" was introduced, by which a settler got 50 acres for himself and 50 more for each "head" he settled on the land, including, under later regulations, members of his family as well as workers and tenants.

Abuse of the "head rights" system by false entries and other dodges laid the foundation for many of the large plantations in Virginia and neighboring colonies. Such plantations became devoted to the cultivation of tobacco, and their initial expansion was made possible by the labor of white indentured servants (see p. 70). Negroes were first landed in Virginia in 1619, but not until almost fifty years later were they reduced from the legal status of servants to slaves. Slavery fastened the institution of the great plantation on Virginia. It was not long before the plantation gentry became entrenched in the Anglican vestries which ran parish politics; in the House of Burgesses, which ran provincial politics; and in the militia, which kept the peace and had first claim on Indian lands. Yet for decades the colony retained its general aspect of small and successful independent homesteads producing a variety of crops, and even in the eighteenth century an independent Virginia yeomanry withstood the competition and moral corruption of the slave system.

When Virginia was made a royal colony in 1625, the King repossessed all lands not in private hands. Later in the 1620s he made Sir George Calvert, the first Lord Baltimore and one of the old stockholders of the London Company, "proprietor" of a huge domain which Calvert called Maryland. This domain was cut from the northerly part of Virginia and extended westward from Chesapeake Bay. Maryland's first settlers came in 1634. The proximity and experience of Virginia saved them many of the usual hardships of pioneering.

Lord Baltimore, a Catholic, had sought his grant as a refuge for his persecuted coreligionists. But the Catholics, when they fled, seemed to prefer the continent of Europe. The few who did come to the new world, though given as a rule large tracts of their own, were soon outnumbered by Puritans and other Protestants allowed to enter by the proprietor. Indeed, in 1649 the intolerance of these newcomers, heightened as it was by the Puritan success in England, impelled Lord Baltimore to ask the local legislature to enact a measure for religious freedom to protect the Catholics and all others who believed in the Holy Trinity. The legislature complied, and though the famous Toleration Act of 1649 was rescinded a few years later and the Anglican Church itself established in 1692, Maryland enjoyed more religious variety than most of the colonies. In other respects, though its origins were altogether different from Virginia's, Maryland developed along its neighbor's lines. Tobacco became king, but at first king of small farmers using indentured servants, not great ones using Negro slaves.

The first settlers of New England had neither friends nor the hope of wealth to sustain them. They had something stronger: their determination to make the country their home and their altar, come what may. Even in Holland things were getting on the Pilgrims' nerves. "We lived here," one wrote, "but as men in exile and in a poor condition." In 1621, moreover, "the twelve years of truce [between the Dutch and the Spanish] would run out and there was nothing but beating of drums and preparing for war. . . . The Spaniard might prove as cruel as the savages of America, and the famine and pestilence as sore here as there, and their liberty less to look out for remedy." It was thus that the Pilgrims undertook to find a way to come to the new world. "The dangers," they granted, "were great, but not desperate. The difficulties were many, but not invincible." They "knew they were pilgrims . . . but lift up their eyes to the heavens, their dearest country. . . ."

Through Sir Edwin Sandys, one of the officers of the London Company who was not a Separatist himself but admired the group, the Pilgrims negotiated for a grant in Virginia and made an arrangement with London capitalists under which the latter would finance the voyage and the settlement by advancing £7,000 against anticipated profits. In return, expecting by then to have paid off the advance with interest, the Pilgrims agreed to work seven years as servants of the company, all produce during that time to go into a common warehouse and fund.

Dickering and other difficulties delayed the Pilgrims' start until November 11, 1620, when but one ship, the little *Mayflower,* set sail. Her one hundred passengers included some of the Holland group and others who were not part of the Separatist community. Atlantic storms drove the Pilgrims far from Virginia, and on December 21, 1620, they landed at Plymouth. Aware that they were out of the jurisdiction of the government of Virginia and the territory of the London Company, they drew up their own "Compact" of government, elected John Carver their governor, and agreed to abide by the will of a majority of the community. Deciding to remain where God had led them, and where the first cruel winter killed half their number, the Pilgrims arranged for an independent if ill-defined grant of land. In 1628 they gave to each survivor private ownership of twenty acres, though it was not until 1641 that they paid off the colony's debts to the London merchants and their heirs. Until 1691, when they were absorbed into Massachusetts Bay, the Pilgrims led an austere but independent existence, sustained chiefly by trade in fish and fur.

"Let it not be grievous to you," the Pilgrims' friends had written to them from England, that "you have been but the instruments to break the ice for others; the honor shall be yours till the world's end." Other Puritans, as their troubles mounted at home, watched the efforts of the Pilgrims in the new world. The Pilgrims' survival hastened the development of the others' plans to leave.

The second company James chartered in 1609 with an extensive grant north of Virginia was reorganized in 1620 as the New England Council. It was from this Council that the Pilgrims eventually got title to their own territory. In 1628 a number of Puritan merchants and others bought from the New England Council the land between the Charles and the Merrimac Rivers, and in 1629 they organized the Company for Massachusetts Bay. Their charter from the king permitted them to exploit the fisheries and other resources. Most important for the future, the charter allowed the establishment of a Company government.

Early in 1629 the Company for Massachusetts Bay was approached by a number of well-to-do Puritans in England who were more interested in their souls than in fish and fur, and who were able to afford the preference. These Puritans induced the Company to sell them its land and yield its charter. In October 1629, the new group elected John Winthrop governor of the Company, and before the end of 1630 a thousand picked settlers, most of them East Anglians, had been carried to Massachusetts. There they promptly laid out the town of Boston and seven other towns to receive the "Great Migration" to follow.

By 1640 about 25,000 persons had journeyed to the colony, though many returned home after their initial harsh experience with the climate, the soil, and their neighbors. Thereafter, as the Puritans themselves ruled England, migration ceased; and though it was resumed after 1660, the number of newcomers remained small. Quakers and members of other independent sects had been excluded as diligently as possible. Catholics were quarantined and deported. By 1689 New England was characterized as a place of "a very home-bred people . . . exceeding wedded to their own way." To which the founders would have been pleased to say, "Amen."

Massachusetts Bay did not escape the usual cruel first years of colonization in the new world. Soon, however, the experience and character of its settlers told, and Winthrop's fears that we should "fall to embrace this present world and prosecute our carnall intentions," seemed about to be realized almost from the start. The settlers quickly established trade with England, exchanging native fish, fur, lumber and potash for necessities and amenities to be had in the mother country. Local industry also started early to produce the materials for shelter, food, and clothing, and to build ships for commerce. Churches, of course, the Saints erected practically on arrival, and in 1636 they organized their first college to train the "learned clergy" of the future. In 1638 John Harvard bequeathed to the new school his library and half his estate and since then it has borne his name.

In 1642 the Saints adopted legislation seeking to further public education below the college level. This legislation proved ineffective, and five years later, after noting that "one chief point of that old deluder, Satan [was] to keep men from a knowledge of the Scriptures . . . by keeping them in an unknown tongue," the Massachusetts legislature required that each town of fifty householders "should at once appoint a teacher of reading and writing, and provide for his wages;" and that each town of one hundred householders "must provide a [Latin] grammar school to fit youths for the university, under a penalty of £5 for failure to do so." Since everyone in early Massachusetts was required to live within a half mile of the town church, these acts covered the education of all the young people in the colony. Moreover, they were copied by the other New England settlements, except Rhode Island.

These Massachusetts laws established a principle of compulsory public education new to the English-speaking world, and one on which American education theory has since built. But the results in the seventeenth century fell far short of the law's intent. School terms commonly were limited to a few winter weeks when boys were not needed on the farms. Teachers were ill-trained and often dissolute; discipline took as much time as any other activity.

The Massachusetts Bay charter established a Company, not a commonwealth, and Winthrop and his board of directors carefully concealed from Charles I their intention of creating an independent state where (as Cotton Mather later explained), "we would have our posterity settled under the pure and full dispensation of the gospel; defended by rulers who should be ourselves." Certain influential Englishmen, however, soon took pains to enlighten their monarch on what was afoot. Among them were Sir Fernando Gorges and the papist, John Mason, both of whom had claims to land in the new world which conflicted with the Puritans' plantation. Charles was far too occupied trying to save his head from Puritans and Parliament in England (he failed, of course) to pay heed to New England's enemies, and Winthrop and his colleagues were left free to proceed as they wished. Yet the questionable charter hung like a cloud over the wilderness Zion—not least because all local land titles existed only under its authority—and malcontents in Massachusetts itself periodically threatened the "elect" with appeals to the English crown to preserve "English liberties" in America.

As the precious charter prescribed, Winthrop and his board soon set up a commonwealth government with a deputy governor, eighteen administrative "assistants," and a general "Courte or assemblie" to legislate for the community at monthly or more frequent meetings. All the assistants were supposed to be freemen—i.e., shareholders in the Company—and all freemen were to sit in the General Court. The charter provision requiring *eighteen* assistants immediately proved embarrassing, for there were not that many shareholders in the whole first group of settlers. Thus some who were not freemen were named assistants, and this tight little group alone manned the General Court. Since the charter gave only the Court the right to induct others into the ranks of freemen, the self-perpetuating nature of the oligarchy was obvious from the start.

Too obvious. In the very first year a hundred votaries of mammon, in their own opinion as "visible elect" as their rulers, demanded to be made freemen with an appropriate voice in the government. Torn between the fear of losing an industrious group of settlers and allowing them to share in Saintly power, Winthrop's oligarchy tried to eat its cake and have it too. The petitioners were granted the coveted title of freemen; but the meetings of the freemen's General Court were restricted to one a year and its functions solely to electing the governor and assistants. The oligarchy would then proceed, unchecked, to exercise all the prerogatives of government, including the assessment and taxation of property. This "compromise" was made in 1630. The next year the assistants ruled that thereafter no one could become a freeman who was not a member of an approved Puritan church.* Three years later, they ruled that no new church could be established without their consent.

This was piety overreaching itself, as the petitioners suspected, and in 1634 they demanded to see the charter which Winthrop had kept locked up. Again the oligarchy squirmed. Winthrop permitted the petitioners to read the charter and acknowledged the powers of the General Court under it. But instead of permitting all freemen to sit in the Court where they would rule by force of numbers, the oligarchy transformed it into a representative body made up of the assistants and two or three deputies elected by the freemen of each of the towns. When, by 1644, the number of deputies threatened to become too large for the assistants to control proceedings, the oligarchy divided the Court into two houses, a court of deputies and a court of assistants, and gave each a veto on the acts of the other, a power the deputies already had over the assistants in the single-house Court.

By an act of 1635, the oligarchy gave unprecedented freedom in local government to the freemen of the separate towns. Thereafter, the general town meeting became characteristic of New England; and to this day in many small communities the entire voting population participates directly in decisions on such important subjects as schools, land use, roads, water supply, and police. Yet this "concession" early in the seventeenth century was made, after all, only to Puritan Church members (which by the law of 1631 all freemen had to be). In effect it extended the sway of the oligarchy over local affairs, and did not allay in the least the conflict for control of the Bible Commonwealth itself between the unanointed visibly successful and the self-anointed "visible elect."

* For all their insistence on church attendance, the Puritans were most reluctant to admit members into their church. Their aim indeed was to keep out all but the "visible elect." Admission, as Curtis Nettels writes, "entailed a threefold scrutiny of the applicant's religious experience: first by the pastor (who might reject the applicant), then by the church officers, and finally by the congregation." This was an ordeal not to be undertaken lightly, especially given the social penalties that would accompany failure in a community such as Massachusetts Bay.

One of the most vigorous blows of the "elect" in this conflict was the promulgation of the Cambridge Platform in 1648. Presbyterians not Separatists in principle, in the new world the Saints had become Separatists—or Congregationalists—in fact. The elders of each Puritan congregation, like the freemen of each New England town, came to rule their own church, subject to the arbitration of disputes by a synod—a general court—of clergymen, which the General Court of the Commonwealth could call. In 1648, after learning that Cromwell had admitted Baptists, Quakers, and members of other "radical" sects into his "New Model" army, the General Court called a synod in Cambridge, Massachusetts, expressly to sever their lingering ties with Presbyterianism in England. Toleration of the sects by Cromwell had confirmed the New Englanders in their belief that in the entire world they alone were now the true Calvinists and Christians, and that Massachusetts Bay had become the "hidinge place" indeed, not only from the tyranny of Charles I but also from the Protector's "pernicious errors." Lest the sects gain a foothold in Massachusetts Bay, the synod went on to confirm the unity of Church and State in the Commonwealth and to make the civil government directly responsible for the enforcement of the religious and other decrees of the Congregational clergy. The "dictatorship of the visible elect" that resulted (to use Perry Miller's characterization) came to be called the "New England Way."

Yet as Professor Miller says, under the Cambridge Platform "New England was no longer a reformation, it was an administration." The basic aim of "completing" the reformation of the Anglican Church in England became subordinated to buttressing the rule of the Congregational Church in New England; at the same time, the "visible" saintliness of the Congregational Church itself became blurred by the appeal of its "elect" to force. As the agents of God grew hidebound, the agents of materialism grew ambitious. At the last, the Restoration of the Stuarts to the throne of England in 1660 and the re-establishment of the Anglican Church immediately thereafter insured the victory of worldly wealth in the Bible Commonwealth. In 1662, fearful of an English investigation of their "tyranny" (after Massachusetts merchants like Samuel Maverick had filled Charles II's counselors with the horrors of the "New England Way"), the Massachusetts General Court accepted the "Half-Way Covenant," by which nonmembers of the Congregational Church once more were permitted to become freemen and participate in civic affairs and to have their *children* baptized into the Covenant of Grace.

Concession had come hard and late to Massachusetts Bay. In its early days it had other ways of bringing to book what Winthrop once characterized as "the mutinous contentions of discontented persons, . . . the seditious and undermineing practices of hereticall false brethren." Among the first of the "false" was Roger Williams. Almost from his arrival in 1631 Williams rebelled against the idea of the government punishing men for their opinions and beliefs. His persistence in this liberal position led the General Court to expel him from the Commonwealth in 1635. The rulers planned to ship him back to England. But in midwinter Williams fled to his friends among the Narragansett Indians. The following spring, on land purchased from them, he established the settlement that grew into Providence, Rhode Island.

Three years after the Williams episode, deciding at her trial that "two so opposite parties could not contain in the same body without hazard of ruin to the whole," the General Court expelled the "heretical" Anne Hutchinson. In 1638 she and her followers established Portsmouth, Rhode Island. In the next five years two other separatists had set up communities near Providence and Portsmouth, and in 1644 Roger Williams got a "patent" from Parliament under which they all might combine under one government. Ten years later, Williams wrote of Rhode Island, "We have long drunk of the cup of as great liberties as any people we can hear of under the whole heaven. We have not only been long free . . . from the iron yoke of wolfish bishops, and their popish ceremonies. . . . We have not felt the new chains of Presbyterian tyrants, nor in this colony have we been consumed with the over-zealous fire of (so-called) godly Christian magistrates." In 1663 Rhode Island received a formal charter by which it could elect its own governor and which barred no one from political life on religious grounds.

In the mid-1630s other groups, seeking better lands as well as broader tolerance, moved from Massachusetts Bay to land claimed by the Dutch in the Connecticut Valley. The Dutch never were able to enforce their claim and in 1639 the towns settled from Massachusetts drew up the "Fundamental Orders of Connecticut" to unite their government. This is held to be the first written constitution in American history. Like Rhode Island's "patent," Connecticut's "Fundamental Orders" were modeled on Massachusetts's government, though the autocratic power of the Governor was curtailed in both new settlements. In 1637 an independent community, centered in New Haven but including other towns as well, was established along Long Island Sound. In 1662, Charles II united this with the older Connecticut settlements to form one colony. Its domestic government became as clerical and oligarchic as Massachusetts's own; but as far as relationships with England went, its charter was as liberal as Rhode Island's. Other Massachusetts men moved north in this period to future Maine and New Hampshire, but they remained under Massachusetts jurisdiction.

The conflict with the Dutch in Connecticut was only one of many experienced by New Englanders. The French to the north actually claimed the whole eastern coast to North Carolina, and persistently molested the Protestants. Most menacing of all were the Indians, who had been given sufficient cause. In 1643 four New England settlements, Massachusetts, Plymouth, Connecticut, and New Haven organized the New England Confederation, which lasted until 1684. Rhode Island was conspicuously omitted, one of the Confederation's objectives being the nurturing and defense of religion. But a military defense league was foremost in the federators' minds. The Confederation's sternest test came in King Philip's War (named for the defeated Indian chief) in 1675, when it virtually wiped out the Narragansett tribe and permanently ended the menace of Indians to southern New England. This war, in which at least a thousand Indians perished, also cost New England about five hundred dead. More than forty towns were either utterly destroyed or so thoroughly burned and pillaged that they remained impoverished for years. The surviving Indians, moreover, moved north, allied themselves with the French in Canada, and helped the French check New England's efforts to expand.

While thus establishing governments and carrying on wars, the early colonists were also rethinking their relations with England. In 1651 Massachusetts let it be known that "Our allegiance binds us not to the laws of England any longer than while we live in England, for the laws of the Parliament of England reach no further." This statement, repeated in other colonies, was recalled by many spokesmen at the time of the Revolution. But well before then, the independence of spirit it manifested was to stand England herself in good stead in her coming conflicts with Spain, the Netherlands, and above all with France, for control of the new world.

Chapter Three

The Contest for
North America

Sixteenth-century ships were small, slow and dirty. They could make only one round trip a year between Europe and the Orient, no more than three between Europe and the new world. Most of them were owned by private merchants and great trading companies, but ruling princes and monarchs also maintained ships of their own. In times of peace, businessmen often leased these ships for commercial voyages or operated them on commission while trading on the ruler's account. In time of war, the prince or monarch might requisition the merchant fleet at a substantial price and combine it with his fleet in battle. In the sixteenth century, merchantmen and men-of-war, merchant captains and naval captains were interchangeable and commerce and war were one.

In the seventeenth century the Dutch led all other Atlantic powers in improving the quarters and especially the diet of crews which characteristically were depleted by scurvy on long ocean voyages. With an eye to greater tonnage, maneuverability, and fire power, the Dutch and others also advanced the design of hulls. Simplicity in rigging was still another objective, the attainment of which cut the size and cost of crews and added flexibility to their assignments. By the eighteenth century, commercial rivalry among Atlantic powers led to such constant fighting that they neglected the development of professional navies only at great peril. At the same time progress in the development of distinctive commercial vessels and commercial services continued. By 1750 the westward voyage between England and America, for example, had been reduced to a month, the frequency of sailings raised to one or more a day, and safety improved to the point where ship insurance was at once an insignificant cost and a highly remunerative business.

In earlier times, in countries of self-sufficient manors and peasantries with few wants, trade had been an occupation largely of ambitious city entrepreneurs; and merchants might prosper or fail with little consequence to the prospects or pride of their fellow men. In the eighteenth century, this innocent conception of trade still hobbled policy-making in the rival Atlantic states. Yet, as commercial competition grew, the heart and sinew of entire nations gradually became involved. Such stirring English songs as "Rule Britannia" and "God Save the King" date from the mid-eighteenth century. Commercial privateers continued to account for most of a nation's naval strength; but specialized fighting squadrons, flying their own ensigns, gradually extended their control over the organization and outcome of hostilities.

In the eighteenth century dynastic rivalries still caused and colored wars, while religious differences, as of old, added bitterness and savagery to campaigns. Yet as wars grew in number and mercenaries were hired to fight them, costs mounted and funds to keep mercenaries in the field became decisive. Since such funds flowed increasingly from the new world and the Oriental trade, the ultimate prize proved to be not Alsace, or Burgundy, or Sicily, or the Spanish, Austrian, or Polish thrones, but India and America and control of the seven seas which tied their wealth to Europe. By the middle of the eighteenth century the ultimate contestants were England and France; the ultimate arbiters not their redcoats or regulars, but their navies, their commerce, and their colonies.

ENGLAND AND HER COLONIES

The contest for the outposts and oceans of the world did not reach its showdown stage until 1756. Mobilization for this contest, on the other hand, had begun under Raleigh and his contemporary, Champlain, even before Britain or France had staked out a permanent position in the new world. By 1620, though "Navigation Acts" to promote maritime strength already had a long and futile history in England, Parliament was enacting measures to force Virginia to ship all her tobacco home, and exclusively in English bottoms.

After the Dutch took advantage of England's civil strife in the 1640s to strengthen their hold on English trade, Cromwell's parliament voted in 1651 to exclude alien ships from English ports and alien goods from English settlements. Cromwell also revived the fighting navy under the redoubtable Robert Blake and in 1652 opened the wars on the Dutch which ultimately cost them New Amsterdam. In pursuing his "Western Designe," he also warred on Spain in the West Indies where Jamaica fell to the English in 1655.

The Navigation Acts of 1620 and 1651 were adopted when the English navy either was in decay or occupied on more mortal missions than port patrol. That these acts would be honored by the colonists or the continental powers without strict enforcement was but a pious hope. After the restoration of the Stuarts in 1660, however, Parliament enacted new and comprehensive navigation measures, which, with later extensions, regulated the economy of the colonies until the Revolutionary epoch.

The basic Acts were passed between 1660 and 1663. They restricted all trade between England and her colonies to ships built in either place and owned and manned by English subjects. With the exception of perishable fruits and wines, all non-English goods destined for the colonies had first to be "laid on the shores of England," where a duty would be collected. On re-export to America in English or colonial vessels, part of the duty might or might not be refunded. Finally, whatever their ultimate market, certain "enumerated" colonial staples—including initially only tobacco, which had been controlled since 1620, West Indian sugar, and a few minor items—could be shipped nowhere but to England whose home merchants would set the purchase price and gain the re-export trade. Not until 1673 were limits put on intercolonial trade itself, nor until 1733 on trade between the colonies and non-English islands in the Caribbean. Before 1660, enforcement of the navigation acts had been left largely to indecisive parliamentary committees. To enforce the stricter Stuart measures, responsible royal officers were appointed.

The new "civil list," however, soon proved far from effective. Many appointees were mere court favorites placed by Charles II

and James II in positions to recoup or enlarge their fortunes at
the colonials' expense. Others were royalist zealots who interfered
intolerably with colonial liberties and England's own. Thus it was
not long before the rising merchants (and the upper aristocracy of
great Whig landholders allied with them) tired of this costly administration and, for many other reasons, of James II himself.

Catholic James, who as Duke of York had secretly housed Jesuit
congregations and later publicly proclaimed his conversion to
Rome, had taken the throne in 1685, the very year in which his
cousin and mentor, Louis XIV, revoked the Edict of Nantes and
resumed persecution of French Protestants. After crushing the
Puritan revolt under the Duke of Monmouth in the year of his
accession, James's "bloody assizes," administered by the maniacal
Judge Jeffreys, suppressed English Dissenters with such venom that
many Anglicans themselves took fright. James also flouted the Test
Act of 1673, which forbade all but Anglicans to hold public office
in England, and placed Catholics in positions of influence and
power. They and he together then appropriated much of the
property of the Anglican Church. These acts alienated even royalist
Tories who believed in the divine right of kings. When in 1688
James fathered a son and the chill menace of a Catholic succession
was felt throughout the land, Tories and Whigs together harried
James out of the Kingdom.

In James's place the Whig Parliament brought in James's
daughter Mary and her Dutch Protestant husband, the ambitious
William of Orange, who ruled England as William III. Thus was
asserted, at least for English constitutional theory, the superiority
of the elected representatives of the "people" over their own
"elected" King.* As elaborated by "the great Mr. Locke," this

* Actually, the "Glorious Revolution" of 1688 was more in the tradition of
ancient Magna Carta in asserting the privileges of the great landed barons
as against the pretensions of the "people's" king. Henceforth, Parliament
declared (fixing a growing custom into law), members of the House of
Commons shall receive no stipend, thus making it difficult for any but the
very rich to sit. To insure this result, Parliament ruled in 1710 that no one
could be a member of the Commons who did not have a yearly income *from
the land* equal to about $15,000 today, a lordly sum for the times. No won-
der, as Daniel Defoe observed, there was a sudden rage among city businessmen to become landed aristocrats. "I dare oblige myself," he wrote in 1728,

theory became one of the pillars of the colonists' own position that since they did not participate in the election of parliamentary representatives in England, their allegiance could be only to their own local "parliaments" and the king *these* parliaments "elected."

In 1689 Parliament enacted the famous "Bill of Rights," by which the practice of their religion by Dissenters became "tolerated" under law; but Parliament at the same time revitalized the Test Act of 1673 excluding Dissenters from public life. In 1701 Parliament also decreed that henceforth no Catholic could be King. While accepting this second measure, the colonists promptly rejected the application of the Test Act to America. "Toleration," they said, was included in Locke's trilogy of "life, liberty, and property," as a subject to be pursued by them in their own way. But King William promptly undertook to show them how wrong they were on the constitutional issue and proceeded to give British administration of colonial life, liberty, and property its nearly final form.

In place of the Stuarts' ill-defined group of administrators, William set up a permanent Board of Trade and Plantations which, in conjunction with the Privy Council, henceforth conducted American affairs. To strengthen the Board's hand, Parliament in 1696 created a system of admiralty courts in America, manned and managed by the home country, before which colonial merchants might be tried without a jury when caught evading the rules of trade. These rules themselves were made stricter in William's time and his successsors', mainly by adding items to the "enumerated" list. Conspicuous among the additions were naval stores and ship masts which were enumerated in 1706. Parliament, on the other hand,

---

"to name five hundred great estates, within one hundred miles of London, which . . . were the possessions of antient English gentry, which are now . . . in the possession of citizens and tradesmen, purchased . . . by money raised in trade; some by merchandising, some by shopkeeping, and some by meer manufacturing; such as clothing in particular."

The Catholic South of Ireland gave sanctuary to James II after the Revolution and Louis XIV continued to use it as a springboard for harassment of England. In the North of Ireland, in turn, the Scotch-Irish Presbyterians who had been settled there eighty years earlier to keep the Catholics down, were proving far too competitive as businessmen. When, for the benefit of absentee English landlords and their mercantile and manufacturing allies, Ireland's economy was crushed soon after the "Glorious Revolution," the stage was set for one of the great migrations to America.

banned the exportation to England of colonial staples, notably wheat, flour, and fish, which competed with England's own.

Under William and Mary and their successors, other restraints were placed on the colonies, allegedly to strengthen the empire. The Stuarts, as early as 1660, had banned the migration to America of England's skilled artisans. Starting with the Woolen Act of 1699 (applied to Ireland as well as America), colonial artisans themselves were forbidden first to export and later even to make many manufactured commodities. In 1684 the coinage of much needed currency was forbidden in America; thereafter restrictions on money, banking, and credit also grew harsher. In 1705, in an effort to direct colonial capital and energy toward the production of certain scarce materials required in shipbuilding, bounties and other inducements were offered. These promoted hemp growing in North Carolina and other poorer parts of the South; and the extraction of pitch, the making of tar, and the cutting of ship timber in New England forests and elsewhere. But in general, it might be noted, cajolery worked no better than confinement, and England continued to have to look outside the empire for much of her supply of these materials; just as the colonists, when so moved, looked away from England for markets.

THE NEW WORLD THEATER

While England strove to keep her rivals out of colonial waters (and the colonists out of theirs), she also maneuvered to keep them off colonial territory.

In 1660 England's holdings in the new world were menaced on the north and west by Catholic France, and on the south and west by Catholic Spain, each with her Indian allies; while England's chief maritime rivals, the Dutch in New Amsterdam, split her colonial domains in two. As early as 1653, Virginia had permitted some of her more intractable settlers to move south and establish independent outposts as buffers against the Spanish and the Indians on Albemarle Sound. Ten years later these outposts were included in the huge grant made by Charles II to eight aristocratic promoters who had been helpful in restoring him to the throne. Reaching from Virginia's southern boundary to the borders of Spanish Florida and westward to the as yet unplaced "South Sea," the new grant was called by its grateful proprietors Carolina.

The owners of Carolina, the leaders among whom had made their fortunes in Barbados, promptly made elaborate plans for peopling their territory with tenant farmers squeezed out of the West Indies by the great sugar plantations. On the rents from these farmers they expected to live comfortably in England. Not before 1670, however, did the proprietors succeed in landing the first contingent of settlers. After a quarter of a century as a fur-trading outpost, Charleston in the late 1690s became the center of a flourishing rice-growing region. In the next thirty years a mixed population of Englishmen, French Huguenots, Portuguese Jews, and African Negroes gave the town the cosmopolitan character it was to enjoy for another century and a half.

The Carolina proprietors had no more success in controlling the turbulent Albemarle settlers than Virginia had had. By 1729 these settlers had grown much more numerous than the population of distant Charleston and its vicinity, but poorer soil and a poorer port limited the Albemarle group's prosperity. In 1729 a combination of troubles prompted the proprietors to sell Carolina back to the Crown. As the proprietors had long since given the Albemarle settlers a separate governor and assembly, George II, now King, proceeded to make two royal colonies of the region, one called South Carolina, the other North Carolina. Three years later, in 1732, George infuriated Spain by granting territory below South Carolina to a philanthropic "trusteeship" headed by James Oglethorpe, a man "driven by strong benevolence of soul," to help those imprisoned for debt in England make a fresh start in America. Oglethorpe named his grant Georgia. The Spanish never conceded Georgia's alienation, and not until the United States purchased Florida from Spain in 1819 was the incendiary southern border of the "convict colony" defined.

While English settlements encroached on Spain to the south, other English ventures took care of the Dutch in what became the Middle States. Even before the Dutch surrendered New Amsterdam in 1664, Charles II, with Parliament's consent, made a grant of their territory between the Connecticut and the Delaware rivers to his brother, the future James II, as yet Duke of York. At the same time Charles added enough other territory to extend James's holdings from Maryland to Maine. In 1673 the Dutch recaptured New York, as James had renamed the place, but returned it the next year.

In 1688, James, now King, joined New York to New England, the more strictly to govern both. But neither James nor that arrangement lasted out the year. Under William and Mary, New York became a regular royal colony with a royal governor and a council appointed by the King, and an elected assembly. New York's repressive history, however, continued to discourage newcomers. The merchants of New York City and Albany controlled taxation and enterprise, while the old patroons, to whose number James had added favorites of his own, remained undisturbed in the enjoyment of their rents from majestic Hudson Valley estates.

Three other colonies were carved from James's unparalleled grant. In 1664, to two of his aristocratic friends who had been among the promoters of Carolina, James sold the territory between the Hudson and the Delaware, which they named New Jersey. In 1702 New Jersey became a royal colony. In 1704 Delaware, heretofore merely the three "Lower Counties" of William Penn's domains, also got an independent charter. The third colony was Penn's own.

Born in 1644, the son of an admiral who had been close to James I, William Penn was converted to the Quaker faith at the age of twenty-three. By then the Restoration bishops had caused the imprisonment of thousands of Friends while three of their missionaries to Boston had been hanged by the Saints. In accordance with their belief, the Quakers simply turned the other cheek. Such evidence of pure faith and practical Christianity held off if it did not humble their persecutors, and by the 1680's the sect had come upon better days. Indeed, Penn himself wished for much more than "a place to hide" for his coreligionists. Dedicated to the idea that man's "native goodness was equally his honor and his happiness," as he wrote in his *Frame of Government,* Penn had moved far ahead of his times in believing in most men's capacity for politics and all men's right to make their own peace with their

Creator. For a grand "Holy Experiment" in republicanism and religious freedom he sought an ample grant in the new world.

Penn's quest was satisfied in 1681 when, as compensation for a debt of £16,000 owed to his father, the Admiral, the Duke of York gave his young friend that part of his territory reaching west from the Delaware River between the borders of Maryland and New York. It was after a half-century of litigation over Pennsylvania's southern border that the Mason-Dixon line was drawn in 1767.

Penn's "Holy Experiment" was an immediate success. Offering some of the best land in the world on the best terms in America, the Quaker matched his known humanity as a leader with manifest liberality as a proprietor. He served as his own first governor assisted by a council of landowners "of the best repute for wisdom, virtue and ability," elected by the taxpayers. On his arrival in America in 1682, Penn found about a thousand Swedes and Dutch settled on his domain. He generously permitted them to keep their land without charge. By then he had also found takers for more than 300,000 of his new acres, mainly among persecuted German sects whose members had had small chance to recover from the carnage of the recently ended century of religious wars. But enough Englishmen, Friends and others, came from abroad or from Quaker settlements in older colonies to give Pennsylvania and especially its seaport, Philadelphia, a permanent English cast. Though a royal colony for a few years under William and Mary, Pennsylvania was soon restored to its founder. Penn's own fortunes sank so low in later years in England that he went for a time to debtor's prison. But his American venture prospered.

While the Spanish thus were pushed back in the south and the Dutch pushed out in the middle, the French in the north and west also felt the surge of England's expansion. The settlement of Pennsylvania itself was viewed by the French as a threat to their claims to the Ohio Valley, and their Indian allies constantly bedeviled the pacific Quakers. In the North, in 1679, New Hampshire was strengthened as an English outpost by being separated from Massachusetts and given a royal charter of its own. Ten years later the first of the series of wars began which ultimately eliminated the French from the North American continent.

Louis XIV had never become reconciled to the removal of his faithful Stuarts from the English throne in 1688 in favor of "Dutch William," and championed the cause of the "Pretender," whom he called James III. William therefore had a powerful personal motive for making war on France. More important, William's continental obligations always outweighed his concern for England. Thus when Louis threatened to overrun the Netherlands in 1689, William led a European "grand alliance" against him. Waged in Europe among princes as the War for the League of Augsburg, this conflict was fought for fur in America as King William's War. At its conclusion in 1697, France had strengthened her claim to the fur-rich Hudson Bay territory. Its sequel, however, began her long decline.

This sequel was the War of the Spanish Succession, or Queen Anne's War, which opened in 1702 (the year Anne succeeded William on the throne) and was terminated in 1713 by the momentous Peace of Utrecht. By one of the provisions of this peace the Bourbons were confirmed in their occupation of the Spanish throne, which they had grasped in 1700 and would hold until 1931. But in the new world, England reclaimed title to the Hudson Bay country, quieted whatever claims France had to Newfoundland, and took Acadia, or Nova Scotia, and St. Christopher in the West Indies from her. The peace treaty, moreover, recognized the Iroquois as British subjects and thereby gave England grounds to claim all their lands, including French territory in the Mississippi Valley as well as the valley of the Ohio.

France's commercial loss was also great, for by the terms of the Peace she surrendered the *asiento* to England. This was the exclusive privilege, once the prize of the Dutch, of selling African slaves to Spanish America. Besides this most profitable trade, Spain also permitted one English ship a year to visit Panama. This was like offering a bunch of golden grapes and inviting the English to take but one. Good manners could not withstand temptation, and with Jamaica and St. Christopher as convenient bases, the English swarmed into Spanish mainland ports. By this time, too, the rest of the British West Indies and Bermuda had all become jewels in the grand crown of empire; while from Bombay, acquired in 1661 as part of the dowry of Charles II's Portuguese Queen, Catherine of Braganza, British power continued to spread over India.

BRITISH AMERICA

The Peace of Utrecht was a magnificent victory for English arms and English diplomacy, one all the sweeter because it marked the humbling of Louis XIV, the paragon of absolutism, by the parliamentary "nation of shop-keepers" he despised. Indeed, the peace terms, while not conclusive enough to subordinate France forever, were too good to last. England's gains were Europe's goad; England's victory made England vulnerable.

The coalition which William led into the war against Louis in 1702 had come together, as one of its own treaties said, "especially in order that the French shall never come into possession of the Spanish Indies nor be permitted . . . to navigate there for the purpose of carrying on trade." English domination in America as a result of this war suited the continental rulers no better than French or Spanish. For almost two hundred years after Charles V in 1519 added the throne of the Holy Roman Empire to that of Spain, rival monarchs had joined one another in a bewildering series of alliances whose common objective was to maintain what came to be called the balance of power in Europe. After 1588 Spain had been slowly put in her place. Next, Louis the XIV's France loomed as the common enemy, the year 1700 marking the zenith of French power. Now it became England's turn. Her victory in 1713, as spelled out in the Peace of Utrecht, began her towering ascent toward Victoria's empire on which the sun never set. But it also made clear that a permanent corollary to the balance of power principle was wanted —one that brought the new world within the principle's orbit.

The first bitter fruit of this enlargement of the balance of power was England's loss of thirteen of her American "plantations," to the success of whose revolt in 1775 many European powers besides France were to contribute materially. Before the American Revolution, moreover, France herself was to try more than once to regain her old-world mastery and, with others, to contain England's expansion overseas.

Yet for a generation after 1713 internal problems occupied both France and England, and they were content to avoid open war. In 1715 Louis XIV died, leaving his bankrupt and starving country-men to recover as best they could under his five-year-old grandson, Louis XV. Actually, under Louis's Regent, the Duke of Orléans, and for a time under Louis himself, France did well. Her aristocrats reclaimed many of the rights they had surrendered to the absolute "Sun King"; and young nobles like the Baron de Montesquieu joined commoners like Voltaire in learning to admire if not to ape British political institutions. French trade and industry also flour-ished, to such a degree indeed that the political frustrations of the prosperous but powerless Third Estate help explain the ferocity of the Revolution which so shocked the world in 1789.

A year before Louis XIV's death, Queen Anne died in England. Her successor was George I, Elector of Hanover, the closest Stuart "cousin" who was not a Catholic. Many English tories preferred the "pretender," James III, and in 1715 (and again in 1745 when "Bonnie Prince Charlie" had succeeded to James's role) they re-belled against the new royal family. George I and George II, neither of whom learned English, spent little time away from their Hanover estates. The Whigs, however, were committed to the succession. While the "Whig Oligarchy" thus was kept busy quieting rebellion, it was also left free to develop those institutions of Parliamentary (aristocratic) supremacy which the French *philosophes* liked so much but which George III and his American colonists both were to challenge fiercely.

In British America this post-Utrecht period of relative peace, and especially the years 1721-42 during which the great Whig, Robert Walpole, virtually governed England, is usually called the era of "salutary neglect." The same conditions which prompted the mother country to forgo war with her rivals also bade her leave her colonies to their own devices. Under this regime, colonial life flowered. To be sure, America was breeding native social and political tensions, largely geographic or sectional in character; but these only grew out of the general prosperity which swelled the pride and the purses of the colonists until the empire could no longer contain them, internal tensions and all.

THE LABOR FORCE

Visions of quick fortunes from local El Dorados and from unob-
structed short routes to China drew European adventurers to the
new world even as late as the eighteenth century; and until well
past the middle of the nineteenth century drew Americans themselves ever westward across the continent. Long before this, however, a more substantial economy had developed in North America
which supported a pleasant style of life in newer towns like Charleston and Philadelphia as well as in Boston, Newport, and New York,
and gave a manorial veneer to the large tobacco, rice, and (toward
the end of the era) indigo plantations of the rural South.

Through most of the colonial period, of course, at least ninety
per cent of the white settlers in the English mainland colonies continued to live in huts, lean-tos, or one- or two-room log cabins on
half-cleared family farms scattered through the sunless forest from
Maine to Carolina. As settlement moved inward from the coast and
from the choice river bottom lands, the migrants gradually lost contact with the civilization of the major ports and the exchange centers
on the navigable streams. Yet the majority of farmers, at least in
New England and the Middle Colonies, managed to save themselves and their families from barbarism and to stake out a col-
lectible claim on the future.

In the towns themselves the majority also worked with their
hands for long hours at occupations—as carpenters, bricklayers,
bakers, weavers, coopers, chandlers, sawyers, sadlers, locksmiths,
and the like—which had engaged their forebears and themselves in
the old world. Families frequently ran to ten or more children; and
their quarters on narrow, noxious streets were likely to be cramped
and cold in winter, tumultuous and hot in summer. After the first
two or three decades of settlement firewood became scarce and expensive. Pigs and cattle had the run of public thoroughfares, and
while towns very early passed laws against littering the streets with
refuse, even in the eighteenth century observance and enforcement
often were lax. Sickness was frequent, epidemics common, fire a
constant hazard.

Nevertheless, eighteenth-century townspeople endured nothing like the sodden segregation of the great cities of later periods. Proximity to the country opened hunting and fishing and other rural recreations to practically all town dwellers. In the towns themselves everything was within walking distance of everything else, the common architecture was engaging, the water front open and attractive, market places lively, taverns frequent, ale and rum abundant and cheap. City laborers' wages ran four or five times those in London and elsewhere, while independent artisans and shopkeepers commanded high enough prices for the frugal early in life to accumulate capital with which to improve their condition and their children's chances.

Many, of course, failed to make good in the American environment and in American terms, and throughout the colonial period (as well as later in American history) the disheartened or disenchanted sailed back to the troubled lands they had fled. But immigration, over and above the growing number of Negro slaves forcibly brought in, far outstripped emigration. The newcomers included British government officials and representatives of London and Bristol merchants, who were to form the nucleus of the higher circles in the colonies. Numerous middle-class artisans, mechanics, and shopkeepers also came over. But most of the immigrants were from lower levels of society and found work as farm laborers, especially in Virginia, Maryland, and Pennsylvania. Preponderant among these poor were Scotch and Scotch-Irish Presbyterians and South of Ireland Catholics, victims of Anglicanism and mercantilism in Great Britain; and pietistic Palatine Germans, victims of the Catholicism and expansionism of France.

Probably half the immigrants each year, and virtually all the non-English ones before the 1730s, entered under some form of "white servitude" into which they had sold themselves to ship captains and "soul brokers" in exchange for their ocean passage. The voyage itself was viler even than on slave ships and on the average a third of the "servants" died. The conditions of servitude in America usually were set forth in an "indenture," or contract, which was auctioned off to employers or their agents on arrival in colonial ports. The term of servitude ranged from four to seven years and sometimes longer. "Very often," according to one expert, servants bound themselves for a second term, and sometimes even for life. During the term employers had the legal right to resell the "indenture"—in effect, the person himself—at any time, and in many other respects to treat the "servant" as a slave.

Many of the contract laborers did not wait for their terms to end before striking out for themselves. Runaways were frequent, and most of those who succumbed to the lure of the forest and the wild life of the frontier went unapprehended. Some who did work out their terms were granted fifty or more acres of land, as their contracts often stipulated, but the available evidence suggests that this provision was frequently unobserved or that the freed servant sold off his grant for a ready pittance. Even in an exclusively agricultural colony like Maryland fewer than 10 per cent of the servants appear to have settled down as free farmers. In Georgia, the Trustees once came to the cynical conclusion that "many of the poor who had been useless in England were inclined to be useless likewise in Georgia." The more northerly colonies also had their rural derelicts, while the towns from the 1650s on faced the problem of pauperism arising from servants "sett att Liberty," who "either through Idleness or sickness become unable to help themselves."

The institution of white servitude survived the Revolution. George Washington was ordering the purchase of servants for his Virginia plantation in 1784; while in Pennsylvania as late as 1793 it was held that tampering with the indenture system would bring severe social and economic dislocations.

EXPORT STAPLES AND THE SPECULATIVE URGE

While most colonial Americans cultivated the soil, the main sources of the gentry's wealth in all the mainland colonies in the eighteenth century had become ocean commerce and land speculation. Even in the overwhelmingly rural tobacco country of Virginia and Maryland tobacco planting was profitable because ocean-going ships visited each season at the great planters' private wharves along the many navigable rivers. In South Carolina and Georgia the rivers were less hospitable to deep-sea vessels, but they called at Charleston and Savannah where the rice was collected for export. When tobacco profits failed, and rice culture exhausted the limited regions suitable to it, land speculation rescued those among the gentry who managed not to succumb to debt.

The Navigation Acts enumerating tobacco afforded the Virginia and Maryland planters a secure market, which became all the more inviting late in the seventeenth century when the West Indies gave up tobacco culture to concentrate wholly on sugar. Yet the tobacco trade had certain drawbacks that were not long in making themselves felt. From the time of James I, who considered tobacco "a corrupter of men's bodies and manners," use of the leaf was periodically discouraged in England by heavy sumptuary duties, and by the 1750s the continent was taking 80 per cent of the tobacco first landed in British ports. Even for this tobacco American planters had no choice but to accept the prices offered by British tobacco merchants. These prices, in turn, often reflected severe depressions in the tobacco trade brought about by continental wars, political manipulation of taxes, and the ordinary ups and downs of business life. In order to maintain their aggregate incomes at such times, planters would devote more and more acreage and slaves to the leaf. But when the market was weak, overproduction only depressed prices further. At the same time, the merchants continued to charge planters exorbitantly for carrying the staple in their ships and for insurance, credit, and local haulage.

When the planters, moreover, ordered foreign wines, silks, books, and other rare or manufactured commodities, the English tobacco merchants served as purchasing agents. Outraged eighteenth-century Virginians estimated the merchants' commissions for this service at 100 per cent. Though scrupulous merchants might be found, Robert Walpole himself noted in the 1730s that the planters were reduced "to a state of despair by the many frauds that have been committed in [the tobacco] trade."

Speculation in land was a natural hedge against the uncertainties of overseas conditions. One of its special charms was that princely land grants—sometimes running to tens of thousands of acres—often could be acquired with little or no cash through political favoritism or chicanery, and illegal private deals with Indian tribes. Indeed colonial assemblies offered bounties and other inducements such as free surveying to gentlemen who would further the security of the established settlements by undertaking to populate the wilderness on the Indian, French, and Spanish frontiers.

The rising demand for timber for use as fuel and potash, and in shipbuilding, house building, and cooperage often made land speculation profitable from the start. Hunger for tobacco land among the established gentry themselves, aggravated by the common belief that it was cheaper to mine plantation after plantation than to maintain the fertility of the land first cleared, also helped push up the price of virgin acreage. Most important was the market provided by the tens of thousands of free immigrants (and runaway servants) who came down the Shenandoah Valley after 1730. Many of them simply "squatted" on God's country, claiming a "natural right" to it, and held off the more or less legal owners at gun point. But large numbers, either singly or in groups, had brought some capital and were eager to buy or rent land.

Had the great tobacco planters kept adequate books of account, nevertheless, they might have discovered that even land speculation did not insure their solvency. The extraordinarily long and cumulative credit allowed them by English merchants, usually with the next year's crop pledged as security, also helped to keep the planters' true financial condition from them. A third factor, no doubt, was the expansiveness of plantation life itself, which could not be constrained by debt, however hopeless. "Such amazing property," observed Philip Fithian, tutor to the Virginia Carters, "no matter how deeply it is involved, blows up the owners to an imagination, which is visible in all." They "live up to their own suppositions," a Londoner commented, "without providing against Calamities and accidents."

Between 1734 and 1756 rising tobacco prices also put a premium on land, and the tobacco gentry enjoyed their "golden age." In that generation, writes Samuel Eliot Morison in his essay on "The Young George Washington," "the traditional Virginia of Thackeray and Vachel Lindsay—'Land of the gauntlet and the glove'—came into being."

Virginia society, to be sure, remained almost exclusively agricultural and those aspects of culture that flourish in populous commu-

nities failed to flower here. "Few Men of Fortune," wrote the
Reverend James Murray in 1762, "will expend on their Son's Education the Sums requisite to carry them thro' a regular Course of
Studies. . . ." William and Mary College (the first colonial college
after Harvard) had been opened at Williamsburg in 1693 and was
well endowed by the established Anglican Church; but few students
spent more than a year there, and that year was usually one of
indolence and sport. Sons of great planters sometimes were sent
to England for study; but many of them remained there permanently. The Scotch-Presbyterian invasion of the Virginia back country brought to that region a taste of Calvinist enthusiasm for reading
and writing and the catechism; but even this soon lost its heartiness
in the wilderness and failed to seed the more settled regions.

Religion itself, moreover, though enriched by periodic "revivals,"
tended to wane. In 1739 the English evangelist, George Whitefield, visited Virginia during the most spectacular of his many
American tours to exhort sinners to repent. Whitefield, like Jonathan Edwards in New England and Theodore Freylinghuysen in
New Jersey, other leading revivalists, preached that all Christian
believers could enjoy a "new birth" if they would genuinely yield
their souls to Christ. Unlike Edwards, Whitefield spoke more of
God's love than Hell's terrors; but his very voice carried like the
trumpets of jubilee to sinners gathered by the thousands to hear that
the Day of Judgment was near at hand.

Whitefield embellished his exhorting with wild laughter, flights
of song, and violent gestures and gyrations that soon had his
listeners shrieking, dancing, and writhing on the ground to manifest that the spirit of the Lord had entered them. The number of
"conversions" mounted wherever Whitefield went; yet the "Great
Awakening," as this first vast revival is called, soon passed. Historians have attributed much importance to it. There can be no
doubt that it gave a strong impetus to the growth of the Baptist
Church, Methodism, and other nonintellectual sects, especially in
the back country. It also set a precedent for later revivals, all of
which lent a characteristic emotional tinge to American religious
observance. Yet between revivals, "converts" in Virginia often
lapsed back to the more secular concerns of the frontier and made
later revivals as much worldly as worshipful meetings.

The established Anglican Church made the most of the "wild and savage" revivals to stress its own "moderately cultivated" demeanor. Few enjoyed the universal upperclass preoccupation with the horse more than the ministers of the Established Church—places reserved largely for the sporting "younger sons" of the gentry. So profound was this preoccupation that Professor Morison undertakes to explain George Washington's personal discipline in terms of his youthful experience with young steeds. Everybody rode for exercise. Horse races, and the gambling that inevitably accompanied them, became daily events. Above all, the hunt, riding to hounds, became the sport of bluebloods, admission to the hunt club the accolade.

Yet few indeed could afford for long this gamy life and its attendant expenditures for clothes, equipages and body slaves, mansions, parks, and wine. Eventually, the Virginians' debts for honorific imports grew so calamitously that Governor Francis Farquier was moved to remark in 1766 that their "Blood . . . is soured by their private distresses." His regretful observation was elicited in part by the first great legislative scandal in American history. In 1766 John Robinson, for twenty-eight years the esteemed Speaker of the Virginia House of Burgesses, was convicted posthumously of having issued " £ 100,000 of retired currency to insolvent planters" in what is judged to have been "a desperate attempt to save the Virginia aristocracy from economic ruin."

Many were not saved by Robinson's largesse. But even among those who crashed, perhaps especially among them, the vast West beckoned more beguilingly than ever, and Virginians' visions of landed wealth grew feverish enough, as Washington's and Jefferson's did, to encompass the entire continent and indeed the entire hemisphere.

The rice planters of South Carolina worked their soil—and their slaves—far harder than the Virginians did and to far better purpose. Like tobacco, the principal markets for rice were on the European continent, and English merchants had hoped to service these markets through the re-export trade. To insure their monopoly, rice was enumerated in 1704, but was found to be subject to spoilage from the long storage and excessive handling necessitated by re-export. Rice was made virtually free once more in 1729 and prices soared. When Georgia assumed the frontier role of buffer against the Spanish in 1732, the rice planters of South Carolina could settle down to business. Suddenly rice became the bonanza crop, the gold and oil of the mid-eighteenth century, and fortunes were made in a season. By the 1750s the planters had extended their fields to Georgia itself and in the next decade proceeded to make that colony a virtual captive of its neighbor.

By the 1750s, moreover, encouraged by a Parliamentary bounty, many rice planters had turned to the production of indigo, which was urgently in demand as a dye by the flourishing English cloth manufacturers. Indigo fortunes soon reinforced rice fortunes, and the port of Charleston, its pastel mansions glistening in the reflected sunlight of the harbor, hummed with trade.

As late as the 1760s the rice and indigo gentry numbered no more than 2,000 families. "Nevertheless," observes Carl Bridenbaugh, the author of southern *Myths and Realities,* "the Carolina Society took its pattern from this gentry exclusively." Many gentry families were West Indian in origin and together they reproduced the culture of a tropical imperial island. On the mainland Negroes outnumbered whites only in South Carolina, and here the ratio was an overwhelming three to one. In Charleston itself, the mid-century population of about 10,000 was equally divided by color, and a sizable proportion of the Negroes were household and body servants. Numerous names among the gentry persisted: Laurens, Izard, Huger, Rutledge, Gadsden, Manigault. Yet it was hardly a static group. "Their whole lives," commented an observer of Charleston at its colonial peak:

> are one continued Race: in which everyone is endeavoring to distance all behind him; and to overtake or pass by, all before him; everyone is flying from his inferiors in Pursuit of his Superiors, who fly from him with equal Alacrity. . . . Every Tradesman is a Merchant, every Merchant is a Gentleman, and every Gentleman one of the Noblesse. We are a Country of Gentry. . . . We have no such Thing as a common people among us: Between Vanity and Fashion, the Species is utterly destroyed.

In Carolina, as distinct from Virginia and Maryland, debt was not endemic. "The planters are full of money," noted Henry

Laurens in 1750. Money, in turn, naturally flowed to land; and even by mid-century, prospective settlers in Carolina complained that "the valuable land is chiefly engrossed by the wealthy." Twenty years later a skeptical visitor from New England wrote that "the rise in value of lands seems romantic, but I was assured they were fact."

The Carolina nabobs had been in no hurry to unload their wilderness estates. Much of the land they preserved in its pristine forest grandeur. The sections they cleared were less for farming or for sale than for the timber trade and for the exploitation of the fabulous red pine whose products—pitch, tar, turpentine, and resin—a Carolinian boasted, "administer more to the necessities and comforts of mankind than any other trees whatever." Thus the newcomers who overflowed into South Carolina after 1750 from already well-filled Pennsylvania and Virginia, were usually forced to the "cutting edge" of the frontier. Here, in the "cowpens" and beyond, many fell to the nomadic life of herdsmen of wild swine and cattle (not infrequently stolen from the Indians) from which civilization had striven for centuries to raise mankind. Some found this life so congenial that they made their fortunes out of meat and skins and tallow; a veritable back country gentry arose in South Carolina on the foundation of the most extensive cattle ranges in the colonies. But most of the settlers continued to slide on the social scale, becoming primitive huntsmen on the prowl for elusive game, including Indians.

Illiteracy was higher in South Carolina than anywhere else in England's mainland colonies, and her foreign-born "Back Parts" had few defenses against the "mixt Multitude" of "white-collar" people carried inland on the stream of settlers like camp-following women. The "Back Parts" complained frequently of white-collar venality to the reigning grandees of Charleston, where all South Carolina government was centered, but to so little consequence that "Finding . . . they were only amus'd and trifled with, all Confidence of the Poor in the Great is destroy'd and . . . will never exist again."

When violence broke out in the South Carolina back country in the 1760s, it was directed (as in North Carolina too) against the "'mercenary tricking Attorneys, Clerks, and other little Officers' who were almost exclusively native-born adventurers of English

descent." In the Revolution, when the Carolina planters fought
England, the non-English "Back Parts," Anglophobe though they
were to the marrow and to the man, chose to fight the planters.
Charleston grandees survived both conflicts and, by measures similar to those of the Virginians, pushed the speculative frontier right
through Spanish Florida itself.

THE SEAFARING NORTH

In the North, ocean commerce played the dynamic role that the
export staples—tobacco, rice, and indigo—played in the South. The
Saints of Massachusetts Bay were first on the waters, but the slavers
and smugglers of Rhode Island and the Quakers and Yorkers down
the coast gave them a mighty run for their money.

With characteristic Saintly good fortune, Cromwell's wars with
the Dutch occupied the world's two major commercial powers just
when the ambitious men of Massachusetts were prepared to forsake
their stubborn soil and "farm the sea." Yankee fur and fish were
welcome in cold and Catholic ports; Yankee clapboard, planks,
staves, meal, and grain were needed in the West Indies where concentration on the production of sugar grew so intense that virtually
every requirement of settlers and slaves had to be imported. Yankee
trade spurred Yankee shipbuilding, and new-world vessels flying
many different flags became common sights at every old-world
wharf. But the Saints themselves did most to spread their fame.
"It is the great care of the Massachusetts merchants," wrote the
"unfriendly but accurate" Englishman, Edward Randolph, as early
as 1676, "to keep their ships in constant employ, which makes them
trye all ports to force a trade."

Yankee prosperity became especially marked after 1713 when
prices obtained in the West Indies began a long upward trend. In
1713, also, England acquired Newfoundland and Nova Scotia and
control of the teeming fisheries in their waters. Along with the
fisheries, came the development of offshore and distant whaling.
Soon Nantucket whalers were ranging from Brazilian shores to the
Arctic Ocean. Fishing and whaling together further spurred shipbuilding—and related industries like rope and sail making—and
drew welcome artisans and mechanics to New England towns from

abroad. Town requirements promoted Yankee agriculture, which was further benefited by improvements in country roads.

As in the South, prosperity fathered indulgence. It is true that Calvin had admonished all believers "perpetually and resolutely [to] exert themselves to retrench all superfluities and to restrain luxury." But by the eighteenth century many Saintly merchants had moved over to the more engaging Anglican communion. King's Chapel, the first Anglican Church in Boston, had been opened in 1688 and promptly became the resort of the rich. For those who would not move so far there was the liberal Brattle Street Church, opened in 1698. "Give an account of thy stewardship," Calvin had commanded the "elect." But those who joined the liberal congregation were specifically exempt from "a public relation of their experiences." They, not God, it seemed, had become the creators of their wealth. They demanded that they be excused from discussing it, if not displaying it, in public.

In the eighteenth century Boston's "codfish aristocracy," and its imitators in the lesser ports, began to affect swords, satins, and solid English broadcloths. Grand brick mansions appeared in the vicinity of Beacon Hill furnished in the best English tradition. In the country, comfortable "colonial" homes supplanted the rude structures of pioneer days, and their owners dressed and drank in conformity with their rise in substance and status. The old requirement that all residences must be within half a mile of the town church had long since broken down, and with its passing went the solidarity of religious observance, the strength of the public school plan. But to the optimists of the day these fallings-off appeared only as temporary costs of growth and prosperity.

Fortunately, indulgence gave the greatest impetus to trade. New England's few staples, notably her catches of cod, competed with England's own. Fish and other staples could be shipped elsewhere, even within the navigation system. But no region that wanted them could supply New England with the luxurious English manufactures the Yankee gentry craved. New England's escape from this predicament took ingenious and illicit forms, including outright piracy of gold. When the Peace of Utrecht in 1713 deprived young Yankee privateers of legal enemies to plunder, peaceful merchantmen of all registries became their prey. New York, in fact, was the open haven of the leading pirate chiefs, the favorite haunt of their crews. But Yankee merchants readily accepted pirate booty to soften the arteries of trade.

New England's major *commercial* voyages took the form of a triangle, with England usually at one of the points. Most lucrative, and least respectable, was the slave triangle, to which staple agriculture outside New England gave such an impetus. Slaves usually were brought to the American mainland colonies in English ships or those of Charleston and other southern registries. Rhode Islanders were by far the most active northerners in this branch of the slave traffic. The characteristic Boston slaving voyage found the Yankees carrying rum to Africa to pay for or otherwise obtain their human cargo. They carried the Africans to the British West Indies, a passage the horrors of which defy exaggeration, and in exchange took on coin, and molasses from which to distill more rum and repeat the program.

Early in the eighteenth century, when British West Indian sugar production began to fall off, Yankee captains took to visiting "closed" French and Spanish West Indies to fill out their molasses cargoes. France and Spain complained to England about this contraband trade. Nagged by her own West Indian capitalists, England also complained to New England, but, under Walpole, halfheartedly. Finally, in 1733, Parliament yielded to the importunities of the British investors in West Indian plantations—who, until the Revolution itself, always carried most weight in American affairs— and passed the Molasses Act forbidding the mainland colonies to trade with foreign islands. This Act was a blow at the Yankees which they well knew how to parry. Smuggling became at once a common and a fine art. England's tightening of the enforcement of the Molasses Act after 1764 was one of the principal goads to revolution in New England.

Commerce and kinship have always walked hand in hand. Just as English mercantile families in the days of Henry VIII and Elizabeth sent their relatives to settle in Spain when the Spanish trade became active, so the New Englanders sent their brothers, sons, and in-laws to the West Indies. As often as possible they also engaged as agents in England members of their families who had resisted the lures of the new world. Failing family connections, religious confreres were sought out; failing these, at least fellow countrymen were preferred to the Dutch or Spanish or Portuguese. Characteristically, family business was enlarged and family ties multiplied by intermarriage among mercantile families.

In no group was the principle of blood being thicker than water more carefully observed than among the Quakers. The Friends' religious beliefs even more strongly than the Puritans' own promoted success in business. Persecution by the dominant sects in Europe and America, in turn, dispersed the Friends' business leaders over the towns of the western world. "There were Quakers," writes Frederick B. Tolles, the historian of colonial Quaker enterprise, "in most of the ports with which Philadelphia had commercial relations. A number of them, like the Hills in Madeira, the Lloyds in London, the Callenders in Barbados, the Wantons in Newport, and the Franklins in New York, were related by marriage to the leading Quaker families of Philadelphia. . . . The intelligence which they received through their correspondence and from itinerant 'public Friends' . . . from Nova Scotia to Curaçao and from Hamburg to Lisbon . . . was chiefly concerned with prices current and the prosperity of Truth." No wonder that Philadelphia, which did not exist until a half century after the founding of Boston, had become by 1755 the leading city in the new world, and "Quaker grandees" Philadelphia's leading men.

Philadelphia's Quaker merchants, of course, also had significant local advantages to build on, in particular an extensive back country populated with industrious farmers. Pennsylvania grain quickly became available for export in large quantities and the farmers themselves offered a thriving market for the imports. The scale of back-country business boosted Philadelphia itself and made Philadelphians all the abler to indulge in English manufactures and other exotic wares.

Quakers might use "plain talk" like *thou* because "the pronoun *you* in the seventeenth century connoted social superiority"; and "keep to Plainness in Apparel As becomes the Truth." Yet, as eighteenth-century travelers noted, while Quakers above "the ranks of *Inferior People* . . . pretend not to have their clothes made after the latest fashion . . . and be dressed as gaily as others . . . they strangely enough have their garments made of the finest and costliest materials that can be produced." Behind the simple façade of their rows of brick houses, moreover, were to be found the most elegant furniture, paintings, rugs, portraits, and paneling in America; while their "plantations," as they called their country estates, came to have elaborate English gardens and other signs of grace.

As early as the 1690s rich Quaker merchants began moving to the Anglican Church to escape the public surveillance of their "stewardship" by the Meeting. Others who simply fell off in their observance became differentiated from tiresome true believers by the epithet, "wet Quakers," of uncertain origin. Still others, influenced perhaps by the Quaker attachment to "Laborious Handicrafts," as against the Puritan stress on the intellect, were drawn to Newtonian science and experimentation. Such men often became Deists, for whom God was little more than the "Heavenly Engineer" who set the world going. Eighteenth-century Deism, far from unknown in Virginia and New England, flourished in Philadelphia. Its apostle was Benjamin Franklin, who said Americans admired their God "more for the Variety, Ingenuity, and Utility of his Handyworks than for the Antiquity of his Family."

Among the more interesting imports of rich Philadelphia merchants were the instruments, materials, and books of the science of their day. To "make their remittances" for these and more decorative worldly goods, the Quakers faced the same problem as the Puritans. Their grain found no kindlier reception in England than Yankee grain; their other staples, no greater English outlets than Yankee fish and wood. Thus they were forced to send their goods and ships to many parts of the world for coin and products that England wanted. In all the trading areas then known, in ships built in their own competent yards, the Friends offered the Puritans stiff competition and often came off with the richer prize.

Nature endowed New York City with the finest harbor in the Atlantic world. Yet as late as 1770 New York ranked fourth among

American ports behind Philadelphia, Boston, and Charleston. The slow development of the Hudson and Mohawk valleys was largely responsible for the city's backwardness, but the pirate taint contributed. New York merchants liked pirate wares, which were cheap and profitable; and pirate crews, who were free spenders. About 1700 Captain Kidd and his "men of desperate fortunes" made New York their rendezvous. Soon after, the governor of the colony pressed the Admiralty in London for a vessel swift enough to "destroye these vermin who have hitherto made New York their nest of safety." But nothing happened for almost a quarter of a century, and conventional trade and traders naturally kept to more orderly Boston and staid "Quaker Town."

Yet New York did grow. By the 1670s flour had outstripped fur as the port's leading export. In 1678, foreshadowing the kind of business sense that was to insure New York's nineteenth-century greatness, the town passed an ordinance insuring by practical methods of inspection the uniform quality of its product. New York flour gradually won a reputation that made Philadelphia look to its own lax laws. After 1720 the pirates were run out of New York waters, and the port became a more active competitor with those of New England and Pennsylvania, whose problem of remittances to England it shared. By then Dutch had virtually disappeared as a common language in New York, though the city retained the brash worldliness and cosmopolitan character with which the Dutch had endowed it when they welcomed ships of all nations to the harbor.

INVESTMENT AND EMPIRE

Though the limitations imposed on colonial manufacturing by the Navigation Acts were observed in America no more than was convenient, manufacturing drew little of the profits of trade. Aside from shipbuilding, only two colonial industries attained importance. One was the distilling of rum for export, chiefly by the merchants of New England. The second was iron manufacture, concentrated largely in Pennsylvania, New York, and Virginia. Stimulated by Parliamentary legislation in 1750, the American output of pig and bar iron was pushed to levels beyond England's. In defiance of the legislation which was aimed at developing colonial raw materials for use by

English fabricators of iron ware, the colonists, especially the Pennsylvania Quakers, built up their own iron fabricating works too. By the time of the Revolution these had become the largest and most efficient in the world.

Colonial manufactures were profitable, few more so than the Pennsylvania iron industry. Yet as a Quaker wrote in 1768, "It is almost a proverb in [Philadelphia] that every great fortune made here within these 50 years has been by land." Northern capitalists, Franklin conspicuous among them, invested heavily in city lots and buildings which appreciated gratifyingly throughout the eighteenth century. More significant were northern speculative investments in the wilderness, which rivaled the southern planters' own. After 1750 Yankee merchants monopolized much of the virgin forest of New Hampshire and Maine; while the holdings of Philadelphians, with Franklin again in the lead, encroached on and sometimes illegally went beyond the borders of Maryland and Virginia.

Unlike manufacturing, colonial land speculation had England's blessing. In the enduring struggle with the French it was the parsimonious Walpole's policy to employ the British navy to keep the enemy away from America and to encourage the Americans to occupy all the land they could before the French already there took it as their own. After Walpole's fall, British and colonial speculators fought for primacy in exploiting the American west, and the conflict between them became one of the principal sources of imperial disharmony. The conflicting land claims of American speculators, in turn, aggravated as they were by vague colonial charters and overlapping boundaries, turned colony against colony in feuds that helped drag out the Revolutionary War and continued long after independence. Within each colony itself, the land problem set section against section, tidewater against "Back Parts," East against West. The growth of litigation over land rapidly raised the income and status of American lawyers. Gradually they supplanted the clergy as the chief spokesmen for their commonwealths, and for each commonwealth's ruling group.

THE CORE OF SECULAR POWER

Colonial society like English society on which it was modeled (with significant exceptions, such as Negro slaves in the place of tenants on the "manors") was stratified virtually from the beginning of settlement. And contrary to common belief, status distinctions became sharper as time passed. Between 1700 and 1760 the population of the mainland colonies grew from about 250,000 to more than 1,500,000, an advance unprecedented in the history of the world and startling to observers abroad. Yet even more striking was the early emergence of a few thousand leading families—a few hundred in each of the colonies—and their aggrandizement in wealth and power and more subtle claims to primacy.

Nowhere was this more apparent than in the structure and tendency of colonial politics. Nominally at the head of the government in each colony was the Governor. In Rhode Island and Connecticut he was elected by the legislature. In Pennsylvania and Maryland he was appointed by the absentee proprietor. Elsewhere (including Georgia after 1752) he was appointed by the King. Assisting the Governor and appointed by him was the Council, or upper house of the legislature. The lower house, usually called the Assembly, was made up of representatives elected by those qualified for the franchise and troubling to exercise the privilege. Local government was organized differently in the different colonies; but even in Virginia, where the Governor appointed the local justices of the peace, the most important local officers, he was likely to be a captive of his appointees who resisted interference once they had their commissions.

The Governor's strength lay in his power to veto legislation. When he was a man of ability and acumen, of course, he could promote legislation in the direction of the King's policy, or forestall or constrain Assembly action before a veto became necessary. But the mutual confidence on which such management must be based dwindled in the eighteenth century. The Assembly's strength lay in its control of appropriations, including those for the Governor's salary and the enforcement of Parliament's as well as its own decrees. In the eighteenth century virtually all colonial assemblies (like Parliament in England) used their control of the purse to usurp control of the entire government. A few families, in turn, used their wealth and status to control colonial assemblies for generations.

The perpetuation of oligarchic control rested on two objective conditions. One was the limitation of the franchise in practically all the colonies to those with considerable property, preferably in land. Religious qualifications for voting were frequent, but with the exception of the almost universal disfranchisement of Catholics and Jews, they were enforced less and less strictly where property qualifications could be met. In Virginia and elsewhere, voters who met the property qualification in each of two or more counties, could vote two or more times, and many were the rugged rides taken by the gentry to exercise this privilege of plural voting (made easier by the spreading of election dates) when contests promised to be close.

The second condition was the withholding of representation in the Assembly from new inland settlements, either by refusing to establish counties and towns in thickly populated areas or by keeping down the number of representatives from such areas. In South Carolina throughout the colonial period the inland settlements had no representation whatever, nor even local courts.

Yet the objective conditions for oligarchic rule tended to be sustained by more subtle sanctions arising from the popular recognition of merit based on family and fortune. Locke's conception of property, on which oligarchic pretensions rested, went well beyond the crassness of mere ownership, exploitation, and accumulation. Property was the foundation of personal liberty, liberty the foundation of moral independence, morality the foundation of welfare. Property carried obligation as well as power; great property carried the obligation of great power exercised for the common good. This idea of aristocracy was scarcely challenged in the eighteenth century until near its end. The idea of democracy did not gain much impetus even in America, until the nineteenth century.

Colonial history is dotted with local rebellions against the ruling oligarchies. The issues between the general population and the gentry were many. One of the most persistent had to do with the supply of money. The chief single need for currency among the general farming population was for taxes, which in their estimation (and usually they were right) were not only too high but unfairly apportioned. In addition, the population generally was in the same relation to the speculators and importing merchants as the planters were to the merchants abroad. That is, they were in debt—for land

and goods. Like all debtors, they clamored for a plentiful supply of currency with which to meet their obligations. Often enough their clamor was heeded; but since paper money had a tendency to be overissued and to decline in value on that account, the gentry grew increasingly conservative about meeting the debtors' demands. Thus taxes went unpaid, mortgages unserviced, loans unredeemed. Collectors, meanwhile, were tarred and feathered and run out of the debtors' vicinity at gun point. Organized efforts at collection or foreclosure often were met by organized armed resistance.

Conflicts over the money supply and taxation were not necessarily sectional in character, though they tended to be most acute where the back country felt the overbearing weight of tidewater and town tycoons. Other political conflicts were largely sectional in origin. One of the most persistent complaints of new settlers on the moving frontier was the failure of the provincial government to protect them from the Indians, the French, and the Spanish. A second was the failure of the government to provide passable roads to markets. A third was the failure of the easterners to establish local courts in the back country and save the settlers days of travel and neglect of crops and cattle to have even minor disputes adjudicated. A fourth was the levying of tithes for the benefit of the established churches, few of whose members and none of whose ministers were to be found in the wilderness. The failure to extend representation and the franchise to the back country grew into a major grievance largely because of the aristocrats' reluctance to allay the back country's other grievances.

Yet the claims of the aristocracy to political place and power were themselves rarely challenged. Probably a fourth or more of the entire white population of the colonies was illiterate; probably a fifth even of the literate knew little or no English, while many more used it only awkwardly. Of the remainder, most of the rustics could imagine no greater peril than having to address constituents in public or to assume effective places in legislative councils. City mechanics and artisans must have had similar misgivings. As late as 1788, in seeking their support, no less, for the Constitution just framed, Hamilton wrote of them: "They are sensible that their habits in life have not been such as to give them those acquired endowments without which, in a deliberative assembly, the greatest natural abilities are for the most part useless." He urged the Constitution upon them because it attached the interest of the merchant, "their natural patron and friend," to the interest of the nation.

The common run of voters were as yet proud to be represented by the great men of their colony. Thus they returned generations of Byrds, Carters, Harrisons, and Washingtons to high office in Virginia; of Van Rensselaers, Schuylers, and Livingstons in New York; of Logans, Norrises, Pembertons, and Dickinsons in Pennsylvania. In Massachusetts, where the franchise was liberally bestowed and where the middle class of artisans, shopkeepers, shipwrights, and small farmers probably were better educated than elsewhere, Hutchinsons, Hancocks, Olivers, Bowdoins, and Brattles all clung to high office generation after generation. Elections often were hotly contested, but the candidates almost invariably were to the manor born. A popular political genius like Sam Adams, the first great rabble-rouser in American history, developed a "machine" of his own which functioned in the Revolution as the famous "Caucus Club." But even an Adams made little headway against the oligarchs until they needed him to help meet the British challenge.

THE CONQUEST OF NEW FRANCE

For all its trappings of wealth and power, the colonial "aristocracy" was distinguished (not demeaned) by the fact that its members worked. Only in South Carolina, where the planters claimed an inability to withstand the heat of the rice fields and where they could afford to lounge in Charleston, was there to be found an American leisured class. Elsewhere, the responsibilities of management—on plantation, ship, or mining estate, in city shop, distillery, or office—devolved upon the head of the house. No greater contrast could be found with New France. French settlers, of course, worked hard, ranged far, traded shrewdly, and fought with skill—but chiefly for the aggrandizement of the Crown at Versailles and the enrichment of its noble sycophants.

French new-world enterprises were directed largely from Quebec. These were almost exclusively of two kinds: the fisheries, which brought Frenchmen into constant and violent conflict with New Englanders; and the fur trade, in which Frenchmen and their Indian allies menaced the frontiers of English settlements from Georgia to Maine. The English colonies, though they carefully nursed their dislike of one another, had grown by 1750 into a veritable nation of nearly a million and a half persons who were feeling increasingly hemmed in and harassed by the maritime activity, the territorial claims, and the border violence of New France. New France itself had scarcely 60,000 persons, many of whom, no doubt, lived for the day of their return to the home country, and most of whose leaders felt this day being hastened by the outward thrusts of their vigorous English neighbors.

Other factors fed this mutual rivalry and suspicion, of which differences in religion were most divisive. Hatred and fear of Catholics was scarcely lessened in New England when French-incited Indian raids, following King Philip's War of 1675, periodically leveled exposed Yankee towns. In 1690, after political problems involving the legality of Massachusetts' charter and the security of her Established Church came to a head in England partly through French-Catholic meddling, Cotton Mather said, "It was Canada that was the chief source of New England's miseries. There was the main strength of the French. . . . *Canada must be reduced*." Two years later, when these miseries culminated in the notorious Salem witch hunts, the distracted accusers' principal charges against John Alden, one of their principal victims, was that "He sells powder and shot to the Indians and the French and lies with Indian squaws and has Indian papooses."

Catholic France was on the minds of eighteenth-century Englishmen—and English colonists—the way Germany was on the minds of twentieth-century Frenchmen. The dynastic and imperial wars of the eighteenth century helped keep the English—and colonial—mind inflamed. These wars were renewed in 1739 when hostilities broke out between England and Bourbon Spain.

When illicit English traders swarmed over the Spanish Main after the Peace of Utrecht, the Spanish created a special Caribbean coast guard and manned it with the roughest pirates they could find. An influential "war party" soon arose in Parliament, which Walpole could not restrain. In 1739, to impress Parliamentary leaders, the "war party" decided to make an example of a certain Captain Jenkins. On testifying before the House of Commons, Jenkins "commended his soul to God and his cause to his country," and swore that the ear he carried in a little box was his memento of a brush with Spain's defenders. Parliament promptly voted to fight the "War of Jenkins' Ear." "They are ringing bells now," commented Walpole. "They will soon be wringing their hands."

Ambitious naval onslaughts on the Atlantic and Pacific coasts of Spanish America between 1740 and 1744 brought the British nothing but disaster. By the time they counted their dead, moreover, the little War of Jenkins' Ear had led to a renewal of the big war for the world. In 1740 Maria Theresa came to the throne of Austria. In the same year Frederick the Great came to the throne of Prussia and promptly attacked a part of Maria Theresa's domains. Bourbon Spain and France soon joined him, and the British and the Dutch moved to assist the Austrians. Frederick and France proved invincible on land in this war, called in Europe the War of the Austrian Succession. But when Spanish and French new-world funds were choked off by the revived English fleet in the American phase of the conflict known as King George's War, a stalemate loomed. By 1748 both sides were ready to admit that the struggle was deadlocked and they signed the Peace of Aix-la-Chapelle restoring the *status quo ante bellum*.

The Treaty of Aix-la-Chapelle was a truce, not a settlement; and even before it was signed both sides had begun to prepare for a showdown. In 1747, with the formation of the Ohio Company of Virginia, England had encouraged colonial land speculators to stake out huge tracts in the Ohio Valley "inasmuch as nothing can more effectively tend to defeat the dangerous designs of the French." In 1749 the governor of Canada dispatched his own man, de Bienville, to occupy the valley, and in the next few years other Frenchmen were sent there to build forts. In 1753 Governor Dinwiddie of Virginia ordered young George Washington west to protest against French activity. Such peaceful tactics got nowhere and the next year Washington, now a lieutenant colonel of the Virginia militia, took

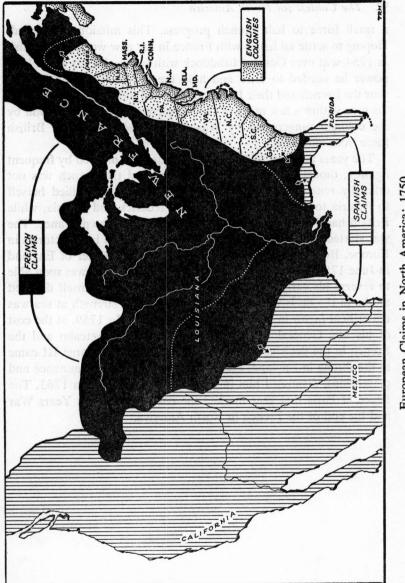

European Claims in North America: 1750

a small force to halt French progress. This mission also failed. Hoping to settle all issues with France in the new world, the British in 1754 sent over General Braddock with two regiments and all the power he needed to seize and hold the valley. But the following year the French and their Indian allies killed the General and routed his men within a few miles of their objective. Only quick action by the colonial rangers led by Washington saved the entire British force from massacre.

The years between 1748 and 1755 thus were marked by frequent fighting, though war between the British and the French was not officially renewed until 1756. By then France had allied herself to Austria to check the ambitions of Frederick and Prussia, while Britain had joined Frederick the better to keep down France. The war started with a series of great Franco-Austrian land victories in Europe. But William Pitt, on becoming chief Minister of England in June 1757, so heavily subsidized Frederick that he was soon able to reverse his early defeats. At the same time Pitt himself directed affairs in the decisive theater in America. Here strength at sea was the critical factor in the mobilization of forces. In 1759, at the cost of his life, General Wolfe took Quebec from Montcalm and the French in the decisive battle of the war. In 1760 George III came to the throne in England. He soon tired of Pitt's predominance and pretensions, dismissed him in 1762, and made peace in 1763. The Peace of Paris that year marked the end of the Seven Years War and the end of the French in North America.

Chapter Four

These United States

In the three-quarters of a century between the Glorious Revolution of 1688 and the glorious Peace of Paris which concluded the Seven Years War, England's rivals on the continent had failed to free their peoples from the autocracy of the Crown, the exactions of the nobles, and the dogmas of the Church. In the same period, the fortunately situated island of England had developed those liberties of movement, thought, and enterprise that would soon win even greater victories than those of the recent great war by means of the Industrial Revolution. Even before the advent of the factory system late in the eighteenth century, machinery had begun to give England such advantages in the manufacture of basic commodities that she could afford to lead the world away from miserly mercantilist ideas to expansive liberalism and *laissez faire*. The world henceforth would be won by cheap goods instead of costly wars, by open markets instead of forced monopolies, by workshops instead of warships.

The English triumph of 1763 marked the end, not the glorious beginning of an era. Yet the "Great Commoner," William Pitt, and his American friend, Franklin, were among the few aware of the rising new forces around them. After all, it was not until 1776 that Adam Smith publishd his revolutionary *Inquiry into the Nature and Causes of the Wealth of Nations,* which systematized and popularized the new politico-economic ideas. And another generation or two were to pass before Jeremy Bentham and John Stuart Mill built into new philosophical systems the ideas of representative government and personal liberty emerging from an industrial and urban society.

In 1762, Horace Walpole wrote: "I am a bad Englishman because I think the advantages of commerce are dearly bought for some by the lives of many more. . . . But . . . every age has some ostentatious system to excuse the havoc it commits. Conquest, honor, chivalry, religion, balance of power, commerce, no matter what, mankind must bleed, and take a term for reason." In England for more than two hundred years men had fought and bled for mercantilist trade. They could hardly be expected to surrender its glittering rewards at the moment of their greatest triumph in its name.

Congratulating themselves on Pitt's crushing of French establishments everywhere, English merchants now looked forward eagerly to encompassing the whole world, including the new world, in a trading and speculating monopoly. Congratulating themselves on Pitt's elimination of the French and Spanish menace in America, influential colonials began eyeing their own continental destiny. Pitt might have reconciled these conflicting British and American aspirations; but with him infirm and out of favor, lesser men only hastened the clash.

As late as 1775, Pitt advised Parliament concerning America: "We shall be forced ultimately to retreat; let us retreat while we can, not when we must." Two years later, "risen from my bed to stand up in the cause of my country," he cried: "You may ravage —you cannot conquer; it is impossible; you cannot conquer the Americans; I might as well talk of driving them before me with this crutch."

FREEBORN ENGLISHMEN

After 1763 the English middle classes became the creators of England's industrial might, the makers of her policy, the guarantors of her greatness. Yet for a generation the nation was embroiled in political crises brought about by the efforts of the great Whig merchants and landlords to cling to their aristocratic supremacy in the House of Commons and to maintain the Commons' supremacy in the country and empire. Until the 1760s the great Whig families had acted as though there were no king and no populace; in this they were abetted by George I and George II whose major preoccupation was their estates in Germany. In consequence Walpole and his Whig successors ran the country. George III, on taking the throne in 1760, proved far less docile. So did his people, who were tiring of Whig corruption. But the Whigs only stiffened their resistance.

George III greatly respected the English Constitution, and especially the role of Parliament in English government. His unswerving support of Parliament, indeed, is what got him into so much trouble with the Americans who had no representation in England and (as they insisted) had parliaments of their own at home. The Parliament George cherished, however, was not the Parliament of the Whig families. To break their hold on the "popular" Commons, George began subsidizing certain members who became notorious as the "King's Friends." But this was a game the Duke of Newcastle, Walpole's heir in command of the Whigs, could play out of far greater experience than the young monarch. The competition between the Crown and the "Government" for Commons votes made it difficult for anyone to remain untarnished. As a contemporary slogan went, the mood was "Everyone for himself, and the Exchequer for us all."*

Yet even in the slough of the late Georgian era, Shakespeare's "other Eden, demi-paradise" remained by far the freest country in the old world. The spirit of individualism, the sense of ownership, the eagerness to participate in political decisions that property was giving to growing numbers of Englishmen, lay dormant on the continent. There the ranks of the educated were closed, debates

---

* Tradition holds that George III was seeking to subvert party, not to say popular, government in England and restore the "tyranny" of the Crown. But "popular" government was far in the future; while "party" government implies modern "party responsibility," which itself implies an organized and active "opposition party" seeking to dislodge the party in power. Such an opposition party did not exist in England until after the American Revolution. The terms "Whig" and "Tory" were seventeenth-century designations for "Low Church" people on the one hand, and "High Church" people on the other. Connection with the Jacobite uprisings in 1715 (see p. 68) tainted the Tories with "treason" in the same way that connection with the American Civil War in 1861 tainted the Democrats. The English Whigs used this taint as zealously as the American Republicans were to do later, with the result that there was no effective *party* opposition to them. Political conflicts took place almost exclusively within Whig ranks and political aspirants—even the great Pitt himself—had to find Whig favor.

went on in salons, political decisions often ignored the debates, and resistance was treated as sedition. In England the ranks were open, the debates public, the decisions subject to remonstrance. Nowhere was the press so militant, public discussion so general, public opinion so influential as in the island kingdom. After England conquered the world with her ships and freemen, English constitutionalism, English industrialism, English liberalism captured the imagination and energies of the world.

After 1763 a few men led England toward revolution at home by agitating through all the channels of public opinion to extend officeholding privileges and the franchise to nonlandowners, and to extend representation to the rapidly growing but politically powerless commercial and industrial cities. Among this radical program's sponsors—some of them as unstable and opportunistic as frustration could make them—American independence found its few friends in the mother country. But for liberal relations short of independence, the colonists claimed many more sympathizers, including Edmund Burke with his "fertile, disordered, and malignant imagination," the redoubtable Charles James Fox, the perceptive Adam Smith, Pitt, and even, had he been able to yield a little less to his pathological stubbornness once he had embarked on a policy, George III himself. Unfortunately, most other Englishmen, not least those embroiled in the power game, gave the "American problem" only passing thought.

"One free people cannot govern another free people," wrote the English historian, James Anthony Froude. This was all the more true of England and America, since Englishmen nowhere were so free as in the new-world colonies. "What do we mean by the revolution?" old John Adams asked reminiscently at eighty. "The war with Britain? That was no part of the revolution; it was only the effect and consequence of it. The revolution was in the minds and hearts of the people . . . before a drop of blood was shed at Lexington."

When in 1750 England passed the Iron Act prohibiting the manufacture of most iron ware in America, Franklin warned: "A wise and good mother will not do it." In 1751 he wrote a pamphlet to prove that in the not too distant future more English subjects would be living in the new world than in the old. This grand growth in numbers, he said, will create a market far beyond England's capacity to supply. Restraint on colonial manufactures will only push up prices and invite foreign competition and costly wars in which the colonies, "kept too low," would be "unable to assist her and add to her strength." Give Americans room and incentive to grow, America's philosopher-statesman advised. Then, he exclaimed, "What an accession of power to the British empire by sea as well as by land! What increase of trade and navigation!"

Franklin went unheeded in London. But London went heedless of the logic of world events. The triumphant Seven Years War which so puffed up the British also capped the prosperity the colonies had been enjoying since the days of Walpole's "salutary neglect." "You cannot well imagine," a visitor wrote from Boston in 1760, "what a land of health, plenty, and contentment this is among all the ranks, vastly improved within these ten years. The war on this Continent has been equally a blessing to the English subjects and a Calamity to the French." Such reports made the English, when the colonists resisted taxation to help pay for the war, feel American cries of poverty to be only the Puritan cant one might have expected. At the same time the prosperity thus reported gave Americans, as Governor Hutchinson of Massachusetts said later, a "higher sense of the grandeur and importance of the colonies." It moved them, in Sam Adams's words, to demand to be made "co-equal in dignity and freedom with Britons."

INDEPENDENCE

To be effective a rise in status must be accepted as well as asserted. Even during the war, however, colonial disenchantment had set in. Supercilious English army officers, largely Anglican, looked down their noses at *all* colonials as declassed Dissenters, and young Colonel Washington himself quarreled bitterly with them over recognition of his superior rank. Even worse were the surly Scots who improved their time on duty studying speculation in American lands with their mercantile and official countrymen long here.

Other wartime experiences were just as offensive to the colonials and more serious. Much of Massachusetts' wartime prosperity had resulted from her supplying enemy forces and conducting business as usual with enemy islands. In 1758 the British had stuck their noses into this unseemly commerce and visited upon Massachusetts that "terrible menacing monster the writs of assistance." These writs authorized customs officers to avail themselves of constabulary aid when searching private warehouses and dwellings for contraband. They were issued for the life of the monarch plus six months, and when George II died in 1760, British officials sought renewals in 1761.

Massachusetts' remonstrance against this interference foreshadowed the Americans' later difficulties with one another. Rhode Island smugglers had been omitted from attack by the writs. "We want nothing," said the Boston merchants, "but to be free as others are, or that others should be restrained as well as we." But certain lawyers took the higher ground that American "natural rights" had been invaded. Their leader was James Otis, Jr., who "first broke down the Barriers of Government to let in the Hydra of Rebellion." Sam Adams became Otis's able second, and together they worked up such a "Rage for Patriotism," that in a couple of years "scarce a cobler or porter but has turn'd a mountebank in politicks."

American land speculators also got a glimpse of the future in 1761. In anticipation of difficult administrative problems arising from the magnificence of her conquests, England that year instructed colonial governors to forbid further land sales in the West. Pontiac's Conspiracy in 1763 brought the bleak future a little closer. The defeat of France had left her Indian allies at the mercy of the colonists who took full advantage of the removal of the French menace from their borders. Early in 1763 the Ottawa chieftain, Pontiac, organized the remnants of his followers for one last blow at France's ancient enemy. Many settlers were massacred; but no colony, for all their recently vaunted prowess as Indian fighters, voted aid to Britain. British forces quelled the uprising, and to forestall any more of the kind, the King issued the inflammatory Royal Proclamation of October 1763. In this Proclamation George III closed to "any purchases or settlements" by "our loving subjects," the vast region between the Alleghenies and the Mississippi from Florida to Quebec.

In five years, nevertheless, thirty thousand white settlers crossed the mountains; and eminent Americans of the future such as Washington, Franklin, and Patrick Henry, organized or reorganized land companies to sell to those who would not "squat." In 1773 even Governor Dunmore of Virginia invested in Washington's land company and in 1774, with an eye on the land bonuses his poor recruits would soon yield up for a song in cash, led a foray of frontiersmen against the Indians in "Lord Dunmore's War." Along with Indian land his men seized a parcel of Pennsylvania territory which Virginia clung to until the end of the Revolution. Indeed it took the Revolution to confirm it to either commonwealth, for in June 1774, Parliament responded to conduct of this sort with the Quebec Act. By this measure the entire territory north of the Ohio River was annexed to the old province of Quebec, thereby voiding the claims of four different colonies to it. Massachusetts was not among them but received a shock as well. For the Quebec Act granted religious liberty to England's newly acquired French Canadian Catholic subjects on Massachusetts' northern border and restored their Roman political and legal institutions. By 1774 Massachusetts was primed to view such a generous measure with dread and suspicion.

By the time of the Quebec Act relations between the colonists and their English cousins had sunk so low that Virginia had already issued the call to the First Continental Congress. This body of representatives from twelve colonies (Georgia alone stayed away) convened in Carpenter's Hall, Philadelphia, September 5, 1774. What brought them together at last was, if not the spirit of rebellion, at least the love of liberty which they and their forebears had nurtured for a century and a half and upon which, in the past decade, England had presumed so carelessly.

The Seven Years War had almost doubled England's national debt and the cost of administering and protecting the vast new American empire won by the war had quadrupled. To help pay the interest on the debt and the cost of administration and protection, Parliament taxed the income of English landowners 20 per cent. The reasonableness of asking the prosperous Americans at least to share the cost of their own protection attracted the landowners' sympathizers, not the less so after Pontiac's Conspiracy showed that the colonists would not defend one another and that the cost of defending them all would not soon decline. As sympathetic as any to the landowners' plight was George Grenville, who became head of the King's government in April 1763.

Grenville's vision was as limited as his administrative zeal was fierce. To defend the American empire, Lord Amherst, in command in the colonies, wanted 5,000 men. Policy-makers in England, perhaps more fearful than Amherst of the quick revival of the French menace and perhaps more sordid in their search for jobs, preferred 10,000 men and Grenville pushed two ill-conceived acts to raise the money for them. The first, the Sugar Act of 1764, renewed the 1733 prohibition on colonial imports of molasses from the French and Spanish West Indies, even though Yankee distillers relied increasingly on these superior if illicit sources. At the same time the Act cut the duty on British West Indian molasses and proposed to make up the difference by new duties on other commodities and vigorous prosecution of smugglers. Despite the example of Walpole and Pitt, who had carefully eschewed stamp taxes, Grenville's second measure proposed the sale of stamps to be affixed to every sort of document, license, bond, or publication in daily use by all who were articulate, in trouble, or in trade. Worse, the stamps had to be paid for in *specie*. Worse still, this requirement came on the heels of the Currency Act of 1764. Passed by Parliament at the urgent behest of English merchants, this Act excused them from accepting depreciated Virginia legal tender notes in payment of debts; it also outlawed any further issue of paper money in America, and thus made specie all the more precious to trade.

Merchant demands for measures like the Currency Act might have reminded Grenville and his increasingly inept successors that it was the mercantilist system they were defending, and that, in Pitt's estimate, British merchants made profits of at least £2,000,-000 a year on colonial commerce. Such profits appeared to Pitt and the colonists to be "tax" enough. The colonists, moreover, had accumulated a war debt of their own of £2,500,000, which domestic taxes would have to underwrite. In the past the colonists had submitted to Parliamentary taxation which they judged, in retrospect, to have been required in the management of a mercantilist empire. The inconvenience and effrontery of the Sugar Act may have been what prompted them to search out broad grounds for its rejection; in any case, they discovered this Act's fatal flaw in its own preamble, which stated as the Act's purpose, "improving the *revenue* of this Kingdom." After a century of conflict with overweening royal governors, for the colonists to admit the *English* Parliament's right to tax them for *revenue* was death. Only their duly elected "parliaments" might exercise the power of the purse: "Taxation without representation is tyranny." The colonists scoffed at the British idea that they (like British industrial cities) were "virtually represented" in Parliament by strangers they never heard of; Pitt joined them in denouncing "virtual representation" as "the most contemptible" idea "that ever entered into the head of man."

"One single act of Parliament," said Otis about the Sugar Act, "has set the people a-thinking in six months, more than they had done in their whole lives before." That was in New England. The fatal flaw of the Stamp Act was that it set people *talking* everywhere. More than talking! In response to the Stamp Act the colonists began to develop the revolutionary machinery by which they ultimately separated from England and set up their own official and independent governments.

In June 1765, Massachusetts issued a call for a Stamp Act Congress, the first intercolonial Congress ever called by Americans, to meet in New York the following October. Here Christopher Gadsden of South Carolina announced that "there ought to be no New England man, no New Yorker, known on the continent, but all of us Americans." In its resolutions the Congress declared that "no taxes . . . can be constitutionally imposed on [the colonies] except by their respective legislatures." Outside Congress, meanwhile, even more significant work was afoot. To resist the Stamp Act's drainage of specie, the most respectable merchants joined in nonimportation agreements, and beyond that combined with the "rabble" in the violent "Sons of Liberty" to see that the agreements were honored. The Sons of Liberty themselves went further, destroying the stamps where they could find them, tarring and feathering luckless stamp agents, and under cover of the idea that men of property could be presumed to be favorites of the royal governors, sacking the homes and warehouses of the rich in general.

The nonimportation agreements so effectively crippled trade that the English merchants themselves forced the repeal of the Stamp Act in 1766. But Parliament at the same time joined in the contest over its rights by asserting in a Declaratory Act its power "to bind the colonies in all cases whatsoever." The next year, with "Champagne Charley" Townshend as Prime Minister, Parliament showed it meant business by imposing new revenue duties in the colonies, on lead, paper, and tea, and permitting snooping customs agents to employ the hated writs of assistance to insure collection. Parliament also acknowledged its intention to use the revenue thus gathered to create a "civil list." This would relieve royal governors and judges of having to appeal to recalcitrant colonial assemblies for their salaries and for funds with which to pay their growing staffs. Such an attack on the colonial "parliaments" was ominous, and unfortunately it coincided with Townshend's dissolution of the New York Assembly for failing to enforce the act for quartering British troops in private homes and inns.

The Townshend Acts bore most heavily on Massachusetts, and for its protests against them that colony's General Court was dissolved in 1768. Violence broke out soon after when a mob attacked customs agents trying to collect Townshend duties from John Hancock's sloop, *Liberty*. This prompted the governor to ask for troops. Redcoats in Boston were sufficient provocation to riot, and it is remarkable that eighteen months went by before there was real trouble. On March 5, 1770, a snowball attack on some of the soldiers brought the unfortunate order to fire, and after the melee four Bostonians were lying dead.

New England seethed over the "Boston Massacre"; but when the new Lord North ministry quickly repealed all duties but that on tea, quiet seemed to have been restored. The earlier violence of the Sons of Liberty had offended many colonial gentlemen of property, and the repeal of the Stamp Act had satisfied most of the other respectable elements in America. When Sam Adams sought outside cooperation for Massachusetts in defiance of the

Townshend Acts, he got the cold shoulder. England's quick conciliatory response to the "Boston Massacre" again took the wind out of the agitators' sails. It had to be admitted, however, that the English had so far failed in their efforts to force the colonists into yielding regular revenue; at the same time the colonists themselves had failed to win their point on the unconstitutionality of the English attempts.

Radicals like Sam Adams found numerous occasions to agitate in the few years after 1770. In 1772 he set up in Massachusetts a network of local "committees of correspondence" to keep the idea of rebellion alive. Similar committees were organized in Virginia by Thomas Jefferson and Patrick Henry, and in many other colonies as well. Still, rebellion languished until December 16, 1773, the date of the Boston Tea Party. To save the East India Company, Parliament had just given it a monopoly of the tea trade of America, in complete disregard of other merchants including those of Boston. Parliament also permitted the Company to use its own local sales agents, so that there weren't even commissions for the established American tea dealers. Once more, therefore, Boston merchants joined forces with the mob and together they dumped the Company's tea.

Men of property elsewhere again were appalled at this resort to violence in Massachusetts, but when Lord North's ministry got Parliament early in 1774 to retaliate with the "Coercive Acts," colonial resentment became general. Known in America as the "Intolerable Acts," these measures ordered the closing of the port of Boston, the quartering of troops on its citizens, and the shipment of capital offenders to England for trial. The Quebec Act, passed at about the same time, only capped these others, and together they prompted Virginia to call for delegates to the First Continental Congress. Just as Congress met in September 1774, George III was writing to certain Americans, "the die is now cast, the Colonies must either submit or triumph . . . there must always be one tax to keep up the right."

The First Continental Congress was elected by special local conventions. Because the conservative elements abhorred extralegal activity and tended to stay away, radicals gained control. Naturally they sent numerous extremists to Philadelphia, but their respect for their betters was shown by the presence there of many mild conservatives as well. This Congress agreed to comprehensive non-importation, nonexportation, nonconsumption action directed against British goods. Its revolutionary step was the creation of the official "Continental Association" to supervise the enforcement of these measures and much else in American life. The Association was given power to publish the names of recalcitrant merchants and to confiscate any British goods they held. After sending a petition to the King for recognition of their rights and redress of their grievances, the Congress agreed to reconvene in a year.

Events brought it back sooner. The country's defiance of the Intolerable Acts prompted the British to appoint General Gage as the new Governor of Massachusetts and to quarter his troops in Boston. The Massachusetts Assembly responded by reconstituting itself into a provincial Congress with a committee of safety led by John Hancock to organize resistance. The committee quickly established munition dumps outside of Boston. On learning of one at Concord, General Gage sent a detachment to confiscate it. Paul Revere anticipated the British and when the redcoats reached Lexington on the way to Concord on April 19, 1775, they found in line to meet them the "minutemen" Revere had roused. Eight minutemen were killed and the British continued on to Concord where the "embattled farmers . . . fired the shot heard round the world." The British accomplished their mission, but on the way back to Boston they were harassed by sharpshooters and suffered 247 casualties.

The Revolution had begun, and the Second Continental Congress convened in Philadelphia, May 10, 1775, to see it through. On June 23 Congress appointed Colonel George Washington commander-in-chief of the American forces. By then Ethan Allen's Green Mountain Boys on the Vermont frontier had taken Fort Ticonderoga; Benedict Arnold had begun preparations for the disastrous assault on Quebec designed to bring Canada in as the fourteenth colony; and the battle of Bunker Hill had been fought and lost.

As yet the country had not faced the issue of independence

squarely. The resort to arms in different sections of the country, however, forced hundreds of thousands to discover that their loyalty to the King and to the Church of which he was the supreme head was stronger than their loyalty to their neighbors; and their number might have been much larger had not the Sons of Liberty and other radical groups intimidated the indecisive. By the end of the Revolution some 70,000 loyalists had fled the country, mainly for Canada; but the total number opposed to independence was probably ten times as great. The rest of the Americans were virtually pushed into independence when Parliament, on December 22, 1775, forbade all future intercourse with the colonies. The exigencies of armed conflict and especially the need for allies hastened the American decision. After the publication of Thomas Paine's *Common Sense,* in January 1776, there was no turning back. "There is something absurd," wrote Paine, "in supposing a Continent to be perpetually governed by an island. . . . England [belongs] to Europe, America to itself." More than 150,000 copies of Paine's pamphlet were quickly sold everywhere in America.

By May 10, 1776, Pennsylvania and other colonies had set up new independent state governments, and on that day Congress advised the rest to do the same. A month earlier Congress had declared the ports of America open to the commerce of the entire world, and soon commissioned hundreds of privateers to prey on the commerce of England. On July 2, a majority of the delegates carried the motion of Richard Henry Lee of Virginia, "that these United Colonies are, and of right ought to be, Free and Independent States." On July 4, the Declaration of Independence was adopted "setting forth the causes which impelled us to this mighty resolution." The words were largely those of Jefferson, but the spirit, as he himself acknowledged, was everywhere in the air. "I did not consider it as any part of my charge," said Jefferson later, "to invent new ideas altogether or to offer no sentiment which had ever been expressed before." By far the greater part of the document is concerned with setting forth the details of the alleged "absolute tyranny" of the King of England. Many of the accusations against him were polemical, and only partially true. The pregnant message of the Declaration, which enlisted it in the coming general onslaught on monarchy and the divinity of kings, is set forth in the section which begins:

> We hold these truths to be self-evident, that all men are created equal, that they are endowed by their Creator with certain unalienable Rights, that among these are Life, Liberty and the pursuit of Happiness— That to secure these rights, Governments are instituted among Men, deriving their just powers from the consent of the governed, That whenever any Form of Government—becomes destructive of these ends, it is the Right of the People to alter or to abolish it, and to institute new Government . . .

For all the brilliance and bitterness of the conflict between the colonies and the government at home in the decade before the Revolutionary War began, the actual hostilities dragged themselves out for seven dreary years. These years were marked by extraordinary bravery, as in the stand of the untrained colonials before British fire at Bunker Hill in 1775; by extraordinarily brilliant maneuvers, such as Washington's on the freezing Christmas night of 1776 when he regrouped his retreating little force, recrossed the Delaware and surprised the British at Trenton; by extraordinary suffering, as endured by the ragged, half starved Continental Army at Valley Forge in the desolate winter of 1777-78; by extraordinary brutality, such as that which characterized the warfare between Carolina frontiersmen and Carolina loyalists which culminated in the great American victory at King's Mountain in October, 1780; and by transparent treason, as in Benedict Arnold's attempt to sell out West Point to the invaders just a month earlier. Yet the greater struggle seemed always to be going on in both governments which barely succeeded in keeping representative forces in the field.

In England enlistments for the "civil war" were so poor that 30,000 German mercenaries had to be hired to fight across the sea. Many Parliamentary leaders hoped a colonial victory would so discredit King George III's "personal government" that they aroused no enthusiasm for the distant conflict. In America virtually all of Washington's energies were given to keeping a token army together. Congress could requisition men and money, but it could not force reluctant states to yield either. By December 1776, the 16,000 troops Washington had taken charge of a year and a half earlier had shrunk to 2,400 bitter-enders. On the 20th of that month the Commander-in-Chief wrote to Congress, "Ten more days will put an end to the existence of our Army." A low point was reached in the spring of 1780 when the British seemed near victory for want of opposition and the Americans near disintegration for want of pay. A congressional delegation then set out for Washington's camp in Morristown, New Jersey, empowered to offer him, as they said, "a kind of dictatorship in order to afford satisfaction to the Army." The sojourners got an interesting reception from General Nathanael Greene and other officers who had similar plans of their own, but sensibly were steered away from the Commander-in-Chief. "He has strange notions about the cause," said Greene, "and the obligation there is for people to sacrifice fortune and reputation in support thereof. . . . I shall not combat his opinions; but leave time and future events to effect what reason will have no influence upon."

So acrimonious were the relations among the independent American commonwealths after 1776 that "time and future events" might indeed have effected a British victory. As it was, the British strategy quite properly was to divide and conquer. British forces occupied New York City in 1776 and Philadelphia in 1777, thus virtually for the duration of the conflict separating New England from the South. In 1777 "Gentleman Johnny" Burgoyne and his unenthusiastic redcoats marched down from Canada to gain control of the Hudson. But the wilderness terrain and militant frontier resistance checked him at the great battle of Saratoga, where he surrendered on October 17. This victory convinced the French that the American side might be the winning one. Until then they had unofficially aided the colonials with men, money, munitions, and ships. In 1778 they made a formal treaty of mutual assistance and greatly increased their contributions. Spain also declared war now on her ancient foe, while other nations of the continent harassed English commerce.

Like Burgoyne in the North, the more able Lord Cornwallis began an assault in the South in 1780. After moving through the Carolinas he reached Yorktown, Virginia, where he expected aid from the British fleet. The French fleet, however, succeeded in bottling him up while at the same time chasing off the approaching British ships, and on October 19, 1781, Cornwallis capitulated. His troops went through the ceremony of stacking their arms to the tune of "The World Turned Upside Down." By then George Rogers Clark, fighting for Virginia and not for the Continental Congress, had secured the Mississippi Valley for the new nation.

Cornwallis's defeat brought about the downfall of Lord North's ministry and in its place the disillusioned George III named many friends of the colonies. This helped the American peace negotiators Franklin, John Adams, and John Jay turn the treaty ending the war into a more brilliant triumph than any won on the battlefield. By the terms of the settlement, which was finally certified in 1783, American independence was recognized. The boundaries of the new nation were to reach south from the Great Lakes and west to the Mississippi. On this great river American citizens were to have equal rights of navigation with British subjects. Beyond these generous though as yet ill-defined borders, Americans were to enjoy their old fishing privileges off Newfoundland and in the Gulf of the St. Lawrence. Two other provisions promptly disclosed the weakness of the American government. First, British creditors were to be permitted to sue Americans for debts owed before the war; second, loyalist property was to be restored. The trouble was that Congress had no jurisdiction over such matters and could only recommend compliance to uncompliant states.

THE NEW NATION

During the Revolution almost everyone agreed that it was the war, not Congress, that had kept the states united, and that something stronger than Congress would be needed after the war to keep them from going their separate ways. Many newly risen "gentlemen of principle and property," who had enjoyed a taste of power during the war and had done well while it lasted, were determined that there should be no separation, that enterprise, opportunity, and progress be nationwide. Many others, "whose personal consequence in the control of state politics," as Washington pointed out, "will be annihilated" by a strong central government, joined the majority of the "people" in their determination that separation should not be prevented by a "tyranny" such as they had recently overthrown.

Of the 3,250,000 people in the United States at the close of the Revolution (excluding Indians who were much in evidence but unenumerated) about one third remained unfree. Approximately 600,000 of these were Negro slaves. During the war, Congress had prohibited the importation of Negroes from Africa and within a decade of the peace every state but Georgia enacted similar legislation. Enforcement, however, was hardly such as to check the activities of slave smugglers. In the same decade New Jersey and the states to the north (all of which had slaves) provided for gradual emancipation. But this only worked well in New England where Negroes were least significant in the labor force. Filling out the ranks of the unfree were some 300,000 indentured servants; some 50,000 convicts who despite state laws against their entry, continued to be landed surreptitiously; American debtors and alleged vagrants sold into involuntary labor by court order; and many thousands of youthful apprentices often let out by their parents to journeymen or master workers for as long as twenty years.

More than a million persons in the new nation thus had neither bodily freedom nor political voice. Another million or so, women who were neither slaves nor servants, had limited legal standing. In the few cities of the day, fashionable ladies often added to the gaiety of life and sometimes to its great decisions. If married, however, they could neither hold property nor will it. Women could neither sue nor sit on juries. Public education and public employment normally were denied them. Inadvertently given the vote in many early state constitutions, women gradually had it taken from them.

In the mid1780s, no more than 400,000 free adult men could be found in the entire United States. Had more of them been settled, literate, alive to great issues, they might be said to have made up the political community. Tens of thousands, however, typically were on the move to distant and isolated places, to the northern frontiers of Vermont and Maine, to the Mohawk Valley of New York, the Monongahela Valley of Pennsylvania, the wilds of Kentucky and Tennessee. "The Americans . . . acquire no attachment to Place," noted Governor Dunmore of Virginia in the 1770s. "But wandering about seems engrafted in their Nature; and it is a weakness incident to it, that they should ever imagine the Lands farther off, are Still better than those upon which they are already Settled." Of many such people, Hector St. John de Crèvecoeur wrote in his famous *Letters of an American Farmer,* in 1782:

> By living in or near the woods, their actions are regulated by the wildness of the neighborhood. . . . The chase renders them ferocious, gloomy, and unsociable; a hunter wants no neighbors; he hates them, because he dreads their competition. In a little time their success in the woods makes them neglect the tillage; . . . to make up for the deficiency, they go oftener to the woods. . . . Their wives and children live in sloth and inactivity; and . . . [all] grow up a mongrel breed, half civilized, half savage.

Large numbers of more settled American farmers were hardly less isolated than such frontiersmen. Even in New England, towns were distant from one another and accessible only with the greatest difficulty. Outside of New England and parts of Pennsylvania where German sects had settled in communities of their own, there were few towns at all. Often families lived miles apart. Most of them were too poor to own slaves or servants or to hire help. Given the usual state of what few roads there were, even men with ample time and money could rarely meet on political or other matters. Nor could they readily correspond. In Virginia in the 1780s, when John Marshall was a young lawyer, scarcely a third of those who made deeds or served on juries knew how to sign their names, and such men were a cut above the general run.

All told, at the close of the Revolution, perhaps 120,000 Americans could meet the property, religious, or other qualifications to vote, though this number rose steadily thereafter through liberalization of the suffrage and growth of population. Fewer still could hold office. Characteristic of this segment of the population were the yeomen of the older sections of the country. Yeoman life in a fairly comfortable Massachusetts family about 1790 is well described in the following account:

> At my grandfather Little's, three daughters . . . and three sons still remained under the paternal roof; there were also three young men, apprentices, learning the trade of shoemaker. Grandsir at that time

carried on a brisk business, as business was reckoned in those days, in a shop near the dwelling—this, and the care of a good sized farm, kept every one busy. Family worship and breakfast over, the "men folks" went to their labor, and grandmam' and the girls began the day's routine. The two youngest girls assisting alternately week by week in the housework and spinning. The weaving was usually put out to some neighboring woman. . . . At dark my work was laid aside. . . . At nine o'clock grandsir and the young men came. Grandsir would set himself in his armchair, before the fire . . . the nuts, corn, and apples passed around, and sometimes a mug of flip was made. After all had become warmed and refreshed, the Bible was laid on the stand, a fresh candle lighted, and the old gentleman reverently read a chapter, then a lengthy prayer was offered, through which we all stood with heads bowed reverently.

Such farmers often were ambitious enough to enlarge their holdings for their sons, confident enough to go into debt for good land, responsible enough to trade some produce for cash to meet interest and taxes. When they could afford amenities, they gave the town merchant or itinerant peddlers their business. In this and other ways their produce entered the channels of trade. Many of them, though without enthusiasm for independence, had served in the Revolutionary Army. Though this experience impelled some of them to seek new land in the West, most of them returned home as soon as possible and stayed there. These men knew their rights and hugged their liberties, but with Jefferson they believed that government best which governed least. They took politics seriously only when they were in trouble or when lawyers like Patrick Henry or professional politicians like Sam Adams stirred them up.

According to the "gentlemen of principle and property," these husbandmen were "turbulent and changing." According to the rising Jeffersonians, it was very hard to awaken them to their rightful power. Eager to assist in stirring them up were thousands of city "mechanics" and city poor, who had found their political voice during the Revolution. Owning little property and on that account usually deprived of the vote, such urban agitators nevertheless joined a zest for politics with leisure for meetings, a love of resolves, a taste for oratory, and a palate for toasts. The yeomen,

enfranchised but not political-minded; the "rabble," intensely political but seldom enfranchised—these constituted the "people" in the
political lexicon of the "rich and well-born." Some of the latter
thought the people must be protected from themselves. Most of
them thought *they* must be protected from the people.

While most of the people in America in the mid1780s continued
to live in the country at discouraging distances from one another,
most of the "gentlemen of principle and property" either resided
permanently in the cities or habitually frequented them. Before the
Revolution, English officials had set the urban social tone. In their
places now were lawyers, merchants, planters and speculators, many
of whom were in fact not as far removed from the people as they
pretended. Not all of them engaged in politics or held political
opinions. Those who did felt privileged by right and by God to
rule, and generally speaking, the people continued to acknowledge
their pretensions.

Philadelphia, with a population of 40,000, remained the nation's
metropolis in the 1780s. Of all the important cities, it had been
hurt least by British occupation and by the defection of leaders
from the patriot cause. Thomas Willing, a loyalist merchant who
stayed on and later became president of the first Bank of the
United States, was one who did well during the war. His success
was abetted by his partner, the "financier of the Revolution,"
Robert Morris, and by his son-in-law, William Bingham, privateers-
man, land speculator, merchant, and banker. Notable among the
newcomers was the Frenchman, Stephen Girard, who settled in
Philadelphia in 1776. When the British left two years later, he
began accumulating the trading fortune that soon made him the
richest man in the country. Benjamin Franklin returned to Philadelphia from abroad in 1785, and with David Rittenhouse and
Benjamin Rush, leading scientists of the day, revivified the American Philosophical Society which he had founded in 1744.

Postwar New York, with about 30,000 people, had become
Philadelphia's nearest rival. Between 1785 and 1790 it served as
the capital of the nation. The British occupied New York for seven
years; by the time they left in 1783, about half of the city's loyalist

Chamber of Commerce had also departed. Here, as in Philadelphia, however, numbers of loyalists remained, and eventually lent leadership and capital to the city's growth. Newcomers such as John Jacob Astor, who arrived from Germany in 1783, and William Duer, who came down from Albany the same year after making a fortune in the war, also pushed the city's business forward. At the same time, brilliant young lawyers appeared. Among them were Aaron Burr, a grandson of Jonathan Edwards; and Alexander Hamilton, an illegitimate West Indian of English descent who in 1780 married a daughter of General Philip Schuyler and thus gained the backing of the old Dutch aristocracy. Both Burr and Hamilton had made reputations as Revolutionary officers. Many New Englanders seeking livelier opportunities also came to New York, foreshadowing a larger migration later. Among these Yankee newcomers were seafarers like Samuel Shaw. As supercargo on the New York ship, *Empress of China,* Shaw was mainly responsible for the success of the voyage that opened the China trade in 1784.

Boston, now the nation's third city, had lost heavily during the Revolution through the departure of loyalist capitalists to England and neighboring Canada. After the war Boston's recovery was retarded by the defection to New York of young men of talent. Young merchants like the Cabots, Lowells, Gerrys, and Higginsons —the forebears of the "Proper Bostonians"—came down from the upstate ports of Salem, Marblehead, and Gloucester to make their mark in the Massachusetts metropolis. But their progress was slowed by Boston's loss of the West Indian trade which the British kept closed to American ships until 1830.

Just behind Boston ranked Charleston, South Carolina, still the chief city of the South and according to travelers, the "most aristocratic city in the Union." Between Charleston and Philadelphia lay a few more or less ambitious Southern ports, of which Baltimore alone fulfilled its early promise. Busier were the new state capitals —Augusta, Georgia; Columbia, South Carolina; Richmond, Virginia—their inland location reflecting the "land office business" brought about by the wearing out of tidewater soil and the push of new settlers to the West.

In an age when colleges were rare and nonclerical students rarer, many of the new leaders were college graduates. When most American adults could scarcely read, they, typically, satisfied a taste for world history and world literature. Often they met to discuss both. Travel, though never easy, was least difficult for gentlemen with good servants, good horses, and ample time. The prospect of whist, wine, and philosophy at their destination frequently sped the journey. More often these men corresponded. It was "as if the war not only required, but created talents" wrote the contemporary historian, David Ramsay. Men whose minds were "weaned with the love of liberty, and whose abilities were improved by daily exercise . . . spoke, wrote, and acted, with an energy far surpassing all expectations which could be reasonably founded on their previous acquirements."

Since some of these leaders did not side with Jefferson on the perfectibility of man, all at least joined with John Adams in acknowledging the "improvability" of the conditions of his existence. This, they believed, would be brought about by the operation not of divine but of natural—Newtonian—law. Natural law may have been made by the Creator of the universe, but as one of the favorite authors of these men, the Scot philosopher Adam Ferguson, said, it could be grasped only by "the mind of man left to itself without the aid of foreign intervention." Revealed religion and its mysteries Washington considered the expendable heritage of "a gloomy age of ignorance and superstition." John Adams once said, "An ounce of mother wit is worth a pound of clergy." "It will never be pretended," he said later, "that any persons employed . . . in the formation of the American governments . . . had interviews with the gods, or were in any degree under the inspiration of Heaven."

If these men rejected revelation and the authority of scriptures, they had to find out about things for themselves. But their practicality was even more purposeful than that. The Revolution had set them free; now they felt obliged to produce rules for the safe exercise of freedom. "Researches of the human mind after social happiness," wrote Washington in 1783, "have been carried to a great extent; the treasures of knowledge acquired by the labours of philosophers, sages, and legislators, thro' a long succession of years, are laid open for use, and their collected wisdom may be happily applied in the establishment of our forms of government." As if to follow out this line of thought, Madison, the same year, wrote to Jefferson who was in Europe, asking for "whatever may throw light on the general constitution and *droit* public of the several confederacies which have existed. I observe in Boinaud's catalogue several pieces on the Dutch, the German, and Helvetic. The operations of our own must render all such lights of consequence. Books on the Law of Nature fall within a similar remark."

When in most Americans the notion of a central government called up only Tom Paine's image of George III, "the royal brute of England," these men and their friends could think of and use more palatable examples from man's long past. When most Americans knew only the reign of forest and field, these men and their friends had a classic and firm idea of the State. Some of them, like Robert Morris and James Wilson were, with Hamilton, in the vanguard of the long and bitter fight for a strong national government. Others, Washington and Madison among them, grew agreeable to it as a necessary evil. Still others, including Franklin and Jefferson, learned only to tolerate it. Sam Adams and Patrick Henry who, of all these leaders, remained closest to the "people," accepted it only grudgingly and under pressure.

"A ROPE OF SAND"

Though the last of the new state constitutions, that of Massachusetts, was adopted by 1780, not until the next year did the first official central government actually begin to function in the United States under the Articles of Confederation. Such Articles had been talked of almost from the opening of the Second Continental Congress in May 1775. In June 1776, even before the Declaration of Independence, a committee, headed by John Dickinson of Pennsylvania, was named to draw them up. Dickinson's draft reserved for the states much of their newly asserted power, but was deliberately careless in hedging the sovereignty of Congress. This caused such dissension that a year and a half passed before new Articles, revised and weakened, were gingerly dispatched by the delegates to their respective commonwealths.

Four more years passed before the latter ratified them—unanimously, as required by the cautious Congress. The delay was caused mainly by speculators influential in a few states which could claim no lands beyond the mountains. Their aim was to force such landed states as Virginia and Massachusetts to yield their holdings to Congress which would then open them to all comers.

Dickinson's draft had given a sovereign national government traditional sovereign power: the power to tax its people, to regulate currency and trade, to raise, equip, and field an army. The approved draft left the nation at the mercy of the states. State legislatures appointed and paid the delegates who were subject to recall at any time. These delegates did not vote as individuals but only for their commonwealths, each of these having one vote in Congress regardless of population or wealth. When Congress recessed, the "executive," consisting of one member from each state and appropriately called "A Committee of the States," could act only when nine members agreed. Congress could ask the states for money, but not collect it; requisition troops, but not enlist them; recommend tariffs, but not enact them. Congress could make treaties, borrow money, issue currency, and deal with Indians outside state borders. But it had no courts or armed corps of its own to enforce its engagements or enactments.

Even before the Articles had been approved, men were working to discredit them. Extremists such as Gouverneur Morris even proposed prolonging the Revolution so that "that great friend to sovereign authority, a foreign war," as he said in 1781, might speed the day when the existing "government would acquire force." Congressional efforts after the end of the fighting to deal with problems arising from the treaty and independence neither raised the standing of the government nor quieted demands for change.

As required by the treaty, Congress made "earnest recommendations" to the states to speed the loyalists' recovery of their property and the payment of prewar debts to other British subjects. But in some states loyalist lands were confiscated even after the end of the war, and state governments winked at the tarring and feathering of "traitors" who interfered. As for the debts, certain Virginians asked, "If we are to pay the debts due to British merchants, what have we been fighting for all this time?"

Such evidence of the contempt in which it was held by its own people seemed only to justify the flouting of Congress by others. England aroused Americans in the old Northwest by finding excuse after excuse for delaying the evacuation of its armed fur-trading posts in new American territory along the Canadian border. Spain at the same time aroused the Southwest by inciting the Indians of Florida against American frontiersmen. Spain also claimed that Britain had no right to grant Americans free use of the Mississippi and the port of New Orleans. While Congress looked on helplessly, Spain played upon southern and western dissatisfaction by offering this privilege only to those who would defect from the United States. Congressional efforts to negotiate other commercial matters with Spain also failed. When John Adams, in turn, tried to get England to grant prewar preferences to the new nation, he was laughed out of court. His mortification was compounded by the pitiful efforts of Americans to retaliate against British restrictions with some of their own. When New York put up tariffs, New Jersey and Connecticut jumped at the chance to profit; when Massachusetts stood the British off, Rhode Island rolled out a welcoming rug.

If Congress could make no headway as a sovereign party to a treaty, it was partly because it failed to gain any strength from independence. Indeed, until Washington prevailed upon the troops to disband in June 1783, Congress was harried from place to place by its own army which impatiently awaited payment. More formal creditors, meanwhile, pressed futilely for $2,000,000 in arrears of interest on the public debt, not to speak of the $40,000,000 principal.

Still other Americans looked to Congress in vain. Though Ethan and Levi Allen in the independent state of Vermont swore that "at all risks . . .Congress shall not have the parcelling of [Vermont] lands," most of the 60,000 settlers there wanted only a nod from the central government to join the Union, but they were ignored. When in 1784 North Carolina ceded her Watauga country to the central government she also passed along responsibility for protecting the 10,000 settlers against the Indians. Congressional futility encouraged separatists there in 1784 to form a distinct state of their own, which they called Franklin. Not until 1788 did they return to the Union. In Kentucky country in the 1780s, those resisting the blandishments of Spain held ten different conventions seeking state-hood. Three of these even had the blessing of Virginia which still claimed the territory. But Congress did no more here than in Vermont. Private interests, even if often selfish ones, saved both the northeastern and southwestern frontiers for the new nation.

If Congress had any genuine authority it was over the "Old Northwest"—the territory between the Appalachians and the Mississippi, north of the Ohio River, which it had acquired from the states on the ratification of the Articles. Here, as elsewhere, development and settlement were left largely to private interests, but Congress at least wrote the rules in creative fashion. A preliminary ordinance for the government of this area was enacted in 1784, but it was held in abeyance until people moved in. To encourage settlement, Congress passed a Land Ordinance in 1785 which provided for surveying the territory into townships and sections. Each section was to consist of 640 acres, and nothing smaller than a whole section was to be sold at auction. The minimum auction price was to be one dollar an acre. Congress hoped to refurbish the treasury by land sales in this region, but the requirement of $640 in cash eliminated most buyers. With sales lagging, Congress yielded to speculative interests which offered but a small fraction of the "minimum" price for huge acreage. When the speculators began to people the region, Congress proceeded to enact a new measure for its government. This was the famous Northwest Ordinance of 1787.

The Northwest Ordinance stipulated that no more than five states be made from the Northwest Territory, tentatively defined the boundaries of each state, and outlined a system of transition governments. When 60,000 free inhabitants had settled within such states they would be admitted to the Union "on an equal footing with the original states in all respects whatever." This Ordinance established the procedure by which almost all future states were brought into the Union. In the Northwest Territory itself, the new states compacted with the older ones to guarantee civil rights, provide for "religion, morality, and knowledge," proscribe entail and primogeniture, and prohibit slavery.

Before settlement could proceed, however, more than laws were needed. Most important, the Indians in the West had to be quieted or removed, and here Congress failed. By 1787, moreover, events elsewhere in the country had given the strong central-government men so many additional occasions to belabor Congress that they felt safe in moving seriously to supplant it. Most of these events grew out of the suddenly declining fortunes of the yeoman farmers. Until 1785 these farmers had enjoyed a long wartime boom. After that date the foreign troops their grain had fed had left for home and the American Army had been disbanded. As trade fell off, worried creditors began to press the farmers for back payments. At the same time the states, under pressure from the holders of their wartime securities, raised taxes on the land and demanded their payment in specie. In 1785 in Massachusetts, a third of the farmer's cash income was going to the government, to be paid out in turn to the state bondholders.

This sudden and seemingly unfair reversal of conditions prompted the farmers themselves to seek redress. Some states made concessions. In New England the ruling oligarchies only made things worse. In 1786 the Massachusetts legislature actually raised taxes on land. This goaded the farmers to resist collection with violence. In the most famous farmers' uprising, Captain Daniel Shays, a veteran of Bunker Hill, led 1,200 men to the court house in Springfield. Governor Bowdoin's militia easily handled matters; but in the next election the farmers voted him out in favor of the aging patriot, John Hancock.

Starting in 1780, numerous conventions for revising the Articles had been proposed by the strong-government men. In 1782 the New York legislature and in 1785 the Massachusetts legislature had taken the lead, but nothing happened. In 1785 Maryland and Virginia differed on the matter of navigation of the Potomac River and Chesapeake Bay, in which Washington himself was interested. A meeting on the question led naturally to general discussion of commerce and the wish for other states to join in. The upshot was a call by the Virginia legislature for a meeting of all the states at Annapolis in September 1786. By then Shay's "rebellion" had turned the "rich and well born" from considerations of mere commercial promotions to an avowed concern for the protection of their very lives and property.

Only five states sent delegates to Annapolis, but among them was New York, and among its representatives was Washington's ex-aide, the indefatigable and brilliant Hamilton. The convention formally was to deal with commerce only; but the opportunity was too good to miss. Strategy suggested prompt adjournment and a ringing call for a new convention to amend the Articles thoroughly. Hamilton wrote the report carrying out this decision; and soon all the states but Rhode Island were preparing to send delegates to the Great Convention in Philadelphia in May 1787.

"A MORE PERFECT UNION"

"No motley or feeble measure can answer the end or will finally receive the public support," Hamilton in New York wrote to Washington in Philadelphia during the Convention. The "public" he talked to worried that the Convention "from a fear of shocking popular opinion, will not go far enough." How far he himself would go he indicated earlier by his proposals to the delegates: A "Governor" of the United States should be elected for life by a method at least two steps removed from the original voters. The Governor of each state, in turn, with an absolute veto on state laws, would be appointed by the Governor of the United States. This was nationalism with a vengeance, and the members of the Convention, many more learned and more lenient than Hamilton, rejected it. "The gentleman from New York," it was said, "has been praised by everybody, he has been supported by none."

Though Jefferson and John Adams were in Europe during the Convention and other personages were absent for various reasons, the meeting was one of great men and great minds. The rather symbolic attendance of Washington and the aged Franklin lent strength and stature to the sessions. In all, seventy-three men had been named, but only fifty-five ever appeared. A mere eight had been signers of the Declaration. On the whole the members were young men, educated, urbane, practical.

The Convention opened on May 25 and unanimously elected Washington presiding officer. Uneasy about the populace and the press, it next voted to keep its sessions secret. The delegates had been sent to Philadelphia to "amend" the Articles. Some held to the letter of their instructions. Others, lest they "let slip the golden opportunity," as Hamilton said, took a freer view. When Edmund Randolph of Virginia announced that he was not "scrupulous on the point of power," Hamilton seconded him and the Convention proceeded to supplant, not amend, the Articles.

The delegates took as their point of departure the so-called "Virginia Plan," sketched out in an address by Randolph on May 29. Virginia proposed a bicameral legislature, membership in both houses to be apportioned among the states according to their free population. Members of the "second house" of this "National Legislature" would be elected by the members of the first, who themselves would be elected by the voters. The "National Legislature" as a whole would elect the "National Executive" and the "National Judiciary."

The flaw in this scheme was its failure to give the national government direct power over the people. But the biggest argument took place over the basis of representation. The small states feared being overwhelmed by the populous ones. Accordingly they offered a counterproposal of a one-house legislature in which the states would continue to vote as units. The "New Jersey Plan," as it was called, had no chance in this Convention. It did, however, contain the clause which survived as one of the pillars of the federal system: "Acts of the United States in Congress . . . shall be the *supreme law* of the respective States . . . or their citizens . . . and the Judiciary of the several States shall be bound thereby in their decisions."

Argument over the representation clause of the Virginia Plan grew so hot in the Philadelphia summer that at one point the small-state men threatened to pack up and go home. Eventually a special committee under Franklin saved the Convention by devising the "Great Compromise." To please the large states, membership in the lower house would be by population; to please the small ones, membership in the upper house would be the same for all.

In apportioning representation in the lower house, the free states wanted slaves given less weight than whites. The South would agree to this only for "direct taxes," which were also to be apportioned by population. The so-called "three-fifths" compromise broke this deadlock. In apportioning both representation and direct taxes, five slaves were to be counted as equivalent to three whites.

Still a third compromise had to be effected before the commercial interests won their point that only a straight majority be required for the enactment of measures regulating commerce. The South, fearful of taxes on exports and interference with the slave trade, wanted a two-thirds majority. For yielding on this, the South got taxes on exports prohibited forever, interference with the slave trade prohibited for twenty years. It also won the point that treaties, commercial or other, to take effect, must be approved by a two-to-one majority in the Senate.

Much has been made of these compromises; but they are conspicuous chiefly because on most other matters the delegates saw eye to eye. Long discussion preceded the decision to make the term of office of representatives two years, senators six years, the president four years, and judges life. But the principle involved provoked little argument: the new government must be protected from popular fancy which might turn out an entire administration at once. Similar fears dictated the indirect election of senators (since made direct by the Seventeenth Amendment) and the president, and the appointment of judges by the president with senatorial approval. The "people" had their directly elected House; beyond that their participation in the government was to be remote.

The Constitution, the framers hoped, would quickly reverse the allegedly desperate tendencies of the times; but, as Madison said, they also self-consciously "built for the ages." In place of the "half-starved, limping government" of the Confederation (Washington's own description), the Constitution established a legislature with unequivocal power to tax the people, to "raise and support Armies," and to "provide and maintain a Navy." It alone could declare war, regulate commerce, coin money, provide for the "general welfare," and "make all laws necessary and proper" to the exercise of such powers. For the enforcement of the laws the Constitution provided for a single, responsible executive, the president. He would be elected independently of Congress and empowered to appoint (and remove, it was later decided) his own aides, checked, to be sure, by the frequent requirement of Senate consent. With the same check, he alone could make treaties. He was also commander-in-chief of the army and navy. Finally, the Constitution created an independent national judiciary headed by a Supreme Court. This court was given original jurisdiction in many matters; most important, it was given appellate jurisdiction over all cases involving the Constitution, federal laws or treaties, even if such cases originated in state courts.

To reinforce the national government was insufficient. The country must also be protected, in Madison's words, from "the mutability of the laws of the states." Most significant, the states were forbidden to make "anything but gold and silver coin a tender in payment of debts," and to pass any laws "impairing the obligation of contracts." If the states retained "residual powers," the national government was supreme in the exercise of those "delegated" to it. From this, two implications may be drawn: (1) Acts of Congress beyond the scope of its delegated powers must be unconstitutional. (2) State acts impinging on Congressional areas of supremacy must also be unconstitutional. In keeping with the theory of checks and balances, moreover, the courts (though Washington once claimed this for the executive) held the power to void unconstitutional *legislative* acts signed by the president. This is the basis of "judicial review," as Hamilton explained it in Number 78 of *The Federalist*. For a long time, with but one exception, only state acts were adversely "reviewed."

On these "remedies," then, there was general agreement in the Convention. The same is true of those provisions which have preserved the Constitution for almost two centuries. Chief among these from the framers' point of view were the built-in checks and balances. No executive could get free enough to become a man on a white horse; on the other hand, no transient upsurge of popular feeling could lawfully unseat the president or overturn the courts.

A second source of the Constitution's longevity is the amending process, closely hedged and sparingly used though it has been. The futility of trying to amend the Articles by the required unanimous consent of the states hastened the Confederation's demise. The promise of the first ten amendments (to serve as a Bill of Rights), on the other hand, assured the Constitution's ultimate ratification; the prompt fulfillment of the promise speeded it to a long life. "I will be a peaceable citizen," said the Constitution's opponent,

Patrick Henry. "My head, my hand, and my heart shall be at liberty to retrieve the loss of liberty, and remove the defects of that system in a constitutional way."

Perhaps the success of the Constitution is to be accounted for mainly by a paradox. Statesmanship prompted the framers to leave many powers to the jealous states. On the other hand, they wrote the document with such generality—no accident, but a significant result of their universal way of thinking—that these powers could be retrieved by the national government when changes in national life made it imperative that they be exercised on a national level. A constitution to be a success, Napoleon said, should be "short and obscure." Most likely he had the American Constitution in mind. Many features of American government and politics which the framers did not clearly foresee have also contributed much to the perpetuation of the form of government they set up. Among these may be noted the two-party system, the enlargement of the role of the Cabinet, the committee system in the House and Senate, the bureaucratic civil service.

The Constitutional Convention, for all its practical conservatism, created a radical government, a free nation among aristocratic ones, a republic among skeptical monarchies. For all its limitations on direct democratic action, moreover, the Constitution did not omit a "democratical branch," prescribed by John Adams as essential to all free governments. Under the Constitution, said John Marshall who rose to prominence during the ratification controversy in Virginia, "it is the people that give power, and can take it back. What shall restrain them? They are the masters who give it, and of whom their servants hold it."

The "people," none the less, proved not as willing to give power as Marshall hoped; and he himself had to acknowledge that "in some of the adopting states, a majority . . . were in the opposition." The secrecy of the Convention did not help matters; the knowledge, moreover, that only thirty-nine of the fifty-five delegates signed the final document heightened suspicion.

The Articles required that "amendments" first be approved by Congress and then by state legislatures. Congress, however, dispensed with voting on the document and passed the issue directly to the states. The Convention, in turn, stipulated that ratification in the states be by special conventions to which the Constitution makers could be elected, and not by the state legislatures. It stipulated further that when nine of the thirteen states acted favorably, the new law of the land would be declared in effect. It was not, in fact, until a month after the Constitution had been declared in operation that North Carolina ratified it. Rhode Island held out until May 1790, when threats of commercial pressure forced its hand.

Delaware, on December 7, 1787, was the first state to ratify. Five days later Pennsylvania voted for the Constitution, but only after a series of Federalist stratagems deeply alienated the losers. New Jersey, Georgia, and Connecticut next came quietly into line. When the Massachusetts Convention met on January 9, 1788, a majority was definitely opposed. The promise of later amendments dissolved some opposition; more disappeared when the sponsors played successfully upon the ambitions of opposition leaders. Even so it was only by a vote of 187 to 168 that ratification won after a month of hard work. Maryland and South Carolina soon made eight ratifiers. While hot contests went on in the key states of Virginia and New York, a second convention in New Hampshire (the sponsors had not dared to allow the first one to come to a vote) made it the ninth state. Presented with this situation and mollified when Washington consented to run for president, Virginia yielded on June 25 after a brilliant debate on both sides. The vote was close, 89 to 79.

In New York, Hamilton led the sponsors' fight. Aware of the strength of the opposition, Hamilton began writing in support of the Constitution as early as October 1787. John Jay soon joined him, and also James Madison of Virginia. Their joint efforts have since been known as *The Federalist*. The articles first appeared in the New York press and were copied in many papers elsewhere. They had little effect on the contest, however. In New York's convention in June 1788, the opposition held a two-to-one majority. News of the sponsors' belated victory in Virginia implied that the new Union would be formed without New York. But even this failed for weeks to dissipate the opposition. Hamilton and the pro-Constitution forces nevertheless succeeded in postponing a negative vote; and their promise late in July to fight for amendments which would constitute a bill of rights at last won enough votes for the Constitution to squeeze through, 30 to 27.

In September 1788, Congress called for the election of the first president in February 1789, the first inauguration the following March. New York City was named the first capital.

"I am not much attached to the majesty of the multitude," Hamilton once said, and "waive all pretensions to their countenance." On another occasion he stated that the "people . . . seldom judge or determine right." On the issue of the Constitution he was correct. A great English Prime Minister once called the Constitution "the most wonderful work ever struck off at a given time by the brain and purpose of man." But the American people had been slow to see it that way.

Chapter Five

An Agrarian Republic in a Revolutionary Epoch

The old Congress had set March 4, 1789, as the date for the convening of the new one in New York City. But it was April 6 before a quorum of Representatives and Senators completed the rough journey to the capital, and April 30 before President Washington, "accompanied," as he said, "by feelings not unlike those of a culprit, who is going to the place of his execution," was inaugurated. To Fisher Ames of Boston, the conservative who had defeated Sam Adams for Congress, the "languor of the old Confederation" seemed to persist. "The people will forget the new government before it is born," moaned Ames. "The resurrection of the infant will come before its birth."

Conscious of their role as republicans in a skeptical monarchical world, the leaders of the first Congress were determined not only to make good but to make a good impression. Vice-President John Adams in particular, fresh from years of attendance at the courts of Europe, was so insistent upon dignified titles and procedures in the Senate that he was promptly dubbed "His Rotundity." "When the President comes into the Senate," the President of the Senate asked his colleagues, "what shall I be? I cannot be President then. I wish gentlemen to think of what I shall be." William Maclay, the irreverent Senator from Pennsylvania, found "the profane muscles of his face in tune for laughter" over the discussion that followed.

But need for getting down to more serious business soon overcame any pompous preoccupation with decorum. The Constitution may have been barren of guides to punctilio, but it was clear as to objectives; and if it hadn't been, the times were making their own

127

disquieting demands. The Constitution gave the legislature power to raise much-needed money; now the actual business of levying and collecting taxes had to be faced. The Constitution established a national judiciary consisting of a Supreme Court and "such inferior courts as Congress may from time to time ordain and establish." Now this provision had to be implemented. The Constitution created a strong executive; now this department had to be organized and manned. Though New York was a gay town whose prosperity added to the diversions everywhere at hand, it remained the capital of a weak nation, one beset by foreign and domestic debts, surrounded by foreign enemies, harassed on its borders by hostile and aroused Indians, on the sea by bold pirates, in alien ports and waters by unfriendly navies. Nor was there to be unity at home.

GIVING MUSCLE TO THE GOVERNMENT

For all its dilatoriness, Congress dealt with each of its Constitutional injunctions during its very first session. Its earliest substantive act, however, was to pass and submit to the states the first ten amendments constituting the Bill of Rights. These were ratified by December 1791.

This promise fulfilled, the new government faced its most urgent initial problem—money for day to day expenses. For this purpose Madison had a tariff bill before the House even before Washington's inauguration. Hoping to get it passed in time to tax the heavy spring imports already on the high seas, he wrote the measure to touch "such articles . . . only as are likely to occasion the least difficulty." The very proposal, however, found merchants adding the anticipated tax to their prices; they gave its passage no encouragement. At the same time, with lobbying and log-rolling tactics that became notorious later, manufacturers combined to delay matters until each got special protection for his own products. Shipowners also got favorable consideration. Imports arriving in American bottoms were to be taxed at a rate 10 per cent below that on goods brought in by foreign carriers. Debate put off the passage of Madison's bill until July 4. Collection itself could not begin until inspectors, weighers, and other port officers—the advance guard of political appointees who later underpinned the party system—were inducted. Henceforth, for more than a hundred years, the customs would yield more in federal revenue than any other single source, and customhouse jobs would be the staple of federal patronage.

While the House was occupied with strengthening the federal treasury, the Senate was working on the structure of federal law enforcement. On September 24, 1789, it passed the first federal Judiciary Act. This measure made explicit the procedure by which federal courts could review and, if need be, annul state laws and state-court decisions involving powers and duties delegated by the Constitution to the Federal Government. It also specified the make-up of the Supreme Court and the system of lower federal tribunals: the circuit and district courts. Attached to each district court were United States attorneys and their deputies to serve as federal prosecutors, and United States marshals and their deputies to serve as federal police. This Judiciary Act created the office of Attorney-General, but the Department of Justice itself was not set up until 1870.

While Congressmen and Senators labored over such basic measures, the President considered appointments to carry them out and to man other positions, major and minor, that must be created. Caution was Washington's watchword. An excellent administrator, he proposed to surround himself only with the best men available. Yet expediency dictated that appointments be spread geographically and that the dignitaries of the different states be appeased. Washington was profoundly aware of the tenuous attachment of many state leaders to the new central government. "A single disgust excited in a particular state" on the matter of patronage, he wrote, "might perhaps raise a flame of opposition that could not easily, if ever, be extinguished. . . . Perfectly convinced I am, that if injudicious or unpopular measures should be taken by the executive . . . with regard to appointments, the government itself would be in the utmost danger of being utterly subverted. . . ."

Though the Executive had been the weakest branch of the old Confederation, its three executive departments established in 1781 —Foreign Affairs, Treasury, and War—continued to function for a time unchanged by the new government. Not before July 1789, did Congress establish a new Department of State; new War and Treasury departments followed by September. As Secretary of War, Washington nominated his old comrade in arms, General Henry Knox of Massachusetts. As Attorney-General he named his fellow Virginian, Edmund Randolph. John Jay of New York continued in charge of foreign affairs until 1790, when he became first Chief Justice of the Supreme Court. At that time, Washington's fateful choice, his neighbor Thomas Jefferson, took over as Secretary of State. Equally fateful was Washington's appointment of his wartime aide, the ardent Alexander Hamilton, as Secretary of the Treasury.

Many years later Jefferson told a story that illuminates the character of Washington's two chief advisors. "At a dinner I gave in 1791 . . . the room being hung around with a collection of the portraits of remarkable men, among them . . . Bacon, Newton, and Locke, Hamilton asked me who they were. I told him they were my trinity of the three greatest men the world had ever produced, naming them. He paused for some time: 'The greatest man,' said he, 'that ever lived was Julius Caesar.' "

More English than the English in his devotion to constitutional monarchy, Hamilton became more zealous than most Americans in his championship of the centralization of power in the executive of his adopted land. He convinced himself that the "people" recognized their natural leaders in his own favorite moneyed class. If he could but bind that class to the "people's" government, the entire nation would be firmly united, the better to face the enemies at hand and realize its mighty future. Hamilton's fight to supplant the Articles had had this as its objective.

Hamilton's first report to Congress on the public debt was ready in January 1790. In it he urged three new bond issues: one to refund the foreign debt, another to call in the bewildering agglomeration of wartime securities issued by the old Congress, the third to refund unpaid state debts which, according to his plan, the new central government would assume. His proposal on the foreign debt passed with scant opposition. Included among the issues to be called in at face value under his second proposal were the certificates, passing in the market at no more than twenty-five cents on the dollar, with which the Army had been paid and which the soldiers had carried to many parts of the hinterland. Even before he made his report, certain of Hamilton's friends learned of this provision and sent fast boats and fast stages loaded with cash to beat the good news to the back country. Madison led the opposition in crying corruption; but their hastily drawn alternative bill was defeated by the House, and Hamilton's plan won.

This victory was acclaimed by those in the cities who felt rich enough to share Hamilton's political philosophy or at least had enough ready money to share its fruits. The opposition came mainly from the South where cash for speculation in securities was scarce. The sectional rift was widened when Hamilton's third proposal, assumption of state debts, came up in April. The South, through the sale of its state lands, had succeeded in paying off most of its wartime obligations. Now it defeated the Secretary's proposal that it help the central government bail out its prodigal sister states to the north. Hamilton, however, was nothing if not resourceful. Ultimately he got Jefferson's backing by offering the South the new capital. In June 1790, "assumption" passed. The other part of the deal gave Philadelphia the capital for ten years, with the permanent site on the Potomac to be ready in 1800.

It is "a fundamental maxim in the system of public credit of the United States," Hamilton said, "that the creation of debt should always be accompanied with the means of its extinguishment." He hardly cared, however, to extinguish the securities the interest on which supplied income to the moneyed families and, more important, served them as collateral for further speculation on credit. In practice, Hamilton undertook only to service, not pay, the debt. Even this took $2,000,000 a year. Since the tariff yielded much less than was needed, Hamilton made two more proposals, both adopted, but not without further sectional strife.

The first of these proposals urged the creation of a national bank, modeled on the Bank of England, which would serve the government for short-term borrowing. Its other features were designed mainly to increase the currency and credit available to the expanding business community. "The farmers, the yeomanry, will derive no advantage from it," complained Representative James Jackson of Georgia, during debate on the measure. Madison took higher ground, declaring that the Constitutional Convention had specifically intended to deny Congress the power to charter companies, and that the bank proposal, therefore, was unconstitutional. The bank bill was approved early in 1791 by a House vote of 39 to 20, all but one of the opposing votes coming from the South. Before the measure received Washington's signature, however, the President questioned Jefferson and Hamilton on its validity. Jefferson, making what henceforth became known as the "strict interpretation" of the Constitution, upheld Madison's argument. Hamilton argued, on the contrary, that the constitutional power to regulate the currency carried with it the "implied power" to establish monetary agencies like the bank. Washington accepted Hamilton's "broad interpretation," and signed the bill in February 1791, chartering the First Bank of the United States for twenty years. In December, the main office of the Bank opened in Philadelphia and in the following years eight branches were established in port cities from Boston to New Orleans.

Hamilton's second proposal, also enacted in 1791, placed excise taxes on various commodities, among them, provocatively enough, distilled spirits. The South thought spirits essential to work in its climate. Among back country farmers who seldom saw coin, whisky had also long served as a medium of exchange. Attempts to collect a tax on western "money" for the benefit of eastern speculators led to violence in 1794. This centered in western Pennsylvania where disgust with the tactics by which the Constitution was ratified in that state had been most acute. To show the world's capitalists, who had invested heavily in the new bank's shares and other United States securities, that a republican government could coerce its citizens in money matters, Hamilton prevailed on the President to call out 15,000 militia against the "Whisky Rebellion." The Secretary of the Treasury naturally rode along. Unfortunately for the demonstration the "whisky rebels" decided to remain indoors when the soldiers arrived. A military farce, this adventure also proved a political fiasco for Hamilton.

Perhaps the apex of his whole program was his Report on

Manufactures, which went to Congress in December 1791. In it he argued brilliantly for protective tariffs, subsidies, and similar aids to infant industries which ultimately would supply the sinew of a great nation. But American merchants were to remain cool to industrial enterprise for another quarter century, and for longer than that were to oppose protective tariffs as a plague on trade. Congress received the Report coldly.

As the country's currency became increasingly tied up in speculation in Hamilton's new government securities, moreover, the more sober merchants became increasingly suspicious of Hamilton's intentions. When the Secretary's bosom friend, William Duer, "the prince of the tribe of speculators," as Madison called him, went to a debtor's cell in the spring of 1792, the merchants' worst fears were realized. Excellent harvests in Europe had already reduced both the demand and the prices for American exports. Duer's collapse, which carried down many other plungers, turned business uncertainty into catastrophe. Hamilton himself had always been the soul of circumspection in avoiding personal gain from public power. But he never succeeded in cleansing his reputation of the mud spattered on him by his opportunistic friends. "I have experienced," he wrote in answer to one of Duer's last requests for aid, "all the bitterness of soul on your account which a warm attachment can inspire."

Additional troubles, meanwhile, were overflowing the Federalists' cup of gloom. The Federalists had pleased many on the northern frontier by admitting Vermont as a state in 1791, and many in the Southwest by admitting Kentucky in 1792. In the Southwest, however, Spain continued to contest the Florida border as defined in the Treaty of Paris, and kept pressure on Washington's administration by refusing to open the Mississippi at New Orleans to western shipping. In the Northwest, England continued to hold military posts and to use them to aid Canadian fur trappers against American entrepreneurs. Spain and England, moreover, if they did nothing to egg them on against the encroaching American frontiersmen, also did nothing to hold the Indians in check. Washington's own efforts to deal with the Indians also failed miserably.

REPUBLICANISM AT HOME AND ABROAD

Hamilton had a vision of the future of the United States that was at once too innocent for his mercenary fellow Federalists and too sophisticated for the "new American" verging on the vast and wonderful frontier. Hamilton was concerned with money only as a medium for national, not personal aggrandizement; capital was the heart, the lungs, the bloodstream of power; capitalists the instruments of progress; the state the directing force. But Federalist capitalists thought, as a rule, on a lower plane, and nursed their substance carefully in the familiar lines of investment.

Yet Hamilton shared with his fellow Federalists their contempt for small farmers, their view of frontiersmen as little better than Indians and, if anything, more troublesome. He knew, as he often stressed, that the "genius of the people" was a central element in the development of national wealth. But his model always remained the English, not the American people, the rising factory hand not the farming and the frontier breed. The instruments of American progress for almost a century were to be rough and crude frontier warriors, huntsmen, prospectors, and land speculators, not manipulators of securities; self-sufficient husbandmen pushing west from clearing to clearing, farm to farm, not cogs in urban industrial complexes. Such men would explore and open to settlement Jefferson's "empire of liberty" that stretched as far as the farthest western horizon and was meant to nurture a society unlike any that the English—or the Secretary of the Treasury—imagined. Hamilton's program and that of the Federalists had a short life, and without the allegiance of Washington, Federalist rule would have been shorter still. The famous General of the Revolution served the same shielding function for the minority party of his day that Grant was to serve after the Civil War and Eisenhower after World War II.

No date marks the beginnings of political parties in the United States. The country, however, had been clearly divided on the Constitution, and the first years of the new government saw opposing leaders attempt to strengthen the opinions and mobilize the votes of their followers. The Federalists at first had great advantages. Above all, they had a strong, clear program, and in Hamilton an imaginative and uncompromising leader. He showed, too, that besides the press and the pulpit the Federalists had the Army and the will to use it. On the local level, a ready-made network of chambers of commerce, units of the Society of Cincinnati, and other going Federalist organizations was quickly supplemented by a grass-roots patronage system affording sinecures to Federalist party workers.

The opposition suffered from the taint of having, in general, fought the Constitution of the very government they aspired to control. Moreover, as their first name, "anti-Federalists," suggests, they had no positive program of their own. Even on the issue of the Constitution, however, the "antis" had had a majority of the voters, and few were lost to the new government. By 1791, Jefferson was writing to Washington of his conviction that the Federalists' "corrupt squadron" menaced the country. To Madison he was writing of his plans to give the majority its voice. Jefferson cherished stability and dignity in government as much as Hamilton. But he insisted that men "habituated to think for themselves"—American "yeomen"—were much more easily governed than those "debased by ignorance, indigence, and oppression"—in short, the natural spawn of great cities. On the yeomen he would build.

Among Jefferson's first steps was his enlistment of the poet of the Revolution, Philip Freneau, to edit a new anti-Federalist paper in Philadelphia, the *National Gazette.* During the winter of 1791-92, Madison wrote a series of articles developing the position of "the Republican Party, as it may be termed."* After the *Gazette's* initial issue in October 1791, sympathetic papers elsewhere began picking up Freneau's thrusts. Jefferson next sought allies, local lieutenants, grass roots clubs, and candidates who could afford the time and money to run for and hold office. Madison, of course, was Jefferson's closest collaborator. Others included Governor George Clinton of New York, who, in opposition to General Schuyler, Hamilton's rich father-in-law, controlled the upstate vote; and Aaron Burr (Clinton had recently helped him defeat Schuyler for the Senate) whose Sons of St. Tammany already were hungering for patronage in New York City.

During Washington's first administration party lines had been clearly drawn by financial and frontier issues. In his second ad-

---

* This party became the *Democratic* Party of our own time. The Republican Party of today was not organized until 1854 (see pp. 181, 193).

ministration, after his unanimous re-election in 1792, foreign policy gave parties "their demarcations, their watchwords, and their bitterness." Some foreign policy problems lingered from the war with England. But the French Revolution, which began a few weeks after Washington first took office in 1789, was the source of most of them, just as the United States was, in important ways, one of the sources of the French Revolution.

The American Declaration of Independence, a monument to the authority of natural rather than Biblical law, was read with enormous enthusiasm abroad. American success in winning freedom from George III heightened French enthusiasm in particular. When Louis XVI, in financial straits because of his expenditures to aid the Americans in their fight against King George, had to call the Estates General for new funds in 1789, the French stage was suddenly set. Such a call had not been issued for 175 years and was a revolutionary step in itself. In a climate heady with constitutional theorizing, it was a dangerous step as well.

At first the French Revolution was welcomed everywhere in America; when Lafayette late in 1789 sent the key of the Bastille to Washington, the President received it as "a token gained for liberty." In January 1793, Louis XVI and Marie Antoinette were executed and the Jacobin "Reign of Terror" began. Shortly after, England and Spain joined the other continental monarchs who had declared war on France to crush the threat of republicanism to themselves. Westerly gales kept this news from crossing the ocean for weeks. In April the evil tidings all flooded in at once. The Federalists, their misgivings over French violence and French leveling having grown steadily, felt confirmed in their detestation of the Revolution. The Republicans held to their detestation of monarchs and monarchy, to their confidence in the aspiring populace of France as against the aristocrats of Britain.

Besides heightening the conflict of American opinion, the news of regicide and war in France opened the conflict over policy. The old French treaty of 1778 obliged the United States to assist France now; to see that she did, the Jacobins sent over "Citizen" Edmond Genêt. Genêt had other instructions as well, including the organization of Jacobin Clubs in America to further the cause of Liberty, Equality, and Fraternity. Just at this time Jefferson himself had begun to sponsor political clubs, called Democratic Societies. By offering the occasion to welcome a true representative of the Revolution, Genêt's visit gave a fillip to the Jeffersonian cause of which the Democratic Societies made the most. So time consuming indeed were the receptions for the visitor after his arrival at the pro-French port of Charleston, that by the time Genêt reached Philadelphia Washington had been prevailed upon to issue the Neutrality Proclamation of April 1793. His mission a failure, and his faction overturned at home, Genêt married a daughter of Governor Clinton and settled down in New York.

The Federalist argument against honoring the French treaty, an argument that hardly bore examination, was that the agreement had been made only with the executed French king. Jefferson (and international law) held that the treaty was with the French nation, but he and his party acknowledged the usefulness of the Proclamation. When the British started capturing American ships suddenly enjoying the windfall business of neutral carriers, Republican sympathy for France was warmed by active hostility toward England. As if to water green American memories, the British in Canada chose this moment openly to incite the Indians to raid the Ohio country where thousands of Americans were newly settling. Recalling the effectiveness of commercial retaliation in the great days of the Revolution, the Republicans now demanded similar reprisals against the hated mother country.

Federalist merchants, on the other hand, were making large profits despite the British and wanted at least to leave well enough alone. To forestall the Republicans they had the President send John Jay as special envoy to Great Britain in April 1794, and to conciliate the West he was instructed to insist that the British give up their border posts. Recalling Jay's abortive negotiations with Spain ten years before when he proved ready to sell out free access to the Mississippi for some miserly commercial concessions, westerners looked with deepest suspicion on his appointment. Jay got the British to consent to evacuate the western posts, which they did by 1796. But this was hedged by so many other privileges left to the British in American territory that the West felt it had gained nothing.

In all other respects but one Jay's mission proved worse than a failure. The sight of Jay making gestures of peace with Britain moved Spain, which had withdrawn from the coalition against France in 1795, to try to woo the United States to her side. Her tactic was to offer to open the Mississippi to American traffic for three years, subject to renewal. This was confirmed in the Pinckney Treaty that year. Otherwise, the most important consequence of Jay's negotiation was to incite the French themselves to join the British in attacks on American shipping. By March 1797, France had captured almost 3,000 American ships she said must have been bound for hostile British ports.

By then the issue no longer rested with the neutral Washington. Long dismayed by the "baneful effects of the spirit of party," the General had seriously considered retirement in 1792. In 1796 there was no dissuading him and early that year he asked Hamilton (who had resigned from the Cabinet a few months earlier) to draft a "Farewell Address." On September 7, 1796, Washington published his version in the newspapers.

Washington expressed his keen satisfaction with many aspects of his two terms. The country had been immensely strengthened by the Constitution, and his administration had set it on a strong national course. Business again was good. On the frontiers (if only for the time being) the Indians had been quieted and western settlement encouraged. Above all, in a war-torn world the United States remained at peace, however precariously. Washington had hoped to top off his accomplishments with the establishment of a national university, a project widely endorsed but not sufficiently so to impress Congress. Only toward the end of his Address did the President discuss foreign affairs. "Taking care always to keep ourselves . . . on a respectable defensive posture, we may safely trust to temporary alliances for extraordinary emergencies." Nowhere did he admonish against all "entangling alliances," a phrase that is Jefferson's, not Washington's. His deepest concern was domestic: the peculiarity of party strife in the United States which had already taken on the sectional character that was to culminate in civil war.

The party battle was in fact near its peak when Washington retired, and his decision intensified it by opening the highest office to the rising political machines. In the electoral college the voting was still by men rather than parties. While the Federalist, John Adams, squeezed by with seventy-one votes in the election of 1796, the Republicans on their first try won the vice-presidency. Their candidate, Thomas Jefferson, received sixty-eight votes.

No one in America had written more or more confidently about the nature of man than John Adams. Jefferson had shrewdly observed, however, that in practice Adams was "a bad calculator" of "the motives of men." His first mistake was to retain in his Cabinet the second-rate Hamiltonians who had surrounded Washington toward the end, and who, with their retired leader's priming, almost pushed the General as well as his successor into war with France. Adams's second mistake compounded his first. Without querying the French Government, he dispatched a three-man mission to try to get French sea raiding stopped. Talleyrand, foreign minister of the Directory that was then running France, refused even to see the Americans until they handed over to his agents a bribe of $250,000. This was but the first of a series of calculated insults to the Americans. The mission itself was ridden with disharmony which Talleyrand's delaying tactics only aggravated. Ultimately the Americans returned home fuming.

In their correspondence, Adams's envoys had referred to Talleyrand's agents simply as X, Y, and Z. When the "X.Y.Z. dispatches" were made public, both parties created a deafening uproar in which one slogan was heard: "Millions for defense, but not one cent for tribute." Congress late in 1798 set up a Navy Department. During the next two years the Navy's new warships and hundreds of privateers carried on an undeclared naval war with France. Money was also voted for an army, but to the chagrin of Hamilton who was aching to take the field of glory once more, this military force was unaccountably slow in materializing and never did enter the unofficial war.

At the time of Adams's election, Madison had written Jefferson: "You know the temper of Mr. A. better than I do, but I have always conceived it to be rather a ticklish one." One thing Adams soon became most ticklish about was the Republican taunt that he was "president by three votes." Other partisan attacks aroused him in the summer of 1798 to hit out at his detractors. Chief among the latter was the Swiss, Albert Gallatin, who had become Republican leader in Congress on Madison's retirement in 1797. Adams also found offensive immigrant French intellectuals who were suspected (rightly, in certain cases) of engaging in espionage, and a group of Irishmen, defeated in their fight for freedom at home, who carried their hatred of Britain to America. Nor could the President ignore such home-grown Republican journalists as Franklin's grandson, Benjamin Bache, called "Lightning-rod Junior."

Adams might easily have overcome his pique; but when for their own purposes, the most violent men of his party pushed the notorious Alien and Sedition Acts through Congress in June and July, 1798, Adams grasped the weapons presented. These Acts empowered the President at his own discretion to expel or jail distasteful foreigners, and exposed to fines and imprisonment American citizens acting openly "with intent to defame . . . or bring into contempt or disrepute" the President or other parts of the government. Though no arrests were made under the Alien Act it did scare hundreds of foreigners into leaving the country. Under the Sedition Act about twenty-five persons, practically all of them Republican editors, were haled before federal courts, jailed, and fined. Many Republican papers were effectively put out of commission.

Madison called the Sedition Act "a monster that must forever disgrace its parents." He and Jefferson viewed it as a naked campaign weapon that must be answered. Their response took the form of the Kentucky and Virginia Resolutions, voted by the legislatures of those states in November and December, 1798. Both sets of Resolutions attacked the Hamiltonian "broad interpretation" of the Constitution and developed the solid state-rights position that later was used to justify nullification and secession. The government, they held, is but "a compact to which the states are parties." The states alone, therefore, and not Federalist-dominated courts, had the right to declare what measures went beyond their "compact" and were unconstitutional. Jefferson, who wrote the Kentucky Resolutions, went farthest: he held that the *legislature* of each individual state had this right "within its own territory."

Looking to the presidential elections of 1800, the Republicans used these Resolutions to open their campaign against the "Federalist reign of terror." Apparently they were effective against an opposition itself torn between peaceful Adamsites, and Hamiltonians yearning to make an occasion for their master to play Caesar. In the elections of 1800, the Republican ticket of Jefferson and Burr won 73 electoral votes; the Federalists, Adams and C. C. Pinckney, won 65 and 64 votes respectively. But who was to be President? According to the Constitution, the House, with one vote per state, had to decide between the tied Republicans. Burr had ambitions of his own and knew well how to promote them. Only after thirty-six ballots, bitterness rising with each one, was Jefferson safely in. The next Congress put an end to this kind of problem by the Twelfth Amendment, ratified in 1804. This Amendment provided that, henceforth, "The electors . . . shall name in their ballots the person voted for as President, and in distinct ballots the person voted for as Vice-President."

The Republicans won not only the presidency but control of both the House and Senate. They did not quite make a complete sweep, however. The lame-duck Federalist Congress, before adjourning in March 1801, passed a new judiciary act which created a whole new group of circuit court judges, and increased the number of district court judges. Adams packed these lifetime judicial positions with Federalist sympathizers. Most important, he named John Marshall Chief Justice of the Supreme Court.

JEFFERSONIAN DEMOCRACY

"I have sworn upon the altar of God eternal hostility against every form of tyranny over the mind of man," Jefferson said in 1800. To his followers, persons counted more than wealth, debate more than dictation, consensus more than conformity. Jeffersonian democracy was not an enthronement of the people, but simply of leaders with profound respect for them. "Of course there can be but two parties in a country," said the Federalists, "the friends of order and its foes." Republicans preferred liberty and opportunity to "order." "If there be any among us who would wish to dissolve this Union or to change its republican form," said the first Republican President in his first inaugural, "let them stand undisturbed as monuments of the safety with which error of opinion may be tolerated where reason is left free to combat it."

It is fitting that Jefferson should have been the first president to begin his rule in the rude capital on the Potomac. On many details he himself had advised the French engineer, Pierre Charles L'Enfant, who planned the city of Washington. As it happened the White House was also designed by a foreigner, the Irishman, James Hoban, while an Englishman, B. H. Latrobe (with the American, William Thornton) designed the Capitol. The Alien Act offered poor hospitality to such men. Jefferson, once he had named his advisors (Madison became Secretary of State and Gallatin Secretary of the Treasury), began by allowing this "libel on legislation" to lapse. He welcomed foreign talent anew. Next he freed all who had been jailed under the Sedition Act and had Congress return their fines. Having thus quickly righted matters of the spirit, Jefferson turned to matters of the purse. He admonished Gallatin to keep the finances so simple "that every member of Congress and every man of any mind in the Union should be able to comprehend them." He undertook to help in this by restoring conspicuous simplicity to the government. He dismembered the diplomatic corps, halted expansion of the navy, actually reduced the army.

Another economy move, entirely unlooked for by commercial New Englanders and others who deemed the President the least dependable repository of national honor, was Jefferson's war on the Barbary pirates. England, while paying tribute herself, connived with the pirates to keep other nations from encroaching on British trade, and when the United States became independent her shipping proved a particularly appetizing target. Washington and Adams had sweetened pirate treasuries with $2,000,000. Jefferson thought it would be cheaper to put a stop to the racket. His economy navy ultimately proved unequal to the task, but Jefferson at least won a significant reduction in tribute although it continued to be paid until 1815.

Jefferson was doubly fortunate in that he took office while American prosperity due to the European wars was at its crest and yet while talks leading to the European peace of 1802 were soon to begin. He was also optimistic enough to believe that prosperity and the looming peace might walk hand in hand, and a year later he had reason to feel that his optimism had been justified.

Especially gratifying evidence was the growth of American population and its movement west. In 1800 under Adams, Congress had passed a generous land act permitting a settler to stake out a 320-acre homestead for an initial cash payment of $160. Under Jefferson, a new act in 1804 reduced the minimum required purchase to 160 acres, and the minimum cash payment to $80. Ohio, admitted to the Union in 1803, was the first state to the growth of which these measures contributed. In the following six years Indiana, Michigan, and Illinois attained territorial status.

The Act admitting Ohio established two precedents of national importance. The Land Ordinance of 1785 had stipulated that the federal government was to grant to each township in the states made from the Northwest Territory 640 acres of land (one section), the proceeds from the sale of which were to be used to support schools in the state. The first such grants of federal land were made in Ohio and established the precedent of federal aid to education. At the same time Congress provided that 3 per cent of the proceeds from the sale of other federal land in the state should be granted to the state for use in the development of roads. This legislation set the precedent for federal aid to transportation.

Jefferson also tried to promote settlement in the southwest. His main effort here was addressed to the resolution of conflicting speculator claims to the Yazoo River region held by Georgia. John Randolph of Virginia accused the President of forfeiting the sovereign rights of Georgia for the benefit of corrupt businessmen. Around Randolph gathered the die-hard state-rights Republicans whose philosophy Jefferson himself had buttressed with the Kentucky Resolutions of 1798. Jefferson, however, as he was to make abundantly clear in the purchase of Louisiana, was no stickler for state-rights or a narrow interpretation of the Constitution where America's "manifest destiny" was concerned, and he had his own bold followers. Yet only in 1814, when Randolph was temporarily out of Congress, could the Jeffersonians vote the funds needed to settle the Yazoo issue. Within the next five years, Alabama and Mississippi became states in the contested territory.

The growth of the American West was not enough to satisfy Jefferson. He was impatient to encompass the entire new world in the United States. "However our present interests may restrain us within our limits," he wrote in 1801, "it is impossible not to look forward to distant times, when our rapid multiplication will . . . cover the whole northern, if not the southern continent." Early in 1803 he finally got Congress secretly to finance an expedition across the continent by Meriwether Lewis and William Clark. Setting out from near St. Louis in July 1803, these explorers returned east in 1806, having traced the Columbia River to its mouth and established an American claim to Oregon country.

By then Louisiana, or New Orleans as the whole western country was often called, had come into American possession. In 1800, secretly plotting to revive France's new world empire, Napoleon had reclaimed Louisiana from Spain. The latter, feeble and pacific, as Jefferson said on learning of the deal, "might have retained it quietly for years. . . . France, placing herself in that door, assumes to us the attitude of defiance." Soon he had negotiators in France trying to buy the port of New Orleans, "the possessor of which is our natural and habitual enemy." By 1803 Napoleon's new world ambitions were tempered by enemies of his own in Europe, and he jolted the American envoys by offering them the entire territory between the Mississippi and the Rockies for $15,000,000. On April 30, 1803, the momentous sale was closed. Louisiana had been conveyed with the boundaries "that it now has in the hands of Spain." If this was vague, Talleyrand, now Napoleon's agent, told the troubled Americans, "I suppose you will make the most of it."

Since Spain had not yielded Florida to France, it was not included in the deal. But Jefferson kept his hopes up. "If we push them strongly with one hand, holding out a price in the other," he said, "we shall certainly obtain the Floridas, and all in good time."

The Louisiana Purchase troubled the Randolph Republicans; but the strongest response came from New England Federalists who saw in the addition of this vast territory the further weakening of their political power in the nation. So distraught were some that they conspired to leave the Union, and so desperate that they turned to Vice-President Burr for help. The latter was to run for governor of New York and, on winning, was to take that great state into a new northern confederation. Hamilton gave this Yankee scheme away. Sickened by this and other offenses, real and imaginary, Burr challenged Hamilton to the duel in which Hamilton was killed. The tragedy occurred on July 11, 1804. Burr, like so many other discredited characters of the day, fled to the West where he ineffectually schemed to divest the United States of New Orleans.

The treason of the "Essex Junto," as Burr's Yankee conspirators were called, almost ruined the Federalist Party even in New England, and in the elections in November, Jefferson carried every state but Connecticut. By then, however, the Napoleonic wars had been resumed. Neutral commerce became increasingly subject to attack by both belligerents and the pacific President found his enthusiasm for office ebbing. By 1806 he was "panting for retirement."

Jefferson was especially jealous of the surplus Gallatin had built up in the Treasury, though he hated to admit that it had come mainly from tariffs on European trade. If America needed a costly navy to protect her commerce from the onslaughts and affronts of warring powers, better have no commerce and no navy. But was not the best defense in fact America's own *internal* development? America's continental destiny would supply the needed land. An "American system" of tariffs and other aids to home manufactures would supply the needed industrial complement. This Jeffersonian vision the President disclosed in his message to Congress in December 1806:

> The question now comes forward—to what . . . objects shall these surpluses be appropriated . . . when the purposes of war shall not call for them? Shall we suppress the impost and give that advantage to foreign over domestic manufactures? . . . Patriotism would certainly prefer its continuance and application to the great purposes of the public education, roads, rivers, canals, and such . . . objects of public improvement. . . . By these . . . the lines of separation . . . between the states . . . will disappear . . . and their union . . . will be . . . cemented by indissoluble ties.

Neither Jefferson nor Hamilton had a doctrinaire attachment to "private enterprise"; both were clear as to national objectives and were ready to use the instrumentalities at hand to reach them. Private business was hardly more important than government in national development. Hamilton was consumed with ambitions for national glory, to the attainment of which individual aspirations were subservient. Jefferson was consumed with ambitions for the glory of the individual; his "American System" would make the state subserve the flowering of the human rather than the national spirit. It was his vision rather than Hamilton's that was to color American continental development and American isolationism for a hundred years—not least in the expansive, industrial epoch after the Civil War.

THE SECOND WAR OF AMERICAN INDEPENDENCE

Secretary of State James Madison was Jefferson's hand-picked successor in the presidency. No one shared the Jeffersonian vision of America's destiny more fully. But before Madison could attempt to bring that vision closer to reality, indeed before he could relieve Jefferson of his presidential burdens, both men had to face up to the more immediate realities of the Napoleonic struggle for power in the old world.

By 1805 Napoleon's victory at Austerlitz had given France control of much of the land mass of Europe, while Nelson's victory at Trafalgar had given Britain control of the seas. This apparent stalemate led only to an uncompromising war of attrition, in which Britain stepped up her attacks on commerce bound for ports other than her own and Napoleon responded with indiscriminate seizures of ships not clearly serving him. Between 1804 and 1807, the United States lost more than 1,000 merchantmen to the British, and about 500 to the French. More aggravating was the British practice of impressment. For her own safety Britain had greatly to expand her navy in which life had become so harsh that sailors deserted at every port. Desperately in need of men, Britain claimed the right to search neutral ships and impress back into service deserters found on them. Often she took aliens as well. Between 1804 and 1807, 6,000 men were taken from American ships. The British sometimes sailed right into American ports for the purpose. In June 1807, an impressment attempt led to fighting between the British warship *Leopard,* and the new and unprepared United States frigate *Chesapeake,* which cost twenty American lives.

To almost everyone but Jefferson, it seemed, this final affront meant war. The President dusted off his own favorite policy which he now called "peaceful coercion." By depriving the belligerents of American goods and American carriers, he would force them to respect neutral, American rights. In December 1807, Jefferson got Congress to vote an Embargo Act forbidding all ships to clear American harbors, and proscribing all exports even over land. Far from ruining Britain or France, this measure ruined only New England and American ports to the south. On March 1, 1809, three days before his retirement in favor of Madison, Jefferson suffered the ignominy of having to sign an act terminating his apparently naïve efforts. He had, however, preserved peace for fourteen months; and time soon showed that his policy might have preserved it until Napoleon's final collapse.

Driven from commerce, American capitalists took some hesitant steps toward manufacturing after 1807. To nip this new development in the bud and keep the American market for themselves, many in Britain (as Jefferson had hoped) began demanding concessions to American shipping. Unfortunately, the British Government took these demands seriously enough only to send emissaries to the United States with the idea of quieting discontent at home. These emissaries so exasperated Madison's administration that the President had them recalled. At the same time he withdrew the American representative in London. By 1810 no formal channels of diplomatic communication remained to the two nations, while a nonintercourse act proscribed trade between them. Bonaparte and the ubiquitous Talleyrand, meanwhile, played their own game with Madison and Congress, thereby accelerating the deterioration of the American economy and aggravating the discomfiture of the American public.

Popular disgust with the international situation was recorded in the by-elections of 1810 and 1811, which saw more than half of the impotent Tenth Congress thrown out. Included among the replacements were brilliant and bristling frontiersmen like Henry Clay of Kentucky, Felix Grundy of Tennessee, and John C. Calhoun of upland South Carolina. Most of them were young enough never to have been British subjects; all of them thirsted for a Jeffersonian American empire of their own. The war in Europe gave them their excuse, European mismanagement in the new world their opportunity.

By 1810 most of the inhabitants of Spanish West Florida were Americans. Bemoaning Spain's inability to protect them from the Indians, they revolted and asked for annexation to the United States. Madison, as unscrupulous as Jefferson in acquiring new territory, had connived with the rebels, and agreed to their request. East Florida was attacked next, but when Spain threatened war and New England threatened secession if war came, Madison recalled the troops. This "treachery" set the southerners impatiently marking time.

To the north there was more trouble with Indians. All along the frontier the tribes had been tricked into making grant after grant to white men in treaties they little understood, until, in 1811, the great Shawnee, Tecumseh, decided a stand must be made. But Governor William Henry Harrison of Indiana Territory, one of the harshest American negotiators, anticipated him. While Tecumseh was away mobilizing his forces, Harrison and his troops attacked the leaderless tribe at Tippecanoe Creek. Finding the ruins of his settlement on his return, Tecumseh swore the survivors to eternal war. Frontiersmen long believed that the British in Canada were supplying Tecumseh with arms and egging on his braves. The cry thus grew loud for the conquest of all Canada (for how else could the British be eliminated from "Our Continent"), and for the conquest of all Florida, lest Spain be used as a catspaw for Britain's reentry.

The handful of frontiersmen who brought this borderland cry to the halls of Congress in November 1811, easterners promptly branded "War Hawks." Taking advantage of the mutual enmity of older members, the War Hawks quickly elected their leader, Clay, Speaker of the House; he in turn used the Speaker's prerogative to name his partisans chairmen of the major committees. Soon the War Hawks had bills before the House for strengthening the armed services, and were telling the world, in Clay's words, that "we could fight France too, if necessary, in a good cause—the cause of honor and independence." Later events helped keep the pressure on the hesitant President who on June 1, 1812, reluctantly sent his message to Congress asking for war on Great Britain.

In his war message, Madison said nothing of Canada and Florida but stressed the accumulation of intolerable British offenses against American citizens, ports, ships, and commerce. A few days later Secretary of State James Monroe was already preparing an armistice offer, while the British, ignorant of Madison's war message, were actually taking steps to meet most of Monroe's terms. But by demanding an end to impressment, Monroe was demanding too much; while the British, yielding only on other maritime matters, were conceding too little. "We are going to fight," wrote frontiersman Andrew Jackson as early as the previous March, "for the reestablishment of our national character . . . to seek some indemnity for past injuries, some security against future aggression, by the conquest of all the British dominions upon the continent of North America."

Confusion in American minds as to the actual objectives of the war muddied strategy from the outset. Canada, it was universally agreed, was the only "tangible" place to engage England. Yet New England, a natural path to the heart of Canada, obstructed the conduct of the war in every way. The South, in turn, fearful that the acquisition of Canada would threaten its political future as the acquisition of Louisiana had hurt New England's, much preferred to have Yankee ships fight the war at sea. The West agreed with Jefferson that "the cession of Canada . . . must be a *sine qua non* at a treaty of peace"; but it was soon shown that the swaggering frontier could not stomach withdrawal of the local garrisons guarding it against the Indians simply to send them skylarking to distant Montreal. Taking Canada, Jefferson had boasted, "will be a mere matter of marching." But it was only after Captain Oliver Hazard Perry had shattered a British flotilla on Lake Erie in September 1813, that Canada could even be successfully approached by land. "We have met the enemy and they are ours," Perry reported, thereby giving the signal for an American force, with naval support on Lake Ontario, to invade York (present Toronto) and burn the Canadian parliament houses. Nothing more substantial came of this expedition, and it gave the British a precedent for burning the White House and the Capitol when they invaded Washington in August 1814.

The conduct of the war on the high seas was adequate. American naval gunners consistently outshot the British, while American privateers captured 1,300 British merchantmen valued, with their cargoes, at $40,000,000. The course of the war on land was no better than the available officers might have led one to expect.

"The old officers," commented the rising Winfield Scott at the outset of the war, "had very generally slunk into either sloth, ignorance, or habits of intemperate drinking." Most of the new ones he thought "coarse and ignorant men," with a sprinkling of educated "swaggerers, dependents, decayed gentlemen, and others unfit for anything else." By 1814, however, some vigorous new commanders had been uncovered, among them Scott himself, his superior, General Jacob Brown, and the violent southwestern free lance, Andrew Jackson. The British also greatly improved their performance. By 1814 Napoleon had abdicated and veterans of Wellington's campaigns against the French Emperor were now free to be sent to America.

The caliber of the fighting thus was raised in all theaters. Since the end of the Napoleonic wars in Europe left little excuse for their American phase to continue, however, the objective of both sides was simply to gain better bargaining positions at the impending peace conference. On learning of England's receptivity to negotiations, Madison early in 1814 sent five peace commissioners to meet with the British at Ghent in Belgium. On December 24, 1814, the Treaty of Ghent was signed. Fifteen days later, before the news had reached America, Andrew Jackson won his memorable victory over the British at New Orleans. The war was indeed over; but Jackson's theatrical career had just begun.

America's peace commissioners at Ghent—among them the poker-playing Clay, the puritanical John Quincy Adams, and the sophisticated Gallatin—were no clearer about their mission than Madison's administration had been about the war. The British opened by demanding western territory to give Canada access to the Mississippi. They seemed determined also to concede nothing on impressment and other maritime matters, including the New Englanders' privilege (granted in 1783 but withdrawn in 1812) to fish in Newfoundland and Labrador waters and dry their catch on local shores. Clay was perfectly willing to trade away New England's fishing privileges to win Canada and other expansive demands of his own. Adams was adamant about the reopening of the fisheries even if he must sacrifice wilderness land.* When the military stalemate left both missions high and dry, they at last agreed simply to disagree. Clay called the Treaty of Ghent a "damned bad treaty." Its terms returned matters to their prewar status and left to later commissions the settlement of boundaries, fisheries, and commercial intercourse.

Before these commissions got far along, the irrepressible Jackson almost brought about a renewal of hostilities. During the war Jackson had defeated and taken a great deal of land from Britain's allies, the Creek Indians, in the Southwest. In 1817, two British adventurers, Arbuthnot and Ambrister, convinced the Creeks they had been robbed. Scalpings followed. Ordered to punish the Indians, Jackson routed their forces, hanged their chiefs, courtmartialed and executed Arbuthnot and Ambrister, and marched on Pensacola. There he ejected the Spanish governor who had given the redmen a haven, and claimed the territory for the United States. England, Spain, and Congress were all up in arms, but peace was kept. This adventure gave Spain just "the push" Jefferson thought she needed to make her realize that she had better sell Florida to the United States before the latter's uncontrollable citizens simply took it. In 1819 the United States, "holding out a price in the other hand," as Jefferson had suggested, closed the deal for $5,000,000. The backwoodsman had become a new force and had begun to make policy in the United States.

The Florida purchase settled the southern boundary permanently, though there were American expansionists even in New England who remained far from satisfied. The absorption of all North America by the United States, said John Quincy Adams in 1819, was "as much a law of nature . . . as that the Mississippi should flow to the sea." Revolts against Spain by the last Spanish colonies in the new world whetted the appetites of "large America" enthusiasts at this time.

* Adams, and the New England position generally, were at a disadvantage because of New England's secession movement which culminated in the Hartford Convention during the war. See the discussion of the Convention and its sequel in Chapter Six.

When these revolts proved almost universally successful by 1823, the United States, with the blessings of Great Britain, took the opportunity "for asserting, as a principle in which the rights and interests of the United States are involved, that the American continents, by the free and independent condition which they have assumed and maintain, are henceforth not to be considered as subjects for future colonization by any European powers." This pronouncement was one phase of what we know as the Monroe Doctrine. The second phase of the Doctrine declared that the United States would consider any interference with the sovereignty and territorial integrity of the new Latin American republics by European powers "manifestation of an unfriendly disposition." Europe thus was explicitly warned off adventures in Central and South America. Many in the United States continued to feel that these southern lands would eventually come under American ownership.

By 1819 the commissions set up by the Treaty of Ghent had also made progress in settling the northern boundary of the United States. Eventually the work of these commissions insured the permanent demilitarization of the Canadian-United States border. Their work also fostered lasting peace between England and the late rebels. For years, however, this peace remained a wary one. "That man must be blind to the indications of the future," said Clay in 1816, "who cannot see that we are destined to have war after war with Great Britain." Congress heeded his appeal that year by voting large appropriations for the Army and Navy even though the nation was faced with a huge war debt and a barren treasury. The large Irish immigration to the United States after the war gave a practical political purpose to keeping anti-British feeling warm.

On their side, many Englishmen never forgave the crude colonials for declaring war on them when England alone seemed to hold the fortress of civilization against the barbarism of Napoleon. Numbers of Englishmen visited America after the war to return to write scathing accounts of their hosts. It was in this period that the *Edinburgh Review* asked the famous question: "In the four quarters of the globe, who reads an American book? Or goes to an American play? Or looks at an American picture or statue?"

Chapter Six

The American Way of Life

"An age is needed to expound an age," said the first great Unitarian divine, William Ellery Channing. By the time James Monroe, the last of the "cocked hats," retired from the presidency in 1825, the age of the founding fathers had been clearly and, as almost always happens in history, ironically "expounded." The Constitution itself, secretly contrived, anxiously promulgated, and reluctantly ratified, had by 1825 survived almost forty years of faction, separatism, sedition, insurrection, war, and expansion. Designed to instill national feeling, to centralize power, to preserve seaboard property, privilege, and caste, the Constitution failed to accomplish any of these things. Yet it was deemed a great success at home, a model for romantic reformers abroad.

To Hamiltonians and Jeffersonians alike, the Constitutional Republic had been a questionable experiment for a nation as large and populous even as the original thirteen struggling commonwealths. Yet this Republic by the mid 1820s had grown to twenty-four states, had more than doubled its area, more than tripled its population, and almost quadrupled its wealth. The eighteenth-century "gentlemen of principle and property" who had set the young Republic on its way distrusted human nature, especially when it was not firmly leashed to a disciplined and informed mind. Insignificant in numbers themselves, they built into their framework of government imposing obstacles to what they considered the inevitable license of the "tyrannical mob." By the 1820s the "people of no importance," their ranks augmented by the continuing immigration of Irish, Scots, and Germans, but principally by an extraordinarily high birth rate, had simply flanked these obstacles and inundated their creators.

153

New York State, her rich back country newly accessible by river and canal, had grown by 1830 as populous as all New England, whence many of her western settlers had come. Pennsylvania, similarly endowed, lagged little behind New York. Virginians, meanwhile, continued to move into Kentucky and Tennessee in numbers sufficient to push their combined population higher than the "Old Dominion's." Virginians also helped settle southern Ohio, Indiana, and Illinois. The northern parts of these states, at the same time, were filling up with Yankees. By 1830, Ohio had become far more populous than Massachusetts, Indiana than Connecticut. To the south, Alabama, Mississippi, and Louisiana were challenging the Carolinas.

Meanwhile, for the first time in American history, cities were growing faster than the farming country. Much the greatest city in the West was New Orleans, the capital of the entire Mississippi valley. Much the greatest city in the country was New York. Elsewhere by 1830, Lowell on the Merrimack, Rochester on the Erie Canal, Buffalo and Cleveland on Lake Erie, Pittsburgh and Cincinnati on the Ohio, and St. Louis on the Father of Waters all had their future teeming growth clearly foreshadowed. Many other sites, less lucky politically and geographically, as yet yielded to none in pride, hope, and tall talk.

"Society is full of excitement," Daniel Webster said in 1823. "Competition comes in place of monopoly; and intelligence and industry ask only for fair play and an open field." In the older states, immigrants, debtors, renters, and recusants were acquiring the franchise and the privilege to hold office. In most of the new ones they wrote the constitutions and manned the governments. Yet the wide open politics only reflected a wide open society. Men were starting out young, marrying early, assuming major responsibilities in their teens. Along with the farms, they were forsaking the mental furniture of their fathers. Threadbare abstractions—be they about God, mammon, government, fate, steam power, or forest fever— were being put to the pragmatic test. Once again men were trying their powers, not simply taking their places.

"The same man," the young French visitor to the United States, Alexis de Tocqueville, wrote home in 1831, "has given his name to a wilderness that none before him had traversed, has seen the first forest tree fall and the first planter's house rise in the solitude, where a community came to group itself, a village grew, and today a vast city stretches. . . . In his youth he lived among nations which no longer exist, except in history. In his lifetime rivers have changed their courses or diminished their flow, the very climate is other than he knew it, and all that is to him but the first step in a limitless career."

Enlightened scholars in their libraries might continue to pore over the chastening past. Man in the open air cared only for the romantic future. History, the lugubrious handmaiden of eighteenth-century politics, was beginning afresh in nineteenth-century United States. And American life, if not American "books, plays, and statues," was becoming the inspiration and guide (and occasional caution, as in Tocqueville's famous report on America to the France of Louis Philippe) for fresh starts across the sea.

"THE ERA OF GOOD FEELINGS"

The years to which historians have given the name "the era of good feelings" were in fact but a sorry interlude between the end of the Second War of Independence and the launching of the American Way. These years were sorriest in New England which gave the era's name its currency.

The War of 1812 had brought great prosperity and a great moral crisis to New England. Until near the war's end, the British blockade left the friendly ports of Massachusetts and Rhode Island alone, and through them funneled the imported iron and other wares for which Yankee merchants made the rest of the country pay through the nose. Yankee farmers and manufacturers at the same time grew rich selling supplies to the Quartermaster of the Army their sons refused to serve. The specie New Englanders thereby drained from the other sections they either hoarded or invested in British rather than American bonds. Mainly on this account, but also because the national administration had allowed the charter of its own Bank of the United States to lapse in 1811, American bonds fetched but 40 per cent in specie value and the government had to suspend specie payments on its debt.

The Hartford Convention of December 1814, "this mad project of national suicide," as John Quincy Adams called it, marked the climax of New England's wartime sedition. Half of New England felt accursed by the profiteers in their midst. The profiteers felt accursed by Mr. Madison's War "against the nation from which we are descended." Reminded by their clergy of "Israel's woes in Egypt," where the Jews "had been the most opulent section," they resolved, like the followers of Moses, "to dissolve . . . their union."

Enough moderates infiltrated the Convention which met at Hartford in December to dissuade it from effecting the "opulent section's" purpose. Secession was postponed. Even the demands of the "moderates" on Congress, however, exposed the working of the sectional virus that sped southern secession later. One of their demands would deprive the slavocracy of representation in Congress based on the Negro population. By such action they hoped to stem New England's precipitate fall into minority status in the national government. A second demand would proscribe the election of successive presidents from the same state, i.e., Virginia. Members of the Hartford Convention threatened to meet again for sterner measures if Congress rejected the moderates' demands, but they were saved from themselves when the end of Mr. Madison's War followed closely on the end of the meeting.

Federalist faithlessness like Federalist finance had failed to deliver the country to its foreign foes. Federalist defeat in the presidential election of 1816 preserved the country from its foes at home. This election is especially significant for the fight Madison had to make against the Randolph state-rights contingent in the Republican Congressional Caucus to effect the nomination of his Secretary of State, James Monroe. Heretofore, the Caucus had been tightly knit and ruled the party with an iron hand. The rift between the state-righters and the nationalists foreshadowed Jackson's fight on "King Caucus" and the ultimate establishment in its place of the convention system of making party nominations. In 1816 the Federalists made one last effort to appear as a national rather than a New England party by nominating Rufus King of New York. Monroe's easy victory buried the Federalist Party forever. Defeat, nevertheless, found New England not yet without stratagems.

Shortly before Monroe's inauguration in March 1817, the editor of the *North American Review,* a Boston magazine so hostile to the war that it had often been called the *North Unamerican,* wrote to the President-elect congratulating him on his "feeling of sovereignty," and inviting him to extend it once again to New England by showing his gracious presence there. Monroe accepted. His journey from Washington proved a triumphal one, but his reception in Boston topped everything he had met on the way.

Having captured the President, as they thought, the New England secessionists proceeded to try to capture his administration. On July 10, 1817, George Sullivan, one of the adornments of the Boston bar and a recent secessionist leader, wrote the President suggesting as Attorney-General in the new Cabinet Daniel Webster, "a rock on which your administration might rest secure against the violence of almost any faction." Otherwise, wrote the comforting Mr. Sullivan, "your administration will be overthrown; because your Cabinet is weak & discordant." Webster, a congressman from New Hampshire at the time, had not attended the Hartford Convention; but as his biographer Richard N. Current writes, he had done "his best to destroy" Madison's "administration and all its works and in particular to sabotage" Madison's War. Without this "rock," in fact, Monroe won an even more sweeping victory in 1820 than in 1816.

It was during the progress of these maneuvers, on July 12, 1817, that Boston's *Columbian Sentinel,* as "Unamerican" in the past as the *North American* itself, wrote: "We recur with pleasure to all the circumstances . . . during the late Presidential Jubilee . . . which attended the demonstrations of good feelings." It entitled the article, "ERA OF GOOD FEELINGS." By then New England had been humbled economically as well as politically; but the rest of the country was enjoying a short-lived boom that prompted it to take up the slogan.

New England's deepening economic difficulties derived mainly from old England. With the war's end early in 1815, Americans rushed to replenish their supplies of European—mainly English—finery and other goods. Imports soared to a record $110,000,000 even at bargain prices. "It was well worth while," Henry Brougham told Parliament the following year, "to incur a loss on the first exportation in order, by the glut, to stifle in the cradle those rising manufactures in the United States, which the war had forced into existence." In 1816, undiminished by the "protective" tariff enacted that year, American imports exceeded $150,000,000. Wreck and ruin among New England's little factories was widespread. England persisted, moreover, in keeping American ships out of their pre-Revolutionary haunts in the West Indies. When New Englanders sought to revive their carrying trade elsewhere, they met England's own merchantmen and Americans from the recently blockaded ports to the south swarming back into business. The commercial blight spread quickly to Yankee shipbuilding and lumbering.

A generation later New England would flower once more as the nation's leader in philosophy as well as finance. But until then, from her sour spirit and her stony soil a new "Great Migration" went forward. Worse, the holier-than-thou Federalist oligarchy offered thanks that "in the vast raw wilderness," the "forester class" it despised found a "retreat sufficiently alluring to draw them from the land of their nativity."

In the meantime the rest of the country prospered. Back in 1793 the Yankee, Eli Whitney, having gone to Georgia to teach school, invented the cotton "gin" (patois for "engine") which made it practical to grow there the hardy but heretofore hard to clean short staple cotton plant. When the resumption of the European wars in 1803 simultaneously cost the South its continental markets for other crops and made England and eventually New England hunger for cotton cloth, cotton planting boomed. Once the wars ended and New England's little factories died, England herself demanded large cotton crops for her own tireless machines. The continental market for American tobacco also revived. Poor European harvests in 1816 and 1817 added to the demand, too, for American pork, beef, and wheat. The debt incurred by the record American imports of manufactures on the heels of the peace added an element favoring export of American agricultural staples by which American merchants balanced their accounts.

This blue-sky combination of factors drew thousands to the West and Southwest. As always in American history, a boom in agriculture brought a boom in land speculation. "I ain't greedy about land. I only want what jines mine," westerners explained. The three hundred or more state and private banks promoted in the years of "financial liberty" after 1811 spurred on the boom. By 1817 such banks had issued $100,000,000 in paper money, much of it unnegotiable even in near-by communities. These "facility notes," as they were called, helped newcomers get started and oldsters enlarge their holdings. But the notes also created obligations on which the "bankers" could foreclose new and old settlers alike simply by withholding further "facilities" at their pleasure.

By 1817 the Second Bank of the United States, chartered the year before, was ready for business. Influential local bankers, foreseeing competition, had written into some western state constitutions provisions against "foreign banks" doing business within their borders. Ill-managed from the first in places where it could do business, the new national bank proceeded to justify local fears by outdoing even the state banks in the lavishness of its loans. These loans, moreover, were made in notes more negotiable than those of the state banks. In retaliation the injured local financiers got their states to try to tax out of existence both the branches and the notes of "the monster." But the legal battles over such measures took time, and with the "monster's" blessing the boom continued.

By midsummer of 1818, the Bank of the United States was at last ready to take deflationary measures. But by then the land boom was already showing signs of petering out, and the national bank's tight-money policy proved as ill-timed as its earlier inflationary lending had been. The financial collapse of 1819 was worldwide. The revival of European harvests and a constricted market after the postwar textile boom combined to create a universal glut both of grain and of cotton. But the depression was most severe in the United States and most sickening in the West.

The crisis of 1819 prompted a number of states to abolish the useless and degrading punishment of imprisonment for debt. States also passed liberal bankruptcy laws, and laws easing the settlement of contracts. Congress, in turn, came to the aid of the West with a new land act in 1820 making it possible for a settler to buy an eighty-acre homestead for as little as $100 in *cash*. The next year Congress passed a Relief Act to assist those whom earlier credit provisions had got into trouble.

Such was the condition and temper of the country when the Supreme Court met in February 1819. In the next few weeks John Marshall delivered three resounding decisions, each limiting the power of state governments, and hence state business interests dependent upon state aid. In the old case of *Marbury* v. *Madison* back in 1803, Marshall had set the precedent by which the Supreme Court has since held the power to declare a federal statute unconstitutional. In 1810 in *Fletcher* v. *Peck,* he had held a state law unconstitutional which attempted to terminate a contract between an individual and a state. Now in *Sturges* v. *Crowninshield* he held a New York Bankruptcy Act unconstitutional simply because it altered the obligations under a contract between man and man without either's consent. Next in *Dartmouth College* v. *Woodward,* Marshall put corporation charters into the same category as contracts and ruled that they could not be changed by unilateral action on the part of the incorporating state. Finally in *McCulloch* v. *Maryland*, a case arising out of state measures designed to tax out of existence the Maryland branch of the Bank of the United States, the Supreme Court placed federal agencies beyond the reach of state law. Far from being "an act of sovereign and independent states," as Maryland contended, Marshall held that the Constitution was an act of the whole people. "The power to tax," he said, "involves the power to destroy. The states," he added, "have no power by taxation or otherwise . . . in any manner [to] control, the operations of the constitutional laws," or "the means . . . plainly adapted" to their "end."

"A deadly blow has been struck at the *sovereignty of the states,*" cried the Baltimore journalist Hezekiah Niles, "and from a quarter so far removed from the people to be hardly accessible to public opinion." Actually, most Americans didn't care. In the older states, subsistence farming remained the rule, agriculture a sacred calling. At the other end of the rainbow, traders, trappers, hunters, and mountain men, "with all the freedom of the lonely wind . . . started from frontiers at which more cautious pioneers were glad to stop

. . . and wandered through the reaches of the outer West." The "more cautious pioneers" themselves were on the move again across the Mississippi, where the fight between free soilers and slavers for Missouri, "like a fire-bell in the night," to use Jefferson's chilling phrase, awakened men and filled them "with terror." In the nearer West, in yet-wild Ohio and Indiana, pietistic Germans, having fled from renewed persecution at home, tried to sustain one another in wilderness communities. While all around them fierce Scotch-Irish isolates who had lost their God, bred from the native terror of storm and flood and fever, of marsh and swamp, turkey buzzard and lurking brave, "a certain jollity of mind, pickled in a scorn of fortune." Business crashes and courts of law affected and impressed them little.

THE WESTERN PRIZE

Englishmen, opined "the Contentious Man," William Cobbett, just before the crash of 1819, would be mad to try and could never survive the life of the western pioneer. "The rugged roads, the dirty hovels, the fire in the woods to sleep by, the pathless ways through the wilderness, the dangerous crossings of the rivers"—all, for what? "To boil their pot in gypsy-fashion, to have a mere board to eat on, to drink whiskey or pure water, to sit and sleep under a shed far inferior to English cowpens, to have a mill at twenty miles distance, an apothecary's shop at a hundred, and a doctor nowhere." Yet as Jefferson had said, Americans found it "cheaper to clear a new acre than to manure an old one," and for that and many less fathomable reasons, almost half of "Yankeedoodledum" (Walt Whitman's word) kept on the move toward the setting sun.

The Lincolns were a typical case. "Virginia John," the rail splitter's distant forebear of Massachusetts extraction and a man of means, had come south from western Pennsylvania before the Revolution. In the rich valley of the Shenandoah in 1778, "Thomas the unstable," the future president's father, was born. Four years later found the family in Kentucky, where Thomas grew up "a wandering laboring boy." In 1806, a Methodist parson is said to have married him to illiterate, illegitimate Nancy Hanks, after which Hankses and Lincolns domiciled together and buried their dead all over the state. Abe was born in 1809 in one of their better log huts. By 1816, the whole tribe had "packed through" to Indiana where, young Lincoln recalled:

> The panther's scream filled the night with fear
> And bears preyed on the swine.

There they lived for ten years before heading toward Illinois, "squatting" the first year in a three-sided shelter, that "darne little half-face camp." "We lived the same as the Indians," some Lincoln relatives said later, " 'ceptin' we took an interest in politics and religion."

The Revolution had vouchsafed Americans a nation of their own, and with it, "slick as a snake out of a black skin," had materialized the image of "Sam Slick, the Yankee Peddler" (like a nation, larger than life) all rigged out in his "long tail'd blue," "lank as a leafless elm," but lusty, "in everything a meddler." About the time of the War of 1812 ("Yankee" having become a sore reproach), "Nimrod Wildfire," "a mighty hunter but a poor farmer," Davy Crockett in the large, had nudged over Uncle Sam.

> We raised a bank to hide our breasts, not that we thought
> of dying
> But that we always liked to rest unless the game is flying.

By 1820 nearly four million likely Nimrods had crossed over Lincoln country, most of them on foot, gun in hand, their few possessions on their backs or saddled on occasional cows. For all the excitement of 1818-19, speculators and their gulls were few among them. The Lincolns' backsliding life remained the common lot of the West, where Methodist circuit riders fought the Demon drink in the forests, and exhorters wrestled with the Devil himself at "camp-meetings, class-meetings, prayer-meetings and love feasts," to get the Lord's sinners to repent, repent.

> Come hungry, come thirsty, come ragged, come bare,
> Come filthy, come lousy, come just as you are

Yet business organization and enterprise were not to leave the West to hunters, sinners, and soul-savers for long. In 1823 Harrison

Gray Otis noted that in New England, "there has been a curious 'revival' in the spirit of men . . . which is quite remarkable. . . . It is amazing to see what is done by the puff on one hand and the panic on the other." New England capital would soon look west for investment opportunities. In the West itself "woods, woods, woods, as far as the world extends" were being leveled, and the character of the country was being transformed. By the 1820s, writes Constance Rourke, the brilliant analyst of *American Humor,* "the backwoodsman became Yankee," but "the Yankee of the legend also absorbed the character of the backwoodsman." No longer just of New England, and no longer a reproach, the Yankee took on the "inflation" of the West: "I am Sam Slick the Yankee peddler—I can ride on a flash of lightning and catch a thunderbolt in my fist." "We Yankees," the new Slick told an English audience, "don't do things like you Britishers; we are born in a hurry, educated at full speed, our spirit is as high as our pressure, and our life resembles a shooting star, till death surprises us like an electric shock."

The fusing, firing elements were cotton, steamboats, and canals; and the impetus they gave to slavery, a bit later, carried into the consciousness of the nation a third member of America's soul-saving "comic trio," the Negro slave of raw southwestern plantations.

> Wheel about, turn about
> Do jis so,
> An' ebery time I wheel about
> I jump Jim Crow.

In New England and elsewhere in the world early in the 1820s wheels and looms and factory belts began to turn again, and cotton suddenly was in urgent demand. Earlier, the cotton planters of South Carolina and Georgia (like the eighteenth-century tobacco planters of Virginia and Maryland) had been forced from the depleted tidewater soil to the piedmont. From there they had pushed many small slaveless farmers beyond the mountains. By 1820 the piedmont itself had become, as a visitor noted, "dreary and uncultivated wastes," and the planter harried the farmers into the hills. In Alabama, Mississippi, Louisiana, Arkansas, and Tennessee, farm after small farm was bought up and combined into great plantations and new bottom land cleared for cotton.

Hand in hand with the spread of cotton went the need for slaves. An able-bodied male field hand cost $350 to $500 in 1800. By 1820 the price had doubled and thereafter continued to rise. After 1808 when the Constitutional prohibition of slave imports took effect, until 1860, 5,000 slaves were smuggled annually into the country, chiefly through Gulf ports. But this hardly met the demand. "It is a practice, and an increasing practice in parts of Virginia," Thomas Jefferson Randolph told the State Legislature in 1832, "to rear slaves" for the Cotton Kingdom. "The exportation [from Virginia] has averaged 8,500 for the last twenty years." Maryland's deliveries in the same period approached those of her neighbor. Henceforth, writes a southern historian, "the sale of slaves became the source of the largest profit of nearly all the slaveholders of the upper South," where manumission sentiment had once been keenest.

Cotton had captured the conscience as well as the capital of the South. Even in worn-out South Carolina where, as a traveler noted in 1826, there remains "finer grazing country [than] any in the world . . . every other object gives place to cotton." Here its cultivation, especially in competition with the Southwest, made no sense. In the Southwest, at the same time, the cultivation of anything else (but sugar on special land) seemed senseless. "Corn, sweet potatoes, melons, and all northern fruit, with the exception of apples, flourish here," wrote a Connecticut missionary in Louisiana in 1825, "though the planters calculate to supply themselves with provisions almost entirely from the upper country."

It was the Cotton Kingdom's growing requirements in food and work animals that first gave to the slack and swaggering West just the impulse it needed to lay down the reel and rod and gun and get serious about farming. Since the siren, speculation, naturally danced along, credit flowed faster and on a much larger scale than earlier. It was not long, therefore, before debt forced the westerner to concentrate almost as single-mindedly as the planter on cash crops. Southern specialization in cotton spurred Western specialization in grain and meat and mules. The marvelous Mississippi River system conveniently tied the two sections together, and for the time being the steamboat tightened the knot.

In 1811, four years after his success with the *Clermont* on the Hudson, Robert Fulton built the first western steamboat, the *New Orleans,* and as in New York, sought a monopoly of western business. In 1824, in *Gibbons* v. *Ogden,* John Marshall dealt the final blow to all monopolies on interstate waters, and by 1830 nearly two hundred steamboats were churning up western rivers and generating a velocity of exchange unimagined a decade earlier. From newly thriving up-river ports such as Pittsburgh and Cincinnati everything from the interior came by steamboat to the levees of New Orleans for distribution to the rest of the South and Southwest or for shipment overseas. And everything from abroad or from the East destined for the South and West paid toll at the great Gulf port.

By 1830, however, changes in transportation had begun to isolate the South. Much earlier many easterners had taken to wondering how best to direct the flow of western produce to their own active ports. One enterprise with this objective was the great "National Highway," authorized during Jefferson's administration in 1806. By 1818 it provided excellent access from Cumberland, Maryland, to Wheeling on the Ohio, and was supplemented by thousands of miles of privately built turnpikes which served as feeders, mainly from the north. But one road, however good, does not make a system; and in any case the turnpikes themselves charged such high tolls that producers of heavy agricultural commodities were discouraged from using them. By 1830 many turnpike companies had become bankrupt and abandoned their roads.

In 1810 the New York State legislature set up a committee to study a canal to the West, but nothing came of it. In 1816, however, when De Witt Clinton again raised the issue, engineering qualms and political quarrels had dissolved in the current prosperity. "Clinton's Big Ditch" was to run an incredible 364 miles (the longest existing canal ran thirty miles) and connect the Hudson with Lake Erie. Completed in 1825, the Erie Canal in the next nine years paid off the state's entire cost (with interest) of $8,500,-000. Two figures explain its success: it cut freight rates between Buffalo and Albany from $100 to $15 a ton, travel time from twenty to eight days. The land boom it started along its path would alone have justified the enterprise.

New York City's success agitated its competitors. But while many Atlantic ports thrust longing little ventures toward the mountains before the panic of 1837, only Philadelphia succeeded in getting its state to complete a western connection. Between 1826 and 1834 Pennsylvania built a complicated $10,000,000 system of waterways and inclined railways to Pittsburgh. Yet some of the failures were even more interesting than the successes. When Maryland refused to dig a canal between Baltimore and the Ohio River, Baltimore businessmen in 1827 organized a private corporation to build a newfangled steam railroad across the mountains. This railroad's first fourteen miles (the earliest in the United States) were opened in 1828. Not until the 1850s, however, did the B. & O. reach the Ohio River. In 1830 Bostonians also turned to the railroad and proceeded to build local lines. In the South in the early 1830s Charleston, Savannah, and Richmond all started railroads with the idea (fruitless, as it proved) of diverting to themselves some of the business of New Orleans.

While the ambitious East eyed the suddenly enterprising West, westerners themselves were finding many reasons to turn away from the South. For one thing, by 1830 the West was producing more wheat, corn, and hogs than the slavocracy and Europe together could consume. For another, as river business grew, river hazards multiplied. All the improvements in western steamboat design, moreover, failed to make low-water sailing safe at any time. This tended to bunch traffic in the flood tide seasons of spring and fall, and the sudden artificial abundance depressed prices. Warehousing at New Orleans in anticipation of better returns was costly and the humidity gradually spoiled crops.

Such considerations tempted westerners after 1820 to embrace Clay's "American System," so named in contrast to the dependence on European markets where failures had intensified the domestic crash of 1819. Clay would have the West support high tariffs in order to encourage eastern manufacturers whose success would insure farmers a growing "home market" for their surplus. At the same time, western support for "internal improvements," by working to reduce the oppressive transportation charges east and west, would give farmers both higher prices for their produce and cheaper factory goods. Though the West soured on Clay because of his restrictive land policy and abandoned him when he championed the Bank of the United States, it backed the rest of his program in Washington and embarked on ambitious state canal and railroad programs. By 1840, 3,326 miles of canals had been constructed in the United States, mainly in the North and West, at a cost of $125,000,000. Most of the money had been supplied by the states, much of the rest by British investors in state bonds. In the middle 1830s western states also turned to railroads, but had little to show for this effort by 1837 other than an excessive debt.

Travel over turnpikes was slow and costly. Canals were much cheaper, but four months in the year the northern routes were frozen. The railroad was to free industry and trade from the weather and the medieval pace of oxen and tow horses. In the western trade, however, canals remained the major carriers for decades. The South continued a valuable customer of the West, and the Mississippi River system supported New Orleans and upriver towns. But by 1840 the East had taken the bulk of the western and especially the northwestern trade. "Samson Hardhead," Yankee and backwoodsman, had triumphed over the planter caste.

In the East, New York City ultimately overshadowed its own thriving competitors and bound both West and South in vassalage to its commercial institutions. The Erie Canal, of course, boosted New York tremendously. But long before the Canal was opened, New York merchants had taken two bold measures. Auctions, which assured rapid turnover of goods for cash, were common in all American ports where ships were anxious to get away. Elsewhere, if bids were unsatisfactory, goods could be withdrawn. In New York City after 1817 purchasers were assured that the highest bid would get delivery. Buyers naturally congregated there; and where buyers congregated, sellers flocked. New York's second innovation, in January 1818, was the establishment of Atlantic packets to run on regular schedules to Europe, "full or not full." Elsewhere exporters remained at the mercy of the weather and the whims of captains.

New York's progress henceforth fed upon itself. But typically her merchants extended a helping hand. New York supplied the entire country with the manufactures and luxuries of the world. To settle their accounts for merchandise from abroad, her merchants boldly sent their ships to New Orleans and other cotton ports and ran the cargo collected there to England and the continent. By 1830 about forty cents of every dollar paid for cotton went north—almost without exception to New York—for freight bills, insurance, commissions, and interest.

THE INDUSTRIAL REVOLUTION

In 1810 Henry Clay told Congress: "A judicious American farmer, in his household way manufactures whatever is requisite for his family. . . . He presents in epitome what the nation ought to be in *extenso*." But in the next ten years changes in the country's situation drove Clay to change his mind. During and after the War of 1812 problems of national defense and security brought about a reassessment of the place of the factory in the American scheme of things. Later on, specialization in cotton in the South and the burst of enterprise in the West transformed both sections into enticing markets for machine-made goods. The fact that American canal and railroad building was financed so largely abroad left Americans free to employ their own scant savings in industrial enterprises which improved transportation inspired. Ultimately the profits from manufacturing, enhanced for a generation after 1816 by protective tariffs, proved both a major impetus and the greatest single source of capital for industrial expansion.

At the start of the eighteenth century production of many common goods had hardly advanced anywhere in the world over the eighth century or earlier. Since then, industrialization has remade man's universe and all his social relations. The publication of Newton's *Principia* in 1687, it has been said, caused young men to fall "in love with that Studie," mathematics, and made "experimenting" the popular diversion of gentlemen. The practical beginning may be placed in the year 1733 when the Englishman, John Kay, invented the "flying shuttle" to lighten the domestic weaver's work and multiply his output. Thirty-five years passed before such men as James Hargreaves, Richard Arkwright, and Samuel Crompton made successive improvements in the spinning of cotton to meet the weavers' insistent calls for more, stronger, and finer yarn. When in 1769 the illiterate Arkwright, "the bag-cheeked, pot-bellied barber," as Carlyle ferociously described him, patented a machine to spin yarn by water power, the age of the factory with its heavy and ever more costly installations was at hand.

Once the early factory machines became available the next major step was the use of steam power to run them. The steam engine had been invented in England in 1702 by Thomas Newcomen, but seventy-five years went by before James Watt, Matthew Boulton, and John Wilkinson worked out the improvements in design that made the contraption useful for more demanding tasks than pumping out shallow coal pits. As important as advances in machine design were improvements in metal-working tools used to produce parts meeting the precise specifications of the new engines. Boulton and Watt built the first practical factory steam engine in 1777 for Wilkinson's iron works. Thereafter, in many countries, including the United States, lonely mechanics toyed with its application to every kind of power problem including the propulsion of boats and carriages. Arkwright began using steam power for spinning in the 1780s. In the early 1800s steam power looms were invented for weaving cloth in factories. These developments multiplied the productivity of individual textile workers more than a hundred times.

Factories are one thing; industrial*ism* is another. Eli Whitney's role in forwarding the whole concept and application of industrialism is even more significant than his invention of the famous gin. The early factories made their great progress and profits by mechanizing hand operations. Whitney, a solitary genius in America, was one among a number elsewhere in the western world who rationalized factory production into something new under the sun. The key to Whitney's work was the development of the principle of interchangeable parts, each made in massive quantities to strict specifications by special-purpose machines, and then assembled into the final product. This was mass, as against simply machine, production. It involved Whitney in continuous experimentation aimed at adapting the operations in industrial production to the unique possibilities of machine work, and designing new machines to produce perhaps odd but ever more readily assembled parts.

Whitney kept continuous and cumulative records of the performance of men, machines, and materials. Correlations of these, and operational corrections based upon them, he made integral parts of the whole production process. In the twentieth century this aspect of mass production has been given the name scientific management. Only in the twentieth century, indeed, has knowledge of chemistry, metallurgy, and psychology itself grown sufficiently to make scientific management feasible on a broad scale. In principle, however, few advances have been made over Whitney's comprehensive concept. This concept he applied in the manufacture of his first twenty cotton gins. He developed it fully in the production of arms for the government. His first contract for 10,000 muskets was granted on the eve of the undeclared naval war with France in 1798. Alas, he was ten years late in making his final deliveries. But those were years of innovation and progress along a path only vaguely indicated by his predecessors anywhere and understood by but a handful of his contemporaries in the United States.

One reason for Whitney's isolation was British secrecy. In 1765 Parliament revived in much stricter form the old Stuart prohibition on the emigration of skilled operatives. In 1774 it took the further step of forbidding the exportation of mechanical models and plans and of machinery itself. After the Revolution these measures were made more comprehensive and enforced more vigilantly.

Yet the most compelling reason for Whitney's isolation was the preoccupation of Americans themselves with nonindustrial activities. "During the general lassitude of mechanical exertion which succeeded the American Revolution," complained the leading engineer in the country, B. H. Latrobe, in 1803, "the utility of steam-engines appears to have been forgotten." In this epoch

American steamboat inventors such as James Rumsey and John Fitch died impoverished and unsung. Fulton himself had to bear the public's jibes at "Fulton's Folly." As early as 1815 John Stevens had made a practical demonstration of the steam railroad but his projects got no encouragement. Oliver Evans, the Philadelphian who indeed anticipated some of Whitney's industrial and mechanical ideas, met only resistance and contempt. Even Whitney himself, when he began to make money after 1810, "remained," as his biographers say, "rooted in the practices and attitudes of the community. . . . His own hard-earned money went into . . . the purchase of stocks of banks, insurance companies, turnpike companies"; into land speculation and a scheme to sell ice in China. "Whitney's money was put out for profit on a particular venture, not for interest in industry."

The first successful American factory, that set up by Samuel Slater in 1791 to spin cotton for the Providence merchants, Almy & Brown, was a tiny affair. Slater had skipped England, as he said, after having had "an oversight of Sir Richard Arkwright's works . . . upward of eight years." His American works had seventy-two spindles, tended by nine children under full-time supervision. Their wages ranged from 12 to 25 cents a day. Slater's yarn was sent to weavers who made cotton cloth on looms at home, though as Almy & Brown complained in 1809, "a hundred looms in families will not weave so much cloth as ten . . . under the immediate supervision of a workman."

By the time of the War of 1812 hundreds of factories like Slater's were at work. Most of them were in New England and were operated by men Slater had trained. These men knew little of keeping accounts, managing labor, developing markets. The banks would have nothing to do with them, and the postwar crash wiped out a great many of them. The American cotton textile industry itself, however, survived and flourished under the leadership of the "new model" factories to which the War's destruction of commerce had turned erstwhile shipping magnates.

The first "new model" factory was opened in Waltham, Massachusetts, in 1816 by the Boston Manufacturing Company which had been incorporated three years earlier by Francis Cabot Lowell,

Patrick Tracy Jackson, Nathan Appleton, and others of their caliber. These men had long since proven their ability to manage hazardous, large-scale enterprises. Taking the long view, they built the first wholly integrated cotton manufacturing plant in the world, with all operations under one roof. The economies of large-scale and integrated production they enhanced by the use of many technological innovations the development of which was made part of the production routine. They integrated their business further by setting up their own selling agencies in place of independent local jobbers.

An original scheme for acquiring and holding labor completed the major innovations of the "new model." The family labor of the older mills was hopelessly inefficient. On the other hand, generations passed before American men were broken to the discipline of factory work. The Boston Manufacturing Company turned to young women, eighteen to twenty-two years of age. These it offered to shelter and feed and to educate after hours in fresh new company dormitories in its own company town. Management expected in this way to attract an upright and ambitious group, the sisters of the Yankee youths who were moving into Ohio and farther west. Its expectations were justified. After the crash of 1837, cheap, docile, immigrant male labor replaced the spirited girls. But until then absenteeism was much lower than in the older plants and productivity much higher.

The Boston Manufacturing Company began operations in one of the very worst of the postwar years for textile companies, but it was an instantaneous success. Annual dividends were so high that by 1822 stockholders had got back more than their initial investment. In the 1820s and 1830s large numbers of new textile corporations began operation. Among these were nine chartered by the group, now known as the "Boston Associates," who had started the Boston Manufacturing Company. This group also chartered insurance companies and banks to keep up and concentrate the supply of capital, real estate companies to take over the best factory sites, and water power companies to monopolize entire rivers by controlling dams and dam sites.

Just as Whitney had rationalized industrialism as a production process, so the "Boston Associates," the Morgans and Rockefellers of their day, had begun to rationalize it as a social force. It was not long before their power was such that their competitors paid toll to them for the use of water, patents, and business services, while they themselves sought new and distant worlds to conquer. "If you are troubled with the belief that I am growing *too rich,*" one of them wrote to a competitor, "there is one thing you may as well understand: I know how to make money, and *you* cannot prevent it." When Ralph Waldo Emerson observed in 1834, "In a former age men of might were men of will, now they are men of wealth," he had the "Boston Associates" in mind.

THE SPECULATIVE SPIRAL

The cotton textile industry was the first mature American industry, one paced not by the individual craftsman but by machines, housed not in the artisan's dwelling or workshop but in segregated factory towns or industrial slums, and supervised not by the owner but by hired professional managers financially accountable to professional capitalists. Other industries showed similar accelerating and centralizing tendencies. But sheer expansion of population and the sheer expanse of land were to keep American business relatively free and open for generations. And the spirit of science, basic and applied, was to keep the frontier of opportunity moving ahead even after the land itself became filled.

Filling up the land, indeed, even in this burgeoning epoch of the industrial revolution, remained America's most significant occupation. Between 1820 and 1837 investment in American industry is said to have risen from $50 to $250 million, most of it representing profits plowed back into new plant and machinery. By 1837 bank notes and discounts reached the stratospheric total of $675 million, most of it representing advances in the price of land forced upward by the surge of settlement, the progress and promise of transportation, and the speculative fever such factors fed. Chicago furnishes as good an illustration as any. Between 1830 and 1840 the population of the United States grew by a third. That of Illinois trebled. That of Chicago multiplied eight times, from 500 to 4,000. In the previous decade, Chicago lands, like most of the unoccupied

public domain, brought $1.25 an acre. By 1832 the price had risen
to $100; by 1834 to $3,500. In 1836 the state legislature approved
a canal to link the city with the Mississippi and began selling millions of dollars' worth of bonds for its construction. In that year a
single *lot* along the proposed route brought $21,400.

As always in such periods debt rose faster than ability to pay;
and as always there came a day of reckoning. The crash of June
1837, grew by 1839 into a world-wide depression, and as in 1819,
the West suffered most. In 1840 Senator Thomas Hart Benton
of Missouri described the situation in his section:

> The goods are worn out, the paper money has returned to the place
> whence it came; the operation is over, and nothing remains to the
> transactions but the 170 millions in debt, its devouring interest, and
> the banks, canals and roads which represent it. The whole of these
> banks have failed once, and most of them twice, in two years; the
> greater part of the roads and canals are unfinished, and of those
> finished, several are unproductive.

In the succeeding years, most of the western states and some in
the older sections repudiated their bonds, and American credit
abroad sank to zero. In 1842 the Rothschilds of Paris said to an
envoy of the Federal Government seeking a loan: "You may tell
your government that you have seen the man who is at the head of
the finances of Europe and that he has told you that they cannot
borrow a dollar, not a dollar."

Yet the depression did not halt western development. In the
1830s tens of millions of acres in the Southwest were opened to
speculators by the violent removal of the Indian tribes. Millions
more became available when Sam Houston and other Americans
helped Texas win her independence from Mexico in 1836. As a
result of the Black Hawk War which began in Wisconsin country in
1831, moreover, the northwest tribes were relieved of more than a
hundred million choice acres.

Settlers, of course, had been moving westward throughout the
1830s. In 1836 Arkansas, and in 1837 Michigan had become states.
But the depression gave a strong impetus to migration to the newly
opened lands. "Fly, scatter through the country," cried Horace

Greeley to New York's poor in 1841, "go to the Great West, anything rather than remain here." Many thousands of easterners took his advice and their number was swelled by the record flow of immigrants from abroad. Between 1839 and 1844 nearly 80,000 newcomers a year entered the United States.

Middle-class Germans took passage at Le Havre or Bremen in cotton ships bound for New Orleans, whence they made their way up-river to engage in trade in St. Louis or Cincinnati and to "make" farms in nonslave territory. Some took up ranching in Texas. English, Welsh, and Scottish artisans and Irish Catholic laborers came principally in ships that had delivered grain to relieve Europe's recurrent famines, and usually landed in New York or Baltimore. Many Irish also debarked at Montreal and Quebec, and from there infiltrated New England. The Irish, the most impoverished and numerous of the new arrivals, multiplied the poor of the port towns; the others more often joined Americans on the trek west.

A pre-emption act passed by Congress in 1841 hastened actual settlement on new lands. By this act Congress at last removed the stigma of lawbreaking from those staking out western claims in advance of government surveys. The act gave "squatters" first chance to buy in their claims at the minimum price when the government survey reached them. In the 1830s and 1840s the riches beneath the rich land of the West also drew the foot-loose and free. Even before 1830 a small army of lead and zinc miners had made Galena, Illinois, appropriately situated at the head of navigation of the Fever River, the prototype of all later Wild West towns. In the early 1840s "copper fever" ran through Michigan, while adjacent areas yielded their centuries-old hoards of coal. Only shortly thereafter thousands from the Midwest joined the rush to prospect for gold in California. At the same time, prospectors for souls were leading the way across the Oregon trail to the country for which it was named, while the Mormons moved on from Illinois to their permanent abode in Utah.

The tremendous pioneering activity of the depression years brought about the admission of Florida and Texas in 1845, Iowa in 1846, and Wisconsin in 1848. Politics more than lack of population postponed the entry of California, Oregon, and Minnesota until the 1850s and of other trans-Mississippi states until the outbreak of the Civil War.

The crash of 1837 spoiled the appetite of the older West for internal improvements, and in the early 1840s (temporarily, as it proved) many states forbade the use of public money to build public transportation. Some of the newer states, peopled by victims from the older ones, did likewise. Since the Federal Government had also long since gone out of the internal improvements business, it was left for private corporations (aided by frequent and lavish public assistance) to project and construct the western railroads of the next generation. Since their own financing had been so conservative, their own banks so cautious, and their own profits so high, the "Boston Associates" and related Yankees were to find new business worlds to conquer in western railroad schemes.

This was a new departure for these Yankees. Heretofore, fearful of not being able to reach markets beyond the mountains with the goods imported in their ships, they had simply discouraged the rapid settlement of the West. When they shifted from commerce to manufacturing, their anti-western attitude grew even stronger for now they feared the loss of their labor supply as well. By 1830, however, the construction of canals and the growth of cities had had a reassuring effect. The old Yankee attitude was well reflected in the resolution introduced in the Senate in December 1829, by Samuel A. Foot of Connecticut, who urged that new western lands be kept off the market until even the poorest land already up for sale had been disposed of. In an effort to strengthen southern relations with the West, the brilliant Robert Y. Hayne of South Carolina denounced Foot's measure. Crying, "Liberty first and Union afterwards," he invited the frontiersmen to join the slavocracy in its recently promulgated doctrine of "nullification." Daniel Webster, now the lion of Massachusetts, leaped to his feet to reply. In a grand effort to wash away the memory of New England's treason during the western-sponsored War of 1812, a memory kept well watered by opposition like Foot's to western growth, Webster thrilled the nation with his purple paean to the Union. Hayne's was the path of "delusion and folly." Cried

Webster, "Liberty *and* Union, now and forever, one and in- separable."

By 1833 Webster's business backers had yielded sufficiently to the warmth of the new spirit to listen patiently when their Con- gressman and future Governor, Edward Everett, expounded the advantages they might reap if they supported western schools. "The learning, religion, and living ministry," he said, "bestowed on the great West by these Colleges, unite in special benefit to mercantile morality. . . . They ask you to contribute to give security to your own property, by diffusing the means of light and truth throughout the region, where so much of the power to preserve or shake it resides." By 1836 Everett's listeners were prepared to unbend a little in practice as well as in spirit. "We shall be pleased," allowed Amos Lawrence, the Boston manufacturer, that year, "to see the best buyers of the large places west and southwest at old Boston to buy our domestic fabrics. . . . At present we do not want to see any but the first class buyer; a year or two hence, we shall be glad to see the second class as we can fix the price to cor- respond to the risks."

Soon the thaw would be complete: "America begins with the Alleghenies," cried the Brahmins of the 1840's. Ours, said Emerson, once the depression had run its course, "is a country of beginnings, of projects, of vast designs and expectations. It has no past; all has an onward and prospective look."

JACKSONIAN DEMOCRACY

On the eve of the elections of 1824, Webster acknowledged that "General Jackson's manners are more presidential than those of any of the candidates." But Jackson had acquired manners only late in life. In the North Carolina town where in 1784 the seventeen- year-old orphan son of a Scotch-Irish immigrant had come to read law, he was long remembered as "the most roaring, rollicking, game-cocking, horse-racing, card-playing mischievous fellow, that ever lived in Salisbury . . . the head of the rowdies hereabouts." In the War of 1812 his soldiers nicknamed Jackson "Old Hickory" after "the toughest thing they could think of." Years later when an opponent expressed doubt over a Jackson threat, one of the General's friends remarked, "I tell you . . . when Jackson begins to talk about hanging, they can begin to look for the ropes." In 1821 "Old Hickory" himself said: "I have an opinion of my own on all subjects, and when that opinion is formed I persue it publickly regardless of who goes with me." One of his opinions, when it was suggested that he was "by no means safe from the presidency in 1824," he expressed this way: "No sir, I know what I am fit for. I can command a body of men in a rough way: but I am not fit to be President."

Others had their own opinion, among them future members of the famous "Kitchen Cabinet," who entered the General in the presidential sweepstakes as early as 1822 with this characteristic announcement:

> GREAT RACING!!! . . . The prize to be run for is the *Presidential Chair*. . . . There have already four states sent their nags in. Why not Tennessee put in her stud? and if so, let it be called *Old Hickory*. . . .

And in 1824 Old Hickory won! And lost! With the collapse of the Congressional Caucus method of making nominations, five different candidates had crowded onto the presidential track. With the death of Federalism, all ran under the colors of the Republican Party. Jackson got the most votes. But he failed to get the required majority in the electoral college. In the House of Representatives, where the decision rested, the Speaker Henry Clay, an also-ran in the election, threw his support to John Quincy Adams who became President.

When Adams promptly named Clay his Secretary of State and hence (as was suggested by the experience of every previous Secretary of State but one) his heir apparent, the Jackson managers cried, "Corrupt bargain." For the next four years they never let the country forget the "chicanery" of the painfully honest Adams as they prepared to defeat him—and Clay—next time. Jackson himself gradually warmed to the idea that the presidency had been stolen from the people and in the next election between

> John Quincy Adams, who can write,
> And Andrew Jackson, who can fight

Old Hickory sallied forth in the people's cause.

In 1824 only 356,000 persons voted. Four years later, aroused by the first modern political campaign in support of the first popular hero since Washington, four times as many enthusiasts went to the polls. Fifty-six per cent voted for the General.

In February 1829, while all Washington anxiously awaited the arrival of the "hero of New Orleans," once more victorious, Webster wrote from the capital: "Nobody knows what he will do. . . . My opinion is that when he comes he will bring a breeze with him. Which way it will blow I cannot tell." For all his having "an opinion of my own on all subjects," the new President really was no wiser.

If there was anything Andrew Jackson had a lower opinion of than Indians, it was speculators. Yet from the first, his violent Indian policy supplied the land on which the speculators of the 1830s fed. Other Jacksonian measures inevitably if inadvertently helped run up the price of land. In 1830 for example, fearful that it would cause "a torrent of reckless legislation" by Congress, Jackson vetoed the so-called Maysville Bill by which the Federal Government would have participated in the financing of a turnpike across Kentucky. The veto left "internal improvements" to the states alone where reckless projects found smoother sailing and reckless promises provided speculators with great talking points.

Jackson's fiscal policies, though motivated by the deepest conservatism, made the financing of speculative state projects easy. These policies had as a principal objective the elimination of the national debt, but they involved the President in long conflicts over the tariff, land policy, and the life of the Second Bank of the United States. Early in his career Jackson had incurred personal debts, which he attributed to the lures of easy money. Most of his business life he devoted to paying these debts off. Jackson looked upon the national debt as though, like his personal obligations, it were a debt of honor or of shame. Though his principal political enemies were eastern high tariff men, Jackson was willing to have the tariff raised to unprecedented highs in order to get the money to reduce the national debt. When his followers in South Carolina declared the tariff of 1832 "inconsistent with [their] longer continuance . . . in the Union," Jackson promised to shoot anyone who seceded, and asked Congress for a "force act" to give him the privilege. On the other hand, Jackson's political friends were westerners dedicated to low-priced and even free public land; but he managed to keep his temper when Congress persistently rejected western proposals for pre-emption and graduation (the policy of reducing the price of public land until ultimately the land for which there were no buyers would be given away).

The high tariffs and the high price of public lands made it possible for Jackson's administration to pay off the public debt in 1835. But by then Jackson's banking policies had made this the most speculative act imaginable. The Second Bank of the United States had become the embodiment of evil to Jackson's followers since it dealt so alluringly in paper money and yet crushed the man who reached for the vision or started a local bank to compete. If the Bank of the United States made strategic loans to politicians, especially near election time, this only confirmed its opponents' belief in the Bank's total depravity.

Yet to the Jacksonians local banks could do no wrong. If *their* politicking was unspeakable, it was also unmentionable. If *they* yielded to the temptation of paper money, it was only to encourage the man whom the "monster" would ignore or strangle. In 1832 Jackson vetoed a bill for the extension of the Second Bank's charter, which expired in 1836. In 1833 he began removing the government's deposits from the Bank to his "pet banks" in the states. Once the national debt had been paid off, a national surplus mounted madly, and so did the Treasury's deposits in the "pet banks." These deposits the reckless banks simply loaned out to speculators whose activities pushed the price of public land itself far higher than the levels which had contributed so handsomely to the surplus in the first place.

By the spring of 1836, the Treasury surplus had risen to $41,-000,000—more than a fourth of the entire circulating medium of the country. Its haphazard dispersal by "pet banks" made some regions drunk with speculative currency, but left others panting for cash even for the most urgent business transactions. Something had to be done. Congress met the crisis by passing an act in July 1836, authorizing the President to distribute the Treasury surplus to the states proportionately to their electoral vote. Jackson began the distribution in January 1837. The transfer of the Treasury's deposits to the states, however, only made the currency situation all the more chaotic; those states with "pet banks," moreover, simply redeposited their shares in these questionable financial institutions.

The speculative upsurge that followed the removal of the deposits from the Second Bank had been checked in July 1836, by another Jackson measure, the famous "Specie Circular." This required that payment for government land henceforth must be in gold or silver. Typically, Jackson hoped that this measure would force the hated eastern speculators to buy land with specie which would be sent west to buttress the shaky "pet banks." Its effect, however, was simply to confirm the view that the notes of these banks were unsound. This conviction itself did check speculation, but the distribution of the surplus in 1837 started it up again in the western states. New projects began once more to jostle one another for authorization and publicity, and land prices resumed their skyward course until the crash of values in the middle of the year.

Martin Van Buren, not Jackson, reaped the harvest of Jacksonian policies. In the elections of 1832 Jackson's opponents had raised the issue of the Second Bank's charter with the hope that a Jacksonian veto of a bill renewing the charter would be unpopular in the country. "The Bank," Old Hickory growled to Van Buren, his Secretary of State and heir-apparent, "is trying to kill me, *but I will kill it*." Jackson's veto of the bank bill apparently cost him no support. In any case he won an easy victory. By the elections of 1836, the prevailing prosperity only heightened Jackson's popularity and he had no trouble putting "Little Van" across.

The Jackson men, who had earlier used the name "Democratic Republicans," became known simply as Democrats in 1836. Their opponents distinguished themselves as "National Republicans" until 1832 when they draped themselves in the heroic mantle of the Whigs—in opposition to the "tyranny" of "King Andrew I," the cruel slayer of the Second Bank. That their name failed to take in the General's followers this doggerel of the time suggests:

> Yankee Doodle, smoke 'em out,
> The proud, the banking faction.

None but such as Hartford Feds
Oppose the poor and Jackson.

When Van Buren took office in March 1837, the speculators besieged the new President to withdraw the "Specie Circular." But the retired Jackson admonished his protégé: "Its continuance [is] imperious now for the safety of the revenue. . . . I have done my duty to my country and my god [and] have given [you] my opinion freely. . . . *I say, lay on, temporise not, it is always injurious.*" The country, however, thought otherwise; and while the Democrats reluctantly renominated "Little Van" for the presidency in 1840, the Whigs swept the elections with a disinterred war hero of their own, William Henry Harrison. Borrowing freely from the Democrats' campaign book, they harped on the alleged "log cabin" origins of their candidate, and carried the day with the slogan, "Tippecanoe and Tyler too!"

If Andrew Jackson's politics consisted in doing battle with the dragons of great wealth, his political opponents sought only to fight Jackson. Democrats and Whigs, nevertheless, had more serious differences. The Whigs became the party of the "neebobs," as Old Hickory called them, who had made their fortunes, and the Democrats the party of those still on the make. If the army of Jacksonians was largely agrarian, it was probably because land was the most ubiquitous of commodities and business in it the most popular of occupations. If the Democrats gained the support of artisans and operatives in the nascent unions that appeared in the commercial and industrial cities in the 1830s, it was probably because their members were aspiring to business opportunities themselves. If the Democrats gained the support of religious revivalists and the evangelical sects that spread through the West in particular after 1820, it was probably because such enthusiasts were championing the virtues of respectability in a wild country. If the Democrats gained the support of the reformers associated with the religious revival— temperance men, popular educationists, fighters for women's rights, abolitionists—it was because the do-gooders were broadening the paths of progress or removing obstacles from them.

Yet this support itself would have been politically useless had not the Jacksonian epoch been marked by great changes in politics itself. These changes derived of course, from the spread of the franchise in the 1820s and 1830s everywhere but in the South. But the franchise itself was only a means to other ends. Above all, the Jacksonians held, only simple men could legislate wisely for the simple multitude. This led to lowering the bars to office as well as to the vote. Other innovations in this period were the direct election of presidential electors who heretofore had been elected by the state legislatures; the popular election of minor judges; the development of the convention system by which popularly elected delegates "fresh from the people" supplanted the legislative caucus for the nomination of party candidates; the development of popular oratory and new methods of campaigning, including stumping the country; the emergence of new types of candidates, showmen or heroes for the multitude, and professional managers to handle their campaigns; the elaboration of the "spoils system" by which the minions of the political managers might be rewarded from the public purse. Most significant, perhaps, was the manufacturing of "issues" with which to engage the interest of the uncommitted voters and to draw them to the polls. Most of these issues were ephemeral and empty; one of them was "abolition," and it sundered the nation.

Chapter Seven

The Victorious North

On learning of Robert E. Lee's surrender to U. S. Grant in April 1865, Emerson wrote in the privacy of his *Journal:* " 'Tis for the best that the rebels have been pounded instead of negociated into a peace. They must remember it, and their inveterate brag will be humbled, if not cured." Three years before, in a public address which Lincoln himself attended, Emerson had been less brutal but no less sure. "Why cannot the best civilization," he asked, "be extended over the whole country, since the disorder of the less civilized portion menaces the existence of the country?"

The American Civil War may almost be said to have begun where the English Civil War had ended two hundred years before. Anglicans and Puritans had settled in America a thousand miles apart and nursed and enlarged their jealousies and hates. Brought face to face by the exigencies of the Revolution, their meeting only confirmed their differences. It was at the Continental Congress in 1774 that John Adams first saw in the flesh well-horsed, saber-rattling, extravagant planters with their flamboyant body slaves. The experience, writes his biographer Gilbert Chinard, "caused Adams more anxiety than he had ever suffered in all his lifetime." Adams himself hastened to report home from Philadelphia how he dreaded "the consequences of this dissimilitude of character," and added: "Without the utmost caution on both sides, and the most considerate forbearance with one another . . . they will certainly be fatal."

Slaver and slave trader, exporter and carrier, cotton planter and cotton spinner: southerner and northerner after the Revolution had ample grounds for mutual understanding. But the interests that drew them together only fanned into flame the forces that
184

drove them apart. Even in their contest for the West they shared a common aim. The planter fearful of the West's voting power, the manufacturer fearful of its drain on his labor supply, both hoped to slow the West's development. Ultimately each was frustrated by a greater need, the planter for land, the manufacturer for markets. Each thus pushed the development of the West in disregard of the other, while the West itself fed well on the needs and the sons of both.

After 1820, indeed, the West became the proving ground for the contending societies of the older sections. Here the vigor and expansive force of free northern capitalism and evangelism confronted the "peculiar institution" and the ideologies and anxieties of the "Cotton Kingdom." Nothing wounded the South more than the defection of her own vigorous sons and daughters to the *free* West itself, where they often met and sometimes married evangelizing Yankees and "formed little islands of abolitionism at an early date." Their going, the historian Dwight L. Dumond writes, "deprived the South of men and women whose combined intelligence, moral courage, and Christian benevolence would have gone far toward modifying the harsher features of slavery . . . and toward keeping alive . . . free discussion" of it. "Having been born and reared in the South," he continues, "many of them as slaveholders, and having made great personal sacrifices by migrating to the free states, they spoke with authority and were given a respectful hearing by the conservative and wealthy class in the North."

Until the expansion of the Cotton Kingdom after 1793, emancipation and manumission had had a long and progressive history in the South. Thereafter, until about 1830, state laws made manumission more difficult and the free Negro himself more susceptible to enslavement even for petty crimes, but the section continued to recognize slavery as evil. After 1830 slavery became unarguable and untouchable, and the free Negro an outcast whose desperate plight was used to illustrate alleged biological deficiences in competence and character of the entire race. Nowhere was the slave system harsher than in the new Gulf states of the Southwest where rough adventurers, battening on the blood of Indians, occupied the best cotton lands or served as overseers for Charleston and Savannah nabobs who might visit their wilderness plantations twice in a decade.

In the North by 1830 slavery had been universally legislated out of existence. The free Negro, however, was little better off than in the South, while Abolitionists, though far from silenced, were scarcely loved. "Depend upon it," advised the confident editor of the *Richmond Whig,* "the Northern people will never sacrifice their lucrative trade with the South so long as the hanging of a few thousand will prevent it." As the Abolitionists' campaign gathered force after 1831, when William Lloyd Garrison began publication of the *Liberator,* their meetings were mobbed, their houses gutted, and their presses wrecked. Their most famous martyr before John Brown was the Reverend Elijah Lovejoy of Alton, Illinois, who was killed in 1837 while defending his printing plant from marauders. "It is as much as all the patriotism in our country can do," complained James G. Birney two years earlier, "to keep alive the spirit of liberty in the *free* states."

In the North, nevertheless, the Abolitionists won a growing number of friends. Attacks like those on Lovejoy brought into their camp thousands who agreed with Birney that "the contest had become one, not alone of freedom for the *black,* but of freedom for the *white*." More numerous and more welcome were the recruits who promoted the Abolitionist doctrine as well as their rights.

At the very time that Professors Thomas R. Dew, George Fitzhugh, and William Harper were propagating the South's "Pro-Slavery Argument" with appropriate evidence from science and the Bible, and others such as John C. Calhoun were adding the evidence of classical history, the greatest of "Revivals" began in the North and especially in the Northwest, under the leadership of the champion of evangelists, Charles Grandison Finney. The "Great Revival" not only sanctioned Abolitionism, it fed on it. For the glory of man and God its converts led the Holy War against drink, debt, and debauchery, against the condition of the jails and the schools, against the infringement of women's rights, against monopolists in general and the Bank in particular. But no grosser sins could they find in Christendom than pride of pigment, property in men, the enslavement of one Christian brother by another.

Evangelical religion also spread rapidly over the Cotton Kingdom at this time and Christianizing of the slave himself became
popular among masters who had their own consolation and salvation to think of. But as growing numbers of southern ministers and
missionaries added to their sin of slave apologetics the sin of actual
slave ownership, their northern colleagues became all the more
certain of the depravity of the "institution." As early as 1838 the
Presbyterians split into an Old School or Southern proslavery
branch and a New School or Northern antislavery one. When in
1844 Northern Baptists and Methodists refused any longer to work
with missionaries who carried slaves with them, the latter seceded
from their national churches and set up independent Southern Baptist and Methodist constituencies. But like political secession in
1860, such intransigence only spurred on the North.

Abolitionism and evangelism both had their ups and downs before the Civil War, but together, as surely as canals and railroads,
manufactures and markets, they turned the West from the South
and made the entire North a section. Always expansive, the South
in the 1840s became militantly so. Yet cotton, besides being a cor-
rupting thing was a confining one. The North had greater freedom
and greater space for its own expansive urge. Many northerners
agreed with Lincoln when he advised in 1856: "Let us draw a
cordon . . . around the slave states, and the hateful institution, like
a reptile poisoning itself, will perish by its own infamy." The South
also agreed that it had to expand to survive; and since it could not
expand beyond the geographical limits of cotton culture, it had
reason for desperation and rebellion both.

THE MILITANT SOUTH

If the South was right about slavery in the middle of the nineteenth
century the whole world was wrong. Great Britain prohibited the
slave trade in 1807. In 1833 she abolished slavery throughout the
Empire. In 1848 France abolished slavery in her colonies. Before
1850 all the Spanish American republics had done away with the
"peculiar institution." In the next decade the Hapsburgs and the
Romanovs freed the serfs of central and eastern Europe. Throughout this period all the maritime nations of the world except the

United States permitted the British Navy to stop and search their ships for slaves, the carriers of whom even the United States had formally agreed to condemn as pirates. Many slave ships escaped search and seizure simply by running up the Stars and Stripes when interception threatened. That the land of liberty should condone such license was an irony few outside the South enjoyed. In the South it was but one more stone in the wall of moral isolation that made the defense of its necessities so urgent.

"We hold these truths to be self-evident," says the Declaration of Independence, "that all men are created equal; that they are endowed by their Creator with certain unalienable rights; that among these are life, liberty, and the pursuit of happiness." A "decent respect to the opinions of mankind," say its authors, prompted them to "declare the causes" of their separation from England. After 1830 Southern spokesmen derided the Declaration and strove to prove it "God's law that fetters on black skins don't chafe." The "very spirit of the age [was] against them," writes Lincoln's biographer, Albert J. Beveridge. All the fiercer, then, the challenge. We must, cried William Lowndes Yancey of Alabama, the very architect of secession, "abandon the law of compromise and . . . adopt the law of the constitution." Yet all the more absolute was the response: We must, cried the gathering voice of the North, transcend the Constitution and follow the "higher law" of the Declaration and the Christian world.

The movement for personal freedom which swept the western world in the first half of the nineteenth century, and nowhere more thoroughly than in the northern American states, the South itself condemned as part of the "radicalism" of the industrial revolution. Southern spokesmen grew ever fonder of comparing the affectionate paternalism of the master toward his "hands"—the word "slave" gradually fell into disuse among respectable planters of the Cotton Kingdom—with the harsh insecurity, the depression breadlines and seasonal unemployment of "free" factory workers. This comparison helped greatly to sweeten for all its denizens alike the image of the "Old South" as the last grand realm of chivalry. In this realm landless shopkeepers, slave traders, artisans, clerks were beneath consideration. But among squire, yeomen, poor white, "nigger," only

the harsh test of a lost war would disclose the chinks in the aristocratic hierarchy.

"In the absolute, certainly," writes W. J. Cash, the author of
The Mind of the South, "there was much of privation and down-
right misery in the lot of the poor white, and often in that of the
yeoman farmer as well. But these people did not contemplate ab-
solutes. They continued always to reckon their estate in terms established on the frontier. As they themselves would have phrased it
from the depths of a great complacency, they found it 'tol'able,
thankee, tol'able.' . . . In every rank," Cash notes, "men lolled
much on their verandas or under their oaks, sat much on fences,
dreaming. In every rank they exhibited a striking tendency to build
up legends about themselves and to translate these legends into
explosive action—to perform with a histrionic flourish, and to strive
for celebrity as the dashing blade. In every rank they were much
concerned with seeing the ponies run, with hearing the band, with
making love, with dancing, with extravagant play." If the great
planter had the fastest horses, the finest music, the courtliest ladies,
the most beauteous black wenches, the grandest entertainments,
the most extravagant play of all—well, was he not chivalry's champion, the proof as much as the pride of the system? "Negro entered
into white man as profoundly as white man entered into Negro—
subtly influencing every gesture, every word, every emotion and
idea, every attitude." As long as the slave submitted (no wonder
the Abolitionist was anti-christ incarnate), all white men on the
land would be lofty—steal, scrape, beg and borrow though one
might from his neighboring cavalier.

And yet, as Cash writes, always men's "thoughts were with the
piper and his fee." The image of the "Old South" was so perfect,
so pure that men need not wonder why nothing like it could be
found elsewhere under the sun. Change could but mar, alteration
blemish its beguiling symmetry. But the physical world itself often
monitored the nodding mind. "If the dominant mood is one of
sultry reverie, the land is capable of other and more sombre moods.
. . . There are days when the booming of the wind in the pines
is like the audible rushing of time—when the sad knowledge of the
grave stirs in the subconsciousness and bends the spirit to melan-

choly. . . . And there are other days . . . when the nerves wilt under the terrific impact of sun and humidity, and even the soundest grow a bit neurotic. . . . And there are other days, too, when . . . hurricanes break forth with semi-tropical fury; days when this land which, in its dominant mood, wraps its children in soft illusion, strips them naked before terror.

"Nor was it only the physical world. His leisure left the Southerner free to brood as well as to dream—to exaggerate his fears as well as his hopes. And if for practical purposes it is true that he was likely to be complacently content with his lot, and even though it was the lot of white-trash, it is yet not perfectly true. Vaguely, the loneliness of the country, the ennui of long, burning empty days, a hundred half-perceived miseries, ate into him and filled him with nebulous discontent and obscure longing. Like all men everywhere, he hungered cloudily after a better and a happier world."

A more concrete ambition also rippled the pool in the southern looking-glass. The Cotton Kingdom was not spread in a single generation from South Carolina to Texas by men content to doze and dream at home. Accosted one day on a steamboat by a representative of the Education Society peddling a "Bible Defence of Slavery," a typical Red River planter shouted: "Now you go to hell! I've told you three times I didn't want your book. If you bring it here again I'll throw it overboard. I own niggers; and I calculate to own more of 'em, if I can get 'em, but I don't want any damn'd preachin' about it." Such men were unusual enough. As late as 1860 hardly 350,000 Southerners owned any slaves at all. Fewer than 8,000 owned as many as 50 slaves. But these men, heading less than 1 per cent of southern families, probably owned a fourth of all hands. Their purchases were chiefly responsible for pushing the slave population from 1,500,000 in 1820 to nearly 4,000,000 in 1860, despite a death rate that claimed every second Negro infant. It was they who were chiefly responsible for pushing cotton production from 335,000 bales in 1820, virtually all of it in South Carolina and Georgia, to a record 5,387,000 bales in 1859, two thirds of it in the rich Gulf states.

As late as 1840 most of the leading southwestern planters lived in log cabins and were as rough-hewn as their surroundings. But it was the rare adventurer among them who did not have his eye on the fine site on the hill where eventually he would build his porticoed mansion and entertain, when at home, like a prince. Often enough, in later times, he was away. "Must have ice for their wine, you see, or they'd die," the notable northern traveler, Frederick Law Olmsted, was informed of Mississippi planters of the 1850s. "So they have to live in Natchez or New Orleans."

" 'And in summer they go up into Kentucky, do they not? . . .'

" 'No, sir. They go North. To New York, and Newport, and Saratoga, and Cape May, and Seneca Lake. Somewhere that they can display themselves. . . . Kentucky is no place for that. . . .'

"I asked," Olmsted reports, "how rich the sort of men were of whom he spoke."

" 'Why, sir, from a hundred thousand to ten million.'

" 'Do you mean that between here and Natchez there are none worth less than a hundred thousand?'

" 'No, sir. . . . Why, any sort of a plantation is worth a hundred thousand dollars. The niggers would sell for that.'

" 'How many Negroes are these on these plantations?'

" 'From fifty to a hundred.'

" 'Never over one hundred?'

" 'No; when they've increased to a hundred they always divide them; stock another plantation. There are sometimes three or four plantations adjoining one another, with an overseer for each, belonging to the same man. But that isn't general. In general, they have to strike off for new land. . . . Old land, after a while, isn't worth bothering with.'

" 'Do most of these large planters who live so freely, anticipate their crops as the sugar planters are said to—spend the money, I mean, before the crop is sold?'

" 'Yes, sir, and three or four crops ahead generally.'

" 'Are most of them the sons of rich men? . . .'

" 'No, sir; lots of them were overseers once.'

" 'Do the grandsons of wealthy planters often become poor men?'

" 'Generally the sons do. Almost always their sons are fools, and soon go through with it . . . if they don't kill themselves before their fathers die. . . . They drink hard and gamble, and of course that brings them into fights.' "

"Next morning," writes Olmsted, "I noticed a set of stocks,

having holes for the head as well as the ankles; they stood un-sheltered and unshaded in the open road. I asked an old Negro what it was. 'Dat ting, massa?' grinning; 'well, sah, we calls dat a ting to put black people, niggers, in, when dey misbehaves bad, and to put runaways in, sah. Heaps o' runaways, dis country, sah. Yes, sah, heaps on 'em round here.' "

But if the ambition to own Negroes and land was concrete, it was also coarse and common, almost Yankee in its crude material-ism, and doomed to crash on the rock of nature. Cotton, like to-bacco, ate up the land. By 1850 there were more abandoned farms in the South than in New England. Soon there would be no new land for plantations. Cotton, moreover, with its requirement of continuous cultivation and its monotonous round of simple tasks, was suited to slave labor working in gangs under the lash of drivers. But what would one do with one's "hands" when the land gave out? The law forbade setting them free. Society frowned on selling them off, and in any case that was only the most brutal evidence of failure. Cotton drew the great planters of the South to invest their capital in unnegotiable labor; their "hands" forced them to con-tinue growing cotton—ultimately on the least rewarding land.

This vicious circle of the southern economy spun out the chal-lenge to southern politics. The Cotton Kingdom must, it must ex-pand—Indians, Spaniards, Mexicans, Cubans must be driven before it. Texas must be annexed, New Mexico purchased, California con-quered, Cuba grasped, Kansas and Nebraska occupied for the boll and the black. That was the South's "right." The Bible made slavery Christian; the Constitution protected property of every sort; the rule of law had its very justification in its guarantees to minorities, its restraints on the mass.

Here was a field for ambition that transcended cotton, that escaped the stigma of self-interest and even, if handled as brilliantly as by Calhoun, that of sectionalism; a field that offered opulent occasions for the oratory which the South adored; for politics, which was its passion; and for power which was its goal. "You slaveholders," cried a disenchanted daughter of South Carolina aristocrats to her own sister in 1860, "have lived so long on your plantations with no one to gainsay you and the negroes only look up and worship you that you expect to govern everybody & have it all your own way—I can see it in Father—in brother John—in Brother Patrick and in you."

American politics between the end of the War of 1812 and the beginning of the War with Mexico in 1846 had been dominated by three issues: the Tariff, Internal Improvements, and the Bank. Over each of them the conflict had been sectional but indecisive. Thereafter, though immense efforts were made to bury it as an issue and ingenious compromises sought to suck out its poison, Negro slavery became the touchstone of party alignments, the divider of the nation; since emancipation the memory of Negro slavery has been the demon of the reconstructed land. As early as 1844 the slavery issue prompted the Democrats to drop the Declaration of Independence from their articles of faith; in 1846 it split their opponents into "Cotton" and "Conscience" Whigs; in 1848 it united the latter and eastern Jacksonians under the banner of "Free Soil, Free Speech, Free Labor, and Free Men"; and ultimately in 1854, it made this "Free Soil" Party the major constituent of the new party of the free farmers of the West who, in the cause of liberty, reclaimed Jefferson's old party name, Republican.

The problem of Texas brought the slavery issue into the open again a generation after the Missouri Compromise of 1820. Since Texas had won its independence from Mexico in 1836, the South and the Texans themselves hankered for its annexation to the United States. Jackson and Van Buren, fearful of upsetting the balance of free states and slave, shied away from the issue. When the Virginian, John Tyler, became President in 1841 on the death of William Henry Harrison, the South took new heart, and when Webster resigned in 1843 as Secretary of State, Tyler began to take steps. In 1844 Calhoun became Secretary of State and promptly worked out a treaty of annexation. When the Senate failed to ratify, Texas became the main issue of the campaign. On this issue the Democrat, James K. Polk of Tennessee, won the presidency and, even before his inauguration in March 1845, Tyler had accepted the mandate and rushed annexation through Congress. He accomplished this by a joint resolution requiring only a majority vote in both houses instead of by a treaty which two thirds of the Senate would have had to approve.

Mexico immediately withdrew its representative in Washington. Polk was more aggressive. The southern boundary of Texas had been in dispute and he ordered "Old Rough and Ready," General Zachary Taylor, to occupy the contested area. He also sent John Slidell to Mexico to settle other long-standing issues and to offer to buy New Mexico and California. Slidell was sent home empty handed. Mexico, meanwhile, had dispatched its own troops to confront Taylor's. Eager as he was to win by conquest what Slidell failed to gain by purchase, Polk's war message to Congress came after the actual outbreak of hostilities in the disputed area.

The Mexican War began in April 1846, with fighting in Texas and California. It ended in February 1848, with the Treaty of Guadalupe Hidalgo after a brilliant invasion of Mexico itself by "Old Fuss and Feathers," General Winfield Scott. By this treaty, Mexico acknowledged the annexation of Texas and for a small sum ceded the disputed Texas territory, all of New Mexico country, and California. If the South anticipated any joy from this triumph, however, it was disillusioned even before victory was won. Soon after the war began, David Wilmot of Pennsylvania proposed in Congress that "neither slavery nor involuntary servitude shall ever exist in any part" of the territory acquired from Mexico. As a proviso to an appropriation bill, this proposal passed the House but was defeated in the Senate. The country debated it for two years; and when California grew to the proportions of a state following the gold rush of 1849, the issue had to be faced in a more serious form. "In the presence of the living God," cried Robert Toombs of Georgia, "if by your legislation you seek to drive us from the territories of California and New Mexico, I am for disunion." Indeed, in 1850 disunion was only averted by the compromise which did in fact admit California as a free state. In return the South got the assurance that in the rest of the Mexican cession "popular sovereignty" would decide whether slavery should be permitted. More important to the South was another provision of the compromise promising a stricter and more vigilantly enforced fugitive slave law.

Although it had achieved its war with Mexico and had won it so brilliantly, the South nevertheless had less new territory than the North to show for it, and fewer new senators and representatives. Having also attained a new fugitive slave law, the South soon learned that it was more effective in making Abolitionists than in reclaiming runaway Negroes. Free men simply would not hunt out other men to return them to bondage.

The South's hopes were buffeted by still other events. A transcontinental railroad had been talked of in the country for a decade before the California gold rush made it seem a practical undertaking. In 1853, to make certain that such a road would follow a southern route, the friendly administration of Democrat Franklin Pierce sent James Gadsden to Mexico to purchase part of the needed right of way west of Texas. This purchase Gadsden made for $10,000,000. The next year, Stephen A. Douglas of Illinois tried to win southern support for a more northerly route favored by capitalists associated with him, by introducing in Congress the so-called Kansas-Nebraska Bill. This measure would organize that part of the Louisiana Purchase beyond Missouri into two territories. In them the Missouri Compromise line marking the northern limits of slavery would be repealed and the decision on the issue left to "squatter sovereignty." Douglas's bill passed, and in the territorial elections in Kansas in 1855 thousands of slave-owning "border ruffians" from Missouri crossed over to vote for slavery. By 1856 an army of northern abolitionists, John Brown among them, had arrived in Kansas to contest the fraudulent vote, and soon there was civil war in "bleeding Kansas." The pro-slavery territorial government remained in control but the South gained nothing from it. In the meantime, the railroad project was shunted aside as slavery itself held the interest of the country.

Cuba, like Mexico, had so long been the apple of the South's eye that in 1854, after an effort to purchase the island from Spain failed, the American envoy joined the American ministers in England and France in issuing the remarkable "Ostend Manifesto." This declared that Cuba was geographically part of the United States and that if it were not obtainable by peaceful means, "by every law, human and divine," the United States had the right to take it by force. The South envisioned Cuba divided into two new

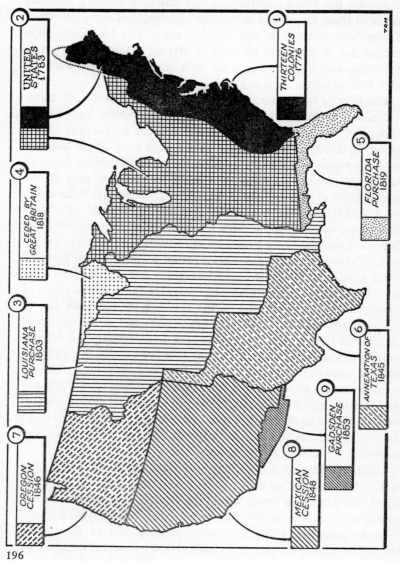

Territorial Expansion of Continental United States

1. THIRTEEN COLONIES 1776
2. UNITED STATES 1783
3. LOUISIANA PURCHASE 1803
4. CEDED BY GREAT BRITAIN 1818
5. FLORIDA PURCHASE 1819
6. ANNEXATION OF TEXAS 1845
7. OREGON CESSION 1846
8. MEXICAN CESSION 1848
9. GADSDEN PURCHASE 1853

slave states. The nation, however, expected nothing but trouble, and Pierce's administration had to repudiate the Manifesto.

After James Buchanan became President in 1857, southern filibustering expeditions designed to conquer northern Mexico and Central America received official sanction. The leading filibusterer was the Tennessean, William Walker, who made himself dictator of Nicaragua in 1855 only to be driven out soon after. In 1858 Buchanan made the formal prediction that in time the drift of events would make Central America part of the United States—a hope entertained in the North as well, where sentiment for a canal across this narrow territory had been percolating. Walker had tried to seize northern Mexico in 1853; in 1858 Buchanan made an offer to buy it; and in 1859 he asked Congress to permit him to send the Army down to restore order and collect debts due American citizens.

By then such foreign adventures had become the last resort of a desperate people. At the time of the Compromise of 1850 the great majority of Americans had hoped, as one headline said, that this was "The Closing of the Drama." Actually it was hardly the closing of the first act, as many other events aside from the expansionist efforts of the South attest. In 1852, after earlier magazine serialization, Harriet Beecher Stowe published *Uncle Tom's Cabin*. Her picture of slave life stirred the wrath of Abolitionists and planters alike. In 1856 on the Senate floor, Preston ("Bully") Brooks of South Carolina tried to kill the eloquent Charles Sumner of Massachusetts for personal remarks during an antislavery speech, while southern sympathizers stood idly by. In 1857 in the case of the Negro, Dred Scott, the Supreme Court not only reversed lower courts which had upheld his free status because he had been brought to a free state; it went on to add that Congress could not deprive persons of any kind of property anywhere in the United States, that the old Missouri Compromise itself, which had set boundaries to slavery, had been unconstitutional all along. Five of the nine Supreme Court Justices at this time were southerners. That was enough, said Horace Greely, to give the decision as much "moral weight" as it would have if it had been "the judgment of a majority . . . in any Washington bar-room."

The year 1858 saw the epic debate between Lincoln and Douglas in the campaign for senator from Illinois. That same year Lincoln made his "house divided" speech. To the South this was a warning that they could never accept Lincoln in the presidency. In 1859 John Brown led the raid on Harpers Ferry, Virginia, where the small Abolitionist band seized the government arsenal with the idea of arming the slaves and leading them in insurrection. Colonel Robert E. Lee and a detachment of United States marines captured Brown, who was hanged on December 2, 1859.

Three days after Brown's execution the thirty-sixth Congress assembled, and it was obvious that the events of the last fateful fifteen years had utterly dissipated the "caution and . . . considerate forbearance" to which John Adams had once looked for the preservation of the Union. "The members on both sides," wrote Senator Grimes of Iowa, "are mostly armed with deadly weapons, and it is said that the friends of each are armed in the galleries." Hate and distrust poisoned the atmosphere, challenges to duels rang through the air, fights on the floor of both houses were frequent. Almost a decade earlier, nearing the end of his own frustrated life, Calhoun had said it was "difficult to see how two people so different and hostile can exist together in one common Union."

THE LAND OF THE FREE

"We moved into a house of our own, had a farm of our own, and owed no one," boasted a typical northern farmer who had settled on the free soil of Michigan in the early 1830's. Such people and their predecessors for two centuries had left the old country not so much for business opportunity as for economic freedom and personal dignity. It was not their idea to make the nation great; they simply wished a chance to measure up to their private Christian capacities untrammeled by the traditions, ties, and periodic terror of Europe and the curse and competition of slavery in the American South. The forebears of Henry Ford came from Ireland in 1832 "with the desire and determination," a descendant wrote later, "to establish homes in which the fullest sense of freedom and independence could be had to the utmost." If many such newcomers promptly sought out their fellow nationals and fellow sectarians, that was but a natural irony in a strange land. Inescapably they also brought with them considerable mental and moral freight which encumbered them in the wilderness and which they would gladly have left behind. But not so the prevailing spirit of thrift, frugality, and hard work in which they "made" their farms, and which they urgently passed on to their offspring.

The generations growing up in the North after 1830, however, were hard to keep down on the farm. In Jackson's time the gates had been cast wide open to the temple of the "bitch Goddess, Success"; henceforth, especially in American cities, social inequalities grew too evident to be blinked at, and ambition and aspiration were molded by them. In Boston, not Webster but the "Boston Associates," in whose pay he was, became the models of ambitious Yankee youths. In Philadelphia about 1840, young Jay Cooke, the future financier of the Civil War, was writing home to the folks in Ohio, "Through all the grades I see the same all-pervading, all-engrossing anxiety to grow rich. This is the only thing for which men live here." And of his own future: "I shall . . . go into business myself," and live in "palaces and castles which kings might own." From New York in the next decade the fame of the first millionaires, of the Astors, Vanderbilts, and A. T. Stewart, spread not only across the country but across the sea.

Vanderbilt, the *London Daily News* acknowledged in an editorial celebrating the Commodore's visit to England in 1853, is the "legitimate product" of his country. Comparing Vanderbilt and America to the Medicis and Florence, the *News* went on: "America was not known four centuries ago; yet she turns out her Vanderbilts, small and large, every year. America . . . is the great arena in which the individual energies of man, uncramped by oppressive social institutions, or absurd social traditions, have full play, and arrive at gigantic development. . . . It is time that the millionaire should cease to be ashamed of having made his fortune. It is time that *parvenu* should be looked upon as a word of honor."

The massive increase in population in the ante-bellum decades was most important in opening up magnificent markets for Americans on the make. Of the 31,500,000 persons in America in 1860, 14,500,000 represented the increase in the previous twenty years.

Of these, ten million lived in the free states of the North and West, and almost half of them had come from abroad. In 1854 alone almost 430,000 immigrants entered the United States, a figure to be reached but once again before 1880. Most of the newcomers settled on farms in the West, but millions swelled the population of the cities, few of which were to be found in the Cotton Kingdom. By 1860, one fifth of all Americans lived in places of 2,500 or more; and of these about half lived in the sixteen cities with a population of more than 50,000. New York by 1860 had passed the million mark, and was followed more or less distantly by Philadelphia, Baltimore, and Boston. New Orleans remained the predominant city of the South, but its western reign was challenged by St. Louis and Cincinnati, each of which could boast more than 160,000 persons on the eve of the Civil War, and by Chicago which had grown to 110,000.

Since the barbarian invasions of Rome, commented the *Democratic Review* in 1852, "no migration has occurred in the world at all similar to that which is now pouring itself upon the shores of the United States. . . . In a single week we have again and again received into the bosom of our society, numbers as great as a Gothic army." These people, like the millions growing up in America itself, had to be transported, clothed, fed, housed, and furnished. This was especially true of the landless millions of the cities. Urban requirements, indeed, led to a revolution in eastern agriculture. As the virgin West came under cultivation, the old land of the East no longer could compete in the world markets for the great export staples, wheat, corn, and hogs. But as cities grew, eastern farmers began producing perishable milk, butter, and cheese, eggs and poultry, fruits and nuts for adjacent urban markets.

Eastern farmers, like the planters of the South, themselves often supplied a market for the western staples. Most of the wheat, corn, and hogs, however, like the southern staples among which cotton, of course, was predominant, went abroad in eastern ships to pay for imports of foreign capital and foreign manufactures. The 1850s were the golden age of the American merchant marine. The magnificent clipper ships gave this age appropriate grace and glamour, but the conventional square riggers were more important economically. Flying the American flag, they carried much of the commerce of the entire world. The millions of immigrants landed on American shores depended on these ships for passage. Their most important inert cargo was English railroad iron which eventually and ironically helped turn America away from the ocean to the bustle and big business of her domestic expansion while England extended her rule of the sea.

In the 1840s and 1850s and indeed in every decade for half a century thereafter, railroad progress held the key to American prosperity. By 1860 a billion and a half dollars had been invested in American railroads, more than 25 per cent of the total active capital in the country. As early as 1840, when the United States had about 3,000 miles of track, it was the world's railroad leader. In the next decade about 5,500 miles were added. Of these the Cotton Kingdom built its appropriate share calculated on a per capita basis; but its lines were scattered, and their track was as shaky as their finances. Most of the new mileage laid before 1850 went to serve the increasingly interdependent economies of the leading eastern ports. In the 1850s Americans built an astonishing 21,000 miles of railroads, most of them tying the East to the distant West. As late as 1850 not a single railroad entered Chicago. In the next five years at least eleven reached there from the East, the South, and the West. By 1857 twelve railroads had crossed the Mississippi, nine of them running from Chicago to prairie towns. By 1860 the railroad reached the Missouri River at St. Joseph.

"While we in St. Louis have been fighting the slavery question," wailed a local paper in 1856, "Iowa and Illinois were industriously occupied in constructing roads through both states, in order to secure the trade of Iowa to Chicago." The slavocracy did see the possibility of obtaining a portion of the Chicago trade by way of a north-south road which eventually became the Illinois Central. But the South actually lost trade to the only section of this road laid before the Civil War.

The Illinois Central's own prewar importance arose from other considerations. The project already had a questionable history when Representative Stephen A. Douglas of Illinois interested himself in it in the 1840s. He had a grandiose plan involving all the states of the Mississippi Valley, slave and free. His idea was to finance construction with the aid of huge federal land grants to each state traversed (except Kentucky and Tennessee where the Federal government owned no land). These grants eventually were to be distributed to the companies that actually laid the road. Costly lobbying in Washington got 3,736,000 acres from Congress in 1850; by perhaps still costlier lobbying in Springfield, a Boston group headed by John Murray Forbes beat Douglas's local backers to the charter for the railroad company which would build the Illinois portion of the road. Before the Civil War, with the Illinois Central grant as the precedent, Congress bestowed about 18,000,-000 additional acres of the national domain to forty-five different railroads. Once the South seceded, the transcontinentals traversing northern routes received far more lavish stakes from Congress.

The railroad tied the North and West into one massive free economy. It did much more. It tied business to politics and both to the life of the individual in a way unknown in America before. The railroad corporation tapped the savings of many thousands along its routes as well as in the money centers of the world; it held the sentence of death over communities reluctant to yield to its demands in exchange for a terminal or track; it could give favors in exchange for favors, withhold service as a threat to a community's integrity, withdraw it as punishment for local political and social independence. No business in the world had played for such large stakes before; none, therefore, had so stimulated the bare use of power.

The growth of cities, heightened regional specialization in agriculture, expansion of the transportation network, and the relation of all these to everyday politics and life lent a vigor and unity to the northern spirit probably unmatched in this epoch anywhere on earth. One consequence of this expansiveness was the hunger for wealth at any price and a deterioration, even outside of the railroads, of business morality. Or so contemporaries complained. In 1857 the *New York Tribune,* in one of many blasts, said that most people never knew how corrupt business commonly was. "From the groceries we daily consume," said this paper, "to the medicines which we consume more rarely; from the apparel with which we cover our bodies to the paint with which we cover our homes, we are constantly embroiled in a network of frauds, such that our whole commercial experience is very little else than a series of impositions."

This spirit of enterprise was to lead to unmatched corruption during the oncoming war. On the other hand, large profits, illicit or otherwise, certainly stimulated the northern economy which eventually overwhelmed the secessionists. In the 1840s and 1850s, besides the growth of the railroads and related industries and significant increases in their efficiency, northern business saw the development of the sewing machine, successful vulcanization of rubber, discovery of the Bessemer process for making inexpensive steel, commercial exploitation of petroleum, perfection of the telegraph, the start of work on Atlantic cables. Actually, few of these innovations used any significant amount of capital or labor before the Civil War. Older industries, however, had become by 1860 almost as highly capitalized as the railroads themselves. In these industries—textiles, shoes, food processing, lumbering, metalwork—many of the new departures of the previous decades became rationalized: integration became more common and more thoroughgoing; improvements in machine tools, and especially in the accuracy of gauges, greatly increased the precision of metalwork and the efficiency of production by interchangeable parts; the principle of the assembly line imposed itself on the flow of materials of all kinds.

Once the province of small groups in New England and scattered entrepreneurs elsewhere, industry in the 1850's had grasped the imagination of the entire country. In that decade, appropriately, the Middle West became the world's leader in the manufacture of agricultural machinery. The performance of American-built threshers and reapers, moreover, was unmatched by any foreign make. For the display of machinery, international fairs had become common in the 1850s. At the Paris Fair of 1854, six men with hand tools competed with four different threshers for half an hour, with these results:

> The six men with flails threshed 60 liters of wheat
> A Belgian threshing machine   150 "   "   "

A French threshing machine	250	"	"	"
An English threshing machine	410	"	"	"
The American threshing machine	740	"	"	"

If practical progress went hand in hand with profound corruption in American life in the 1850s, together they inspired broad movements of social reform and amelioration. One field for reform was labor conditions. During the prosperity of the 'fifties, factory labor worked twelve to sixteen hours a day. At the same time the flood of immigrants to the plants kept wage levels down; while ignorance, illiteracy, and inexperience kept the wage earners from organizing to better their condition. As bad as the factories were, home conditions usually were so much worse that men may have preferred to remain on the job. "Many families," the Board of Health of Holyoke, Massachusetts, a typical factory town, reported in 1856, "were huddled in low, damp, and filthy cellars, and others in attics which were but little if any better, with scarcely a particle of what might be called air to sustain life. And it is only a wonder (to say nothing of health) that life can dwell in such apartments." When the railroad boom burst in 1857 and a new depression visited the northern economy, simple starvation was commonly added to other curses of the laboring life. Simple and often very spasmodic charity was all the laboring class received. At the same time the South's export markets held up. "The wealth of the South," chortled the section's leading economist, "is permanent and rich; that of the North is fugitive and fictitious."

Yet, so their Christian brothers of the North believed, the four million slaves of the benighted South were far worse off than the poorest unemployed free men in factory towns, who could, it seemed, call their souls their own. The poor of the cities might break one's heart and draw one's compassion. Slavery tried men's souls to the utmost. The Abolitionist crusade enlisted those with the greatest power of selfless dedication. The majority found a softer approach more in keeping with their own prospects and personalities. In the North, despite the rush of industry and urbanism, most people continued to live off the land, independently, face to face with their neighbors and their God. The views they came to hold on slavery Abe Lincoln expressed as early as 1845, when he wrote:

I hold it a paramount duty of us in the free States, due to the Union of the States, and perhaps to liberty itself (paradox though it may seem), to let the slavery of the other states alone; while on the other hand, I hold it to be equally clear that we should never knowingly lend ourselves . . . to prevent that slavery from dying a natural death —to find new places for it to live in, when it cannot longer exist in the old.

Fearful of secession, disunion, and disorder, the "smart" businessmen in the North preferred conciliation and compromise, despite the South's successful opposition to the protective tariff, transcontinental northern railroads, and opening of the public domain to speculators. "What business have all the religious lunatics of the free states," cried James Gordon Bennett of New York's conservative *Herald,* on the eve of an antislavery meeting, "to gather in this commercial city for purposes which, if carried into effect, would ruin and destroy its prosperity? . . . Public opinion should be regulated." But the men on the land were dedicated to nonextension of slavery to the territories, and to fighting if necessary to keep them free. Again Lincoln spoke for the majority when he said in Peoria in 1854:

The whole nation is interested that the best use shall be made of these Territories. We want them for homes of free white people. This they cannot be . . . if slavery shall be planted within them. Slave states are places for poor white people to remove from, not to remove to. New free States are the places for poor people to go to, and better their condition. For this use the nation needs these Territories.

"Free society!" a southern editorial said in 1856. "We sicken of the name! What is it but a conglomeration of greasy merchants, filthy operatives, small-fisted farmers and moon-struck theorists? . . . The prevailing class one meets is that of mechanics struggling to be genteel, and small farmers who do their own drudgery; and yet are hardly fit for association with a southern gentleman's body servant." Lincoln expressed the grander spirit of free men when he said after the war had begun: "I consider the central idea pervading this struggle is the necessity of proving that popular government is not an absurdity. . . . If we fail, it will go far to prove the incapability of the people to govern themselves." This view was not as humane as the official Abolitionist position; it had nothing to do with being one's brother's keeper, especially if his skin was black; it even permitted one to dally, as Lincoln did, with the idea of the Negro's congenital inferiority. Yet it added a spiritual cubit to the slogan, "Vote yourself a farm," which helped Lincoln and the Republicans sweep the election of 1860, and sweep the South into secession even before the inauguration of March 1861.

CIVIL WAR

In its first presidential campaign in 1856 the Republican Party was such an anathema to the South that it did not even appear on the ballot in eleven slave states. At the same time the promise of genuine popular sovereignty in the territories won Buchanan and the Democrats the vote of Indiana, Illinois, and three other free states as well as the solid South with the exception of Maryland. The Democrats won the election, but the Dred Scott decision two days after his inauguration in 1857 gave Buchanan the excuse he needed to allow Kansas in particular to remain in proslavery hands. As the relations between the sections deteriorated thereafter, it was clear that no proslavery Democrat could win the presidency in 1860 and that no "free soil" Republican could conciliate the South.

The planters nevertheless insisted on a Democratic proslavery candidate in 1860, and to get one they split their own party. This made it all the easier for the Republicans to win the election even though they again failed to be named on the ballots of ten southern states. The Republican victory sundered the Union. Lincoln received only 39 per cent of the popular vote, the lowest ever for a victorious candidate; but he carried every state in the populous North and won a clear majority of the electoral college. Within a month and a half of the election, South Carolina adopted its ordinance of secession and by February 1861, was followed out of the Union by Georgia and five Gulf states: Mississippi, Florida, Alabama, Louisiana, and Texas. That month delegates met at Montgomery, Alabama, established the Confederate States of America, adopted a constitution, and named Jefferson Davis of Mississippi, provisional president, and Alexander Stephens of Georgia, provisional vice-president. President Buchanan simply prayed for their eternal souls.

Many in the cotton states had grave misgivings over the precipitate action of their leaders, and indeed nursed these misgivings throughout the coming war. Many of them were ex-Whigs who assumed the Democratic label for convenience after the breakup of their own party. They included Louisiana sugar growers and Kentucky hemp growers, who had sought high tariff protection, as well as southern railroad promoters interested in federal aid for internal improvements. Even some of the richest parvenu cotton planters in the black belt of Alabama subscribed to what they considered the "broadcloth party" to show that they were men of substance and no longer Jacksonian climbers.

After the Civil War these southerners with Whig traditions were to play important roles in building the kind of "road to reunion" they preferred. But as yet they had to yield to the fire-eating Democrats of their section who had nursed dreams of glory for a long time. In 1855 one of the fire-eaters, Senator James H. Hammond of South Carolina, boasted: "Without the firing of a gun, without drawing a sword, should [the Northerners] make war upon us, we could bring the whole world to our feet. . . . No, you dare not make war on cotton. No power on earth dares to make war on it. Cotton is King." In 1861 others of his ilk looked forward to the time when Cuba would fall into southern hands and Central America and Mexico would be occupied, while northern poltroons quaked at the thought of violence and warfare. These fantasies did not materialize, and indeed South Carolina was chagrined to find eight of the more northerly slave states, including Virginia, quite undecided on whether to affiliate with the Confederacy or not. South Carolina's view of the north seemed justified however. Lincoln acknowledged in his inaugural address that "the government will not assail you. You can have no conflict without being yourselves the aggressors."

Secessionists did not know Lincoln was scheming to place the Confederacy in the unfavorable aggressive position. When the Confederacy was organized, it grasped control of Federal property within its borders, but two key forts remained in the hands of loyal garrisons, Fort Pickens off Florida, and Fort Sumter off South Carolina. These forts soon needed their periodic provisioning and replacement of arms. Some advisers warned Lincoln that Union vessels in Confederate waters would lead to the charge of provocation, a charge that might cost the Union the wavering border states. Lincoln decided to send Sumter "provisions only" and to inform the governor of South Carolina that no arms would be landed unless resistance was encountered. The Confederacy thus had the unenviable choice of permitting the world to see how hollow were its claims of sovereignty or of firing the first shots.

On April 12, 1861, before the "provisions" arrived, Major Anderson in command of Fort Sumter refused the last Confederate demand to evacuate, and General Beauregard opened fire on him. In two days Sumter fell. Lincoln replied by calling for 75,000 volunteers to enforce the laws of the land and by ordering Confederate ports blockaded. Soon after, Maryland, Delaware, Kentucky and Missouri chose to remain loyal to the Union, while Virginia, North Carolina, Tennessee, and Arkansas allied themselves with the rebel cause. Thus did the Civil War open.

Neither the North nor the South boasted an army, the machinery for raising one, or the instrumentalities to finance military operations. The North had railroads, factories, money, men. But it took two years to organize them into a war machine. The South by comparison, had nothing—except generals and the awareness that the war must be fought on its own soil. The South's best chance of victory lay in a quick attack while it had unity and peak strength. Yet its object was independence, not conquest, and it began the war on the defensive. The North's best chance lay in delay until it could mobilize its overwhelmingly greater resources. Yet delay looked like acquiescence, while a quick victory would bring around many disaffected elements within the Union. Thus the North attacked before it was ready, and then, chastened, hesitated to move again in time.

When Virginia joined the Confederacy, the rebel capital was moved from Montgomery to Richmond. The first fighting after Sumter took place in July 1861, when Union forces under General McDowell attempted to invade Virginia and were repulsed at

Bull Run by Beauregard and Joseph Johnson. The decisive factor was the firmness of the brigade led by Thomas J. Jackson, before which Union forces broke and ran. Henceforth the Confederate commander was known as "Stonewall."

Lincoln attributed defeat to the rawness of the northern recruits. He promptly replaced McDowell with George B. McClellan whom he named General-in-Chief and ordered to organize, equip, and train an effective fighting force. McClellan's product was the superb Army of the Potomac; but he seemed to love it too much ever to risk it in battle. While McClellan hovered around Washington in the early spring of 1862 offending everyone with his arrogance and procrastination, George H. Thomas and Ulysses Simpson Grant were gaining control of the Mississippi above Vicksburg, while Admiral David Glasgow Farragut captured New Orleans at the river's mouth. The next year, on July 4, 1863, after months of tough campaigning, Grant took Vicksburg and split the Confederacy in two.

In the Eastern theater, McClellan at last made a move in April 1862, when he took the Army of the Potomac to Virginia with Richmond once again the Union objective. On June 26 he was met by Lee who had just taken command of all Confederate forces, and in the Seven Days' Battle was driven off toward the seacoast. McClellan had not been defeated, but the administration was discouraged and Lincoln removed him. Lee, however, soon took the offensive, marching north to sever the Union's east-west railroad lines. He so badly defeated McClellan's successors that McClellan was reinstated. On September 17 he met Lee at Antietam, Maryland, and inflicted casualties severe enough to send Lee back to Virginia to recuperate. When McClellan failed to pursue, however, he was once again removed from command.

On September 22, 1862, just after Antietam, Lincoln issued his Proclamation emancipating the slaves, as of January 1, 1863, in all areas then in rebellion against the United States. Besides inducing many Negroes to take up arms for the North, this measure won Europe's moral support for the Union cause. Heretofore the Confederacy had held the favor of the ruling groups in England and the continent even though the Union blockade had effectively deprived the rebels of much material benefit from the anti-democratic foreign sources. The Union, on the other hand, had held the interest of the middle classes abroad and the moral weight of emancipation gave their voices more weight in European councils. Foreign anticipation of Confederate success reached its nadir in July 1863, when to Grant's triumph at Vicksburg was added Meade's conquest of Lee at Gettysburg, Pennsylvania.

After Vicksburg and Gettysburg the Confederacy was hemmed in from the west and the north by Union arms, and on the east and the south by Union ships. By then southern reserves were spent, famine spread over many rebel states, and ruin faced the proud slavocracy. Much bitter and brilliant fighting took place, however, before the rebels recognized their doom. After pinning the Confederacy down in Chattanooga in November 1863, Grant was given command of all Union forces in March 1864. His successor in the West was William T. Sherman who soon fought his way from Chattanooga to Atlanta and in September 1864, began the march through Georgia. "I propose," Sherman announced, "to demonstrate the vulnerability of the South and make its inhabitants feel that war and individual ruin are synonymous terms." At the same time Philip Sheridan was despoiling the Shenandoah Valley of Virginia up which Jubal Early had led Confederate forces the previous July and almost captured Washington. By September Grant had already been engaged more than four months on the bloody campaign that ended the war, the campaign to take Richmond, so magnificently defended by Lee.

On April 2, 1865, Lee evacuated his battered capital, seeking more tenable ground in the mountains. But Sheridan cut him off and on April 9 at Appomattox Lee surrendered to Grant. The rebels had indeed been "pounded instead of negotiated into a peace." The men in blue, said one Southerner late in 1865, "destroyed everything which the most infernal Yankee ingenuity could devise means to destroy; hands, hearts, fire, gunpowder, and behind everything the spirit of hell, were the agencies which they used." And Emerson's "best civilization" was about to be "extended over the whole country" with a vengeance.

Chapter Eight

The Defeated South

In August 1883, an unknown farmer "chosen," according to Henry Grady's *Atlanta Constitution,* "from the rank and file," stood up to speak before the Georgia State Agricultural Society. "We must get rich!" he cried to a responsive audience. "Let the young south arise in their might and compete with [the Yankees] in everything but their religion and morals. Don't mind old fogies like myself and others of the same age who are sulking in their tents. We have the cotton and can make cheaper goods than they can. We have the wool and will have sense enough to use it. We can make iron at less cost than they can. . . . Get Rich! Sell everything marketable and live on the culls. . . . Get Rich! If you have to be mean. The world respects a rich scoundrel more than it does an honest man. Poverty may do to go to heaven with. But in this modern times. . . . Get Rich! and emigrants will pour in; capitalists will invest."

In the 1880s the whole dead Confederacy seemed to have fallen in love with Henry Grady's vision of an industrial "New South" which itself "had fallen in love with work." Indeed more. As people everywhere began lifting themselves from the slough of the depression of the 1870s, the "New South" became the hope of the entire nation and Grady was its prophet. Fifty years after he had first seen Henry Grady, Josephus Daniels recalled, "What a radiant and charming and accomplished man he was!" The *Atlanta Constitution* under Grady's editorship grew into one of the largest and most influential newspapers in the country, North and South. When Grady personally brought the message of southern opportunity to Chicago, or Pittsburgh, or to abolitionist New England itself, he was welcomed with an enthusiasm that matched his own and glowed

211

212 *The Defeated South*

long after his departure. "We have wiped out the place where Mason and Dixon's line used to be," Grady told the capitalists of the New England Club in New York, "and hung out a latchstring to you and yours." Then, as if to prove the reality of the new fellowship, he went on: "We are ready to lay odds on the Georgia Yankee as he manufactures relics of the battle field in a one-story shanty and squeezes pure olive oil out of his cotton-seed, against any down easterner that ever swapped wooden nutmegs for flannel sausages in the valleys of Vermont."

An army of northern publicists followed Grady home to the South in this period and returned eager to back his play. A. K. McClure, a leading Pennsylvania newspaper publisher and Republican leader, discovered that Atlanta was "the legitimate offspring of Chicago" with "not a vestige of the old Southern ways about it." "Effete pride" was gone; among "the more intelligent young men of from twenty to thirty years," he found numerous "potent civilizers." Congressman William D. ("Pig Iron") Kelley, Representative of the Pennsylvania steel kings, announced that the New South was "the coming El Dorado of American adventure." The popular after-dinner speaker and railroad lawyer, Chauncey M. Depew, told the Yale alumni that "The South is the Bonanza of the future. We have developed all the great and sudden opportunities for wealth . . . in the Northwest States and on the Pacific Slope." In the South lay "vast forests untouched; with enormous veins of coal and iron. . . . Go South, Young Man." Grady himself thus was soon able to report: "Every train brings manufacturers from the East and West seeking to establish themselves or their sons near the raw material in this growing market." Then with arms flung wide in welcome, he exclaimed, "Let the fullness of the tide roll in."

Northern capital had reasons of its own for rushing South in the 1880s, reasons the South dared not inspect too closely. "The South," young Henry Watterson of the *Louisville Courier-Journal* told the world in 1887, "having had its bellyful of blood, has gotten a taste of money, and is too busy trying to make more of it to quarrel with anybody." Unfortunately the facts had already begun to quarrel with the South. The very year in which Watterson wrote, "Pig Iron" Kelley himself had to acknowledge that "apart from the

New South, by which I mean the country around . . . the rapidly developing iron industries . . . the same wretched poverty prevails among the Southern people now, twenty-two years after the close of the war." If the South was "making money," who was getting it? Where was it going? "Mr. Grady in his great Dallas speech," young Tom Watson wrote in his *Journal* in 1888, "thinks that 'Plenty rides on the springing harvests!' It rides on Grady's springing imagination. Where is this prosperity?" And Watson continued with notes for a speech of his own that Grady's *Constitution* would fail to print: " 'New South' idea. If it means apology, abject submission— sycophancy to success—perish the thought. . . . Shame to Southern men who go to Northern Banquets & glory in our defeat. . . . Unpaternal, parricidal."

Like Grady's desperate old "rank and file" farmer, many in the defeated section felt that if they were to cling to life they must cleave to the victors, that they must "out-Yankee the Yankees," as Watterson advised. Their grief they would anesthetize in work and dreams, their guilt in "that 'hardness ever of hardiness [the] mother.' " Yet other southerners—their ranks mushroomed in the depression of the 'nineties—were coming around to see, as Watson noted, that "In Grady's farm life there are no poor cows . . . lands all 'Rich—Richer—Richest.' Snowy cotton, rustling corn. In reality —barren wastes, gullied slopes—ruined lowlands . . . Gin house on crutches. Diving down in the grass for cotton." The New South was one more Northern trick; the New South's failure one more Southern defeat. "The Past!" cried Watson. "There lie our brightest and purest hopes, our best endeavors, our loved and lost. . . . Come back to us once more oh dream of the old time South!"

THE WRATH OF WAR

"A foreigner studying our current literature," complained the carpetbagger novelist Albion W. Tourgée in 1888, "without knowledge of our history, and judging our civilization by our fiction, would undoubtedly conclude that the South was the seat of intellectual empire in America, and the African the chief romantic element of our population." But literature recovered much more readily than life.

There are no accurate figures on the cost of the Civil War to either side, even where figures might be meaningful. Union deaths may be put at 360,000, Confederate at 260,000. Numerically, Confederate losses were near enough to those of the Union, but actually they were overwhelmingly greater, representing a fifth of the productive part of the Confederacy's white male population. Thousands more in the South died of exposure, epidemics, and sheer starvation after the war, while many survivors, aside from the sick and the maimed, bore the scars of wartime and postwar malnutrition and exhaustion all the rest of their lives.

Lincoln's government spent almost four billion dollars on the war. Much of this served to give a fillip to northern industry. Confederate expenditures were only about one half those of the Union, but these were an utter loss in an utterly lost cause and only the beginning of the drain on the South. In the North a few unfortunate exceptions marred the general wartime boom. For example, the cotton textile industry broke down. In the South the exceptions were the rare successes in an environment of desolation. Rebels who ran the northern blockade, Confederate privateers who had preyed on Yankee shipping, southern merchants who had been canny enough to demand gold or goods for food and clothing, or who had catered to the invading soldiers, all faced the postwar years with some capital. But the South as a whole was impoverished. At the end of the war, the boys in blue went home at government expense with about $235 apiece in their pockets. The boys in gray found the South's hand tragically empty. Some of Lee's soldiers, the historian Dixon Wecter writes, "had to ask for handouts on the road home, with nothing to exchange for bread save the unwelcome news of Appomattox."

Military destruction in the Confederacy was thorough. Yet the war was not fought everywhere, and the South lost most in indirect damage. Land, buildings, and equipment, especially of slaveless white farmers who had gone to "hev a squint at the fighting," lay in ruins. Factories, halted for repairs, remained broken down or were simply forsaken. The one billion dollars of Southern banking capital in 1860 was wiped out, and with it the credit system on which the section was peculiarly dependent. Worst of all as far as the future was concerned, the labor system was utterly disorganized.

In the disruption of southern life few suffered more than the ex-slaves. Free and footloose Negroes became a problem to Union officers in captured Confederate territory early in the war, and eventually large numbers were gathered in so-called "contraband camps" where deaths from the elements, epidemics, and crime ran as high as 25 per cent in a few months. The Emancipation Proclamation magnified the problem, but it took Congress more than two years to cope with the crisis. In March 1865, Congress at last created the "bureau of refugees, freedmen, and abandoned lands," known since as the Freedmen's Bureau. Abetted by private northern philanthropy, the Bureau did nobly at the start, but after Appomattox it was swamped as were other resources. More "contraband camps" were opened and their population multiplied. During the first two years after the war, a third of the Negroes died in some of the camps.

Poor white and planter often were left little better off than the ex-slave. As early as 1862 famine forced all Confederate commonwealths to set up statewide systems of relief, but by 1865 these had collapsed in the general ruin. The harvest of 1865, moreover, proved almost a complete failure so that, as one Freedmen's Bureau official reported, it was "an every-day sight . . . that of women and children, most of whom were formerly in good circumstances, begging for bread from door to door." In the four years after the war the Freedmen's Bureau issued about twenty-one million rations, fifteen million to Negroes and as many as six million to whites.

The moral cost of war and defeat and ultimately of Reconstruction added its poison to the sapping brew.

> Furl that Banner, softly, slowly! . . .
> For its people's hopes are dead!

Rebel losses in youth and talent were proportionately much greater than the devastating total of human losses itself. The weakening of purpose, morale, and aspiration among the survivors was depressing enough to make many envy the dead. In Georgia in 1865, a reporter noted that "aimless young men in gray, ragged and filthy, seemed, with the downfall of the rebellion . . . to have lost their object in life." In Mississippi alone it was estimated that there were ten thousand orphans.

The war destroyed the instrumentalities of social control in many parts of the South. Churches, schools, courts, functioned poorly if at all. At the same time heartless bands roamed the countryside, led by ex-Confederate guerrillas like Jesse and Frank James who never gave up the fight against the victors and their society. War inflamed the spirit of riot in such men; defeat banked the spirit of reconstruction in the vast majority. "These faces, these faces," cried a northern observer on a visit to New Orleans in 1873. "One sees them everywhere; on the street, at the theater, in the salon, in the cars; and pauses for a moment struck with the expression of entire despair."

THE POLITICS OF FREEDOM

To many in the North the end of hostilities, for all the devastation of the land and life of the vanquished, did not mark the end of their mission, and by 1873 the wrath of "Reconstruction" had been added to the terrible war.

"Reconstruction" of the Union, not reconstruction of the South, had been the official purpose of the war. Lincoln was sympathetic to this purpose, and when by December 1863, four rebel states had succumbed to Union arms, he was ready with a full-scale program to restore them to their "proper and practical relation" with the loyal commonwealths. "Finding themselves safely at home," Lincoln said, "it would be utterly immaterial whether they had ever been abroad."

As President, just as when he was a candidate, Lincoln held the Union to be indestructible. Citizens might rebel, but states could not break away. Rebels, in turn, could be restored to full citizenship by *presidential* pardon. Lincoln was ready to pardon all but the highest Confederate officials if the former rebels would swear allegiance to the United States and agree to comply with United States laws and proclamations, including the Emancipation Proclamation. By 1864 a sufficient number of people (Lincoln specified at least 10 per cent of a state's 1860 electorate) in Tennessee, Arkansas,

Louisiana, and the new commonwealth of West Virginia, had met the President's conciliatory conditions and proceeded to form new state governments. They also signified their return to the Union by once again electing men to Congress.

But these men never were seated. Under the whip of Senator Charles Sumner, the Massachusetts orator, and Congressman Thaddeus Stevens, the Pennsylvania irreconcilable, Congress had worked up its own "Radical" reconstruction program. In many instances, with "boldness and consistency," as his home town paper in Lancaster, Pennsylvania, put it, Stevens had flouted segregation conventions and laws. Stevens was determined that his ideas of social equality, advanced even for the North, be forced upon the "conquered provinces." "The whole fabric of southern society," he declared, "*must* be changed . . . though it drive her nobility into exile. If they go, all the better." Sumner said, "If all whites vote, then must all blacks. . . . Their votes are as necessary as ·their muskets; of this I am satisfied. . . . The nation is now bound by self-interest—ay, self-defense—to be thoroughly just. . . . Mr. Lincoln is slow in accepting truths."

In the presidential election of November 1864, the Stevens-Sumner cabal tried to gain control of the Republican machine and carry their own man to the White House. In this they failed. The new Union Party, made up of "conservative" Republicans and "reconstructed" Democrats such as Andrew Johnson of Tennessee, captured the Republican machine. On the Union ticket Lincoln and Johnson won. Many Radicals had come around to supporting this ticket during the campaign because they did not want to alienate local Republican bosses and otherwise damage the machine they hoped soon to control. But in the lame-duck Congress that opened after the election, in December 1864, they promptly resumed their war on the President's conciliatory policy.

One of the Radicals' first measures was the Thirteenth Amendment: "Neither slavery nor involuntary servitude . . . shall exist within the United States." This amendment was ratified before the end of 1865. For strategic purposes it was milder than many Radicals would have liked. A second Radical measure established the Freedmen's Bureau. By seeing to it that the Bureau was manned in the South by their own nominees, the Radicals planned to assure themselves control of the Negro vote. A third Radical move was the rejection of all the men elected to Congress by Lincoln's reconstructed states. In March, the Radicals went home more determined than ever to save the South from a return to slavery and their party from the President. "There's ample public opinion to sustain your course," Wendell Phillips, the Abolitionist, advised Sumner, "it only needs a reputable leader to make this *evident*— So when the Senate closes . . . sound one bugle note . . . and set the tone for the summer. We have six months to work in . . . & if you'll begin an agitation—we will see that it reaches the Senate room."

The Radicals' determination did not turn Lincoln from his deeply considered, compassionate course. It was in his second inaugural, on March 4, 1865, after the departure of Congress, that he spoke the famous words: "With malice toward none, and charity for all . . . let us . . . bind up the nation's wounds . . . care for him who shall have borne the battle and for his widow and his orphan, . . . do all which may achieve and cherish a just and lasting peace."

Lincoln called it "providential" that Congress was out of session when Lee surrendered at Appomattox on April 9, 1865. "If we were wise and discreet," the still hopeful President told his Cabinet on April 14, "we should . . . get . . . the Union reestablished before Congress came together in December."

But Providence seems to have looked aside. That same evening the Great Emancipator, at long last the hero of the victorious Union and, ironically, the last, lorn hope of the South, was assassinated at Ford's Theater in Washington by the mad John Wilkes Booth.

"While everybody was shocked at [Lincoln's] murder," said the Indiana Radical, George W. Julian, "the feeling was nearly universal that the accession of Johnson would prove a godsend to the country." Universal, that is, among the Radicals. "Johnson, we have faith in you," cried jubilant Ben Wade of Ohio. "By the gods there will be no trouble now in running this government." A self-taught tailor, Andrew Johnson had been as outspoken an enemy of the nobby planters as Stevens himself. More than once during the war he referred to them simply as "traitors." Since then some suspected that he had become tainted with Lincolnism. But as a Democrat from a rebel state he had few claims on the people and none on the Republican Party, and the Radicals felt certain they could discount the power of his office if he chose to use it against them.

Use it Johnson did. Early in May 1865 he recognized Lincoln's governments in the four presidentially-reconstructed states. Later that month he offered amnesty to most of the citizens in the seven states Lincoln had not organized, and ordered this "white-washed" electorate to write new constitutions which would repudiate the state's war debt and abolish slavery. Under the new constitutions the voters would then elect new state governments. To the consternation of the Radicals, the President permitted each state to determine its own suffrage. When Congress met in December 1865, all the rebel states but Texas had reconstructed themselves on Johnson's terms.

The President, of course, expected trouble. The South had played blindly into Radical hands by its frighteningly quick adoption of the "Black Codes." Enacted in 1865 and 1866 in every Confederate state but Tennessee, these Codes regulated the Freedmen's life with varying degrees of severity. Often they gave him the right to sue, to give evidence, to go to school, to marry. Most states limited his property rights and forbade his working as artisan or mechanic. Nowhere could he hold public office, vote, serve on juries, or bear arms. Worst of all were provisions, such as that in Georgia, which warned that "all persons strolling about in idleness" would be put in chain gangs and contracted out to employers. Stevens was quick to make political capital of the South's ill-considered haste in voting the "Black Codes." As early as September 1865, he announced, "Let all who approve of [our] principles tarry with us. Let all others go with copperheads and rebels."

By such tactics the Radicals fragmented the Congressional opposition and dominated the session that opened in December 1865. Their first move was once more to exclude men elected in the rebel states. The Radicals then pushed through a bill extending the life of the Freedmen's Bureau, but they failed to override Johnson's veto in the Senate. In March 1866, they succeeded in enacting over Johnson's veto a Civil Rights Act forbidding states to discriminate among their citizens as they had done in the "Codes."

The great test came on the Fourteenth Amendment. Doubtful themselves of the constitutionality of the Civil Rights Act, and fearful that a later Congress might repeal it, Radical leaders decided on an amendment to insure its legality and long life. The first section of the Amendment in effect declared Negroes citizens and then prescribed that: "No state shall . . . abridge the privileges or immunities of citizens of the United States; nor shall any state deprive any person of life, liberty, or property, without due process of law; nor deny to any person, within its jurisdiction, the equal protection of the laws." The second section did not give the Negro the vote, but penalized a state for withholding the privilege by reducing its representation in Congress. The third section effectively disqualified from office all rebels who before the war had taken the Federal oath of office. Finally, the Amendment held the Confederate war debt, the debts of the rebel states, and all claims for compensation for loss of slaves "illegal and void." In June 1866, this omnibus measure, perhaps the most far-reaching of any added to the basic law of the land, passed both houses by large majorities. In July a new Freedmen's Bureau Act was passed over a second Johnson veto.

The Radicals demanded that the southern states ratify the Fourteenth Amendment as a condition for representation in Congress. Johnson thought the Amendment itself unconstitutional and advised the states to reject it. Tennessee alone failed to follow his advice and re-entered the Union. When the last of the rejections arrived, Congressman James A. Garfield of Ohio declared: "The last one of the sinful ten has . . . with contempt and scorn flung back into our teeth the magnanimous offer of a generous nation. It is now our turn to act." Harping on actual and alleged race riots in southern cities, the Radicals swept the by-elections of 1866. One of the features of the campaign that year was the first appearance of the Grand Army of the Republic, the redoubtable G.A.R., as a political force. The Radicals also unveiled the tactic of "waving the bloody shirt," the shirt of Union men who had fallen in the war brought about by the Democratic Party's alleged treason. The soldier vote helped give the Radicals such a large margin of control in Congress that they no longer needed to fear presidential vetoes. Their victory the Radicals took as a mandate.

Their first step in an attempt to revolutionize the government was to degrade the Supreme Court. In 1866 that tribunal had decided that "martial rule can never exist where the courts are open." Nevertheless, in March 1867, over Johnson's veto, the Radical Congress threw out the governments of all Confederate states but Tennessee, and cast the rest of the South into five military districts, each under a Congress-appointed general empowered at his own discretion to declare martial law. At the same time Congress voted that the Supreme Court had no jurisdiction in these matters and forced it to abandon a case testing the validity of this so-called First Reconstruction Act.

The main task of each general under the First Reconstruction Act was to arrange for new constitutional conventions in the states in their districts, delegates to which would be elected by universal adult male suffrage, Negro and white. Such conventions would create state governments under which Negroes could vote and hold office. As soon as these governments convened they were to ratify the Fourteenth Amendment as a condition for their return to the Union and the return of their representatives to Congress. All but three states—Mississippi, Texas, and Virginia—complied in time to participate in the presidential elections of 1868. The three laggard states were readmitted in 1870. In many states armies of occupation protected the new governments until 1876 and 1877.

Having brushed aside the Court, the Radicals next tried to subordinate the Executive. Two measures of March 1867, had this as their objective. The first, the Tenure of Office Act, deprived the President of the power to remove federal officers without the Senate's consent. The second, the Command of the Army Act, forbade the President to give the army orders except through General Grant. These measures left the President at the mercy of Radical officeholders and divested him of his constitutional role as Commander-in-Chief. But the Radicals wanted more. When in

defiance of the Tenure of Office Act Johnson tried to remove
Secretary of War Stanton, he was impeached in the House and,
between March and May 1868, tried in the Senate. At the end,
thirty-five Senators voted to throw Johnson out, one vote short of
the two thirds needed for conviction.

Johnson was through anyway. In the election of 1868 the
Democrats preferred to run Horatio Seymour of New York. The
Radicals got the Republicans to run Grant, but even so they were
lucky to win. Indeed, for all the great hero's as yet untarnished
fame, he might have lost had it not been for the Union League.
Union League Clubs had been organized in the North in 1862 to
spread Union propaganda. After the war, it was said, they existed
"for no other purpose than to carry the elections." The League,
one Negro said, is the "place where we learn the law." "I can't
read, and I can't write," said another. "We go by [League] instructions." Grant won by 305,000 votes. Seven hundred thousand
Negroes and 625,000 whites had been made eligible to vote in the
seven hastily reconstructed states. In five, at least, the Negroes voted
heavily for Grant.

The Negro's role in winning the election made the Radicals all
the more resentful of the acts by which former rebels, in Louisiana
and Georgia in particular, barred ex-slaves from the polls. The
Radicals decided that the Fourteenth Amendment's penalties for
disfranchising the Negro were inadequate. Thus when Congress re-
convened early in 1869 it lost little time in passing the Fifteenth
Amendment: "The right of citizens of the United States to vote
shall not be denied or abridged . . . on account of race, color, or
previous condition of servitude." This amendment was declared
ratified in March 1870, and helped sustain "black reconstruction"
during which the freedman enjoyed an illuminating taste of power.

The new state constitutions written by the mixed, so-called
"black and tan," conventions of 1868 and 1870 were liberal in
social as well as political provisions. Above all, most of them
prescribed free public education for Negroes and whites—an innovation for both races in most of the South and one more honored
in the observance there than in many northern commonwealths with

similar laws. By 1877, 600,000 Negroes were enrolled in southern elementary and secondary schools, and Fisk, Howard and other Negro colleges had got their start. "The great ambition of the older people," said Booker T. Washington, "was to try to learn to read the Bible before they died." For them hundreds of night schools were opened. Carpetbaggers from the North, some of whom used the schools simply to dispense Radical doctrine, helped man the new institutions. They may have taught the whites that "schooling ruins the Negro"; but they also taught the ex-slave to read and write.

In politics as in education, carpetbaggers swarmed down for plums and propaganda. But the South also sent thirteen Negroes to the House of Representatives and two to the Senate. Other Negroes gained federal administrative posts and acquitted themselves well. In South Carolina in 1868, Negro state legislators outnumbered whites eighty-eight to sixty-seven. Elsewhere they constituted sizable minorities. Even in South Carolina, leadership in the legislature remained with northern newcomers and their southern "scalawag" collaborators, but the Negroes' role had much symbolic significance —for both races.

The South under "black reconstruction" is almost universally depicted as a howling Babylon of corruption. Stealing, to be sure, was widespread, though the most conspicuous stealing (the fine furniture, carriages, jewels, and golden trinkets purchased at public expense for private enjoyment) was likely to be the least costly. Conventional political swag passed openly over the counter; building contracts, road work, printing jobs, the outfitting of public edifices, all went for sums shockingly above value received. Similarly, millions in state bonds were sold to aid politically sponsored railroad enterprises that never laid a mile of track, or to assist other business corporations whose officers merely pocketed what they received.

For all this and more, between 1868 and 1874 the eleven Confederate states piled up debts of nearly $125,000,000. To service the new obligations and for many other often obscure purposes these states levied taxes that were probably the highest in the country, the overwhelming burden of which fell on the old planter caste. Yet a considerable part of the crushing total of debts and taxes can be explained by the highly inflated currency in which it is usually evaluated. Northern bankers, moreover, sold southern state bonds at discounts as high as 75 per cent, so that a sizable portion of the borrowed money never reached the South. Many of the genuine social reforms of the "black reconstruction" legislatures, moreover, did cost money and were worth what they cost. Millions of dollars were also spent to relieve suffering among the starving and homeless of both races.

Many whites and Negroes of the new ruling class could not even sign their names. As might have been expected from the riffraff of conquerors and conquered alike and from even the best of the recent slaves who looked elsewhere in vain for sympathy and status, large numbers of legislators and administrators disported themselves in gross and bizarre fashion. For all the corruption, it appears to have been such conduct on the part of invaders from the North and their ex-slave friends which did most to complete the moral rout of the planter class and its hangers on. Desperate to regain power, many southern leaders in the late 1860s joined the Ku Klux Klan and similar secret organizations dedicated to "white supremacy." By violence and terror they sought to destroy the Negro's voting power and with it carpetbag misrule.

After 1869 many of these white organizations engaged in such random pillage and murder that respectable elements in the South abandoned them in horror. But the organizations themselves persisted. At the same time the Radicals in Washington renewed their own offensive. In 1870 Congress enacted the so-called Force Act. Besides imposing harsh penalties for infringement of the Fourteenth and Fifteenth Amendments, this Act gave original jurisdiction in all cases arising under the Amendments to Radical-controlled federal courts rather than to questionable southern state courts. When in the elections of 1870 white southern Democrats nevertheless recaptured the governments of Tennessee, Virginia, North Carolina, and Georgia and made notable gains elsewhere, the Radicals proceeded to enact the Ku Klux Klan Act. This gave federal courts original jurisdiction in all cases involving conspiracies or violence against the freedmen and also empowered the President to suspend *habeas corpus* and to declare martial law in any terrorized community.

These acts marked the high point of the Radicals' fight to insure the Republican Party the Negro vote. Both failed. Grant promptly used the Ku Klux Klan Act to send troops to South Carolina to protect the federal courts from "white supremacy" vigilantes. But subsequent requests by beleaguered carpetbaggers for military assistance were denied. A congressional commission seeking to justify military interference made a public report instead, which helped to justify the white South's discontent. This report became very popular among northerners who were repelled by Radical corruption in their own section and who had grown fatigued, as Grant put it later, by the "annual autumnal outbreaks in the South" brought about by carpetbagger aggressions. To conciliate this growing "liberal Republican" group before the presidential elections of 1872, Congress passed an Amnesty Act restoring to good political standing all southerners except about five hundred of the topmost Confederate leaders. Congress also permitted the Freedmen's Bureau to expire.

With the South out of the Union during the Civil War the Federal Government had lost little time enacting measures that the ante-bellum southern opposition had persistently helped to defeat. These included high tariffs on manufactures, free homesteads for free farmers, and lavish land grants for transcontinental railroads across northern routes. Though most of the Radicals had been long-standing leaders of the antislavery agitation, and many of them Abolitionists dedicated to Negro freedom and equality, one of their significant motives in insisting on the Negro's right to vote was the protection of these material fruits of victory from the return of southern Democrats to Congress and the presidency. In this the Radical "Stalwarts" had been most successful. Indeed, by 1872 they had not only protected but had gilded the fruits of victory. "The House of Representatives," said ex-Congressman Stevenson of Ohio in 1873, "was like an auction room where more valuable considerations were disposed of under the speaker's hammer than in any other place on earth." Naturally, the politicos there and in the Senate got their share.

By the elections of 1872, however, many northern businessmen were ready to join with political reformers in "throwing the rascals out." Prominent among these businessmen were import merchants who traditionally were free traders and who, in addition, were being mulcted by the tariff collectors in New York and other ports for the benefit of the Radical political machine. Commercial bankers who financed the import merchants' operations also were ready to protest. So were many lawyers, who were alienated by the corruption of the courts and the low caliber of politically appointed judges. Opposition to the Radicals also drew some northern Democrats who had been outraged by the corruption of their own local party bosses, of whom Boss Tweed of New York City was the most notorious. Such bosses usually shared the "boodle" with their Radical opposite numbers.

Representatives of all these discontented elements convened in Cincinnati on May 1, 1872, formally organized the Liberal Republican Party, and nominated Horace Greeley for the presidency. The futility of the reformers became obvious at this first meeting. So many different "causes" were represented in the Liberal Republican movement that internal dissension disrupted it almost before it began. Unfortunately, its candidate, Greeley, underscored the movement's weakness. For thirty years, as editor of the *New York Tribune,* Greeley had supported with unflagging enthusiasm about as many contradictory programs as the "Liberals" represented.

The Liberal Republican movement not only failed to develop political momentum, it also dissipated the momentum of the reviving national Democratic Party. The Democrats' only chance in the election of 1872 was to join up with Grant's opponents. Since most of these were absorbed in Liberal Republicanism, the Democrats had little choice but to endorse the Liberal candidate. Greeley had once referred to northern Democrats as "the treasonous section of Northern politics." But the Democrats of 1872 closed their eyes to the past and gave Greeley the nomination. Greeley's campaign quickly became a pathetic farce. The Stalwarts, who had again nominated Grant, swept to an easy victory.

The elections of 1876, however, proved another story. After the Amnesty Act of 1872, white southern leaders went about reclaiming their hold on southern state governments. Their tactics included typical Klan violence against the Negro, and economic reprisals against those who voted. But many Negroes had grown tired of the carpetbaggers and scalawags and often needed little persuasion to stay away from the polls. The Panic of 1873 weakened the Republican hold on the white electorate, and in 1874 the Democrats, augmented by victorious white supremacists from the South, gained control of the House of Representatives. Even during the campaign of 1872 there had been reports of vast scandals in Grant's first administration. After their congressional victory in 1874, the Democrats, through Congressional investigations, revealed just how deep these scandals ran. By 1876 the Republican national administration stood revealed as the most corrupt in American history. By then only three southern states, Florida, South Carolina, and Louisiana, remained in Republican hands.

To save what they could of their tainted machine, the Radical politicos decided to conciliate the honest core of the business community by running as their presidential candidate the impeccable Republican reform Governor of Ohio, Rutherford B. Hayes. The Democrats countered with a reformer of their own, Governor Samuel J. Tilden of New York, an outstanding corporation lawyer who had recently sent Boss Tweed himself to jail. With the votes of four states missing, Tilden held a popular majority of 300,000 and an electoral plurality just one vote short of victory.

Given the candidates involved, it seemed as though the reform elements could not lose the election; given Tilden's vote, it seemed as though the Republicans could not win it. But Tilden never got the one electoral vote he needed and the reformers themselves were fairly soon sold out. Three of the missing states were Louisiana, Florida and South Carolina, and the delay in each was caused by a conflict between the Radicals and the resurgent Democrats over the legitimacy of their respective ballot counts. The Radicals, who were still protected by the military, saw to it that the questionable Republican ballots were sent to Congress to be tallied; in Congress other Radicals saw to it that these Republican ballots were accepted. By these means Hayes won what was certainly the most tainted victory of his life.

So tainted indeed was Hayes's election that by February 1877, a Democratic movement to thwart his inauguration had grown strong enough to frighten experienced observers with the thought that "the terrors of civil war were again to be renewed." Taking the lead in forestalling violence was a key group of new southern political leaders. Democrats in name only, they had been Whigs almost without exception before the war. Their sympathy was with commerce and transportation as much as with agriculture. These southerners aimed to combine with regular Republicans to win federal aid for southern railroad development and to draw northern investment capital to southern industry. Their goal was a "New South" rather than restoration of the "Old South." Hayes, not Tilden, became their man. Enough Democratic votes were thus available to the Republicans in Congress to effect a settlement of the election dispute and allow Hayes's inauguration in March.

To insure the new southern leaders' continuance in power and to reassure the entire country, Hayes in 1877 recalled the last of the federal troops from the South. "Black Reconstruction" was ended forever. The Negroes themselves retained their legal political and social rights until these so-called New South Democrats were overthrown within fifteen years of their ascent. But these Democrats themselves scarcely gave the Negroes the opportunity to exercise their rights.

THE ECONOMIC UNDERTOW

While many in the North had been trying to reconstruct the Union by extending to the South the familiar political privileges of freedom, many Southerners had sought to reconstruct their section by restoring the familiar economic disabilities of slavery. This reactionary tendency was intensified after the failure of the industrial "New South" had become apparent in the late 1880s. But the fact remains that industrialism had been tried only because of the prior failure of the old castes to restore their "Old South" to reality, and the inability of northern capitalists to make money in the agrarian South themselves.

In September 1865, Union General Francis C. Barlow, "an able man without many illusions," who had seen service in the South, advised some Boston investors: "Making money [in Georgia] is simply a question of being able to make the darkies work." That alone, however, was to prove far from a simple question even for planters experienced with slaves if not with free Negroes. Yet ex-abolitionist carpetbaggers with little business experience flocked to the South after the war to educate the defeated in northern enterprise and energy; for them it proved impossible to solve the "simple question" of how to profit from former slaves. General Barlow's protégés invested $65,000 in an excellent Georgia plantation of about 6,000 acres. At the end of a year one of them exclaimed of "these imperturbable blacks": "The more I see of them, the more inscrutable do they become, and the less do I like them." At the end of the second year, frustrated by the climate, the caterpillars, and the falling price of cotton, as well as by the liberated Negro's personality, they were ready to slink away. "We sold the plantation for $5,000 and were glad to be rid of it," they wrote in 1867. "What a d—d piece of business the whole thing is."

By 1865 northern enterprise and energy had defeated secession. For a long time thereafter they failed to conquer the South. For an equally long time the South failed to conquer itself. When John Watson, Tom Watson's father, returned from the war to his decayed Georgia acres, the first thing he did was to tell his hands they were free and then invite them to continue on as before. The next day, "not a negro remained on the place . . . every house in the 'quarter' was empty." John Watson nevertheless went right ahead to mortgage a future crop and build a grand new mansion. After the new house was foreclosed in 1868, "my father," reports young Tom, "used to be virtually paralyzed for weeks by what he called 'the blues.' "

Unlike Watson's Negroes, most of the ex-slaves, though given to unpredictable flights to exercise their liberty, retained "a definite attachment to the place" where they had worked. They continued to look to "the 'well-raised' gentlemen"; unfortunately, the latter characteristically looked to the past. For months after Appomattox, some extremists even succeeded in concealing from their slaves that they were free, and clung to the "peculiar institution" to the bitter end.

One of the first economic needs of the South was a restoration of trade and transportation. Aware of this, the Federal Government removed all restrictions on the exchange of commodities between North and South and between the South and Europe by July 1865. Soon after, it returned all rebel railroads, many of them in better condition than before the war. River and road, however, remained the South's main domestic carriers, and twenty years of solid Republican rule were to pass before the South received a fair share of the river and harbor improvement pork barrel. In that period many navigable southern streams remained unusable for commerce. As for wagon roads, the South was left to its own traditional devices. Typically, the best road near New Orleans was rebuilt with an eye more to horse racing than hauling.

The South required capital even more urgently than markets and the means to reach them. Federal postwar policy, however, only ate up what capital had escaped the wrath of war. Ordered immediately after the war to confiscate Confederate *government* property (which amounted to 150,000 bales of cotton and little else) Union agents, their zeal stimulated by commissions of 25 per cent, swarmed over private as well as public warehouses. Most of their loot they sold off on their own accounts. On what it received, the Federal Government realized about $34,000,000, much of which it eventually returned to some 40,000 persistent southern claimants. But this was only a small fraction of the total loss and in any case came far too late. What such physical confiscation began, confiscatory taxes completed. In but three years after 1865 a so-called revenue tax on cotton, one of many federal levies, took $68,000,000 from the South—far more than the total expenditure on a dozen years of relief and reconstruction by all public and private northern agencies combined.

Confiscation and confiscatory taxation, terroristic in themselves, hastened the onset of a much more frightful economic disease which in any case would probably have brought "apathy stealing over the energies of the people," to use Tom Watson's phrase. This was "sharecropping" and its corollary, "the crop lien."

Before the war most southern plantations had been heavily mortgaged. When pressure for service on the debts was resumed after the war by creditors with their own backs to the wall, the fear of imminent foreclosure stirred many planters to an unwonted show of activity. The federal raids and levies nipped this in the bud. Forced sales had already become regular monthly features at nearly every Southern courthouse; now the door was opened wider to the carpetbaggers who snatched up the land only to fail in their ill-considered endeavors. Some planters fended off the day of judgment by selling part of their land in order to finance cultivation of the rest; others leased out acreage for a monthly rent. But scarcity of money had put the planters in straits in the first place. Naturally it also limited the number of cash transactions. The upshot was the system by which the planter "could obtain labor without paying wages and [the] landless farmer could get land without paying rent." For his services in the process of production each was to take, instead, a share of the *forthcoming* crop.

The rub was that to get this crop into the ground both parties to the agreement had to borrow, and since they had no other security they had to borrow on what they *hoped* to produce. Only against this *forthcoming* collateral would the supply merchant advance the required seed, fertilizer, food, clothing, tools, and fencing. Risks under this system were so great that northerners who supplied the supply merchant charged exorbitant prices for goods and very high interest for credit. These exactions and oppressive charges for transportation, insurance, and other commercial functions, the merchant passed on to the southern landlord and cropper. The merchant also added his own high profit and interest and on occasion a generous tithe to reward himself for his literacy at the expense of borrowers who could not read his books. Under this regime the South, instead of being aided by northern capital, became more firmly enchained to northern creditors while the sharecropper was enslaved to the merchant.

The South fell into the catastrophic sharecrop and crop-lien systems largely because of capital starvation. These nails were driven more deeply into the coffin of the southern economy because they offered a kind of solution to the labor problem as well.

Both Negroes and whites were unfamiliar with a free-labor market, but many planters undertook at first to hold on to their workers by offering keep and cash. To protect the Negro from being packed off as soon as the crops were in, Freedmen's Bureau officials insisted that such arrangements be confirmed by written contracts. These usually provided for a wage of $10 to $12 a month, less the cost, determined by the planter, of "quarters, fuel . . . and substantial rations." In exchange the freedman agreed "to labor faithfully . . . six days during the week, in a manner customary on a plantation." In the hope that the Negro would stay at least until the harvest was over, the planter was usually willing to sign. The Black Codes, in turn, made it hazardous for the ex-slave to wander.

Far from strengthening the free-labor market, however, the Black Codes went far toward destroying it. The pay for "convict labor" created by enforcement of the Codes went to the state not the worker, and when a state was in want of cash, state police simply rounded up "vagrants" and hired them out. Since convict pay was so much below the prevailing wage, there was always a ready market for the "vagrant" Negroes. "Employers of convicts pay so little," an Alabama paper complained as late as 1889, "that it makes it next to impossible for those who give work to free labor to compete with them. . . . As a result, the price paid for labor is based upon the price paid for convicts." The system had another attraction. In the 1870s the Tennessee Coal, Iron, and Railroad Company began paying a regular annual rental of $101,000 for the state's convicts. "One of the chief reasons which first induced the company to take up the system," the Company's general counsel explained, "was the great chance which it seemed to present for overcoming strikes."

But the wage system failed on plantations for other reasons. Often there simply was no money for it. When there was, the planter usually found good prior uses for the cash. "The freedmen have universally been treated with bad faith," wrote General W. E. Strong from Texas in 1866, "and very few have ever received any compensation for work performed." The conduct of the freedman, however, often did not help matters. Emancipated, the Negro quickly learned to resent working "in a manner customary on a plantation." In protest he would leave.

Sharecropping ultimately stabilized labor relations. The surviving old planters were quickly liquidated in the postwar South. Through sharecropping, the plantation—with little of its ameliorating paternalism—was preserved. Southern land was divided into large numbers of small "holdings" which gave the illusion of small independent farms. Actually, many "holdings" formed parts of single plantations which, through foreclosures, gradually fell under the control of supply merchants or their creditors.

These businessmen were quite aware of the legend and the dream of the Old South. In aspiring to the political and social eminence of the old planter caste they yearned above all else to become large landowners. The weak credit system made the tendency toward monopolization of land strong. Dictation by the supply merchant made concentration on a single *cash* crop even stronger. Lest the crop fail, moreover, the merchant assumed a degree of control over the entire life of the cropper and his family that an oldtime overseer would hardly have thought worth the effort. For the cropper himself, as "Pitchfork Ben" Tillman of South Carolina put it, the whole system kept men on a "lazy 'descent into hell' "—"like victims of some horrid nightmare," added the more imaginative Tom Watson, "powerless—oppressed—shackled."

The end of the slave system had left the Negroes most numerous on the fattest land of the old "black belt." Most of them found it easier than the old slaveless yeoman farmers to adjust to the inertia and interference of the new system. This lingering servility, in turn, recommended the Negro to the landowner and the merchant. White croppers were likely to be "ornery." When times failed to improve, the rub of poverty gave a higher luster to the white farmers' dream of the "Old Time South." Led by men like Tom Watson, Ben Tillman, James K. Vardaman of Mississippi, and Hoke Smith of Georgia, they looked down upon the new business "planters" as something worse by far than their Damyankee models, as parvenus, usurpers, betrayers of the Lost Cause. All the greater, then, the parvenu's hunger for black "help" to authenticate the new plantation life. "White labor," said an Alabama planter of 1888, "is totally unsuited to our methods, our manners, and our accommodations." "Give me the nigger every time," said another in Mississippi. "He will live on less and do more hard work, when properly managed, than any other class, or race of people. . . . 'We can boss him' and that is what we southern folk like."

The fact that the white farmer on poorer soil outproduced the Negro cropper on the rich black-belt land hardly helped the situation. "The Negro skins the land," went a southern saying, "and the planter skins the Negro." But the poor white was his own "bottom rail," and when debt caught up with *him,* as it inevitably did after crop prices began their own descent into hell in the 1880s, he was simply turned off the land. As cropping took an ever "blacker" hue, the dispossessed white farmer turned sour, until, like Grady's carefully chosen rank and filer, he grew "willing for almost anything to turn up which gives promise or possibility of change." Even the white man's factory was better than the black man's kind of farm.

Poor white degradation was deepened by yet another heritage which postwar chaos exacerbated, the absence of public schools. "In 1876," wrote an old southerner years later, "I stood in Fayetteville, North Carolina, and saw white youth after white youth turned away from the polls because they could not read and write, while my horse-boy and other Negroes taught by Northern teachers, were consistently admitted to the ballot. And I swore an oath that so long as my head was hot, I should never cease from fighting for schools until every white child born in the State had at least the surety of a common school education—and a chance to go as much further as he liked."

"The factory and the school, then!" writes W. J. Cash. These alone offered the poor white the hope of salvation. Yet fifty years after the end of Reconstruction the South had much the highest white illiteracy rate in the country, and not until World War II would the factory make an impression on the prevailing poverty. A vigorous cotton manufacturing industry did arise in the South after the Civil War. Yet as Francis B. Simkins, a historian of the section, says, "if all . . . spindles of the Southern textile industry had been concentrated in one state in 1880, that commonwealth would have ranked only seventh among the cotton manufacturing states of the country." After 1880, the building of factories in the

South became a civic mission to which white doctors, preachers, lawyers, professors, and a veritable army of old generals and colonels lent their capital, their energy, their names and reputations. Textiles continued to grow fastest. In the depression of the mid-1880's southern iron began to compete successfully with Pittsburgh's. At about the same time, the North Carolina tobacco manufacturing industry responded hopefully to the country-wide fad of cigarette smoking. A bit later the cottonseed oil manufacture spurted upward. As late as 1900, the vaunted New South nevertheless accounted for a smaller *proportion* of American manufactures than did the Old South in 1860.

The South raised itself industrially by its own bootstraps. But more significant than southern enthusiasm in the long run was northern capital, though it never did flow in with the rush that Grady's oratory seemed to inspire. After the violence that marked the labor disputes in the "free" North during the depression of the 1870s, the labor appeal of the South acquired importance. "Money invested here," wrote a North Carolina paper in 1887, "is as safe from the rude hand of mob violence as it is in the best United States bond." Shortly after, the *Southern Manufacturers' Record* promised that "long hours of labor and moderate wages will continue to be the rule for many years to come." An Alabama publicist in 1886 offered this additional security: "The white laboring classes here are separated from the Negroes . . . by an innate consciousness of race superiority. This sentiment dignifies the character of white labor. It excites a sentiment of sympathy and equality on their part with the classes above them, and in this way becomes a wholesome social leaven."

That was what the New South campaign aimed to bring about. Unfortunately for its promoters, as late as 1900 fewer than 4 per cent of the people in the important textile state of South Carolina were as yet engaged in manufacturing, while 70 per cent remained occupied with agriculture. The ratios in the rest of the South were little different. And what did the southern white industrial family gain? "Their power," writes a southern historian about the section's factory owners, "was peculiarly Southern. Unconsciously copying the planters, they established their workers in villages which resembled the slave quarters of old. In return for this 'benevolence' they received a feudal obedience."

After the business crash of 1893 conditions grew worse. In 1894 J. P. Morgan fostered a new flow of northern capital into the reorganization and consolidation of southern railroads, coal, iron, steel, and other industries. The discovery of oil at Spindletop, Texas, in 1901 opened gigantic new areas for investment and development. Henceforth not only were southern mill hands and other industrial workers held in bondage, but the entire section lived in peonage to the North. Even federal emergency relief funds for victims of flood, drought, and famine long discriminated against the late rebels. Differentials in tariff, transportation, trust, and banking policies bore the South down, while its own desperate capital needs only added burdens. "We must induce capital for manufactures to come here," intoned one unoriginal southerner as late as 1897, "by offering cheaper money, cheaper taxation, cheaper labor, cheaper coal, and cheaper power, and much more public spirit." And the cost of these fine inducements fall on whom, asked the forgotten poor white farmers? On them "out of all proportion to the value of their property or their ability to pay."

While the shifting currents of freedom lifted the Negro from slave to sharecropper, the economic undertow in the South drew the white farmer and white worker alike to the brink of slavery. As the South gradually became inured to industry, the life of its factory hands grew harsher until in the 1930s they began to look out for themselves in their own unions. Much earlier, in the Agrarian Crusade of the late 1870s and 1880s, and the Populist Revolt of the 1890s, the southern farmer was to unite once more with the western agrarian in striving through the intercession of the national government to win a more favorable place in the national scheme of things. In fact, he gained little from either movement except a degree of local power. Since this power proved inadequate to lift the "white trash" from the economic slough, the white man used it largely to shove Jim Crow into the social ghetto.

A series of Supreme Court decisions, beginning with that in *United States* v. *Reese* in 1875 and ending with the *Civil Rights*

Cases of 1883, made discrimination against Jim Crow easy. In these cases the Court ruled that while the Federal Government might continue to protect Negro citizens from discrimination by state acts, it could not protect them from the acts of private individuals even if the latter were organized. This was practically an invitation to lynch law. Even state acts, moreover, could discriminate on grounds other than race or color in protecting *civil* rights; and could discriminate on grounds of race and color themselves in protecting *social* rights. Thus did the Court sanction the literacy tests and other restraints on the Negro's civil rights, and the flood of Jim Crow segregation measures curtailing his social rights. Until the late 1880s there was little love lost between the races. After that the white southern farmer became the avenging spirit of the "Old Time South"; he in particular made freedom a nightmare for the descendants of the old-time slave.

Chapter Nine

The Wild West

The persistent southern preference for cheap money, low tariffs, commodity banks, and railroad regulation drove the *New York Tribune* to lament in 1879 that "the South is not yet ready for the new civilization." During the next decade Henry Grady made it his mission to correct this condition. In self-protection, the *agrarian* South began once again to reach out for its own "most valuable ally," the agrarian West. "United politically," a Mississippian argued in 1878, the South and West "are invincible. They can defy the world, the flesh, and the devil."

The West that was to respond like "a regular Baptist camp meeting chorus" to the southern agrarian appeal after 1880 was far different from that which had temporarily joined with the slavocracy fifty years before. With its iron ore, coal, steel mills, lake steamers, and railroad grid, the old West was well on its way to becoming the very heart of the Mark Hanna–McKinley country. Eventually the new West would also prove a natural habitat for the civilization of big business and finance whereupon it too would desert the South. For some time, however, the "Wild West" remained politically and economically as far from "ready for the new civilization" as the Georgia pine barrens or the clay hills of Mississippi.

THE COUNTRY AND THE PEOPLE

As late as 1860 not a single state had been organized on the great plains beyond the Mississippi valley except for Texas. In the awesome country of the Rockies and the Sierras and in the forbidding Great Basin between these ranges, political organization had scarcely begun. Even news of the slavery controversy and the Civil War often failed to reach or interest men in this distant wilderness who had ancient and more absorbing interests of their own.

238

In despair their prototype, the Spaniard Coronado, first described the dizzying plains of the West as the "North American desert," and for more than three hundred years his epithet stuck. This uncharted expanse, extending well into Mexico and Canada, seemed as boundless and inhospitable as the ocean. More depressing was its almost complete lack of timber for fuel, houses, fences, barns. Fructifying rainfall scarcely ever watered any part of this country. Instead, violent hailstorms and crushing falls of snow as dry as sand periodically assaulted it, driven by constant, howling winds that often surged to gale velocity. Sucked dry in their passage over the lofty mountain barriers, themselves crowned with snow the year round, these winds brought extremes of heat and cold to the plains that alternately froze the infrequent rivers in their courses and parched their beds.

For white men, whose technology, tradition, imagery, and outlook had long been conditioned by the forests, streams, regular rainfall, and rolling hills of western Europe and eastern America, here was a country to be shunned. Before the opening of the first transcontinental railroad in 1869, most of the people journeying to the salubrious woodlands and watercourses of Oregon and California went by ship around the Horn. This was the favorite route of the clippers, which could make the long voyage from Boston or New York to California in a hundred days and sometimes less. Few undertook to cross the "desert" by wagon train, and so strewn with wrecks and carcasses were the plains that they merited their chilling fame. Of one particular region around Nevada, Mark Twain exclaimed, "The desert was one prodigious graveyard."

Yet, like the high mountain ridges and clear mountain streams that the western trappers plied so successfully, the arid, treeless plains teemed with life. The native grass and livestock of the plains, said William Gilpin, the first territorial governor of Colorado, are "spontaneously supported by nature as is the fish of the sea." Hundreds of millions of herbivorous jack rabbits and prairie dogs fed on the prevalent grass; tens of millions of carnivorous wolves and coyotes fed on the rabbits and the dogs. Most important and most picturesque were the overwhelming buffalo herds. The Plains Indians lived off the buffalo. His flesh was their food, his skin their clothing, his hide the sheltering cover of their tepees. Their daily round of life revolved around the buffalo hunt, and their ritual and worship were dedicated to its success.

For countless centuries, the Plains Indians had stalked the buffalo on foot and lived precariously or starved while the herds multiplied. Then sixteenth-century Spaniards brought the horse to the new world. The horse greatly extended the Plains Indian's hunting range, carrying him as a trespasser to tribal lands not his own and intensifying tribal warfare. As the Indians' ability in the hunt grew, the buffalo herds diminished and tribal wars for the precious beast grew more frequent and bloody. To survive, the Indians became ever more nomadic, more violent, more hostile to trespassers of any kind—and better riders and fighters.

George Catlin, who spent most of his mature life painting Plains Indians, said the Comanches were "the most extraordinary horsemen that I have seen yet in all my travels, and I doubt very much whether any people in the world can surpass them." The neighboring Sioux, Cheyenne, Blackfeet, and Crows could not afford to be much less efficient than the Comanches. A little to the south, the Osage, Pawnee, and related tribes also took well to the horse, the hunt, and the warpath. To the southwest, on the more authentic desert of Arizona and New Mexico, rode the formidable Navajos and Apaches.

These Indians, said Catlin, "all *ride* for their enemies, and also for their game." Besides a magnificent horse, the red man's equipment included the murderous short bow, no more than two and a half or three feet across and superbly adapted to horseback, and a quiver of a hundred barbed arrows. But more important than his gear was the Indian himself and his relation to his mount. "We were surprised, incredulous, almost offended," said visitors to Kansas in 1854, "when a young officer . . . deliberately asserted that our mounted men, though armed with revolvers, were in general not a match in close combat, for the mounted Indians, with their bows and arrows." But it was soon proved that Indian tactics would carry the day.

Riding outside rather than atop his horse, with both hands free, one to feed the bow and the other to release it, and shooting under the neck or belly of his mount while remaining virtually invisible himself, the Indian would circle madly, frighten ill-trained army horses with his blood-curdling yells, and render "any certain aim with the revolver impossible, while his arrows are discharged at horse and man more rapidly than even a revolver can be fired." Not until after the Civil War, when the repeating revolver and the breech-loading rifle became regular army equipment, were the Plains Indians at a disadvantage.

In 1860 about 250,000 redmen, not all as violent as the fighting tribes, held the "desert" and the mountain country. Approximately 175,000 whites, 90 per cent of them male, were also scattered over the vast area. Their number soon was augmented by deserters from both armies in the distant war. Except for the 25,000 Mormons settled in Utah, these whites, like the Indians, were almost always on the move. They prospected, hunted, trapped, drove cattle and sheep, guided and sometimes misguided emigrant trains bound for California and Oregon, scouted for the army, hauled the overland freight, carried the overland mail, gambled, drank, and wenched when occasion offered, and traded and fought with the redmen. Some of them, like Kit Carson and Jim Bridger, were as free on a horse and as sharp on a trail as any native.

While inhabitants of the older sections were making the United States a powerful member of the concert of nations and keeping the country abreast of developments in science, philosophy, literature, and the arts, the Wild West was living an extraordinary life of its own that entered most profoundly into the American spirit and mythology. Even before the Civil War was over, the culture of cowboys, rustlers and roundups, of six-shooters and branding irons, warpath and council fire, wide-open mining towns, posses and sheriffs, had imposed itself on the Great American Desert. After the war, it implanted itself so resoundingly in the American consciousness that its echoes are heard to this day.

REMOVING THE INDIAN BARRIER

The fate of the "Digger" Indians of California following the Gold Rush of 1849 foreshadowed later events in the nineteenth century that almost cleared the redmen from the Wild West. In a decade the ferocity of California prospectors, miners, outlaws, and adventurers had reduced the Digger population from 150,000 to 30,000. From the very beginning of white settlement in North America, the paganism of the natives had served as a justification for Christian violence. In the nineteenth century United States government policy only confirmed the Indians' growing conviction of "the fatal tendency of their new environment."

In 1851 Congress formally terminated the policy of "One Big Reservation" on the whole expanse of the "desert" and forced treaties upon the Plains Indians corralling them onto limited reservations. This deprived them of their traditional hunting grounds, and worse, crowded them onto the lands of other tribes which offered them no welcome. In the meantime administration of Indian affairs, heretofore a function solely of the army, was given in part to the new Bureau of the Interior, created in 1849. The army deeply resented this shift of responsibility, and the open corruption of the new department brought the Indians to open rebellion against the reservation policy. At the mercy now of rapacious officials as well as touchy soldiers, the Indians were either starved on the reservations or killed in open country. In the 1850s a Western settler wrote: "It was customary to speak of the Indian man as a Buck; of the woman as a squaw. . . . By a very natural and easy transition, from being spoken of as brutes, they came to be thought of as game to be shot, or as vermin to be destroyed."

The treaties of 1851 and later had been made only with nominal Indian leaders and rump groups. Thus it became one thing to set aside Indian reservations and another to force most of the redmen onto them and to keep them there incarcerated by the army. Trouble was constantly brewing, and in 1862 when regular army units were recalled from the plains for Civil War service and replaced by inexperienced recruits, the earliest of the so-called Indian wars of the plains broke out. The next five years saw scores of futile battles, which ultimately convinced a parsimonious Congress that the cost of subduing Indians was too great and subjugation itself too slow.

In 1868 new treaties assigning new reservations were made with the war-weary Indians. "All who cling to their old hunting grounds," warned General Sherman, "are hostile and will remain so till killed off. We will have a sort of predatory war for years—but the country is so large, and the advantage of the Indians so great, that we cannot make a single war end it." As Sherman anticipated, between 1869 and 1876 over two hundred pitched battles were waged between the army and the Indians. It was during a conflict with the Sioux in the latter year that General Custer made his "last stand" against Crazy Horse and Sitting Bull in the battle of Little Big Horn.

Extermination of the buffalo demolished the remains of Indian society and Indian hopes. A buffalo stampede was perfectly capable of overturning a train and as western railroad building progressed, buffalo hunting became a regular feature of it. "Buffalo Bill" Cody got his reputation by killing some 4,000 buffalo in eighteen months as a hunter for the Kansas Pacific line. Buffalo shooting next became a popular and devastating western "sport," and then in 1871 changed to a still more devastating business. A Pennsylvania tannery had found that it could work the hides into commercial leather, and skins, heretofore hardly worth retrieving, suddenly were valued at $1 to $3 apiece. Between 1872 and 1874, the annual carnage was 3,000,000 bison. By 1878 the southern herd had vanished, while a tiny remnant of the northern herd had fled to the Canadian woods.

The final act of violence against the Indian was in a way the summation of his history. When Columbus discovered North America probably a million aborigines occupied the area now comprising the United States. Grouped in 600 distinct nations, few of which numbered as many as 2,000 persons, their entire existence was arranged and ordered by the tribe. With the coming of the horse, small groups of Plains Indians broke off to hunt independently and only once a year in the summer did they reunite for tribal festivities which eventually grew into "a frightful conglomeration of rites and customs" known, inaccurately, as the Sun Dance. This sacred ritual lasted for days. It reaffirmed happy tribal unity, and was replete with offerings to the buffalo. In 1884 the United States Government prohibited the Sun Dance and other Indian religious practices. In 1890 while a Dance was nevertheless in progress on the Sioux reservation, troops appeared and the Indians ran. The troops followed, and in the battle of Wounded Knee they massacred the half-starved survivors of the once-fierce tribe. By then there were hardly 200,000 Indians left in the United States.

Three years before Wounded Knee, Congress had passed the

Dawes Act which defined our basic Indian policy until 1934. This Act broke up tribal autonomy even on the reservations and gave each Indian head of a family 160 acres as his own to cultivate. After a probation period of twenty-five years, he was to have full ownership and full American citizenship. By 1924 all Indians had been granted full citizenship.

The Dawes Act dramatically reversed Indian policy as a result of widespread humanitarian opposition to the old extermination policies. Its consequences, however, were disastrous. The division of the land left the Indians with far less than they had heretofore held, even on the reservations. Moreover, the poorest land was chosen for them; the best sold off to white settlers. Worse, even where they had good land, their inexperience with property left them vulnerable individually to the same kind of sharp practices that had cost them so dearly as tribes. They had neither the tradition nor the incentive to cultivate what lands they retained. Pauperization grew like a weed.

It took those responsible almost as long to learn something of the Indian's history and traditions as to exterminate him. The Indian Reorganization Act of 1934 again reversed Indian policy in the light of greater knowledge, and under men like John Collier the Office of Indian Affairs succeeded in restoring tribal unity and tribal incentive on a wide scale. For the first time in at least three centuries the Indian population began to grow again, and by 1955 the once "vanishing Americans" numbered 400,000.

MINING COUNTRY

The thirty years after the outbreak of the Civil War were to disclose the mineral wealth and organic treasure concealed by the "desert." The earth's most productive wheat lands, once the secret of their cultivation was learned, covered the Dakotas and eastern Montana. In the farther reaches of these states, and in future states to the south and west, spread seemingly boundless grazing lands soon to become the source of most of the world's beef, mutton, hides, and wool. Other plains and mountain regions held some of the world's largest and purest veins of copper and iron ore, some of its most extensive deposits of lead and zinc, and valuable seams of coal.

Beneath the lands of Texas (and elsewhere in the West, as time proved), lay incredibly large fields of petroleum and natural gas.

For generations, the forest-oriented nation which claimed the territory had even less use for its resources than the Indians who roamed it. Americans had plenty of land elsewhere. American needs in fuel and structural parts, the major uses of coal and iron, remained well supplied by the wood that still covered much of the older areas. Copper was almost useless to a nation with little demand for electric wire. Pennsylvania petroleum, burned almost exclusively as an illuminant rather than a fuel remained more than adequate to the pre-automobile age. In America's mid-nineteenth-century economy, conventional investments continued to reward capital adequately; men of means thus were content to leave to prospectors with little standing and less credit the searching out of new opportunities for wealth. Such prospectors hardly concerned themselves with the future requirements of organized society; they followed unflaggingly only the most ancient of lures—the precious metals, gold and silver.

The first prospectors in California had a fine code and fine camaraderie. "Honesty was the ruling passion of '48," wrote one of them. In a year, however, the California crowds thickened, and "murders, thefts, and heavy robberies soon became the order of the day." Conditions grew steadily worse during the 1850s as even the fabulous discoveries at Sutter's Mill and elsewhere began to run thin.

In July 1858, the first claim was staked out in Colorado and in six months 100,000 "yondersiders" from California and "greenhorns" from Kansas, their wagons blazoned "Pike's Peak or Bust," swarmed into the region around present-day Denver. They found gold, but very little of it; many swarmed right out again, their wagons now proclaiming "Pike's Peak and Busted." Some remained to strike it rich in other sections of Colorado; some, as in California, turned to farming, shopkeeping and other activities which developed Colorado's varied economy and aspirations to statehood. Thousands joined the army of prospectors, among them George Pullman who is said to have got the idea for his "sleepers" from miners' double-decked bunks.

For those infected anew with gold fever, failure in Colorado only magnified the rumors of the 'fifties about Nevada. Numerous small Nevada strikes kept up the prospectors' confidence. Then in the spring of 1859, the Comstock Lode bonanza on Davidson Mountain was struck (though it was ten years before its full value was known), and in a few months 20,000 men with their horses, mules, picks, shovels, and pans, their whisky, cards, and camp-following women, had congregated in the wild country around. There they threw up "the wondrous city of Virginia," which looked "as if the clouds had suddenly burst overhead and rained down the dregs of all the flimsy, rickety, filthy little hovels and rubbish of merchandise that had ever undergone the process of evaporation from the earth since the days of Noah."

The Comstock Lode was richer in silver than gold, and as an old Spanish proverb says, "it takes a gold mine to develop a silver mine." In 1868 four men with the equivalent of the required gold mine at last began operations on Davidson Mountain: the miner, John W. Mackay, whose "business is mining—legitimate mining," as he said; the top-flight mine superintendent, James G. Fair, much envied for his "fine nose for ore"; and their two speculating partners from California, James C. Flood and William S. O'Brien. As late as 1867 ancient Mexican methods for reducing "pay dirt" to precious metal had hardly been improved upon. By such methods it cost $50 to get $200 in silver out of a ton of high-grade ore, and even then the yield was but 65 per cent. In the next ten years, new methods cut costs to $10 a ton and upped yields to 85 per cent. Early in the game Mackay and his partners set up their own modern reducing mills. By transforming mining into a big business, they were able to take $150,000,000 from Davidson Mountain. Before it petered out in 1880, the Comstock Lode had yielded a cool $306,000,000.

The foundations of Idaho were laid in 1860 when the cry of gold brought some 15,000 prospectors to the Nez Percé Indian reservation in the Boise district. In 1864 a strike at Last Chance Gulch, modern Helena, brought some 20,000 miners and camp-followers into wild Montana. In 1867 Wyoming provided a short-lived scene of action. In the southwest by 1863 notorious Tombstone had become the center of mining operations in Arizona and

New Mexico. The era of the prospectors' West was drawing to a close when in 1874 gold was discovered on the reservation of the Sioux Indians in their sacred Black Hills of South Dakota. Here, Deadwood grew to rival Tombstone in vice, violence, and lasting fame.

At the start of the next decade the first copper seam was discovered in "the richest hill on earth," conventionally known as Butte, Montana. By 1890 annual copper production, reflecting the spread of electricity, exceeded that of gold in dollar value; by 1900 copper production approached that of gold and silver combined. At this time, aided by the demand for storage batteries, the annual production of lead was nearing that of silver in value. Missouri remained the principal source of lead; but after 1880 sizable quantities came from Colorado and Idaho. In 1901, in time for the commercialization of the automobile, "Black Gold" poured onto the western scene from the unprecedented oil gusher at Spindletop, Texas.

Large amounts of capital were needed to exploit these new metals and minerals. Soon financiers like Henry H. Rogers and the Rockefellers of New York, the Guggenheims of Philadelphia, and the Mellons of Pittsburgh were controlling the policies and profits of the "desert." East and West had again been bound together.

Even before mining became big business, western railroad magnates had taken control of the long-distance hauling of miners and their equipment. As in mining itself, however, this businesslike centralization of function grew only gradually, and before it matured transport and communications enjoyed their own exciting history.

Agitation for rapid cross-country mail deliveries began in 1850, but sectional disputes delayed a decision on the route until 1857. That year, shrewdly choosing the long "oxbow route" to satisfy southern congressmen, James Butterfield and William G. Fargo got the first transcontinental mail contract. Service in their sturdy Concord coaches along the 2,795-mile route west from St. Louis began in September 1858. Passengers were carried on the three-week trip for $200.

By 1858 the firm of Russell, Majors, and Waddell, which had

been organized in 1855 without subsidy, was operating 3,000 "prairie schooners" carrying freight to the West. William H. Russell, one of the partners, was an enthusiast for the central as against the oxbow route to California, and to prove its superiority he organized the "Pony Express." By April 1860, Russell had set up 190 stations between St. Joseph, Missouri, and San Francisco. At each station the mail pouches were switched to a fresh pony and whisked away. At its peak the Pony Express had eighty riders always in the saddle, forty racing west and forty returning. They made the run from the Mississippi to San Francisco in the fantastic time of ten days.

Russell had proved a geographical point, but the costs of the Pony Express made it a business catastrophe. After only a year and a half, moreover, modern technology killed any chance the venture might have had. For in October 1861, the transcontinental telegraph was opened. The Russell firm, meanwhile, suffered setbacks and in 1862 sold out to tough Ben Holladay. In 1866, Holladay sold out to Wells Fargo, which had previously bought out Butterfield. There was no room for competition in this costly business, and Wells Fargo itself survived as a local carrier only by working in conjunction with the railroads.

Though the mining country was wide open and offered a haven to every kind of refugee from society, it early developed its own legal code covering personal crime and property relations. This code was honored more in the breach than in the observance; but not until 1866 did Congress extend its own justice to the West, and then only by declaring that the mining country was free to all, "subject to local customs or rules of miners." This declaration put a premium on vigilantism, but the gradual settlement of the Wild West and the extension to it of transportation and communication facilities eventually strengthened more formal government.

These facilities themselves, nevertheless, offered the desperadoes of the country their last glowing opportunity. Express and mail holdups became daily affairs, while practically with the first railroad western news seemed incomplete if it did not report a "Great Train Robbery" somewhere. Yet the year 1881 saw an end even to this phase of western life and lore. That year the railway and express companies joined with the Governor of Missouri to place such a high price on the head of Jesse and Frank James that one of his own men shot Jesse in the back for the reward.

THE CATTLE KINGDOM

While the violence and brutality of the mining camps and mining towns kept more staid Americans out of the mountain country, the violence and bestiality of the trail, the range, and the cow town kept them off the plains. Tombstone, Arizona, and Deadwood, South Dakota, had nothing on Dodge City, Kansas, the "Cowboy's Capital," where twenty-five men are said to have been killed in the town's first year. Nor were Abilene, Kansas, or Laramie, Wyoming, anything like agricultural market towns. The rancher and the cowboy, like the prospector and the miner, nevertheless, helped claim the Wild West from the Indian and furthered the ultimate settlement of the last frontier.

With the annexation of Texas in 1845, ranching and cow punching came into American life full grown. The bit, bridle, saddle, and spurs, the lariat, chaps, and five-gallon hat of the traditional American cowboy, are all Mexican in origin. Mexicans often did not bother to brand their beasts; thus when Americans from Mississippi, Alabama, and Tennessee began trickling into Texas in the 1820s, many of them simply put their own brands on what they took to be wild herds and set themselves up as "cattle kings." Other Americans, drifting desultorily into Kansas and Nebraska as trappers, traders, soldiers, or sheer adventurers, also gathered up spirited horses and herds of "wild" cattle that had wandered north, and began the range cattle industry in that region. But compared to those of Texas, the northern herds were insignificant.

In the 'fifties some of the more enterprising Texas ranchers tried to drive their cattle to market, westward all the way to Colorado and California and northward to Illinois. But redmen everywhere harassed herds and herders; the few steers that got through arrived so lame, thin, and tough they couldn't command a price even approaching the cost of the venture. While cattlemen awaited more accessible and attractive markets, their herds grew. During the Civil War, Union control of the Mississippi River and its tributaries where stock might water, halted all Texas drives even of a local character, and by 1865 as many as 5,000,000 longhorns crowded the almost limitless Texas range.

Fear of cattle rustlers and horse thieves set the ranchers again looking for markets once the war was over. When they learned that $3 or $4 Texas steers might bring $40 a head in the upper Mississippi Valley where wartime demand had decimated the herds, they decided to try the drive north again. The drives of the 'fifties had been attempted all the way to the abattoirs. Late in 1865, the Missouri Pacific was opened to Sedalia, Missouri, and when the grass turned green on the plains early the following spring, the first of the "long drives" to a railhead town began.

Ill-chosen trails, molestation by Indians and by farmers who had followed the railroad west, and poor facilities at Sedalia all contributed to the failure of these early postwar drives. Then in 1868, seeing a fortune for himself if he could control the place where northern buyers and Texas and western breeders could get together, Joseph M. McCoy, an enterprising Illinois meat dealer, took the first real steps to organize the cattle business. Turned down by the Missouri Pacific when he asked for special rates on bulk shipments of cattle east, McCoy got good terms from the Kansas Pacific to Kansas City and from the Hannibal & St. Jo on to Chicago. Next, after much looking, he picked Abilene on the Kansas Pacific as his first "long drive" terminal. There he built a hotel for the cowboys, and barns, stables, pens, and loading chutes for the cattle. In 1868 Abilene received 75,000 steers. Three years later it handled 700,000, a record that was to stand for a long time. As the Kansas Pacific was extended westward, new towns took the cattle leadership. Ellsworth, Kansas, succeeded Abilene in 1872; Dodge City succeeded Ellsworth three years later. Farther north in Wyoming the Union Pacific also moved into the business first at Cheyenne and then at Laramie.

The "long drive" to the successive railhead cow towns grew into romantic fable. In fact, as one veteran writes, "it was tiresome grimy business." For two months of hazardous travel five or six cowboys, each with pony, lasso, and six-shooter, had to keep under control a thousand head of hungry, thirsty, touchy steers. "The caravan started forth each morning at 'sun-up.' . . . The animals throughout their daylong march, nipped at the grass . . . but at the evening halt they set themselves to a solid meal. . . . Two hours after dark the cattle one by one sank down to sleep, to rise again at midnight and to browse until . . . two o'clock, when all vitality ebbs and the Death Angel frequently calls dying men. . . .

"All through the darkness men of the 'night herd' . . . rode about the animals and constantly serenaded the beasts. . . . This . . . was done partly to hold the cattle under the compelling spell of the human voice, and partly to disabuse from the mind of any fearsome member of the herd suspicion that either a puncher's silhouette against the sky-line or else the noise of his moving pony might represent a snooping dragon. The rider, when 'singing to the cattle,' as his vocal efforts were styled, disgorged all the words he knew set to all the tunes he could remember or invent, but omitted any sound or inflection which might startle. Sacred airs were usual . . . but the words . . . well might have surprised the clergy. . . . Accounts of horse-races, unflattering opinions of the cattle, strings of profanity, the voluminous text on the labels of coffee cans, mere humming sounds . . . were poured on many a night into the appreciative ears of an audience of cloven hoofs. . . . But man and horse were ready to wake like a shot and to act the instant that a steer started to 'roll his tail,' an infallible sign of confident expectation to disregard both distance and time."

The "long drive" even to railhead towns did grown steers as little good as it did the cow punchers. In the 1870s, therefore, when the buffalo were wiped off the plains and with them the Indians, changes followed in the cattle business. Only year-old baby steers were driven to the now open range which extended from western Kansas all the way to Montana. These were then sold to northern "feeders." At little cost the latter would graze the steers on the lush grass for three or four years when they would be prime for the market.

Only after 1878, when the return of prosperity following the crash of 1873 raised beef prices, did the "open-range" cattle industry come into its own. In the next seven or eight years millions of steers and thousands of cattlemen swarmed on the "limitless plains." With water so crucial, "range rights" along a stream became the most precious part of the cattle ranch, and often enough had to be defended with rifles. Even where grazers might respect one another's territory, the cattle didn't; and here again rules had to be established for the recording of brands and the disposal of mavericks. Where ranches, as a rule, covered as many as forty square miles and could not be adequately policed, rustling, of course, became common. To impose law and order was one of the objectives of the numerous stock-growers associations which were organized in the 1870s and which eventually became the hidden governments of the states cut from the range. An important business objective of the associations was to reduce competition by making it difficult for newcomers to become members and dangerous for them to operate without joining up.

Association men were aware of the rapidity with which the range, endless though it seemed, could become overstocked to the peril of all growers. This justified their objectives if not their methods. But nothing could stifle the news of the profits to be made. After four years of virtually free grazing, $5 steers commanded $45 to $60 a head. Prospective ranchers flocked in like prospectors to the mines, and cattle company stocks boomed in America and abroad. Hundreds of Englishmen and Scots came to the range, usually to wind up needing money from home and hence to become the celebrated "remittance men" of western pulp fiction. Between 1879 and 1886 thirty-six "American" cattle companies with a combined capital of $34,000,000 were floated in Great Britain alone. Then the "cattle bubble" burst. By 1885 the open range did in fact become overcrowded, and a series of natural disasters followed. The winter of 1885-86 was one of the most severe in history; the next summer was a veritable furnace. Together this winter and summer destroyed most of the feed and many of the cattle, while the surviving steers proved of such poor quality that, despite the biting world shortage of beef, prices crashed.

Long-term developments at the same time conspired to ruin the range. In the 1880s ever larger numbers of sheep were herded across the plains, making the atmosphere noxious to "cows" and cowboys alike and consuming the roots as well as the precious grass itself.

Farmers, moreover, began homesteading the plains and fencing in the cattle range. They kept their own cattle herds, bred them carefully, regulated their feed, and thus produced a much finer quality of beef than the open range could supply. By 1887 the cowboy had begun to sing,

> I little dreamed what would happen
> Some twenty summers hence
> When the nester came with his wife and kids
> His dogs and his barbed-wire fence.

Fencing in the open range closed out the last frontier.

THE "NESTER" ON THE PLAINS

"These fellows from Ohio, Indiana, and other northern and western states," an old trail driver complained in the 'seventies, "—the 'bone and sinew of the country,' as politicians call them—have made farms, enclosed pastures, and fenced in water holes until you can't rest; and I say D——n such bone and sinew!" Impending changes in western agriculture threatened to end the cattle boom. Perhaps the most important of these changes was the mass production of barbed wire fencing, patented by three different inventors in 1874. One cattleman expressed the feelings of all when he wished that the "man who invented barbed wire had it all around him in a ball and the ball rolled into hell."

The Homestead Act of 1862 had opened the prairies and the plains to free settlement under liberal conditions, but much of the best land was appropriated before homesteaders could get to it. Other circumstances further limited the Homestead Act's usefulness. The quarter-section (160 acres) offered free by the Act was suitable to successful Mississippi Valley farming and would have been lavish in New England. On the arid, treeless plains, a quarter-section was at once too large and too small. The independent settler could not afford the cost of breaking enough of the 160 acres to grow a paying crop, plus the cost of irrigation, buildings, equipment, taxes, and hired help. In 1871 the Department of Agriculture estimated that wood fencing alone for a quarter-section farm cost $1,000 in the treeless West. The large farmer or farming corporation, on the other hand, which could afford to buy costly machinery so useful for cultivating the level expanse of the plains, found that a mere quarter-section hardly justified a fraction of the required investment.

Recognition of these problems prompted the passage of the Timber Culture Act of 1873, while two other measures, ostensibly for similar purposes, were lobbied through later by special interests. These were the Desert Land Act of 1877 and the Timber and Stone Act of 1878. On the theory that trees brought rain, the Timber Culture Act offered an additional quarter-section to the settler who would put at least 40 acres of it into timber. This act proved a farce and was repealed in 1891. The Desert Land Act offered occupancy of a full 640-acre section at twenty-five cents an acre, with the privilege of getting clear title to it in three years at an additional one dollar an acre, provided the holder could prove he had irrigated the plot. Thousands of farmers took the bait but gave up trying to irrigate long before the three years expired.

The Desert Land Act in effect was the cattlemen's ruse for getting private title to the public grazing range. Cattlemen registered thousands of dummy entries in the names of cowhands and then got the latter to testify that they "had seen water on the claim." The Timber and Stone Act was legislation that lumbermen borrowed from the cattlemen's book. Applying to land "unfit for cultivation," this Act offered a maximum of 160 acres of rich timber land in California, Nevada, Oregon, and Washington at $2.50 an acre— "about the price of one good log," as a historian has commented. Since aliens who had simply filed their first citizenship papers were eligible for these grants, a land office business in them was done right in eastern waterfront courthouses. There for from $10 to $50 apiece, thousands of alien seamen were induced to register claims and then sign them over to lumber company agents.

Between 1862 and 1900, 80,000,000 acres appear to have been registered by homesteaders, though even this figure is inflated with dummy registrations by which speculators built up large holdings. In the same period railroads, land companies, and the states which had received grants of federal land for educational purposes sold more than 520,000,000 acres to settlers. For these lands they charged from $2 to $10 an acre, fair prices for these sites which were more likely than free homesteads to be near transportation and markets. The purchasers, moreover, often got credit for equipment as well as land from companies eager to sell.

After 1868 when the Union Pacific neared completion, the railroad placarded Kansas and other states on the edge of the frontier with advertisements calling their lands "Better than a Homestead." In the next decade, this road and the Burlington each spent over a million dollars to advertise their lands abroad. Like all other landed railroads, land companies, and western states, they also sent agents scouring the continent for settlers. Steamship companies engaged in carrying foreigners to the new world abetted the promoters. Though the first settlers in a new region on the moving frontier always came from adjacent states, a few figures indicate the success of overseas advertising campaigns. The census of 1880 reported 73 per cent of Wisconsin's population to be of foreign parentage, 71 per cent of Minnesota's, 66 per cent of the Dakotas', 44 per cent of Nebraska's. In the next decade, a record 5,250,000 immigrants landed in the United States. Many remained in the teeming ports of entry and others got no farther west than the mills of Pittsburgh and Cleveland. Millions, however, found their way to the farmlands of the plains. Between 1860 and 1900 the land held by American farmers more than doubled from 407,000,000 to 841,000,000 acres, while the proportion of land actually under cultivation rose from 40 to almost 50 per cent. The plains and their immigrant settlers contributed markedly to these figures.

But before the plains could be brought under cultivation, obstacles never met before had to be overcome. Not even rude log cabins could be raised on the treeless plains; the first shelters were dank, dark sod huts. For fuel, in a region which covered some of the coldest parts of the country, the first settlers used dried buffalo dung and hay in special stoves designed to burn slowly. An acre of sunflower plants, it was claimed in the 1870s, would yield enough stalks for a year's supply of fuel, and the plant became widely grown. Mechanical well-digging equipment was not made practical until the 1880s, and water for domestic purposes presented another problem to those at any distance from the infrequent rivers. The prevailing aridity posed even greater difficulties for actual farming. Even when wells could be dug the required 200 or 300 feet, there remained the problem of getting the water to the surface. Windmills to harness the power of the strong prevailing breezes caused much talk in the 1870s, but were a long time becoming cheap enough for the average farmer. The ultimate solution, to this day satisfactory neither from the point of view of dependability or cost, was "dry farming." After each precious rainfall, the fields must be harrowed to form a mulch of mud over the deeper moisture on which roots might continue to feed.

The growing crop needed water. But there would have been only a poor crop to nourish had not other innovations been made first. The sod of the plains resisted the old-fashioned plow. In 1868 James Oliver of Indiana began improving the chilled-iron plow but ten years passed before it became an efficient tool. In the same period the mechanical tractor was foreshadowed by the practice of mounting numerous plowshares on a sulky and cutting many furrows at once. After 1874 mechanical grain drills also speeded up planting. In a region battered without warning by hailstorms, wind storms, and flash frosts, however, the farmer's welfare depended less on how much he could plant than on how quickly he could harvest. Only after 1880 did the "cord binder" offer practical assistance. The old time eastern farmer dared not plant more than eight acres of wheat in a season; by 1890 the cord binder and related equipment permitted a single western farmer to count on harvesting 135 acres.

But it took a revolution in wheat culture as well as in milling to make such a harvest worth while. Eastern farmers grew soft-kernel winter wheat which traditionally was milled by grinding the husks between two millstones. These farmers usually planted their crop in September or October and harvested it in June or July. Even the first farmers of Wisconsin and Minnesota, however, had found that the early winters killed the seed before it could sprout. On the plains the winters proved even more severe, and here, in addition, the moisture required by soft winter wheat was lacking.

Spring wheat, planted in May and harvested before the first frosts, was known to farmers before 1860. But the known varieties lacked hardiness, and their tough husks could not be milled economically. In the 1860s, after a long passage from Poland, via Scotland and Canada, a hardy new type of spring wheat appeared on the plains, and by the end of that decade a new milling process suitable to it had been brought over from Hungary. This process employed a series of revolving rollers instead of the old millstones. In 1872 or 1873 Mennonite settlers from the Crimea also introduced into Kansas a hard *winter* wheat known as "Turkey Red." This too became commercially feasible through the new milling process.

Both of these hard wheats soon proved most profitable to the millers and most in demand by bakers. The new milling process, perfected by the development of chilled steel corrugated rollers in 1879, permitted a much higher yield of good flour, and the high gluten content of this product allowed more bread to be made than from like amounts of soft-wheat flour. By 1879 Illinois had led the wheat states for twenty years; by 1899 it had fallen out of the first ten. The leaders then were the hard-wheat states of Minnesota, the Dakotas, Kansas, California, and Nebraska. Oklahoma and northern Texas also were developing rapidly as wheat states.

The epochal improvements in wheat growing and milling naturally put increasing pressure on the cattle range. During the 1870s the farmers more and more loudly demanded that the ranchers fence in their cattle. Ranchers, when not urging the "nesters" to move, demanded that farmers bear the cost of fencing the cattle out. The farmer invasion of the range and the cattle invasion of the farms often brought gun battles to the plains.

Joseph Glidden, one of the three independent holders of the patent, set up the first barbed wire factory in DeKalb, Illinois, in November 1874. The next year Glidden's eastern supplier of ordinary wire bought a half interest in the firm and in 1876 began mass production. That year 3,000,000 pounds of barbed wire were sold at about $20 per hundred pounds; by 1890 the price per hundred was down to $4, and virtually all the arable land of the plains had been fenced in.

Wheat has always been a favorite frontier crop. It pays off on extensive cultivation where land is cheap; it requires much less labor than most other crops; it grows in a tough concentrated form making it eminently "storable, haulable, and saleable." Wheat, more-over, thrives on newly broken soil where humus content is high. Though the settler on the plains produced other commodities such as cattle and sheep, wheat was his staple from the start. Even if nature did not encourage him to grow wheat, the new farm machine technology would have stimulated its extensive cultivation; and all other motivations failing, the farmer's creditors would have pushed him into his most obvious cash crop.

A disastrous series of grasshopper invasions literally ate out the American West early in the 1870s. But soon after, everything seemed to conspire to make the new wheat country take on the characteristics of the El Dorado that the railroad advertisements pictured. Starting in 1875, Europe suffered one harvest failure after another. In 1877-78 the Russo-Turkish War closed Russia's wheat ports and left the rest of the continent more dependent than before on American grain. On the continent as in the United States itself, industrialism was drawing millions from farms to cities where they had to be fed by imports from America. To this may be added the chance factor that for eight years prior to 1886 the plains enjoyed such plentiful rainfall that geologists were predicting the permanent moistening of the region.

The market for wheat in the 1880s was so strong that as American production grew, the prices American farmers received kept rising. One dollar wheat had become a golden reality and its continuance seemed a reasonable expectation. Such prices and prospects encouraged farmers to mortgage their land to the limit to raise cash for expansion. The banks themselves, sharing the current optimism, interpreted the limit liberally.

Wise heads knew the West was riding for a fall. By the mid-1880s, India and Australia had entered the wheat market and Russian production had revived. Tariff barriers were rising in Europe. Overproduction in the United States itself was another ill omen. But as buffalo had drawn the Indian to the virgin West, as gold had drawn the prospector, and grass the rancher, so wheat had drawn the farmer. Prosperity might disappear, but the wheat grower had come to stay, to face the age-old problems of nature as well as an engulfing industrial civilization.

Chapter Ten

Tooth and Claw in the World of Business

Domination of the New South with its pretensions to aristocracy and the New West with its pretensions to self-reliance was only one phase of a revolution in the victorious North that had begun long before the Civil War and has not ended yet.

For half a century before 1860, northern industry had been altering the course of American life. Canals and steam railroads had begun to draw the outlying countryside into the orbits of growing cities. The rise of corporations and of markets for their securities upset old-fashioned ideas of property and its control. The increasing mobilization of machinery in factories revolutionized the terms and conditions of labor. At every stage politically entrenched planters and their commercial allies had sought to obstruct these epochal changes. After 1860 northern captains of industry at last were set free; after the victory of 1865, which they claimed as largely their own, they felt justified in prescribing their objectives and philosophy for the entire nation.

THE CAPITALIST IMPULSE

"The people had *desired* money before his day," said Mark Twain of Jay Gould, "but *he* taught them to fall down and worship it." After the Civil War, the vogue of Herbert Spencer gave pseudo-scientific sanction to this materialist philosophy. Through analogies with Darwinian biology, which took the world by storm in 1859, Spencer undertook to demonstrate that just as nature worked automatically in "selecting" her elite, so society neared perfection to the degree that it allowed its elite free play. "There cannot be

259

more good done," he wrote, "than that of letting social progress go on unhindered; and immensity of mischief may be done in . . . the artificial preservation of those least able to care for themselves." Cupidity Spencer defended as part of the universal struggle for existence; wealth he hallowed as the sign of the "fittest." This was Calvinism conveniently bereft of conscience, a philosophy of success without the saving grace of stewardship.

Most prominent among Spencer's disciples was Andrew Carnegie. The young Scotch Presbyterian had early lost his Christian faith and failed for a long time to discover a substitute justification for his secular calling. "Man must have an idol," he noted in 1868 for his own guidance. "This amassing of wealth is one of the worst species of idolatry—no idol more debasing than the worship of money . . . To continue much longer overwhelmed by business cares and with most of my thoughts wholly upon the way to make more money in the shortest time, must degrade me beyond hope of permanent recovery." Carnegie, nevertheless, was impelled to acknowledge that "I was determined to make a fortune," and "nothing could be allowed to interfere for a moment with my business career." It was on encountering Spencer, he reports in his *Autobiography,* "that light came as in a flood and all was clear. Not only had I got rid of theology and the supernatural, but I had found the truth of evolution. 'All is well since all grows better,' became my motto, my true source of comfort."

"The progress of evolution from President Washington to President Grant," Henry Adams observed, "was alone evidence enough to upset Darwin." But no one listened to the skeptical New Englander. "I perceive clearly," wrote the more sympathetic Walt Whitman, "that the extreme business energy, and this almost maniacal appetite for wealth prevalent in the United States, are parts of amelioration and progress, indispensably needed to prepare the very results I demand. My theory includes riches, and the getting of riches." So confident, indeed, did American businessmen become in the inevitability and benevolence of this theory, that they felt the urge to give its operation an unphilosophical boost. Spencer forbade restrictive, "meddling" legislation; if trusts and combinations proved to be the natural results of free competition, worshipers of competition could not logically prohibit them. But certainly there could be no objection to legislation that furthered the objectives of business success. Unrestricted competition might be the life of trade, but once the "fittest" had proved themselves in such competition, what could be wrong with helping them with government patents, subsidies, tariffs, loans?

After the Civil War, businessmen themselves became more numerous in Congress than at any other time in American history. Until the agricultural depression of the mid-1880s, they and their party colleagues had little trouble voting high tariffs and hard money, which served to heighten the profits and thus the spirit of enterprise. After that, through the rigging of the rules of procedure, little effective regulatory legislation was permitted to reach the floor of Congress. "Czar" Thomas B. Reed, Speaker of the House after 1889, raised the manipulation of these rules to a fine art. After 1903, Speaker "Uncle Joe" Cannon, showed only a shade less virtuosity until he was overthrown in 1910. The Senate, meanwhile, came under the spell of Nelson W. Aldrich, who first appeared there in 1881. Though openly contemptuous of "the purchasables," as Aldrich called the voters and their local party bosses, he was re-elected to four more six-year terms.

Aldrich believed that geographical representation in the government had become anachronistic; he hoped to see the upper chamber, at least, manned officially by senators from each of the great business "constituencies"—steel, coal, copper, railroads, banks, textiles, and the like. In fact if not in theory this millennium had indeed been realized, and from Senator George Hearst, father of William Randolph, it had received its appropriate accolade: "I do not know much about books; I have not read very much," acknowledged the Senator to his colleagues in 1886, "but I have traveled a good deal and observed men and things and I have made up my mind after all my experience that the members of the Senate are the survivors of the fittest."

The Supreme Court also had its Spencerians, though it took some time for them to be heard. All the justices of the Court in 1865 had been born before 1820, when industrialism had scarcely made an impression on American life. Two of them had been born during

Jefferson's first administration, no less than three as long ago as the eighteenth century. It was this archaic court that had interpreted the Fourteenth Amendment so narrowly that the reconstructed states had had no difficulty in curtailing the privileges and immunities of freedmen. At the same time, however, it also permitted the states to regulate business. The only dissenting voice was usually that of Stephen J. Field, at sixty, one of the younger justices.

Field was the first to bring business corporations under the rubric, "persons," in interpreting the Fourteenth Amendment. He also took the next logical step: to declare that no corporate "person" could be deprived of property by a state without "due process of law." Since legislative (or commission) limitations on railroad rates or other business decisions might reduce a corporation's profit or the value of its plant, such limitations, Field held, were unconstitutional under the Fourteenth Amendment. By 1882, the makeup of the Court finally had caught up with the spirit of Field and of much of the country. That year Horace Gray of the industrial state of Massachusetts, a firm believer in progress through Spencerian freedom, was appointed to the Court and for the next twenty years dominated its proceedings. In that period many of the earlier regulatory decisions were overturned.

In 1902, ironically enough, Gray was succeeded by Oliver Wendell Holmes, one of whose more famous observations, made in a dissenting opinion in 1905, was that "The Fourteenth Amendment does not enact Mr. Herbert Spencer's *Social Statics.*" Before that, however, and for some years thereafter as well, the Court acted as if the Amendment had. Between 1890 and 1910 only nineteen Supreme Court decisions based on the Fourteenth Amendment involved Negroes, while 289 dealt with corporations. Most of these helped sustain capitalist impulse after the Civil War.

THE WARTIME SEEDBED

At the outset of the war in 1861, northern business had been depressed, and on the whole it remained so for another year and a half. By the end of 1862, however, a general boom had begun which weathered the end of hostilities and continued for almost another decade. Writing from Pittsburgh in 1863, Judge Thomas

Mellon, the founder of the aluminum fortune, declared that "such opportunities for making money had never existed beiore in all my former experience." When, that year, his elder son James, then a young lawyer in Milwaukee, asked parental permission to enlist, the judge ordered, "Don't do it. It is only greenhorns who enlist. Those who are able to pay for substitutes do so, and no discredit attaches." And he added, "It is not so much the danger as disease and idleness and vicious habits. . . . I had hoped my boy was going to make a smart, intelligent businessman and was not such a goose as to be seduced from his duty by the declamations of buncombed speeches." The judge carried the day, and indeed he himself resigned from the bench in 1870 to resume business life.

In the same period, Armour and Morris laid the foundations for their great meat fortunes, Pillsbury for his in flour, Rockefeller for his in oil. It was army demand that first stimulated the mass production of machine-made shoes and men's ready-to-wear clothes. The wartime depletion of farm manpower pushed the demand for reapers far above the productivity of the farm machinery factories. One of the greatest gainers from the wartime boom was the telegraph industry. At the war's end, Western Union was operating 50,000 miles of telegraph line, and a merger in 1866 brought this figure up to 75,000.

The war boom in the North gave a stimulus to extravagance which set the tone for the "gilded age" to follow. More significant from a business standpoint was the stimulus windfall gains gave to speculation, and speculation to the availability of capital for investment in new enterprises. During the war, a writer in *Harper's Monthly* wrote of the New York Stock Exchange:

> The city exchanges and their approaches are already crowded with a mass so frenzied by the general passion for gain that almost all regard for personal safety and respect for personal propriety seems lost. . . . The number of brokers has more than quadrupled in a few months, such has been the enormous increase of stock-jobbing. Their aggregate business, in the city of New York alone, has arisen from twenty-five to more than a hundred millions a day.

At about the same time, the *Independent* reported that in New York alone there were "several hundred men worth $1,000,000 and some worth $20,000,000 while twenty years back there had not been five men in the whole United States worth as much as $5,000,000 and not twenty worth over $1,000,000."

The year after the war ended, the *Commercial and Financial Chronicle* summarized the lasting consequences of the war boom: "There is an increasing tendency in our capital to move in larger masses than formerly. Small business firms compete at more disadvantage with richer houses, and are gradually being absorbed into them."

If the end of the war found the older North with bigger ideas than ever and more complex institutions for carrying them out, it also found the new West teeming with grandiose opportunities and men equal to them. Of Leland Stanford, one of the builders of the Central Pacific Railroad who had gone to California from New York in the 1850s, an enemy once said: "No she-lion defending her whelps or a bear her cubs, will make a more savage fight than will Mr. Stanford in defense of his material interests." The country was now full of fighting men like Stanford.

THE GREAT RAILROAD BOOM

More than any other kind of business activity, railroad building and railroad operation dominated the boom after the Civil War. Actual construction employed more capital and more men than any other industry; it also created a vast market for steel rails and for other iron and steel products such as machinery, tools, car trucks, and wheels. The demand for railroad ties and wood for rolling stock revolutionized the lumber industry. The need for provisions, clothing, and blankets for the army of construction workers simply extended the markets that the great meat packers, shoe manufacturers, and textile factories had found among the wartime army of soldiers. Even the transportation of Irish "paddies" and Chinese "coolies" from overseas to work on the railroad noticeably stimulated ocean commerce.

Though railroad construction was held back during the Civil War, about 4,000 miles of lines were built. Between 1865 and the crash of 1873, 30,000 miles of new track were opened. Most of these were in the East and the Old Northwest where trunk lines were being extended to the Mississippi valley and a network of feeder lines opened up. Practically all of this building was privately financed through security issues floated mainly on the New York Stock Exchange. None of it had any land grant concessions; little of it had other government assistance.

As important as railroad building in the older areas was railroad consolidation. By putting together a string of independent roads Commodore Vanderbilt extended the New York Central to Buffalo in 1869. The next year he added the Lake Shore and Michigan Southern and completed the coveted link with Chicago. The Commodore, a notable system builder, probably was also the ablest railroad manager of the period. In 1871 he opened the first Grand Central Depot in New York from which passenger trains made the 965-mile run to Chicago in the then incredible time of twenty-four hours. By 1870 the Pennsylvania Railroad also reached Chicago, and in 1871 it leased a connection from its old terminus in Philadelphia to the key city of New York.

The Erie and Baltimore & Ohio, the other two trunk lines, suffered in the growing competition. The Erie became a stock-manipulator's football, kicked around by successive managements under Daniel Drew, Jim Fisk and Jay Gould. The Baltimore & Ohio had excellent and aggressive management under president John W. Garrett, but it failed to reach New York. In the South and Middle West consolidation also was the rule. Cincinnati became the major link between the two sections.

More spectacular than railroad construction and consolidation in the older areas were the transcontinentals. After a decade of surveys, debates, discussions, and sectional threats, in 1862 Congress chartered the Union Pacific to build westward across the continent from Omaha, Nebraska. Soon after it granted to the Central Pacific, a California corporation chartered in 1861, the privilege of building eastward from Sacramento. To both companies Congress made land grants of unprecedented generosity. The companies were also to receive lavish loans for each mile of track actually laid. In return these roads, like others that received government assistance, were required to carry the mail at low rates and to be on call for the movement of troops.

Despite government guarantees both companies had great difficulty in raising money to begin construction. Between December 1862, and February 1863, the Central Pacific, which was financed largely in the Far West, maintained a stock-selling office in San Francisco and in that period could sell only twelve or fifteen $1,000 shares. Charles Crocker, of the Central Pacific's "Big Four" then went to Virginia City, Nevada, the mining El Dorado, to sell stock. This is what he reported: "They wanted to know what I expected the road would earn. I said I did not know, though it would earn good interest on the money invested, especially to those who went in at bed rock. 'Well,' they said, 'do you think it will make 2 per cent a month?' 'No,' said I, 'I do not.' 'Well,' they answered, 'we can get 2 per cent a month for our money here,' and they would not think of going into a speculation that would not promise that at once." The Union Pacific, promoted mainly by eastern capitalists, had little better luck in New York, Boston, or elsewhere.

Both companies managed to begin construction on a shoe string in 1863, and the next year they faced failure. Only a new law in 1864 saved them. This measure doubled each road's land grant. More important, Congress agreed to accept a second mortgage as security for the promised loans, thus allowing the roads to offer the private money market new first mortgage bonds with their lands as collateral. The new bonds sold better than the old in Europe as well as at home. Even so, large amounts of Union and Central Pacific securities and those of other roads in the distant West had to be disposed of to the towns, cities and states along the route. Some ambitious local governments gladly bought the bonds; others bought them under pressure of blackmail and bribery. About $500,000,000 in railroad securities were disposed of to public bodies. Land grants aggregating the size of Texas also were made by local governments to favored lines.

The new law of 1864 was eased through Congress by the distribution to influential members of stock in Crédit Mobilier, the construction company which was to build the Union Pacific. The California Big Four, made up of Crocker, Stanford, Collis P. Huntington, and Mark Hopkins, organized a similar construction company to build the Central Pacific. Construction companies had been used earlier in the building of canals, but the stakes this time were much higher and the procedure more questionable. By means of such companies, a Congressional investigation later reported, "the persons who under the guise of a corporation that was to take the contract to build the road held complete control of the corporation for which the road was to be built." This investigation disclosed that Crédit Mobilier was paid $73,000,000 by the Union Pacific for an estimated $50,000,000 worth of work, the difference going to the identical directors of both companies. The Big Four's construction company was paid $121,000,000 for work evaluated at $58,000,000.

The chance to make such fortunes, shady though they were, before any track was open to traffic was what impelled the promoters to push the construction of the roads. By the spring of 1869, when the Union Pacific had laid 1,086 miles of track, and Central Pacific 689 miles, the roads met at Ogden, Utah. Although both roads had to be virtually rebuilt some years later, the feat of crossing the wild plains and the enormous mountain ranges remains one of the great engineering accomplishments of history.

Before the crash of 1873 three other transcontinentals had been chartered and given land by the federal government. Of these only the Northern Pacific was ever completed to the coast, and its arrival in Oregon was delayed until 1881. In 1885 the Boston-financed Atchison, Topeka and Santa Fe completed its route to California. The last of the great transcontinentals, built largely without government aid, was James J. Hill's Great Northern. Hill had come to St. Paul from Canada in 1856 and at the end of twenty years had become a transportation agent for Mississippi traffic between the United States and Canada. The crash of 1873 had hurt the small St. Paul and Pacific Railroad, and in 1878 Hill got the help of Canadian financiers to acquire the line. By 1890 he and his associates had pushed 2,775 miles west through North Dakota and Montana, and in 1893 the Great Northern reached Puget Sound.

By then, the United States had the immense total of 170,000 miles of railroad capitalized at almost $10,000,000,000. In 1867 the railroads did a total of $330,000,000 worth of business; by 1893 this figure was $1,200,000,000. Along with the growth in mileage, investment, and volume, came many improvements in service and safety. In 1864 George M. Pullman built the first sleeping car. Four years later, George Westinghouse introduced the air brake. By 1875 the refrigerator car had been developed, especially for carrying meat. Succeeding years saw the acceptance of the standard gauge throughout the country, the shift from wood-burning to coal-burning engines, from iron to heavy steel rails.

As the railroads improved their speed, service, and safety, other transportation systems declined. The competitive practices of railroad managers furthered their success. Where water rivals were present, as on the Mississippi, the Lakes, canals, and the ocean coastal routes, the railroads regularly cut their own rates even below cost to get the available traffic. Whatever losses were incurred at such places the railroads recouped by charging exorbitant rates at noncompetitive inland stations.

THE INDUSTRIAL NATION

Railroading was but the first factor among many that made the United States industrial leader of the world. Though less dramatic, the widespread use of the corporate form in business, which facilitated the amassing of capital from domestic and foreign sources for single industrial objectives, significantly aided American economic growth. By limiting the liability of capitalists to their actual investments and keeping their personal fortunes safe in the event of misfortunes to their companies, the corporation encouraged risk-taking and the development of resources which might otherwise have remained dormant.

The corporate form had many questionable attributes. It enabled unscrupulous plungers to employ other people's money in nefarious schemes. By making it easy to separate the ownership of a company from its management, it encouraged both to evade social responsibility. The corporation put the impersonal stockholder where the resident owner-manager used to be; it put the statistical profit and the statistical dividend ahead of the welfare of the worker and the community. Moreover, since corporate charters themselves were often political grants with special favors and since corporate business was often large enough to impinge on politics in other ways, business graft paid out by corporations grew to much greater proportions than would have been possible under a regime of small, personally owned enterprises. But these conditions were the defects of a system which, while it was extraordinarily wasteful of both natural and human resources, nevertheless added immensely to both natural and human wealth and eventually to social welfare.

The development of industrial corporations led, in turn, to the rapid expansion of the activities of the stock market after the Civil War, and was, in return, stimulated by this expansion. Until 1929 the stock market was the pulse of industry. It created a vast and ready money market for new enterprises and for the expansion or consolidation of old firms. When the stock market and the associated money market was vigorous and healthy, business was likely to be humming. The confidence a lively market inspired helped to keep business strong. When that confidence was misplaced, the market felt it first and thus served as a barometer of storms ahead. Without the stock market, for all its faults, American industry could not have grown with the speed and resiliency it has displayed.

While the daring, deviltry, and defiance of leading entrepreneurs and speculators promoted the huge expansion of American industry after the Civil War, engineers and production men contributed their share. These men often were in conflict with the business leaders for whom they worked; where they wanted to build the best plant and make the best product, the businessman often wanted to make only the quickest profit, and not infrequently the two objectives met head on. Nevertheless it was in this postwar epic that some of the greatest technological gains were made, and that new productive uses were found for inventions of earlier periods. Invented in 1846, Elias Howe's sewing machine waited until the Civil War to be adapted to factory production of ready-to-wear clothes and shoes. Electricity was known in the eighteenth century, but it was not harnessed to industry until the 1870s. The Bessemer process for making steel was invented in America by William Kelly in 1847, nine years before the Englishman, Henry Bessemer, sought United States patents for a similar process and the "converter" in which to employ it. But not until 1866 did Bessemer steel find general commercial use. Thirty-six thousand patents had been granted to American inventors between the opening of the Patent Office in 1790 and 1860. In the 1870s alone, 140,000 patents were granted, and in the 1890s the figure rose above 300,000.

Nowhere was the spirit of innovation, enterprise, and growth more evident than in the newest industry of all, the production and refining of oil. This industry also produced John D. Rockefeller, the toughest competitor in the country with the clearest grasp of the idea that the natural end of competition is monopoly. "This movement," Rockefeller himself said somewhat later:

> was the origin of the whole system of modern economic administration. It has revolutionized the way of doing business all over the world. The time was ripe for it. It had to come, though all we saw at the moment was the need to save ourselves from wasteful conditions. . . . The day of combination is here to stay. Individualism has gone, never to return.

Born in 1839, Rockefeller, at twenty, had entered into partnership with an Englishman, Maurice B. Clark, as wholesalers of grain, hay, and meat in Cleveland. The business flourished during the Civil War, by the end of which Rockefeller had a fortune of approximately $50,000. The partnership had ventured in oil as early as 1862. In 1865 Rockefeller and Clark dissolved their business, and Rockefeller went into the oil business with Samuel Andrews who knew something of refining.

By then the knowledge that "rock oil" had a bright industrial future was more than ten years old. Seepages of oil had been noted in many parts of the world for centuries. Gradually it gained a mystical reputation as a medicine. In the United States early in the 1850s Samuel M. Kier, in Venango County, Pennsylvania, successfully marketed the local seepages as a cure-all. But Kier had also begun to refine some of the surface oil into kerosene. He also designed lamps to burn it conveniently, and he advertised kerosene widely enough to prepare the market for the new lamp fuel. Whales had grown scarce and whale oil, the world's major illuminant, threatened to soar to $5 a gallon.

Kier did not know how to find supplies of oil sufficiently large to meet a demand which could become tremendous. The first practical steps toward this accomplishment were taken by a young Dartmouth graduate, George H. Bissell, who sent "Colonel" E. L. Drake to the Pennsylvania oil region to begin the first deliberate drilling in 1857. Such a novel enterprise encountered scorn and difficulties, but in August 1859, "Drake's Folly" near Titusville, Pennsylvania, at last gushed in.

Oil is quite appropriately known as "black gold," not only for the fortunes it made but also because of its lure for the prospector. By 1864 wildcatters, as oil prospectors were called, had so covered the district around Titusville with oil derricks that annual production exceeded 2,000,000 barrels. Eight years later the oil regions covered 2,000 square miles in Pennsylvania, West Virginia, and Ohio, and annual production had soared to 40,000,000 barrels. Organized in Cleveland with a capital of a million dollars in 1870, Rockefeller's Standard Oil Company was refining a fifth of the total output.

Where many of the early producers and refiners were taking 100 per cent profits and living high, as wildcatters and prospectors often do, Rockefeller was satisfied with dividends of 15 to 30 per cent. The rest of the profits he reinvested in the business. In its first two years Standard Oil's capitalization rose 150 per cent. Unchallenged in Cleveland, the company controlled about 20 per cent of the refining facilities of the entire country. In 1872 Rockefeller helped organize the South Improvement Company with the objective of capturing the other 80 per cent. His method was simple. In addition to rebates on his own shipments, he demanded that the railroads, in exchange for his own voluminous business, pay him as well a portion of the rates collected from the other refiners. Word of this proposal leaked out and the South Improvement scheme had to be abandoned. The business panic the next year, however, so weakened refiners already overextended in trying to compete with Rockefeller that in succeeding years he was able to buy up their plants at favorable prices. By 1879 Rockefeller had quietly completed his arrangements with the railroads and the new pipe-line systems, and controlled about 90 per cent of the refining capacity of the country and most of the world market for his products.

Similar tendencies were observable in other basic American industries after the war, though their development was much slower than Rockefeller's. Not until 1867 did steel produced by the Bessemer process challenge the better grades of iron in the American market, and not until 1870, under protection of new high tariffs, did American steel rails challenge England's. Early in the 1870s the rich iron ranges of the Lake Superior region were opened. The steel industry's greatest surge, however, came only after Andrew Carnegie dedicated himself to it.

After a successful railroad career, Carnegie entered the steel business in 1872, but held off from the Bessemer process. "Pioneering doesn't pay a new concern," he said; "we must wait until the process develops." A trip to England the next year convinced him of the soundness of Bessemer's method, and on his return he could talk of nothing else. He promptly organized a new firm, Carnegie, McCandless & Company, and built the J. Edgar Thomson Steel Works near Pittsburgh, shrewdly named after the president of the Pennsylvania Railroad. On terms of complete intimacy with Vanderbilt, Huntington, Gould, and other railroad men, including Tom Scott of the Pennsylvania for whom he had worked for many years, Carnegie ignored the depression and "went out," as he said, "and persuaded them to give us orders."

Carnegie opined at one time that "the man who has money during a panic is a wise and valuable citizen." Speaking of the depression after 1873, he added, "so many of my friends needed money, that they begged me to repay them [for their stock]. I did so and bought out five or six of them. That was what gave me my leading interest in this steel business." A British Iron Trade Commission reported some time later on Carnegie's further achievements: "Modern iron making . . . became firmly established [in America] when Andrew Carnegie . . . recognized . . . the necessity for the successful iron producer to control his own material, and it gained international importance when this wonderful man joined to plants and mines the possession of railroads and ships."

By 1890 Carnegie was described as being in "almost absolute control of the steel-rail business in the Pittsburgh district." By then three other steel giants, the Tennessee Coal and Iron Company in the South, the Illinois Steel Company in the Middle West, and the Colorado Fuel and Iron Company in the mountain region, had grown up as if in readiness for the colossal merger of 1901 which created the United States Steel Corporation.

THE INDUSTRIAL DISCIPLINE

The business epoch that closed with the panic of 1873 was the most productive the world had yet seen. When prosperity returned after 1878 the new giant firms that had been created during the depression put the unprecedented productivity of the earlier decade altogether to shame. In virtually all industries, moreover, productivity increased more than investment and much more than employment. There were two major reasons for this. The first was the steady improvement in power supply and in the application of science to production. Not only was invention given renewed impetus, but whole new realms of science, such as chemistry, were yielding their treasures to industry.

The second major reason for the leap in productivity lay in the reorganization of the manufacturing process itself. We have already noted the development of manufacture by interchangeable parts and assembly-line techniques. Now specialization of processes and machines was carried forward. The degree to which this was pushed is clear from the manufacture of shoes. Once one man made the entire shoe. In the 1880s, ranging alphabetically from "binders, blockers, boot-liners, and beaters-out" to "taggers, tipmakers, turners, and vampers," shoe-making involved about sixty-five distinct factory tasks.

Such intensive specialization made it possible to reduce the cost of production greatly—but only when plants were operated at or near their maximum capacity. And operation at this level fre-quently was suicidal. The opening of a new railroad line, a boom in immigration, a burst of exports, a rise in the protective tariff, any promise of a new market led to expansion and mechanization. But each new market was soon exploited, and left in its wake more costly plant and equipment (usually purchased with borrowed money on which interest continually had to be paid) available for work but with no work to do. Thus the *Bulletin* of the American Iron and Steel Association said in 1884, "Indeed it might almost be rated the exception for half the works in condition to make iron to be in operation simultaneously." The National Association of Stove Manufacturers reported in 1888: "It is a chronic case of too many stoves and not enough people to buy them."

This was a constant hazard of American business life. One consequence was the closing of many independent plants. In 1880, the country had almost 2,000 woolen mills; by 1890, only 1,300. In 1880 there were 1,900 manufacturers of agricultural implements; in 1890, only 900. A second consequence was the movement toward pools, trusts, and holding companies by which a few firms could control output, prices, and market areas of entire industries so that a satisfactory level of profits would be assured to the survivors of the competitive struggle.

Pools usually were created in emergencies, and collapsed when the emergency passed. They allowed independent entrepreneurs to retain a semblance of their precious individuality and to express it if need be. This was both their attraction and their flaw. When pools failed, they were supplanted, typically, by trusts, of which the first in this epoch was that organized by Rockefeller in 1879 and reorganized in 1882. By the trust device the stock of many competing companies is turned over to a mutually agreed upon group of trustees in exchange for trustee certificates. Ownership of the stock remains in the original hands, but management of the enterprises represented by it is concentrated in the hands of a single board of trustees. The decade after the founding of the Standard Oil trust saw the formation of the Cottonseed Oil trust, the Salt trust, the Sugar trust, the Leather trust, the Cordage trust, and many others. Not all were strictly trust arrangements, but this became the characteristic epithet for any large combination whose objective was to restrain cutthroat competition.

Of the so-called Sugar trust, Judge Barrett of the Supreme Court of New York once said: "It can close every refinery at will, close some and open others, limit the purchases of raw material, artificially limit the production of refined sugar, enhance the price to enrich themselves and their associates at the public expense, and depress the price when necessary to crush out and impoverish a foolhardy rival." Many other evils were attributed to the trusts, not the least being the political power implicit in such huge and over-bearing organizations. In time, moreover, many persons came to question whether the trusts actually achieved the economies of large-scale operation that their organizers claimed would benefit the public. Yet the trust supplied a viable business answer to the problems of brutally competitive companies. Similar situations faced business in the rising industrial nations abroad and similar solutions were tried. In Europe such arrangements usually had the overt sanction of the state. In the United States where free competition had become the accepted path to progress, the government was forced to give tacit sanction to consolidation while at the same time new legislation seemed to impose restraints on the monopolistic tendencies of business combinations.

The American trusts of the 1880s and early 1890s were insignificant compared to those organized after the crash of 1893. Still the new centralized enterprises presented unusual problems of control. Among these were the sheer mechanics of transmitting directions and results between a central board of directors and scattered plants. More significant were problems of financing the greatly enlarged operations. In time mechanical problems were solved by the invention or improvement of office machines and methods. New specialists in the money markets, mainly the growing insurance companies and the investment bankers, met the enlarged financial requirements of big business.

Among the new office devices were the typewriter, which first appeared in 1867, and the office adding machine, made practical in 1888. More fundamental were the expansion of telegraph facilities and development of the telephone. By 1878 Western Union operated 195,000 miles of telegraph lines and had control of 80 per cent of the telegraph business. In 1881, at a cost of nearly $25,000,-000, the company bought out its two main competitors and their 200,000 miles of wires. This accomplished, President Norvin Green told his stockholders that Western Union "has attained such magnitude and strength that it is no longer necessary to buy off any opposition. Competition may be a popular demand, and it may be good policy on the part of your Company to indulge competing lines between the principal points. This would not materially interfere with remunerative dividends." How wrong he was became clear in two years when John W. Mackay, the Comstock Lode millionaire, organized the Commercial Cable Company and in 1884 laid two new transatlantic cables. These competed for overseas business with Western Union. Soon after, Mackay set up the Postal Telegraph Company to compete for overland business. A disastrous rate war forced the two wire services to agree to end effective competition in 1887.

A strike in 1883 which shut down telegraph wires called the attention of the country to the fact that the telegraph, as *Harper's Weekly* said at the time, had "come to be as . . . important as the . . . mail." So central had it become, indeed, that by 1900 seventy-five bills demanding the establishment of a competing government system had been introduced in Congress. Such bills never passed; one reason was the friendly relations between the company and government officials. "A liberal use of the franking privilege," a government committee reported in 1900, "gives the corporation power in legislation."

In 1876 Alexander Graham Bell patented the telephone. The next year Western Union, which first scorned Bell's invention as an "electrical toy," decided it had better enter the telephone business. Backing a rival patent by Elisha Gray, Western Union organized the American Speaking Telephone Company. It proceeded to use all its political influence to block franchises the Bell Company was trying to obtain from localities, and it succeeded in keeping the new system out of the railroads altogether. Under the direction of Theodore N. Vail, the Bell Company was not awed by these activities and proceeded to sue Western Union for infringement of patents. Its case was so good that the telegraph company settled out of court in 1879. By then Western Union had hastily set up some 56,000 telephones in fifty-five cities, and for the equipment and franchises in these cities Bell paid handsomely.

In the next ten years the Bell Company was beset by competitors, some legitimate, some simply blackmailers. To buy them out cost the Bell system about $225,000,000. At the same time improvements in the telephone instrument and in the wires patented by the Bell Company kept it invulnerable to competition. One of the major innovations was the development of long-distance telephone service after 1884. To expand this business, the Bell directors set up a new corporation, the American Telephone and Telegraph Company. In 1900 this became the overall holding company of the entire Bell system, with a capitalization of $250,000,000. At that time 1,350,000 Bell telephones were in use in the United States. Service still cost New Yorkers as much as $240 a year. At such rates, A. T. & T.'s profits were the envy of all the industries it served.

THE LIMITS OF LABOR ORGANIZATION

In order to accumulate the immense capital required for the exploitation or importation of coal, iron, and other basic raw materials, and for the construction of railroads, factories, and power machinery, great social sacrifices have to be made. These naturally fall most heavily on farmers and workers since such groups constitute the overwhelming mass of the population. Even in free countries these groups have traditionally borne their burdens with little protest. Often enough, silence among industrial workers has resulted from poverty itself, from poor nourishment, ill health, overwork, and a pervasive lack of energy and aspiration, and from the formidable political, legal, economic, and social forces arrayed against them.

Nevertheless the history of industrialism is also the history of labor organization. In the early days of the factory system in the United States the goals of the few and scattered labor unions were more political and social than economic. Their objectives were not so much to improve working conditions as to enlarge opportunities so that their members would soon be able to work for themselves, not for others. They demanded abolition of imprisonment for debt, of chartered "monopolies," and of compulsory militia service. But the "first and most important . . . object for which they were contending," as one group said in 1829, was free public education for all. By this means their children would be enabled to take their independent places in society. The panic of 1837 destroyed the early labor movement, and the rapid territorial and agricultural expansion of the country in the following twenty years offered few opportunities to rebuild it before the panic of 1857.

Unions flourish, normally, during prosperity when labor is acutely in demand. The Civil War boom in the North (enhanced, as far as labor was concerned, by the recruitment of many workers into the armed forces) thus spurred labor organization, and in the postwar prosperity union membership reached a peak. Three of the four Railroad Brotherhoods were organized in this period. The earliest national labor organization in the United States was the National Labor Union, formed in Baltimore in 1866 under the leadership of W. H. Sylvis. At its height in 1872 this organization represented about 650,000 workers. But there were no workers among its leadership and its objectives—political action, monetary reform, social welfare legislation—were farfetched.

The crash of 1873 put the National Labor Union and virtually all other labor organizations out of business. The trough of the depression was not reached until 1877. In that year, following a series of earlier pay cuts, unorganized railroad workers across the country struck spontaneously against new wage slashes. Violence flared from New York to St. Louis, and when local militia in many areas fraternized with the workers and refused to fire on them, federal troops were called out. More than a hundred persons were killed in the strike, but after two weeks the workers capitulated. The Railroad Brotherhoods played an insignificant role in the uprising. The repression of union activities following it was so severe that by 1878 fewer than 50,000 American workers were organized.

A second national labor organization had been created in 1869 in Philadelphia under the leadership of Uriah S. Stephens, a tailor. This was the Noble Order of the Knights of Labor, a secret, fraternal society whose major aim, again, was not to fight for better working conditions in the factories but to organize the entire country into a chain of co-operatives owned and operated by the workers. Everyone was welcome to the Knights, Negro and white, immigrant and native, skilled and unskilled. But it made only halting progress until the energetic machinist, Terence V. Powderly, became Grand Master in 1878, on the eve of the return of prosperity. Powderly ended the Knights' secrecy, made its stand known on political issues of the day, and set up as many as thirty co-operatives in manufacturing, mining, and distribution.

Powderly would not stand for strikes and other labor violence. But many of the unions affiliated with the Knights thought otherwise. When in 1885 a number of such unions struck Jay Gould's railroads and forced the hated speculator to recall a wage cut and rehire union men he had fired, the Knights' fame spread like wildfire. Within a year, despite himself, Powderly found his organization grown from 100,000 to more than 700,000 men. The collapse of the Knights, however, was not far off. On May 3, 1886, during a strike at the McCormick Harvester Company in Chicago, anarchists were holding a public meeting at Haymarket Square in the vicinity. Someone—it has never been established that he was an anarchist—threw a bomb that killed a policeman. In the riot that followed, seven more policemen and four civilians were killed. The Knights had nothing to do with the riot, but the organization had become associated in the public mind and in the minds of many of its members with labor agitation to which the riot was attributed. The public rebelled, many members quit, and dissension in the organization hastened its end. Powderly's co-operatives, meanwhile, floundered.

One factor that speeded the Knights' disintegration was the existence of a competing organization to which many of its disaffected members could turn. This was the American Federation of Labor, founded in 1881 by the London-born, New York cigarmaker, Samuel Gompers. The Federation was a union of craft unions, the way the United States was a union of states. It had no interest in the Negro, the unskilled, the ordinary immigrant. Member unions had to adhere to a rigorous code: they must employ full-time professional organizers to enlarge and discipline their memberships; and dues (a share of which went to support the parent A. F. of L.) must be collected regularly to finance ordinary operations and strikes.

The Federation, in its early days, dallied with political programs and sheltered some socialist thinkers. But Gompers quickly set the tone of business unionism. The welfare of labor, he believed, was inextricably connected with the welfare of capital; the goal of the A. F. of L. under his leadership and after was to employ the major weapons of labor—the strike, the boycott, picketing, and so forth —to gain concrete goals without overthrowing or reforming the system. These goals included shorter hours, higher wages, improved working conditions, above all, recognition by industrial corporations of the union, collective bargaining, and the "closed shop" for the affiliated crafts. By 1900 considerable progress had been made. Membership had been pushed to 550,000. Even the Carnegie Steel Company had recognized the union in 1890 (though the A. F. of L. was thrown out in 1892 after a bloody strike at the Company's Homestead plant). Elsewhere many craft union members had gained the eight-hour day and higher wages as well.

Homestead was not the only brutal strike in which the A. F. of L. became embroiled. After the panic of 1893 workers all over the country fought violently against loss of jobs, pay cuts, the stretching out of hours, and other business practices. One of the worst of the thousands of strikes of the depression years occurred at the company town of Pullman, near Chicago, where the builder of railroad sleeping cars owned the stores, the power plant, the workers' houses and everything else. Here wages were average, rents high, store prices exorbitant. In 1894 Pullman fired a third of his labor force, cut the wages of most of the rest by 40 per cent, but failed to reduce house rents or any other workers' costs. The Pullman workers walked out, encouraged by Eugene V. Debs' American Railway Union. In sympathy Debs men refused to move any Pullman cars on the railroads. Violence quickly developed and President Cleveland sent federal troops nominally to protect the mails in the Chicago area, but actually to break the strike. The Pullman workers, Debs, and affiliated A. F. of L. crafts lost the strike; moreover, the attendant violence cost them the support of the public, and made it easier for corporations to use their own traditional weapons against striking unions: the blacklist, the lockout, the employment of armed strikebreakers, factory espionage, court injunctions.

"When bad men combine," Powderly said in 1878, quoting Edmund Burke, "the good must associate, else they will fall, one by one, an unpitied sacrifice in a contemptible struggle." In the next two decades the "bad men" of business had combined in huge and growing corporations which each year employed a growing proportion of the industrial labor force. But despite the A. F. of L. —or possibly because of its limited nature and aspirations—the "good men" of labor clung to traditional individualism and suffered for it. By 1898 more than 17,000,000 persons worked in American factories. Of this number, a mere 500,000 were members of labor unions. Every phase of common and statute law continued to discourage labor organization and the use of labor's weapons in industrial conflict. But labor itself had scarcely awakened to its opportunities.

THE POLITICAL WEAPON

The severe conditions for survival in the brutally competitive business world of the 1870s and 1880s go far toward explaining many of the social evils that flowed from the extraordinary economic expansion of those decades. Explanation, however, was lost on many who felt that the new industrial community conspired to grind them down. Staple farmers in the South and West felt especially injured after their incomes began to fall steadily in the late 1880s despite their own unprecedented productivity. It did little good to tell them that the railroads were cutting each other's throats in highly competitive areas, when the farmers themselves happened to be in regions where monopolistic conditions permitted the railroads to recoup their losses. Nor were such farmers likely to be convinced that rough industrial rivalry forced businessmen to combine in trusts for self-preservation when the upshot for the man on the land was simply higher prices. The protective tariff, in turn, might have been essential to the success of many American industries in their early stages, but to the unhappy husbandmen protection seemed but a vicious device. Although the farmer sold at low prices in a free world market, he was forced to purchase his manufactured goods at prices artificially kept up at home.

Perhaps worst of all was the apparent manipulation of the national monetary system. With commitments made for years in advance, business insisted on a stable currency. But in a country like the United States, with populations growing explosively and productivity per man rising even faster, a stable currency was certain to be deflationary. As money became relatively scarce, its value rose; as the value of money rose prices fell. This indeed was one of the factors that drove businessmen toward consolidation. But individual farmers could hardly organize as efficiently as industrialists especially since the farmers were at the mercy of world conditions while industry could do much to regulate the environment in which it lived at home.

In the 1870s and 1880s business politics sought to keep the protective tariff as high as the public would tolerate and to maintain the flow of public largesse to the railroads. Gradually, however, business came under political attack from the frustrated farmers of the West and South. First organized in the Granger movement in 1869, and then in the Alliance movement of the 1880s, the farmers succeeded in forcing the states to enact laws regulating railroad rates and outlawing trusts. They also forced state legal departments to initiate suits to break up monopolistic combinations.

At the same time farmers organized co-operatives of their own to market and finance their crops independently of railroad-dominated elevators, warehouses, and financial institutions. Most of the farm co-operatives quickly failed for lack of managerial ability. Business, moreover, subjected them to the most severe competitive tactics. In turn, much of the regulatory state legislation was soon repealed by local politicians upon whom business lavished money. The surviving legislation, moreover, was either ignored with impunity by railroads and trusts, or was eventually declared unconstitutional by the Supreme Court.

The farmers' efforts to fight the tariff and currency issues in federal politics suffered as disastrous a fate as their fight on the railroads and trusts in the states. Indeed no significant tariff or currency reforms were won until Woodrow Wilson's first administration.

Long before that merchants and other groups dependent on the railroads had joined with the farmers to carry the fight from state to federal politics. Between 1874 and 1885 some thirty measures for federal regulation of interstate railroads had been introduced in the House. A few were permitted to pass, only to be killed in the Senate. Then in 1886, the Supreme Court declared that all state efforts to regulate "fares and charges" on interstate railroads were unconstitutional. To fill the void created by this decision, Congress passed the Interstate Commerce Act in 1887.

The jubilation in rural areas occasioned by the Act soon proved premature. The Act established an Interstate Commerce Commission which, in some cases, could issue "cease and desist" orders to the railroads, but the Commission had to go to the courts for enforcement. In the courts the railroads proved masters of obstructionism, procrastination, and delay while they continued to practice the very abuses which the Commission tried to end. Between 1887 and 1905, sixteen cases under the Interstate Commerce Act eventually did find their way to the Supreme Court. In fifteen the Court decided in favor of the railroads.

The farmers and their small business backers in the older sections had just as little success in controlling the trusts. By the late 1880s agitation for federal regulation in this field grew as strong as that for intervention against the railroads. The result was the Sherman Anti-Trust Act of 1890. Senator Aldrich himself had acknowledged that the Interstate Commerce Act was "a delusion and a sham . . . an empty menace to great interests, made to answer the clamor of the ignorant and the unreasoning." Of the enactment of the Sherman Anti-Trust Act one of its leading architects, Senator Orville Platt of Connecticut, said: "The conduct of the Senate . . . has not been in the line of honest preparation of a bill to prohibit and punish trusts. It has been in the line of getting some bill with that title that we might go to the country with." "What looks like a stonewall to a layman," commented Finley Peter Dunne, the leading humorist of the age, "is a triumphal arch to a corporation lawyer."

Business-minded Republicans and Democrats in Congress had combined forces to protect the railroads and trusts from effective regulation. By 1890 farmers and merchants in the South and West and in older sections of the North had formed a new party of their own. This they called the People's Party. By then industrial labor, which had enjoyed rising real wages during the epoch of falling prices in the 1870s and 1880s, was also on the verge of worsening conditions. The Populists sought to enlist labor in the People's Party. In the elections of 1892 the Populists ran General James B. Weaver for President on a platform that comprehensively stated the complaints of American minorities against the two major parties. When Weaver polled over a million popular votes and carried twenty-two votes in the electoral college, the old parties took genuine notice of the uprising. The next elections followed the business crash of 1893, and depression aroused the protest of bitter need. So eager were the Populists for victory that they allowed themselves to be maneuvered into supporting the popular panacea of "free silver" as their major campaign slogan. When the Democrats nominated the westerner, William Jennings Bryan on a "free silver" platform, enough Populists deserted the People's Party for the Democratic Party to kill the immediate political chances of the reform movement.

Grover Cleveland, a Democrat, had held the presidency during the depression. In 1896 the Republicans were able to hold the Democrats up to the nation as the cause of the business debacle. William McKinley of Ohio was the hand-picked candidate of his friend Mark Hanna, boss of the Republican machine. No one could match Hanna's success in raising and spending money for a campaign. With the Democrats won over to the "wild schemes" of the Populists, business had never felt more willing to give. McKinley swept the election. Business seemed to have weathered the political storm with no more than token acquiescence to the popular will. If there was any doubt, McKinley's administration proceeded with high tariffs and deflationary currency legislation to prove that business had again prevailed. All efforts to strengthen the Interstate Commerce Act and the Sherman Anti-Trust Act were easily put off.

Chapter Eleven

"Morganization" and the Middle Class

"The nation is made—its mode of action is determined," said Professor Woodrow Wilson of Princeton in 1897. Then the Professor asked, "Where do we go from here? What we want to know is what is the nation going to do with its life, its material resources, and its spiritual strength? . . . How is the nation to get definite leadership and form steady effective parties? . . . How shall we settle questions of economic policy? Who is going to reconcile our interests?"

Some years later, risen now to Governor of New Jersey, Wilson thought he had found a part of the answer. In an address before the American Bar Association in 1910, he said: "Most men are individuals no longer as far as their business, its activities, or its moralities is concerned. They are not units but fractions; with their individuality and independence of choice in matters of business they have lost their individual choice within the field of morals. They must do what they are told to do, or lose their connection with modern affairs. . . . They cannot get at the men who ordered it— have no access to them. They have no voice of council or protest. They are mere cogs in a machine which has men for its parts.

"And yet there are men," Wilson went on, "with whom the whole choice lies. There are men who control the machine . . . and . . . who use it with an imperial freedom of design. . . . There is more individual power than ever, but those who exercise it are few and formidable, and the mass of men are mere pawns in the game."

When Wilson spoke in 1897, hardly a dozen American corporations, other than railroads, were capitalized at more than $10,000,-

000. In the next five or six years the number of such corporations rose to three hundred. Approximately fifty of these were capitalized at more than $50,000,000, seventeen at more than $100,000,000, and one, the United States Steel Corporation, at almost $1,500,-000,000. Despite the Sherman Anti-Trust Act, consolidation played a much larger part than growth in this dramatic concentration of industry. Among the railroads, where consolidation had begun earlier than in manufacturing, more than a thousand once independent lines had been merged by 1904 into six huge combinations with capital of almost $10,000,000,000. The basic policies of large corporations were now made by a handful of bankers and financiers. Towering over these "Lords of Creation," especially in times of financial crisis, loomed the isolated, imperious figure of John Pierpont Morgan.

The railroader, James J. Hill, complained that corporations were consolidated to manufacture nothing but "sheaves of printed securities" for the benefit of the promoters. The promoters themselves claimed more serious objectives. "With a man like Mr. Morgan at the head of a great industry," his friend John B. Claflin told a group of bankers assembled to honor the financier in 1901, "as against the old plan of many diverse interests in it, production would become more regular, labor would be more steadily employed at better wages, and panics caused by over-production would become a thing of the past." Economic instability arising from the vagaries of politics would also be guarded against. "As the business of the country has learned the secret of combination," said the *Bankers' Magazine* in 1901, "it is gradually subverting the power of the politician and rendering him subservient to its purposes. . . . That [government is not] entirely controlled by these interests is due to the fact that business organization has not reached full perfection."

In the next ten years, "Morganization" was to reach if not perfection at least a "harmony of interests" that approached it. By 1912, there was still room at the top in American business and society, but never in the history of the United States was it so carefully reserved for the congenial clubmates, churchmates, and cliques of the ruling oligarchy. A plunger like John W. "Bet-a-million" Gates, whom Morgan had used as a negotiator from time to time, was driven out of the Tennessee Coal and Iron Company in 1907 for threatening to upset the "harmony" in steel. The next year, the upstart Irishman, Thomas Fortune Ryan, was compelled by Morgan to sell his controlling interest in the Equitable Life Assurance Society to keep "hands that might prove injurious," as Morgan said, from manipulating the Society's funds.

The Genteel Tradition in power as in poetry reached its apex in this prewar epoch. Its defenders were drawn all the more closely together by the new stirrings among Negroes for recognition and respect as workers and voters, and by the flood tide of the "new immigration" to the land of opportunity and the dignity of man. As early as 1895, in his *Unguarded Gates,* Thomas Bailey Aldrich, the genteel poet incarnate, reviewed the tradition—and the threat.

> Wide open and unguarded stand our gates,
> Named of the four winds, North, South, East, and West;
> Portals that lead to an enchanted land
> Of cities, forests, fields of living gold, . . .
> A later Eden planted in the wilds,
> With not an inch of earth within its bound
> But if a slave's foot press it sets him free.
> Here, it is written, Toil shall have its wage,
> And Honor honor, and the humblest man
> Stand level with the highest in the law. . . .

> Wide open and unguarded stand our gates,
> And through them passes a wild motley throng—
> Men from the Volga and the Tartar steppes,
> Featureless figures of the Hoang-Ho,
> Malayan, Scythian, Teuton, Kelt, and Slav,
> Flying the Old World's poverty and scorn;
> These bringing with them unknown gods and rites,
> Those, tiger passions, here to stretch their claws.
> In street and alley what strange tongues are loud,
> Accents of menace alien to our air,
> Voices that once the Tower of Babel knew!

> O Liberty, white Goddess! is it well
> To leave the gates unguarded? . . .

Between leaders of finance increasingly conscious of their exalted estate and submerged masses of foreign and Negro labor increasingly aware of the relative permanence of their low condition, the fringes of a new urban middle class became clearer. This class feared both plutocratic tyranny and proletarian anarchism and socialism. The contrast of these extremes with the American tradition of individualism and democracy afforded middle-class spokesmen a simple yet striking theme and they made the most of it. The development of new national magazines financed mainly by the advertisers of middle-class commodities gave these spokesmen a powerful forum; but the churches, women's clubs, and other organizations helped keep the ball of tradition and reform rolling.

Tens of thousands of small businessmen, crushed or cornered by consolidated giants or merely conscious of their loss of business primacy, constituted the rank and file of the urban middle class. Wilson was to become their political hero. But ministers, professors, journalists, artists, professional men, and thousands of prosperous and newly leisured women gave the characteristic tone to the middle-class revolt. "Ladies, you have chosen me your leader," suffragette Sarah P. Decker told the ladies of the General Federation of Women's Clubs at her inauguration as president in 1904. "Well, I have an important piece of news for you. Dante is dead. He has been dead for several centuries, and I think it is time that we dropped the study of his inferno and turned attention to our own."

With no profits at stake in sweat shops, tenements, slums, saloons, unsafe factories, or in precious contacts with politicos who disposed of franchises, licenses, and other privileges, "Progressives" like Mrs. Decker could attack the political and social as well as the economic sins of plutocracy. The political leader these reformers took closest to their hearts was Theodore Roosevelt, who shocked gentility by entertaining Booker T. Washington, a Negro, at the White House; by appointing Oscar Straus, a Jew, to his Cabinet; and by inviting Mrs. Decker herself to an otherwise stag conference of governors in Washington in 1908. As early as 1899 the young "Rough Rider" was already talking of "heading some great outburst of the emotional classes which should at least temporarily crush Economic Man."

SCIENCE AND SCARCITY

It was the business collapse of 1893 that gave the bankers their opportunity to Morganize the American economy. Their watchwords were scarcity and stability, the one buttressing the other. Growth there would still be; the home market for capital, like the home market for goods (the sanctity of the protective tariff was one of the shibboleths of the age) remained, in their opinion, the best in the world. But the dynamo of American expansion was henceforth to be operated cautiously, and only on the say-so of the "Money Trust."

Yet one of the underlying causes of the 1893 collapse (one far more significant than Morgan's idea of the irresponsibility of the average businessman) had been the continuing rise in productivity in manufacturing and communications brought about by the systematic harnessing of science to industry. The power implicit in this relationship was scarcely understood by men whose whole orientation was to finance. They might sit immovably on the nation's money boxes, or spread themselves across the channels of credit. Yet new worlds of industry and trade, unconceived by them, would swim into view. "The deeper insight we obtain into the mysterious workings of Nature's forces," observed the great German inventor, Werner Siemens, just before the crash of 1893, "the more we are convinced that we are still standing only in the vestibule of science, that an immeasurable field still lies before us. . . ." In the recovery years after 1897, the relations of science and industry grew closer, and even in Morganized industries productivity soared once again. But science's main role then and since has been to create entirely new industries and new products—which the bankers, typically, refused for years to underwrite.

In the period before the first World War, ideas for many of the new applications of science to industry continued to come from mechanics actually employed in factories. But increasingly, the country's scientific schools made their impact felt. As Siemens noted, "theoretical" science and scientists were claiming the attention of alert businessmen in venturing onto the "immeasurable field." As early as 1850 Harvard University had established the

Lawrence Scientific School. The next year Yale's Sheffield Scientific School began instruction. Ten years later, Massachusetts Institute of Technology opened its doors, soon to be followed by the Columbia University School of Mines. Later on in the century, under provisions of the Morrill Act of 1862 providing federal land grants to support higher education in "agriculture and mechanic arts," engineering schools were established in most land-grant states. In the meantime, West Point, for almost half a century the only American source of trained engineers, continued its work; while old Rensselaer Polytechnic Institute in Troy, New York, expanded its curriculum, to join the others in the development of applied science and the preparation of men to use it in business.

Business management itself, meanwhile, was feeling the impact of scientific ideas. Before 1881 not a single book on management by an American could be found in the Technology Division of the New York Public Library. By 1900 there were twenty-seven; by 1910, two hundred and forty. Perhaps the first management school in the country was the Wharton School of Finance at the University of Pennsylvania which received its initial endowment in 1881. The Babson Statistical Service for management was started in 1900. In 1908 came the momentous founding of the Graduate School of Business Administration at Harvard where men were to be trained to study the science of management systematically as well as to function as managers in industry.

An even more significant event took place in 1911, when Frederick W. Taylor published his book, *Scientific Management*. As early as 1882, as a steel foreman, Taylor had been struck with the inefficient operations of his men. It was then that he began his first minute analyses of individual industrial jobs and the assignment of precise costs to each operation. To control costs scientifically, and thereby to cut them, he urged greater mechanization, the standardization of fractions of operations, and piecework incentive-wage payments. Taylor had a hard time selling his ideas during business prosperity; but during the economic doldrums after the panic of 1907, "scientific management" grew in fame and application.

Of these developments in management, Louis D. Brandeis said in his Commencement Day address at Brown University in 1912, significantly titled *Business—a Profession:*

The once meager list of the learned professions is being constantly enlarged. Engineering in its many branches already takes rank beside law, medicine and theology. Forestry and scientific agriculture are securing places of honor. The new professions of manufacturing, of merchandising, of transportation and finance must soon gain recognition. The establishment of business schools in our universities is a manifestation of the modern conception of business.

The most important application of the new findings of science was in the field of electricity. The economy of wood, iron, coal, and steam still dominated American and world industry in the 1890s, but it was proving increasingly wasteful and unwieldy. Factories remained awkwardly tied to the coal mines. Factory operations still were slowed down by overheated machines, the rapid dulling of cutting edges, the multiplicity of steps required to shift from one phase of production to another. But electricity had begun to change all this.

Electricity was first widely used in communication; and until the 1880s its role in telegraphy and the telephone remained its main commercial function. After Edison perfected a reasonably priced incandescent bulb in October 1879, electricity became widely used in illumination. Edison believed most strongly in direct current, but this could be transmitted great distances only at great cost. Alternating current made long-distance transmission of electric power practical. George Westinghouse (the inventor of the railroad air brake) and William Stanley developed the first alternating current generators and transformers; their work became applicable to a great range of uses after 1888 when Nikola Tesla, an immigrant from Serbia, devised the first inexpensive motor employing alternating electric current. Westinghouse soon bought Tesla's patent. In 1893 Westinghouse dramatized the progress of electric illumination by lighting up the Chicago World's Fair.

The third practical application of electricity was in urban transportation. In 1880 the 18,000 urban street cars in the United States were hauled by 100,000 horses and mules at about six miles an hour, a pace that severely limited the expansion of cities. As pressure for speed grew, steam transport was tried on elevated railroads in New York City, starting in the 1870s. Success here led to the construction of the first "el" in Chicago in 1893. But urban steam railroads could not be extended indefinitely. As trains became longer, heavier locomotives were needed to pull them. Heavier locomotives, in turn, required sturdier elevated structures whose cost became prohibitive. Widespread enmity against the "els" and the steam engine also was aroused by their cutting off of light and air, their noise, their smoke, and the fires caused by their flying sparks. The urban steam engine's successor was the electric trolley car. The trolley systems were far more flexible than the steam railroads. Cars were powered individually, eliminating the use of locomotives altogether. They could be run singly or in trains, and switched from track to track with ease. Single track lines on the streets thus supplanted the unsightly elevated structures.

The foremost name in electric traction is Frank Julian Sprague who made the first practical demonstration of citywide trolley service in Richmond, Virginia, in 1888. In getting this system going, Sprague had to solve innumerable engineering problems. He invented the first satisfactory electric car motors, the first dependable trolley poles and wires. Equally important, he worked out systems of traffic control which kept the trolley cars moving. Perhaps most difficult for Sprague was the problem of overcoming the hostility of capitalists who had large investments in the steam elevated lines and who fought franchises and other privileges for the new system. But as it became obvious that the trolley was here to stay, the financiers gradually relented. After 1900 Sprague's system began to be used on new urban subways as well as on surface lines, and by 1912 there were 40,000 miles of electric railway and trolley track in the United States, representing an investment of $5,000,-000,000. The bankers at last had begun to look to urban electric traction to re-enact the dynamic role of the old interurban steam railroads as a profitable user of investment capital. But, typically, the new-fangled automobile was about to end the trolley car's growth just when the bankers had accepted it.

Of all the applications of electricity, perhaps the most far-reaching was its use in industry, and especially in the automobile industry. By 1914 about 30 per cent of American factory capacity had become electrified. Electricity freed the factory from the river valley and the coal field. Factories could now be set up near raw materials, markets, or ports. Inside the plant, electricity made the "straight line" system of production all the more efficient, smoothed out conveyor belt and assembly line procedure. It also put a premium upon plant specialization, upon standardization of jobs and products, and hence upon scientific management. It made possible such a simplification of operations that unskilled and illiterate workers could be employed on jobs for which the machine, so to speak, did much of the thinking. The new technology thus permitted the employment in industry of the masses of new immigrants who poured into America after 1900 and of the Negroes who flocked north for work. For the automobile age the new technology and the new sources of labor became crucial.

Americans had long been prepared for the production of automobiles. From the nation's earliest days carriage manufacture had trained skilled artisans in the fabrication of bodies, wheels, and springs. Since Eli Whitney's time the assembly of interchangeable parts had become an established technique in various lines. Since the 1850s, the manufacture of farm and factory machinery and railroad locomotives had promoted familiarity with the problems of engines. In the 1880s and 1890s, bicycle manufacturers had shown the practicality of pneumatic tires. By then petroleum refining had become a science which could deliver good gasoline on demand. But it was electricity's contribution to mass production that made the automobile commercially feasible just when America needed a new means of rapid transportation.

Like all new industries, the automobile industry had a hard time getting financed. The insurance companies abhorred it as a field of investment and also refused to cover its product. In 1904, Charles Platt, president of the Insurance Company of North America, exclaimed, "I'll never insure a gasoline can on wheels, the noisy stinking things!" A bit later, when he was trying to induce the House of Morgan to back the prospective General Motors, the promoter William C. Durant boasted that 500,000 automobiles would soon be sold each year. "If he [Durant] has any sense," said Morgan's partner, George W. Perkins, "he'll keep such notions to himself if he ever tries to borrow money." A few years later, after he had succeeded in setting up General Motors and invested heavily in plant expansion, Durant again had to borrow money. Again Morgan turned him down, as did most of the other bankers. Durant was so hard pressed that he finally capitulated to a combination of Lee, Higginson & Company of Boston and J. & W. Seligman & Company of New York. Included in their terms was the requirement that Durant surrender the management of the company to the bankers' trustees for the duration of the loan.

General Motors was an effort to control competition in the automobile industry in which by 1910 over sixty firms were producing cars for the market. What kept General Motors in trouble was its failure to include Ford. By 1908 Henry Ford had become one of the automotive leaders. The next year he produced his first Model T and soon was in a class by himself. The first Model Ts sold for $950, not much lower than competing brands. By 1913, Ford had cut the price of Model Ts to $550 and in 1914 he got them out for less than $500. Between 1909 and 1913, Ford production leaped from 10,000 to 168,000 cars, the latter figure one third of the entire industry's output. In 1914 Ford produced 248,000 cars, almost one half of all the automobiles made. His profits that year were more than $30,000,000, 20 per cent above the record of the year before.

The shoestring phase of the automobile industry obviously was over. In 1915, the wholesale value of all automobiles produced in the United States was $700,000,000, a figure greater than the gross passenger revenue of all American railroads that year. After World War I, automotive busses and trucks added to the competitive pressure on the older carriers. In early automobile days, the lack of paved roads retarded the growth of the automotive industry; but between 1915 and 1925 annual public expenditures on roads and highways rose from nearly $300,000,000 to over a billion dollars, and represented a highly salutary subsidy to the automobile makers.

The manufacture of automobiles had not become a commercial activity until 1897. After the introduction of Model T twelve years later, the industry led other fields of manufacturing into the routine application of science and technology. Automobile manufacturers spurred on constant advances in the production of glass, rubber, and steel alloys, from which body and engine parts and tires were made. They also promoted the application of chemistry in the petroleum industry, seeking not only improved fuels but also improved lubricants both for the automobile engine and the automotive factory's machinery. Ultimately the automobile manufacturers became the largest users of each of the commodities that went into the automobile. The leader in automotive progress continued to be Henry Ford, who distrusted big city bankers as heartily as the bankers distrusted Detroit.

In the decades around the start of the twentieth century electricity thus was transforming American life. Besides the automobile industry, it made possible the development of phonographs and moving pictures, and the experiments that led to radio and television. It also was responsible for basic improvements in photography and high-speed composition and printing, all of them essential to the success of national consumer magazines like the *Ladies' Home Journal* and the *Saturday Evening Post*. Both magazines passed the million mark in circulation during the first decade of the twentieth century. Yet to the bankers, these new areas of economic life, like automobiles, remained speculative and unstable and thus questionable fields for investment. Capital failed to be drawn to them, even though the older key industries, such as railroads and steel, flour milling, meat packing and farm machinery, and oil and sugar refining, no longer required most of the new savings of the nation.

After the return of prosperity in the late 'nineties, these savings grew tremendously in banks, trust companies, and insurance companies. If continuing advances in productivity (even in banker-controlled industries) were not to result in ever higher unemployment among a growing population, new outlets for both capital and goods had to be found. These might be sought abroad, a disquieting prospect to "America for Americans" bankers accustomed to importing capital, not exporting it to exotic lands. Or they might be sought at home, by raising the purchasing power of the mass of the population—an equally disquieting prospect to those who believed that the wages of labor must be calculated like the cost of raw materials and held to the lowest possible levels.

It is true that outlets for capital and goods were sought abroad more actively than at any earlier time. In the twelve years between 1900 and 1912 American foreign investments tripled. Yet at the end of that period these investments were about equal to the capitalization of a single American company, the United States Steel Corporation. In the same twelve years, exports of American manufactured commodities (other than foodstuffs) approximately doubled, but the ratio of such exports to total exports remained fixed at about one third. In an article in *Scribner's Magazine* in 1902, called "The American 'Commercial Invasion' of Europe," Frank A. Vanderlip, then Vice-President of the National City Bank of New York, boasted: "We have been successfully meeting competition everywhere. America has sent coals to Newcastle, cotton goods to Manchester, cutlery to Sheffield, potatoes to Ireland, champagnes to France, watches to Switzerland, and 'Rhine wine' to Germany." Yet the total of such exports, like the exports of capital, failed to become imposing, or even adequate enough to sustain the expansion of American industry.

As for the expansion of the home market, if high not low wages had to become the goal of industry, spending not saving had to become the goal of the population. Yet hard work, frugality, and thrift remained the sacred commandments of American morality (appropriate ones in a society once painfully short of capital and labor); and it was difficult to divest people of such drives. Spending, conspicuous consumption, and active leisure involving the purchase of goods and services had become essential to a society suddenly short of markets and effective purchasing power. Yet even in the 1950s the guilt implicit in indulgence remained an important point of attack of the advertising industry.

Advertising tried hard to develop the home market. In the early 1890s Cyrus H. Curtis, publisher of the *Ladies' Home Journal,* asked a convention of pioneer advertising men, "Do you know why we publish the *Ladies' Home Journal?*" And he answered his own question: "The editor thinks it is for the benefit of the American women. That is an illusion that is a very proper one for him to have. But I will tell you; the real reason, the publisher's reason, is to give you people who manufacture things that American women want and buy a chance to tell them about your products." By the 'nineties business—especially the new lines—had become keenly aware of the consuming public. An index of manufacturers' efforts to impress their goods upon the new buyers is the number of widely publicized trade-marks. From a skimpy 170 or so in 1870, their number had grown to many thousands by 1910.

As early as 1876, the poet Bret Harte commented on a particular trade-marked product:

> One Sabbath morn, as heavenward
> White Mountain tourists slowly spurred,
> On every rock, to their dismay,
> They read the legend all the way—
> SAPOLIO.

The manufacturers of Sapolio soap spent about $15,000 for advertising in 1871. Twenty-five years later they were spending more than $400,000 annually. By then, Ivory Soap ("It Floats"), Kodak cameras ("You press the button; we do the rest"), and Schlitz ("The Beer that Made Milwaukee Famous") had all become part of the permanent baggage of the public consciousness. By 1899, "Uneeda Biscuit" was a common phrase in every magazine and every household. By 1903 Cadillac was making a big splash with its "smartest of runabouts . . . speed range four to thirty miles an hour." Well over a hundred million dollars a year was being spent by then for newspaper advertising alone; while as much as 72 per cent of the space of magazines was taken up with product promotion.

Yet it is a commonplace that while advertising can make goods known and even create wants, it cannot supply the wherewithal for buying. In the period before World War I industry showed some awareness of the need to spread purchasing power in the new era of rising productivity. Higher wages were granted to skilled workers, and the first tentative steps toward so-called "welfare capitalism" were taken. Corporations sought to reduce the number and severity of industrial accidents and to maintain injured workers' purchasing power through insurance programs compensating those forced off the job.

But only a few employers acted from an appreciation of the new conditions, and even these usually went only half way. When progressive management paid higher wages, it dissipated the social benefit with the speed-up, the stretch-out, and other devices to raise production proportionately higher than before. Though labor unions tended to stabilize employment and insure a steady rise in mass purchasing power, management also spent millions financing union-busting organizations. The unions themselves, moreover, increasingly took on the character of closure groups whose aim was to monopolize the benefits of unionization for a rising "aristocracy" of skilled workers.

Engineers and young entrepreneurs with little capital of their own to lose might look to new industries to engage the energies, imagination, and savings of the nation. Publishers, advertisers, and rising distributors of consumer goods might look to new methods to stimulate sales (and production) in a rich and growing market. Financiers naturally looked to financiering to occupy and reward the accumulating funds of the middle and upper classes. In the 1870s and 1880s, as we have seen, mergers (involving the creation of new security issues) were made in American industry mainly to check cutthroat competition among highly mechanized firms. The depression of the 'nineties greatly intensified such competition among the surviving companies, each of which hoped to keep its costly machinery fully occupied despite the weakness of the market. It was to bring such competition under control that Morgan led the depression drive for consolidation and combination. The return of prosperity after 1897 made it all the easier for the bankers to float the large issues of new securities of consolidated firms, and mergers began to be actively sought simply for the profits involved in marketing stocks and bonds. Between 1898 and 1903 the number of consolidations reached a peak not to be approached again until similar circumstances brought about similar activity in the late 1920s, and the number of persons owning corporate stock doubled.

As a justification for large-scale stock promotions the ideal of sheer "bigness" itself became attractive. The supposed economies of large-scale operations were magnified; at the same time the opposition of family-owned firms to selling out to consolidated corporations (whose competition they increasingly feared) was dissipated. The failure of the federal government to enforce the antitrust acts seemed to give great mergers legislative and judicial sanction. Though many states also had antitrust statutes and though some states tried to enforce them more strictly than the federal government, their work was nullified by the many states with no antitrust laws. In competing for corporate business, the lax states reduced restrictions in corporation charters to the disappearing point. They permitted interlocking directorates, nonvoting stock, holding companies, and other devices broadening the gulf between ownership and management and promoting the centralization of control. New Jersey was the worst offender. So attractive did its corporation laws become after 1889 that each of the seven largest trusts, as of 1904, with an aggregate capital of $2,500,000,000, and with control of approximately 1,528 plants in every section of the land, had a New Jersey charter.

As the investment bankers enlarged their control over the economy, the ruling oligarchy naturally became smaller and smaller. Topped by Morgan and Rockefeller, it included in the end almost no one but their associates and allies. A climactic struggle between the Morgan and Rockefeller camps began in 1901. Allied with Morgan were George Fisher Baker's First National Bank of New York, the New York and the Mutual Life Insurance Companies, such Morgan-created combinations as the International Harvester Company and United States Steel, and the Hill railroad empire. The major strength of the opposing camp, of course, came from Rockefeller's Standard Oil millions. But this camp had other gigantic resources as well. Most of these were supplied by the investment banking house of Kuhn, Loeb & Company, headed by Jacob H. Schiff. This was the only American firm that could compete with Morgan in the capital markets of Europe. Other Rockefeller financial institutions in New York included the National City Bank and the Hanover National Bank. Also associated with Rockefeller were the Harriman railroads.

The struggle between the two titans was joined in 1901 when Harriman and Hill, backed, of course, by the full strength of their associates, both sought to acquire control of the Burlington Railroad which owned the best connection with Chicago from the West. The contest took place in Wall Street, and the first round was won by Hill and Morgan who captured a controlling interest in the Burlington. But Harriman and Schiff replied by buying up a majority of the shares in Hill's key railroad, the Northern Pacific. Both sides recognized that the struggle was deadlocked when it was discovered that the Rockefeller group virtually owned the Northern Pacific while the Morgan group had managed to retain a majority of the voting stock. Neither group wanted a fight to the finish. Indeed the justification of banker management lay precisely in the avoidance of such fights. The alternative was perfectly clear. Together the erstwhile opponents set up the Northern Securities Company in which their railroad interests were combined.

The Wall Street fight for control of the Northern Pacific had brought a tremendous boom in that company's shares, which carried the rest of the market to new highs. When the fight ended, not only Northern Pacific but the whole market suddenly collapsed and thousands were ruined. The entire operation was a spectacular one that had caught the imagination of the country. Most impressed, perhaps, was President Roosevelt, who found in the Morgan-Rockefeller war just the right occasion to blast the characteristic irresponsibility of the topmost business leaders. He also found in the Northern Securities Company just the right consolidation to attack under the Sherman Act. In a decision as spectacular as the creation of Northern Securities itself, the Supreme Court dissolved the company in 1904. But this hardly deterred the bankers and their allies from cementing by other means, such as stock ownership in each other's companies, their joint control over the money market, the major industries, and the transportation services of the country.

Olympian in their economic power and their contempt for government and politics, the great financiers also moved a few steps forward in society. By the turn of the century a number of them had been admitted to the august Union Club, the oldest in New York. Others had entered the even more exclusive Knickerbocker Club, which had been founded in 1871 by young aristocrats impatient at once with the growing membership of the Union and its long waiting period. For those who couldn't quite make this grade, Morgan himself, in 1891, had founded the magnificent Metropolitan Club. This, in its way, was as exclusive as the others, fortune more than forebears supplying the key to its portals. While club life was lending a gentlemanly sheen to their own day-to-day routine, the giants of American finance were also giving a monarchic gloss to their families by marrying their daughters to the impoverished nobility of Europe. Those who didn't marry counts married cousins and kept wealth and the control of wealth at home.

Family life itself, moreover, had taken on a roseate, not to say a golden tinge. Describing the Morgans on the eve of the twentieth century and on the eve of his own marriage to the banker's daughter, Louisa, Herbert Satterlee writes:

Mr. Morgan's house was just where he wanted it to be and it suited his mode of life. Mrs. Morgan was well and they had their unmarried daughters, Louisa and Anne living at home. . . . He himself was in good health. His friends were nearby. The people in his social world were of his own kind, and the bankers and business men with whom he came into contact had, for the most part, the same standard of ethics and point of view that he himself had. New York was still a friendly, neighborly city and was a pleasant place in which to live. . . . At midnight, when the bells and horns proclaimed the beginning of the New Year, he was looking forward with the eagerness of a much younger man to the great possibilities of the century that was about to begin.

Mr. Morgan himself saw the New Year in while sitting isolated, as usual, playing solitaire. A few months later he was to build a temporary ballroom to accommodate 2,400 persons for Louisa's wedding. Most of the year he spent in Europe where, in the exasperated opinion of Roger Fry, curator of paintings at the Morgan-dominated Metropolitan Museum, he "behaved like a crowned head," going about buying the "gilt-edged securities" of continental art. The decades around the turn of the century, the golden age of millionaire collectors of companies and counts, were also the golden age of millionaire collectors of masterpieces. Private and public museums bulged with the sure things of Europe's past and fraudulent reproductions of them, while domestic artists, like domestic swains, languished in obscurity.

THE CRACKS IN THE WALL

While Mr. Morgan played solitaire on New Year's Eve, 1899, *The New York Times* studied its crystal ball. "The year 1899," said the *Times'* leading New Year's Day editorial, "was a year of wonders, a veritable *annus mirabilis* in business and production. . . . It would be easy to speak of the twelve months just passed as the banner year were we not already confident that the distinction of highest records must presently pass to the year 1900. . . . The outlook on the threshold of the new year is extremely bright."

The *Times'* expectations were not to be denied for almost four years. Ripples of dissatisfaction with Morganization, however, were already becoming apparent in 1901 when barely suppressed alarm greeted the revelations of the amount of "water" in the financing of the billion-dollar steel company. Alarm turned to consternation with the revelations in 1903 of fraud in connection with the flotation of the "Shipbuilding Trust"; and consternation turned to panic when thirty-seven other new combinations went bankrupt that year at a cost of $600,000,000 to investors. A dozen other trusts, capitalized at an additional half-billion dollars had to acknowledge financial difficulties. From 1904 to 1906, moreover, Morgan's own special pet, the vaunted United States Steel, failed to pay common-stock dividends.

A spectacular investigation of New York insurance companies in 1905 by a legislative committee counseled by the brilliant lawyer, Charles Evans Hughes, disclosed incredible irregularities in the financiers' handling of insurance funds and sent many of the lesser financial fry to jail. The Morgans and Rockefellers, both deeply involved in the revelations, escaped punishment by the law, but fell a few more notches in public esteem. The Panic of 1907 marked a kind of culmination of their decline. As a result of the collapse of security prices during this panic, Morgan was able to secure control of the Tennessee Coal and Iron Company for less than half its real value. The Rockefellers, in turn, bought up large holdings in copper and other areas. It was widely supposed, indeed, that the Panic had been induced by the great bankers simply for the purpose of acquiring key and competitive properties cheaply. But the fact that the economy in general failed to recover from the crash until war orders began pouring in from Europe in 1915 indicated that business had been in a fundamentally unsound condition. Morgan himself earned the plaudits of the financial community during the panic by his success in mobilizing funds to shore up shaky banks—of his choosing. But the revelation of his power in this connection only spurred the drive for a reorganization of the country's entire banking system giving government administrators responsible to the voters the power that "Morgan the Peerless" exercised as he alone saw fit.

As middle-class opinion turned against the bankers, they themselves insisted, quite accurately, that they had not seized power in response to any social crusade. Thus they disclaimed responsibility for social welfare. For the welfare of their own companies, however, they had publicly assumed obligations, and on the credit of such obligations they had mobilized billions of dollars of the public's money. For their failure to maintain the integrity of such investments they could not escape blame. A hairline crack of distrust, moreover, prompted the envious or suspicious to try to broaden the fault, and eventually an attack was made on the bankers' entire structure.

Even the objectives which the bankers themselves saw as embodying their greatest virtues were turned against them. Economic stability throttled opportunity and depressed real wages for a rapidly expanding population. Business "harmony," in turn, only dulled initiative and enterprise. "It is a well known fact," the Investors' Guild wrote in a Memorial to President Taft in 1911, "that modern trade combinations tend strongly toward a constancy of process and products, and by their very nature are opposed to new processes and new products originated by independent inventors." More telling was the testimony of the *Engineering News* at about the same time:

> We are today something like five years behind Germany in iron and steel metallurgy, and such innovations as are being introduced by our iron and steel manufacturers are most of them merely following the lead set by foreigners years ago.
>
> We do not believe this is because American engineers are any less ingenious or original than those in Europe, though they may indeed

be deficient in training and scientific education compared with those of Germany. We believe the main cause is the wholesale consolidation which has taken place in American industry. A huge organization is too clumsy to take up the development of an original idea. With the market closely controlled and profits certain by following standard methods, those who control our trusts do not want the bother of developing anything new.

We instance metallurgy only by way of illustration. There are plenty of other fields of industry where exactly the same condition exists. . . .

If the engineers needed specific evidence, they had only to point to Morgan's refusal to finance General Motors, and the failure of General Motors after Lee, Higginson & Company did advance funds to keep pace with Ford and other independent companies.

In the plants and on the railroads which the bankers did operate, moreover, the accident rate reached its peak between 1903 and 1907. Industrial deaths numbered tens of thousands, injuries hundreds of thousands a year. On the railroads, as in the factories, absentee managements concerned first and almost exclusively with financial expediency, stinted gravely on the installation of available safety devices and spent little or nothing on developing new ones. But safety was only one of the problems of industrial employment. Child labor, deathly long hours, filthy surroundings, brutal foremen, and other evils all added to the needless toll. Incredibly noxious conditions in what the workers called "home" only aggravated the social cost of stability.

Though Mr. Morgan found New York at the turn of the century a "neighborly city," it must have been that with a vengeance for the 30,000 persons crowded into a single New York East Side district of five or six blocks. This notorious "District A," one of many such, had a greater density of population than any similar area anywhere in the world, even in teeming India or China or the densest slums of Europe. But much more depressing than New York were the conditions in absentee ownership towns which the bankers never saw.

In many such towns, as in the slums of New York, the majority of the population had come to be made up of the "new" immigrants, the "uprooted," who had been drawn from Europe by the glittering promises and grimmer devices of agents of American industry, land-grant railroads, and steamship companies. The so-called "old" immigration from Britain and western Europe had reached its peak of almost 640,000 in 1882. Thereafter, immigration fell off steadily to a twenty-year low of 229,000 in 1898. When it revived again, with the revival of prosperity in the United States, most of the new-comers were drawn from the impoverished countries of central and southeastern Europe. By 1910 such immigrants, along with Negroes migrating from the South, made up about two thirds of the total labor force in twenty predominant American industries. On the whole ignorant of English and unable to read or write their own language, these immigrants tended to associate with their own countrymen in the port cities in which they landed or in the factory towns to which they were herded by corporate representatives on arrival. All the circumstances of their life conspired to make them hostile to American institutions, which in fact offered them no protection from exploitation and no alternative to it. This hostility became increasingly reciprocated by Americans over whom the alien tide swept.

Genteel American spokesmen, segregated from immigrant slums in the great cities or distant from cities that were almost nothing but industrial slums, denounced assertions that there was poverty in the United States. "No facts to bear out these assertions are offered," said William Graham Sumner, Yale's notable Spencerian sociologist. In 1904, Robert Hunter, in his volume *Poverty,* offered this comment after a most careful investigation: "I have not the slightest doubt that there are in the United States ten million persons in precisely these conditions of poverty, but I am largely guessing and there may be as many as fifteen or twenty million!" And then he asked the brutal question, "But ought we not to know?" and added, "To neglect even to inquire into our national distress is to be guilty of the grossest moral insensitiveness."

THE PROGRESSIVE MOVEMENT

While the Morgans and the Rockefellers disclaimed responsibility for social welfare and the stockholders in their companies as well as corporation law itself countenanced their disclaimer, public sentiment increasingly held them to account. Their financial empires had become the dominant power in the country; the callous disregard of these empires for democratic traditions and for human life itself aroused Theodore Roosevelt's "emotional classes" in particular to invoke the "higher law" of Christian humanity in defense of the "general welfare" against the "malefactors of great wealth."

One of the first needs of this defense was concrete information about what was really happening in the new America. In the first decade of the twentieth century, this information was supplied in startling fashion by the "muckrake" magazines. The foremost of these was *McClure's,* named for its brilliant publisher, S. S. McClure, whose galaxy of writers included Ida Tarbell, Lincoln Steffens, Ray Stannard Baker, and William Allen White. *Cosmopolitan,* edited by John Brisben Walker; *Everybody's,* edited by E. J. Ridgeway; *Arena,* edited by B. O. Flower; and *Hampton's,* edited by Ben Hampton, all offered similar platforms to writers like David Graham Phillips, Charles Edward Russell, and Thomas W. Lawson. The name "muckraker" was first pinned on these journalists in 1906 by President Roosevelt. In a fit of pique, he contemptuously compared them to John Bunyan's "Man with the Muck-Rake," who when offered "the celestial crown . . . could look no way but downward" and continue "to rake the filth on the floor." Some of the writers disavowed this appellation; but most of them wore it as a badge of honor.

The first muckraking articles probably were those by Ida Tarbell on the Standard Oil Company, and Lincoln Steffens on "The Shame of the Cities," both published in *McClure's* in 1902. Other notable performances included Baker's three articles on "The Right to Work," beginning in *McClure's* in January 1903, which examined in detail the relations of labor, capital, and government; Lawson's "Frenzied Finance," which began in *Everybody's* in July 1904; and Phillips's series on "The Treason of the Senate," starting in *Cosmopolitan* in March 1906. These journalists, a later critic has written, "traced the intricate relationship of the police, the underworld, the local political bosses, the secret connections between the new corporations . . . and the legislature and the courts. In doing this, they drew a cast of characters for the drama of American society: bosses, professional politicians, reformers, racketeers, captains of industry. Everybody recognized these native types; . . . but they had not been characterized before; their social functions had not been analyzed."

The muckrake magazines reached immense audiences for the times. Between 1903 and 1906, the circulation of *Hampton's* rose from 13,000 to 440,000; in the same few years *Everybody's* was transformed from a store sheet of John Wanamaker's to a national magazine with a circulation of 735,000. Between 1900 and 1906, *McClure's* circulation jumped from 370,000 to more than 750,000. These figures lagged behind those of conservative consumer magazines like the *Ladies' Home Journal* and the *Saturday Evening Post,* but the muckrake magazines outstripped the old journals of opinion, such as *Harper's, Scribner's* and *Century,* each of which had leveled off at about 150,000 subscribers.

The muckrakers' research was supplemented by that of other groups, notably national and state legislative committees. As early as 1898 Congress had set up the Industrial Commission to study the relation of the new trusts to immigration, agriculture, labor, technology and other subjects. Its report, in nineteen thick volumes, remains a mine of information; around the turn of the century it supplied much of the basic data for the work of social critics like John R. Commons and Thorstein Veblen. The most thoroughgoing use of the legislatures' investigative function was made in the state of Wisconsin during the governorship of Robert M. La Follette from 1901 to 1906. Other reform governors copied La Follette's employment of the faculty of the state university as a "brains trust," and imitated what became famous as the "Wisconsin way."

The muckrakers' work in publicizing their findings was also supplemented by vigorous special groups whose leaders appealed to specialized audiences. Most important among these were the clerical preachers of the "Social Gospel," whose "muscular Christianity" included all phases of reform; and their women parishioners, who were especially adept at organizing reform committees to see "Progressive" action through. The Social Gospel movement went back to the 1870s, but its leaders, such as Washington Gladden and

Walter Rauschenbusch, continued to have great influence. Among their most enthusiastic converts were Tom L. Johnson, the millionaire traction magnate, who became the "best mayor of the best governed city in the United States" (in the opinion of Lincoln Steffens), during his reign in Cleveland from 1901 to 1909; and Samuel M. ("Golden Rule") Jones, an early oil millionaire who virtually emulated Johnson in Toledo from 1897 until his death in 1904. Jones's successor was Brand Whitlock, who carried on Jones's reforms for eight more years. Johnson, Jones and Whitlock all took on national importance because of their overwhelming success in routing the corrupt machine politicians in Mark Hanna's own state.

The spearhead of the middle-class women's activity was the General Federation of Women's Clubs, which had been organized in 1889; and the main plank in the women's program was women's suffrage. By 1910, however, more than eight million women and nearly two million children (under sixteen) had entered the labor force (which totaled about thirty-eight million), and factory and general working conditions occupied much of the Progressive women's attention.

Though they were fighting the evils of consolidated monopolies of enterprise and opportunity, the Progressives were forced to acknowledge that only in union was there strength. Their first field of attack was child labor, and the first "child labor committee" was organized in 1901 by the Rev. Edgar G. Murphy of Montgomery, Alabama. In 1904 a National Child Labor Committee was formed, and by 1910 twenty-five state and local committees were affiliated with it. Other Progressive organizations joined in the fight, among them the National Consumers' League and the General Federation of Women's Clubs. As a result of this combined assault forty-three states adopted child-labor laws between 1902 and 1909. Old laws going as far back as 1813 had dealt perfunctorily with child labor in the factories; the new ones were much more comprehensive, and not only covered hours and conditions of labor in numerous kinds of business but also set minimum ages for leaving school.

Women's working conditions next occupied the Progressive reformers. Under the slogan "let us be our sisters' keepers," the state and national federations of women's clubs assumed leadership in this field. Until 1908, the courts, while permitting regulation of child labor as part of the police power, frowned on controls over women's working conditions as interference with the freedom of contract. Then, in the case of *Muller* v. *Oregon,* the Supreme Court reversed its negative position and virtually all the states enacted new laws in this field. Other areas of Progressive legislation included laws for workmen's accident compensation, laws for the regulation of tenement and factory construction, laws setting standards of public health, and local minimum-wage laws.

But by 1910 the Progressives had ample reason for skepticism about legislation. Effective enforcement commissions did not become common until after the first World War. Until then, legislation may have meant something to politicians needing public support and to agitators needing concrete objectives. Among working women and children, slum dwellers, the maimed and the diseased, little improvement in conditions was noted before the 1920s and 1930s.

One of the products of organized reform is organized resistance, especially on the part of those made to foot the bill. Factory legislation was promptly fought by organized businessmen, chambers of commerce, and similar militant associations whose members would have borne the burden of taxation and other costs as well as bureaucratic interference with their freedom to conduct their enterprises as they alone saw fit. Business resistance to reform was strengthened by business connections with the traditional patronage- and privilege-dispensing politicos in the cities and the states. A growing awareness of the political road block turned the Progressives to a concerted attack on traditional political practices.

The Progressives' chief target was the monopoly the regular party machines had over naming candidates for office; the chief reform they offered was the direct primary, by which, presumably, the registered rank and file of each party would elect the party candidates. By 1916 direct primary legislation had been enacted in forty-five states—the holdouts being Rhode Island, Connecticut, and New Mexico. Other Progressive political reforms included the "initiative," by which the voters themselves could propose legislation; the "referendum," by which the public would have the privilege of accepting or rejecting laws already passed by the legislature; and the "recall," by which the voters could fire undesirable public officials before the end of their terms.

Though these reforms were adopted in numerous states, they did not lastingly improve state or local government. The direct primary, in particular, served largely to screen out of possible candidacy for office those who could not afford to campaign without the resources of their party's war chest. On the other hand, the Progressive movement did draw able men and women into politics for a few years and also served to remind the entrenched party hacks that the voters, on whom they ultimately depended, were in a rebellious mood and that greater attention might henceforth be given to satisfying them on candidates and conduct in office.

The kingpins of the party machines in the states were the United States senators who were elected by the state legislatures. On the national scene, one of the major Progressive demands was for the direct election of United States senators by the people. An amendment to this effect (the Seventeenth Amendment to the Constitution) was pushed through Congress in May 1912, and ratified one year later. This Amendment was a signal Progressive victory, but its effect on the Senate and the state machines remains ambiguous. The drive for women's suffrage also resulted in an amendment, the Nineteenth, after local campaigns for the enfranchisement of women by the states showed little progress. By 1914 only eleven states had granted women the right to vote. The campaign for a national amendment took on greater force after World War I, during which American women had made many sacrifices, and Congress finally yielded in June 1919. Ratification came in 1920, in time for women to participate in the presidential election. Women, organized in the Women's Christian Temperance Union, had a leading role in the enactment of a third Progressive amendment, the Eighteenth, or Prohibition Amendment, which went into effect in January 1920, after almost a century of agitation.

Business opposition to Progressive social legislation in the cities and the states was led mainly by "small business"; in an atmosphere of growing public antagonism to Morganization, the giant corporations preferred that local interests carry the ball rather than appear themselves in overt opposition to social welfare. But when the Progressives in the national theater began agitating for the tightening up of control over railroads, for the demolition of trusts, and reductions in the tariffs, big business took notice. When President McKinley was assassinated in 1901 and Theodore Roosevelt became President, many of the bankers and their satellites expected the worst. Throughout his career, the Rough Rider had chastised "big financiers" and mocked their "glorified pawnbrokers' souls." He had been nominated for the vice-presidency in the campaign of 1900 (when McKinley was re-elected) mainly as a move by the professional politicians to immobilize him in an empty if honorific position. Suddenly he had become the chief of state at a time when the "emotional classes" looked for just such a leader as he.

Roosevelt's reign lasted until 1909, and proved Elihu Root correct when he surmised that the Rough Rider's "bark is worse than his bite." By limiting his role largely to sloganeering, Roosevelt effectively took the wind from the sails of men like Robert La Follette who became a United States Senator in 1906 and tried to accomplish on a national scale what he had achieved in Wisconsin. Characteristic of T.R.'s work was the Pure Food and Drugs Act of 1906. This Act was a sop to consumer groups. It was worse than useless for insuring sanitation in food processing and purity and honest labeling in drugs, since it prescribed no effective means of enforcement and yet blocked the early enactment of more stringent regulation in its field.

But even the passage of the Pure Food and Drugs Act, such as it was, over the political minions massed against any extension of federal power, represented a kind of triumph for Roosevelt. Unlike most of the more thorough reformers, T.R. was a professional politician of considerable experience. He had served three terms in the sordid Assembly of the New York State Legislature; he had been a member of the federal Civil Service Commission for six years under Presidents Harrison and Cleveland, and was also McKinley's Assistant Secretary of the Navy until he quit to organize the Rough Riders to fight the Spanish in Cuba in 1898 (see Chapter Twelve). On his return from the war, he won the governorship of New York. Roosevelt's experience reinforced his native political savvy. Rarely did he plump for the whole loaf or nothing (as Wilson was to do later); when he saw that he could wheedle half a loaf only, he grasped it—with such shouting that his followers were willing to believe that he had slain the dragon of privilege even when he had merely begun its domestication.

In the period between the election of Grant and the re-election of McKinley the two-party system of American politics had degenerated into a quadrennial contest for control of political jobs. Business not politics had assumed the dynamic role in American development, and both parties prostrated themselves before their masters. T.R.'s role, and that of the Progressives in general, was to recall the political genius of the American people from its long slumber. The real invigoration of the role of the state in fulfilling its constitutional obligation to "promote the general welfare" was not to come until the depression of the 1930s. But Roosevelt and the Progressives reminded the nation and the nation's business leaders that that obligation had not been permanently suspended.

Two dramatic actions of Roosevelt's during his first administration, fairly insubstantial in themselves, had great symbolic force in this connection. In the first he ordered his Attorney-General to attack the Morgan-Rockefeller Northern Securities combine in 1902. This had the startling effect of bringing the imperial J. P. Morgan himself on a hasty visit to the White House to find out just how far the power of the nation was going to be employed against the heretofore fairly unmolested business community. When, in 1904, the Supreme Court by a mere 5 to 4 vote dissolved the Northern Securities Company, Roosevelt thundered for all to hear, that "The most powerful men in this country were held to accountability before the law."

T.R.'s second dramatic performance also came in 1902. By October of that year the mine workers in the anthracite pits, most of which had become "captive mines" of the Morgan-dominated Reading Railroad, had been on strike for months. Conditions in the mines and mining towns had been atrocious in the 1870s when the bankers first took control, and they had gone from bad to worse. Led by the able John Mitchell, guiding genius of the United Mine Workers, the miners demanded improvements all along the line. The operators, headed by George F. Baer, Morgan-appointed head of the Reading road, were immovable in their unwillingness even to recognize the existence of the union; negotiation with it was out of the question. At one stage in the strike, Baer made the sanctimonious statement that "The rights and interests of the laboring man will be cared for, not by the labor agitators, but by the Christian men to whom God in His infinite wisdom has given control of the property interests of the country."

This was sound Morgan doctrine and was underscored by the great financier himself when he returned from one of his trips to Europe in August. By then the deadlock in the mines had existed for four months. Winter was imminent and the nation's anthracite coalbins were empty. By October "coal riots" had broken out in various northern cities. Roosevelt demanded that the strike be arbitrated; the operators would yield on nothing until the workers went back to the pits. The workers themselves, "having in mind our experience with the coal operators in the past," as Mitchell put it, remained just as adamant as Morgan and company. At last, on October 13, Morgan made a second trip to the nation's capital, which unaccountably seemed to have returned to Washington from Wall Street. He and Roosevelt finally were able to agree on an arbitration commission which ultimately awarded the workers a 10 per cent wage increase and other concessions. The Rough Rider had triumphed again, and a grateful people could look forward to their winter's heat.

Ever since childhood Roosevelt had been a lover of the great outdoors, epecially the American West. Conservation of American forest, mineral, and water resources was a subject very close to his heart and from the day of his taking the presidency he had worked to enlarge the areas to be preserved from wasteful exploitation by big business. During his first administration, Roosevelt also set up a Bureau of Corporations, a kind of forerunner of the Federal Trade Commission, to do continuing research into the affairs of the titans of the business world, and to make its findings public. He also established the Anti-Trust division of the Department of Justice and created a new Department of Commerce and Labor, with a pro-labor Secretary of cabinet rank.

The middle class obviously enjoyed Roosevelt's reaffirmation of federal power against the plutocrats, especially as he seemed also to quiet the clamor for Socialism among the workers and radical intellectuals. Even big business recognized the merit of Roosevelt's work in this latter connection; at any rate, leading millionaires contributed handsomely to his 1904 campaign fund. In the election that year, Roosevelt defeated the Democratic candidate, Judge Alton B. Parker of New York, by more than two and a half million votes, polling an unprecedented 56.4 per cent of the ballots cast.

The major legislation of T.R.'s second term included, besides the opening-wedge Pure Food and Drugs Act, the Hepburn Act of 1906, and the Aldrich-Vreeland Act of 1908. The first of these gave the Interstate Commerce Commission power to set maximum railroad rates; but such rates remained subject to court review. The Hepburn Act also extended the Commission's regulatory domain to railroad terminal facilities, refrigeration cars, and warehouses. The Aldrich-Vreeland Act, a forerunner of the Federal Reserve Act of 1913, was enacted as a consequence of the Panic of 1907. Its main objective was to broaden the base for the issuance of bank currency in times of financial stringency. It permitted banks to issue currency against reserves not only of federal bonds, as in the past, but against state and local securities and commercial paper. More adequate financial legislation had to wait a few years.

Roosevelt would have given much for a national crisis that might have permitted him, like his cousin later, to seek a third term. The best he could do was to hand-pick his successor, his friend and Secretary of War, William Howard Taft, of Ohio. In the elections of 1908 Taft won easily over the perennial candidate, William Jennings Bryan, to whom the Democrats had returned after the demolition of the conservative Parker four years earlier. Roosevelt himself, finding that his personal estate had shrunk to the point where he had better go to work, made numerous journalistic connections and then, in 1909, set out to hunt big game in Africa. Taft's allegiance to Progressivism was soon shown to be thin indeed. The political news annoyed T.R., and letters from such Progressives as his son-in-law Nicholas Longworth and his friend Henry Cabot Lodge complaining of social coldness at the White House made things worse. After Roosevelt's return in 1910 his split with Taft widened rapidly. At heart Taft was a conservative jurist. An immense figure physically, he was not as jovial as he looked. As a symbol of Progressivism he was an uncomfortable and compromising pigmy.

Taft had the misfortune of permitting the Republican old guard to pass a new high tariff act (the Payne-Aldrich Act of 1909) just when the whole country was complaining of the high cost of living which the bankers' "stabilized" economy helped to bring about. This act contemptuously ignored the Republican Party's platform pledge of tariff revision. So incensed were certain western agrarian Progressives over Taft's betrayal—notably La Follette, Beveridge of Indiana, Bristow of Kansas, and Dolliver and Cummins of Iowa —that they fought their own party leaders in one of the most brilliant debates ever to occur in the Senate. The "insurgents" lost to Aldrich and his company of "regulars," who had Taft's (and the lobbies') encouragement; but the impact of their rebellion shook the Senate old guard to its foundations. When Taft then announced to the public that the Payne-Aldrich Tariff Act, the highest yet, was the best ever enacted, he shocked the Republican rank and file as well.

The year after the tariff fight in the Senate, insurgent House Progressives, chiefly insurgent Republicans, tried to unseat Republican Speaker "Uncle Joe" Cannon, who ruled the chamber with an iron hand largely through his chairmanship of the Rules Committee. This Committee had absolute control over what legislation would be brought to the floor of the House. The Speaker also had the power to name the members of all other committees, and of refusing to recognize any member who wished to address the House. Taft gave the House insurgents no more aid or sympathy than he had given those in the Senate, and Cannon managed to save his speakership; but in March 1910, the insurgents succeeded in stripping the Speaker of much of his absolute power. Taft's role in this melee cost him most of the Progressive support he had managed to retain after the tariff fiasco.

The final rupture between Taft and the Progressives occurred when Interior Secretary Ballinger, more or less on a technicality, reopened to private exploitation certain of Roosevelt's "conserved" coal lands in Alaska in which Morgan and the Guggenheims were interested. Such open perversions of Progressive policies made Taft seem the embodiment of reaction. But Progressives in the Cabinet and in Congress during Taft's administration managed to extend regulatory and reform legislation beyond Roosevelt's own limits.

Where T.R.'s attorneys-general had brought forty-four suits against the trusts in seven years, Taft's brought ninety suits in four years, and these attacked much bigger game and brought much heavier fines. Under Taft, Congress in 1910 also passed the Mann-Elkins Act which at long last gave the Interstate Commerce Commission the power to suspend railroad rates it found objectionable, and to do so without first going to the courts. This made government regulation effective for the first time. Despite the cry of "socialism," Taft's administration provided the country with parcel post and postal savings banks. It also took steps greatly to improve safety on the railroads and working conditions in the mines. It established a separate Department of Labor (and of Commerce), and a Children's Bureau to set child-labor standards and to oversee child-labor conditions on a national scale. Above all, in exchange for votes on the high tariff of 1909, Taft's congressional contingent yielded on the Sixteenth Amendment to the Constitution insuring the legality of the income tax. This amendment, also passed in 1909, was ratified in 1913.

By then Woodrow Wilson of New Jersey had become President, and Progressive legislation in the national theater was on the verge of becoming stronger than ever. Progressive legislation had not been the aim of those who groomed Wilson for the White House. But Wilson, a transplanted Virginian who once said that, "The only place in the world where nothing has to be explained to me is the South," was capable of discerning which way the winds of political power blew and of acting accordingly. The idea of a strong executive appealed to Wilson as much as it did to Theodore

Roosevelt; but strength in office implied that the leader's voice be "lifted upon the chorus and that it [be] only the crown of the common theme." Despite Taft, the "common theme" was still Progressive in tone and Wilson had long since adopted it.

The most exciting candidate for the presidency as the elections of 1912 loomed had been Robert M. La Follette of Wisconsin, the most successful Progressive of them all as Governor of Wisconsin and the most militant as United States Senator. La Follette hoped to get the Republican nomination. The party leaders were certain they could stop him, but far less certain that he would not then run on a third party ticket. Their fears were aroused by the fact that as early as January 1911, La Follette's supporters had formed the National Progressive Republican League to force his nomination as the "logical candidate." The Progressives were determined either to capture the Republican Party nomination or to run an independent candidate of their own, preferably the man from Wisconsin.

Unfortunately for the Progressives, the Republican Party refused to be captured. Far worse, some slick party leaders prevailed upon Roosevelt himself "to head off La Follette" by entering the contest for the "third party" nomination against him. Roosevelt cogitated this move for a long time, then suddenly announced that his hat was in the ring. La Follette support suddenly melted away. Roosevelt, after all, was far more the public incarnation of Progressivism than was the Senator. Above all, T.R. was unmatched as a campaigner. He was especially eager to campaign in 1912 because the old guard who had retained control of the Republican Party renominated Taft. Roosevelt had come to consider his old friend little better than a Judas.

The Democrats had their own "La Follette" in William Jennings Bryan, their own "Taft" in the arch-conservative Champ Clark. A deadlock between these stalwarts opened the way for "Dr. Wilson." And the split in Republican ranks insured Wilson's victory. In the election Wilson polled almost a million and a half fewer votes than Roosevelt and Taft together. His percentage of all votes cast was no more than 41.8. But he had none of Lincoln's concern over being a minority president. "This is not a day of triumph," he said at the conclusion of his inaugural address. "It is a day of dedication. Here muster," he added in good Progressive language, "not the forces of party, but the forces of humanity. . . . I summon all honest men, all patriotic men, to my side. God helping me, I will not fail them, if they will but counsel and sustain me."

Had the Republican Party stalwarts had their way, Taft would have won the election. That he didn't was a measure of the concessions the Progressive spirit had forced upon the rulers of the country. The middle class had found the flaws in "Morganization" and had applied political remedies to them. In Wilson's first administration these remedies were made all the more stringent. Wilson's three major accomplishments were the Underwood Tariff of 1913, the first since the Civil War to lower the tariff appreciably against foreign competition with American manufacturers; the Clayton Anti-Trust Act of 1914, which explicitly outlawed monopolistic business practices and established a Federal Trade Commission to see that they remained inoperative; and the Owen-Glass Act of 1913, which created the Federal Reserve System to give the whole nation, under government supervision, a flexible currency adapted to the seasonal needs of the farmers as well as the long-term needs of the business world.

Before these vigorous measures could be properly tested, the first World War began in Europe. Many of the leading Progressives were isolationist to the core and in this they reflected the popular spirit of the country. To some of them, however, such as T.R. himself, the Progressive movement at home had had its counterpart in the Messianic impulse abroad. To them the American way of life was the obvious model for the less happy universe and the war was a heaven-sent opportunity for America to reorder the world in her own image. In its way this spirit was as much a part of the American tradition as its isolationist antithesis.

Chapter Twelve

The Messianic Impulse

> Take up the White Man's burden—
>   Send forth the best ye breed—
> Go bind your sons in exile
>   To serve your captive's need:
> To wait in heavy harness,
>   On fluttered folk and wild—
> Your new-caught sullen peoples,
>   Half-devil and half-child.

So Rudyard Kipling addressed the American people in February 1899. Kipling himself had neither love nor sympathy for the "new-caught sullen peoples" of the world.

> Take up the White Man's burden. . . .
> And when your goal is nearest
>   The end for others sought,
> Watch Sloth and heathen Folly
>   Bring all your hope to nought.

It was to save and strengthen their own souls that he urged the White Men of the West to shoulder their obligation.

> Comes now, to search your manhood
>   Through all the thankless years,
> Cold, edged with dear-bought wisdom,
>   The judgment of your peers. . . .
>
> Take up the White Man's Burden—
>   Ye dare not stoop to less—
> Nor call too loud on Freedom
>   To cloak your weariness.

In February 1899, the United States had just humiliated Spain in what Theodore Roosevelt was to call "the most absolutely right-eous foreign war" of the nineteenth century, and the Senate was debating the acquisition of the Philippines as part of the spoils of victory. Few in America, least of all the expansionists themselves, thought of making the distant islands a territory and ultimately a state, or of making the "little brown brothers" out there citizens. But could a democratic republic become an empire and rule a sub-ject people? This question agitated Americans from President McKinley down. Kipling's poem, urging the White Men of America to "have done with childish days," helped to justify, indeed to impel an affimative answer.

Appropriately enough, "The White Man's Burden" first appeared in *McClure's* magazine, the leading organ of the "muckrakers" who were soon to pick up the "White Man's Burden" at home. Roosevelt sent advance copies to Henry Cabot Lodge, remarking that it was "rather poor poetry, but good sense from the expansionist stand-point." Lodge himself thought more highly of the poetry and the sense. "I like it," he wrote back. On publication, American news-papers gave Kipling's poem first-page play: and from the United States it "circled the earth in a day and by repetition became hackneyed within a week."

THE WORLD AND THE UNITED STATES

From the time of the Crusades in the eleventh and twelfth centuries until the spread of Communism in our day, the history of Western Christendom had been the history of expansion. To account for this is to explain the whole nature of the "White Man" of the Western World. He would spread "civilization," but also fly from it. Duty drove him as much as daring, faith as much as science, power as strongly as trade, pride as relentlessly as profit. In the pulse-quickening history that this complex of motives brought about, the discovery of America itself had been but one incident.

After the discovery of America, the rivalry of the western powers spread to other parts of the world and gradually brought about the enslavement or exploitation of the colored peoples of the southern climes. Britain's triumph over Napoleon in 1815 at last knocked the French out of the old contest for empire; while the triumph of the industrial revolution in Britain assured her world supremacy for a century.

Yet, like the other institutions of western civilization, the industrial revolution itself gradually spread across Europe, and after the fall of prices following the panic of 1873, competition for world markets grew especially intense. Besides markets, all industrial nations began to look for colonial sources of raw materials and colonial outlets for investment capital. To protect far-flung empires they also enlarged their navies. And, lest their ships, as Admiral A. T. Mahan put it, "be like land birds, unable to fly far from their own shores," they sought additional colonies for naval coaling stations and repair bases. Soon Oceania, the coastal lands of the eastern Pacific, the interiors of Africa and China, Latin America, indeed all the world, once more became the stage of the imperial drama.

The upsurge of colonialism and navalism heightened international suspicions, and all the great countries of Europe began to expand and modernize their armies. Between 1870 and 1890 British military expenditures rose 300 per cent; French, 250 per cent; Russian, 400 per cent; Austro-Hungarian, 450 per cent; German, 1,000 per cent. The same period saw seething diplomatic activity which brought about a constant reshuffling of alliances in consideration of the new international realities.

In an environment of world-wide competition, nationalism seemed to thrive; and explorers, missionaries, travelers, doctors, artists, poets, and scientists all leveled their own country's version of Christian culture at the colored peoples of the appropriated lands. Britain's "White Man's Burden" was matched by France's *mission civilisatrice,* and Bismarckian Germany's *Kultur.* Soon Italy and Russia joined the great adventure for "a place in the sun." And by the 1880s the United States was being readied, as an American missionary said, to join "the Christian nations" who "are subduing the world, in order to make mankind free."

As recently as the 1850s, the Americans, Commodore Perry and Townsend Harris, had opened Japanese ports to the trade of the western world. From a mere market for western goods, Japan quickly became an apt mimic of western industrialism. Even before the 1880s she had shown the transparency of *white* claims to divine appointment to civilize the colored peoples of the world by herself joining the imperial fray.

Russia established her Pacific outpost of Vladivostok in 1860. After selling Alaska to the United States in 1867, Russia turned her hungry eyes in earnest toward the crumbling Chinese Empire, and especially to the province of Manchuria, which thrust itself into Russian Siberia like a thumb in the eye. At almost the same time, Japan too turned to nibble at the Manchu colossus, where England and France had enjoyed special privileges for decades. In 1876, Japan recognized Korea's independence from China and hoped to make the new nation a sphere of interest of her own. Ten years later Britain annexed Burma; and soon after, France completed the organization of French Indo-China.

These white incursions did not deter the Japanese from declaring war on China in 1894, as a result of which she grasped much new territory. Defeat in this war marked the beginning of the Chinese people's revolt against the futile Manchu dynasty and against the foreigners who took such overbearing advantage of it. Startled by the speed and decisiveness of Japan's victory, Russia, in concert with Germany and France, forced the Nipponese to disgorge some of their new acquisitions; but when ten years later Japan decisively defeated the Russians themselves, she established her ascendancy in the Far East.

The Russo-Japanese War of 1904-05 had tremendous consequences. Defeat in the East turned Russia back toward expansionism in Europe, and opened the chain of events in the Balkans that eventually led to the first World War. This defeat also weakened the Russian Czardom and the allegiance of the Russian people to it, and set the stage for the Russian Revolutions of 1905 and 1917. The Russo-Japanese War marked the first conquest in modern times of a western nation by a "backward" eastern one, of a white people by a colored one. Japan's rapid industrialization became a model for colored nations all over the world; Japan's victory exposed the vulnerability of the *white* imperialists.

The Russo-Japanese War was terminated, strikingly enough, by the Treaty of Portsmouth (New Hampshire). The peacemaker was President Roosevelt. His justification for entering into the far-off conflict was American concern for the security of her new Philippine possessions. Of all the aspects of the war, this is perhaps the most intriguing. "In terms of world history," writes Hajo Holborn, the author of *The Political Collapse of Europe*, "the greatest significance of the events of 1905 was the first emergence of a system of world politics. Never before had European, American, and Asiatic policies interacted as they did in this fateful year. . . . The world received in 1905 a first glimpse of the future global age."

THE "LARGE AMERICA" IDEA

In 1868 Secretary of State Seward, having just seen the Alaska Purchase barely skin through the Senate and the appropriation for completing it barely pass the House, complained that "the public mind" refused "to entertain the higher but more remote questions of national extension and aggrandizement." In succeeding decades the main role of the United States in world affairs was as an exporter of grain and beef to feed the rising industrial population of Europe; as a refuge for the excess of this population brought about by the rising standard of living attendant upon industrialization; and as an importer of speculative capital for the completion of its vast railroad network, the exploitation of its fabulous mineral deposits, the organization of its cattle kingdom. After 1865 the American merchant marine itself, once the king of the seas and the pride of the nation, was permitted virtually to disappear. And with no trade to protect, the navy languished. The American navy in the 1880s ranked no higher than twelfth in the world, behind Chile.

Yet "national extension and aggrandizement" had already had an overpowering history in the United States in the agrarian age, complete with "White Man's Burden" mythology; and as a rising industrial nation, the United States was soon to find its avid expansionists, its imperial theorists and actors, its latter-day carriers of the Messianic impulse. In 1870, albeit unsuccessfully, President Grant argued for Senate approval of the acquisition of Santo Domingo in these terms: "The people of San Domingo are not capable of maintaining themselves in their present condition. . . .

They yearn for the protection of our free institutions . . . our progress and civilization. Shall we refuse them?" Santo Domingo had to wait thirty-five years before becoming a "protectorate" of the United States. But elsewhere in the Caribbean region and in the Pacific the United States had already begun its noncontiguous expansion.

In the 1850s, after Perry and Harris had promoted our trans-Pacific interests in Japan, a guano craze swept over American agriculture (guano is a rich fertilizer made from the excrement of sea fowl), and in 1856 the government permitted naval officers to raise the flag on Pacific islands where guano was to be found. By 1880 about fifty islands had thus become "appurtenances" of the United States, some of which became exceedingly valuable in the age of air transportation. By 1880 American businessmen like Minor Keith and Daniel Guggenheim had also laid the foundations of private American empires in Latin America. Keith built railroads in Costa Rica and then, in typical imperialist fashion, turned the heretofore self-sufficient economy of the little country to the intensive production of bananas to supply his railroads with freight. In this way he started what was to become the vast domain of the United Fruit Company. The Guggenheims began operating copper and silver mines in Mexico and South America, thus starting that family's foreign activities.

In two areas such early imperialist adventures involved the American Government in disputes with other nations. One of these was Samoa, in the southern Pacific; the other, Hawaii in the northern Pacific. Events in Cuba in the 1860s and 1870s also interested American officials, but little was to be done about that island for another twenty-five years.

Like many Pacific islands, Samoa offered a haven for shipwrecked mariners and a refuge to more fortunate vessels caught in Pacific storms. As early as the 1830s ships of many nations had begun to deposit missionaries there. After the completion of the first transcontinental railroad in 1869, Grant sent an emissary to the Islands to help develop the excellent harbor of Pago Pago into a way station for American trans-Pacific commerce. British and German interests on the island, however, soon effected the American emissary's deportation, and henceforth relations among the United States, the United Kingdom and Germany grew more belligerent. After the Spanish War in 1899 the United States finally acquired Pago Pago harbor. Germany got most of the remainder of Samoa and the British were compensated elsewhere in the Pacific and Africa at Germany's expense.

Samoa presented an early occasion for the display of American ambitions as a world power. It also exposed the problems such ambitions brought. As Cleveland's Secretary of State Gresham said, this venture was "the first departure from our traditional and well established policy of avoiding entangling alliances with foreign powers in relation to objects remote from this hemisphere."

The Hawaiian islands are more considerable than Samoa, and nearer to the American west coast. Missionaries from New England had settled there as early as 1820, by which time the islands had already become a pleasant rendezvous for ships in the China trade. Between 1840 and 1860 about four hundred American whaling vessels visited the islands each year, and many among the crews jumped ship and remained in Hawaii. Many Hawaiians, voluntarily or otherwise, signed on American vessels and eventually settled in California. For this and other reasons the native population rapidly declined. French and British mariners had also frequented the islands, and the governments of their countries began early in the nineteenth century to show an interest in acquiring them. In 1842 Daniel Webster, then Tyler's Secretary of State, effectively terminated these designs by assuring the islanders that while the United States would not annex them, political meddling there by any other nation would "dissatisfy" us.

By the 1850s it had been discovered that sugar could be grown successfully in Hawaii and after 1876 the new staple was admitted free of duty to American ports. The treaty by which this was arranged reiterated the American position that no third nation would be permitted to meddle in the islands. Relations between the two lands grew closer in 1884 when this treaty was renewed, though ratification was withheld by the United States Senate until 1887 when Hawaii agreed as part of the treaty to yield Pearl Harbor and to permit the United States to build a naval base there.

Between 1875 and 1890, Hawaiian sugar exports to the United States came to represent 99 per cent of all Hawaiian exports. The danger of this concentration on a single staple for a single market was made abundantly clear in 1890 when Louisiana sugar growers prevailed upon Congress to give them special advantages. These were incorporated in the McKinley Tariff which removed the duty on other foreign sugar, thus allowing it to compete with Hawaii's, and at the same time gave the American growers a bounty of two cents a pound. The McKinley Tariff disrupted the Hawaiian economy and heightened anti-American sentiment among the surviving Hawaiian population. This sentiment had been fed earlier by descendants of the American missionaries who by 1890 had come to control three fourths of Hawaii's arable land. They had also introduced Oriental contract laborers to work in the sugar fields. Worst of all, they had extracted a constitution from King Kalakaua by which they virtually controlled the government.

King Kalakaua died in 1891 when the sugar depression had brought anti-American feeling to a peak. When his successor, Queen Liliuokalani, persisted in the idea that Hawaii should be governed by Hawaiians, the American business community responded in 1893 by forming a Committee of Safety headed by Sanford B. Dole. The Committee's main objective was annexation by the United States. With the connivance of J. L. Stevens, the American Minister, and the protection of the United States Marines, Dole's Committee overthrew "Queen Lil" and rushed a commission to Washington where a treaty of annexation was written. When President Cleveland refused to submit this treaty to the Senate, Dole's provisional government proclaimed the Hawaiian Republic in 1894 and named Dole president. The Republic was annexed in July 1898, during the imperialist upsurge following the outbreak of the Spanish-American War. On April 30, 1900, Hawaii was granted full territorial status. By 1958 the agitation for statehood (along with Alaska) had made considerable headway.

The United States' early ventures into noncontiguous expansion scarcely engaged the emotions or sympathy of the American people. Yet a few American officials had joined with the independent business expansionists to prod a reluctant government into enterprises involving distant lands. The leading official imperialist after Seward's time was James G. Blaine, a worshiper of Henry Clay and one of the founders of the Republican Party. Though often a candidate for the nomination, and once, in 1884, the party's standard bearer, Blaine, like Clay, never won the presidency. But he used his lower offices to forward American foreign interests, especially in Latin America.

Blaine's interpretation of the Monroe Doctrine was characteristically aggressive. Keeping Europe out of Latin America was not good enough for him; United States goods and ideas must be forced in. Latin America was selling to the United States twice as much as it was buying, and well over 85 per cent of Latin American goods were entering duty free. Blaine wanted at least equal treatment for United States exports. As Harrison's Secretary of State in 1889, Blaine brought representatives of eighteen Latin American nations to Washington in the first Pan-American Conference. When the delegates failed to make trade concessions, he threatened to place tariffs on Latin American goods. His threat was fulfilled by the so-called "reciprocity" provisions of the McKinley Tariff Act of 1890. This Act implied that the United States would reciprocate for good treatment abroad; in fact it meant that we would reciprocate for bad. Few Latin American countries, however, increased either their trade with or their tenderness for the United States.

In support of his "Large America" policy, Blaine became one of the earliest advocates of a new and powerful navy. On his urging, Congress established the Naval Advisory Board in 1881 and the Naval War College at Newport in 1884. The Board and the College both served admirably to spread "big navy" propaganda. Captain (later Admiral) A. T. Mahan became President of the College in 1889. Three years before he had established himself as the world's leading philosopher of navalism and imperialism by a series of lectures at the College which were published in 1890 as *The Influence of Sea Power Upon History 1660-1783*. Such was the state of American opinion at the time, this classic-to-be went three years before finding a publisher.

In the 1880s Congress authorized the construction of nine new cruisers and the first modern American battleship, *Maine*. To calm foreign anxieties over American intentions, the new navy was described officially as one of "seagoing coastline battleships." In the epochal Naval Act of 1890 this fiction was put aside and the concept of a "navy second to none" appeared. By 1898 only Britain and France outranked the United States in naval power. With the Ocean Mail Subsidy Act of 1891 Congress also took the first step since the Civil War to rebuild the merchant marine. When the panic of 1893 suggested to American business leaders that the American market for goods might not be growing as rapidly as heretofore, some of them also turned their eyes abroad for customers. By 1897 the Annual Report of the State Department's Bureau of Foreign Commerce stated that "what may be termed an American invasion of the markets of the world" had begun.

THE SPANISH WAR

While the United States prepared her navy and her factories to implement Blaine's expansionist policy, a series of international incidents threatened to take the country beyond expansion into war. These incidents served to ready the American mind for violence when war came.

Two incidents arose over the Canadian fisheries. A treaty defining American rights in eastern Canadian waters (and Canadian rights in neighboring American waters) had been approved in 1871; but finding the terms irksome, the United States told Canada in 1883 that we were terminating the treaty as of July 1, 1885. Canada retaliated promptly by taking American fishing vessels found in her waters after that date. Ill feeling over this issue was aggravated a few years later when American sealers in the Bering Sea, contending that Canadian seal-fishing methods were exterminating the herds, got American government cutters to remove Canadian schooners from the area.

At the time of the first incident Henry Cabot Lodge, then a young Congressman from Massachusetts, declaimed: "Wherever the American flag on an American fishing smack is touched by a foreigner the great American heart is touched." The *Detroit News* was more explicit. In February 1887, it said:

> We do not want to fight,
> But, by jingo, if we do,
> We'll scoop in all the fishing grounds
> And the whole Dominion too.

Fortunately cooler heads prevailed in both matters, the first of which was settled by a working arrangement in 1888 and the second by an arbitration treaty in 1892.

Two South American episodes proved more inflammatory. During a revolution in Chile in 1891, the United States detained a rebel steamer that had come to California to buy arms. The rebels won out anyway and hostility toward the United States was rife. In October 1891, the captain of the U.S.S. *Baltimore,* then in Valparaiso, carelessly allowed his crew of over a hundred to go ashore, and to go unarmed. A riot broke out between the American sailors and some Chileans, and two Americans sailors were killed. News of the fray found many in the United States eager to take up the cudgels. Among them was Theodore Roosevelt, whose intimates taunted him thereafter as "the Chilean volunteer." Just in time a full apology came from Chile.

More serious were the consequences of an old boundary dispute between British Guiana and neighboring Venezuela. The dispute flared anew in the 1880s when gold was discovered in the contested region. In 1887 Britain and Venezuela broke off diplomatic relations, and United States' efforts to restore harmony only made things worse. In July 1895, Richard Olney, Cleveland's Secretary of State, reminded Lord Salisbury, the British Foreign Minister, of the "noncolonization" clauses of the Monroe Doctrine. The United States, Olney said, considered Britain's presence in South America "unnatural and inexpedient." He continued: "Today the United States is practically sovereign on this continent, and its fiat is law." When Salisbury replied in unconciliatory language, Cleveland got Congress to appropriate money for a commission to settle the boundary and advised the British that efforts to grasp territory not allotted to Guiana would be considered by the United States "as a wilful aggression upon its rights and interests."

Twenty-six governors promptly pledged the President their backing. "WAR IF NECESSARY," cried the *New York Sun.* If war came, said Theodore Roosevelt, he hoped he might "have a hand in it myself." "The bankers, brokers, and anglomaniacs generally," he wrote to Lodge, seemed to favor "peace at any price. . . . Personally I rather hope the fight will come soon. The clamor of the peace faction has convinced me that this country needs a war."

Britain's growing concern over the rise and rivalry of Germany, and her desire on that account to court the United States, helped avert armed conflict over this issue. But young American inflammables like Roosevelt and Lodge soon found a new situation ready to their hand. This was the latest Cuban insurrection against Spain, which had begun in 1895. An earlier Cuban revolt in 1868 had found Americans looking on with considerable indifference. By 1895, however, the world, the United States, and Cuba itself had all greatly changed. The aggressive imperialism of Britain, France, and Germany, highlighted in this connection by France's efforts to build a canal across Panama in the 1880s, made the likelihood of Cuba's control by a vigorous power much greater than before. In the United States, active and dedicated groups were themselves pushing expansion, navalism, and imperialism, which called for coaling stations, strategic harbors, and protected bases. Our own interests in a Caribbean canal also had matured. In Cuba, finally, American-financed sugar growing had become as depressed as in Hawaii. In 1884 Cuban raw sugar commanded a price of eight cents a pound. In 1895 it brought two cents and the Cuban populace suffered.

Rebel tactics in 1895 included deliberate attacks on American property with the objective of forcing the United States to intervene to restore the order that Spain was too weak to maintain. Spain herself played into rebel hands early in 1896 by sending over the notorious General Weyler whose brutal strategy earned him the name "Butcher." American indignation over Weyler's inhumanity was itself inflamed by a Cuban junta in New York, made up of exiles from the earlier insurrection, who were agitating for Cuban autonomy. Joseph Pulitzer of the *New York World* and William Randolph Hearst of the *New York Journal* also chose this occasion to s.age a rough contest for circulation. The main tactic of each journalist was to outdo the other in stories of Spanish fiendishness. Others in America, among them Roosevelt and Lodge, were spoiling for a fight.

President Cleveland had said in 1896 that he "feared there were some outrages upon both sides, if the truth were known," and he refused to be manipulated by the zealots. In March 1897, however, McKinley became president on a platform that called for Cuban independence. When Spain recalled "Butcher" Weyler and offered other reforms, McKinley seemed ready to reverse his position, but a series of events played into the hands of the war party. Most important was the blowing up of the *Maine* in Cuban waters on February 15, 1898, with the loss of two officers and 258 crew members. Immediately after the disaster Captain Sigsbee of the *Maine* wired that "Public opinion should be suspended until further report," and a prompt inquiry failed to blame Spain. Even before the inquiry was completed, however, Congress appropriated $50,-000,000 for national defense and the cry, "Remember the *Maine*," whipped up the country. On February 25 Roosevelt, now Assistant Secretary of the Navy, in consultation with Lodge, now Senator, cabled Commodore Dewey in command of the Pacific fleet: "Keep full of coal. In the event of war Spain, your duty will be to see that the Spanish squadron does not leave the Asiatic coast, and then offensive operations in Philippine Islands."

Many old guard Republicans in the Cabinet, in Congress, and in Wall Street urged McKinley to continue negotiations with Spain. But the President yielded to the war press and the jingoes, and on April 11 delivered a militant message to Congress. He was obliged to refer to Spain's capitulation on the matter of Cuban reforms, of which he had been aware for two days. But he buried this in his address. This made it easier for Congress to interpret the message as a demand for a declaration of war. The formal declaration came on April 25, two days after the duly warned Commodore Dewey had set sail for Manila Bay.

Dewey's fleet arrived May 1 and on that morning, after giving the famous order, "You may fire when ready, Gridley," the Commodore blasted the futile Spanish fleet he found there. The next step in the campaign, "offensive operations in Philippine Islands," had to wait until enough men had been mobilized. By July 25 about 10,000 American troops had at last reached the Philippines, under the command of General Wesley Merritt. Supported by Filipino insurrectionists under Emilio Aguinaldo, whom Dewey had helped arm, Merritt took Manila on August 13.

By then the "splendid little war," as John Hay called it, had already come to a close in the West Indies. In May the Spanish fleet there, under Admiral Cervera, had been bottled up in Santiago harbor by Admiral Sampson. Sampson, however, could do no damage until a military expedition took the city and forced Cervera out under the American fleet's guns. Overcoming incredible inadequacies in arms, shelter, clothing, and provisions, 16,000 men under General W. T. Shafter finally left Tampa, Florida, on June 14, and arrived in Cuba June 22.

Typical of this army was the First Volunteer Cavalry Regiment, the "Rough Riders," who had no horses. The rest of the Americans were a motley crew under energetic officers who knew little or nothing of war. After the wild melee on San Juan Hill on July 1, Roosevelt wrote home to Lodge, "We are within measurable distance of a terrible military disaster." The defending Spaniards, however, were even more spent than the Americans, and on July 3 Cervera thought it the better part of wisdom to escape if he could. American guns destroyed Cervera's wooden-decked ships. Two weeks later the Spanish army in Cuba capitulated, and on July 25 Puerto Rico fell.

Spain already had begun to seek a peace treaty, and on August 12 hostilities were declared over. The four months' war cost the United States almost 7,000 men, 90 per cent of whom died of disease. Spain's losses in the fighting were much higher. In addition, according to the terms of the peace treaty signed in Paris December 10, she surrendered the remnants of her once imposing new world empire. But ratification of the treaty by the United States Senate was long delayed.

A WORLD POWER

Every justification has been offered for America's going to war with Spain because no clear justification can be found. It was, different people said, America's duty to liberate Cuba, America's destiny to grasp new markets and new lands, America's obligation to bring western culture to the dark places of the earth, America's providence to Christianize the heathen. But why in 1898? "When we Yankees have once set our souls upon a thing," an expansionist of the 1850s once said, "we always have it." Throughout the 'nineties Americans seem to have set their souls upon having a war. Perhaps an editorial in the *Washington Post* just before the start of the war with Spain gave the clearest explanation: "A new consciousness seems to have come upon us—the consciousness of strength—and with it a new appetite, the yearning to show our strength. . . . The taste of Empire is in the mouth of the people even as the taste of blood in the jungle." Finley Peter Dunne, America's leading political wit, put it this way:

"We're a gr-reat people," said Mr. Hennessy earnestly.
"We ar-re," said Mr. Dooley. "We ar-re that. An' th' best iv it is, we know we ar-re."

The resolution by which Congress formalized its declaration of war on Spain included the Teller Amendment which pledged the United States to leave Cuba to the Cubans. Soon after, McKinley said: "By our code of morality," annexation of territory "would be criminal aggression." By July, however, he was singing a different tune. Early that month the joint resolution annexing the Hawaiian Republic was signed, and two weeks later McKinley demanded Puerto Rico and Guam as part of the conditions for an armistice in the war. Next, the "city, bay, and harbor of Manila" were added to the President's demands. Ultimately he refused to consider any peace terms that did not include the cession of all the Philippine Islands. Spain finally yielded, for an indemnity of $20,000,000. "There was nothing left for us to do," McKinley told a gathering of Methodist ministers later, "but to take them all, and to educate the Filipinos, and to uplift and civilize them, and by God's grace do the very best we could by them as our fellow men for whom Christ also died."

"The question of the Philippines," writes Richard Hofstadter, the author of *Social Darwinism in American Thought,* "was some-times pictured as the watershed of American destiny." He proceeds to quote John Barrett, former Minister to Siam, who wrote during the great debate on the issue:

> Now is the critical time when the United States should strain every nerve and bend all her energies to keep well in front in the mighty struggle that has begun for the supremacy of the Pacific Seas. . . . The rule of the survival of the fittest applies to nations as well as to the animal kingdom. It is cruel, relentless principle being exercised in a cruel, relentless competition of mighty forces; and these will trample over us without sympathy or remorse unless we are trained to endure and strong enough to stand the pace.

To fight this position anti-imperialist groups formed the Anti-Imperialist League in November 1898. One of the League's leading spokesmen was William Jennings Bryan, who in December told the press: "This nation cannot endure half republic and half colony—half free and half vassal. Our form of government, our traditions, our present interests and our future welfare, all forbid our entering upon a career of conquest." On February 22, 1899, Bryan said again: "The forcible annexation of the Philippine Islands is not necessary to make the United States a world-power. For over ten decades our nation has been a world-power. During its brief exist-ence it has exerted upon the human race an influence more potent than all the other nations of the earth combined, and it has exerted that influence without the use of sword or Gatling gun."

By then the issue was past arguing. The Senate had debated the treaty hotly for three months. In the midst of the debate, on Decem-ber 21, 1898, McKinley had ordered the War Department to extend the military occupation of Manila to the entire Philippine archipel-ago. The Filipinos, led by Aguinaldo, resisted this move, and their armed defense quickly took the lives of American soldiers. News of the Filipino "insurrection" swayed enough senators for the an-nexation treaty to pass by a mere two votes on February 6, 1899. It took the army three years to make the annexation good against Aguinaldo's forces; and suppression of his resistance cost more in men and money than the war with Spain itself.

Until May 20, 1902, moreover, Cuba itself remained under the dictatorial rule of General Leonard Wood who efficiently rebuilt the island's economy and enlarged its social services far beyond their range under Spanish control. His denial of self-rule to the Cubans, however, was suspect from the start; and suspicions were confirmed by the Platt Amendment to an appropriation act in Congress. This Amendment limited Cuba's autonomy in relation to the ordinary powers of a sovereign government, and permitted the United States to intervene in the island's affairs when it pleased "for the protection of life, property, and individual liberty." Congress required Cuba to incorporate the Platt Amendment in any constitution it drew up and also to accept a treaty with the United States reiterating the Amendment's terms.

The presidential elections of 1900 pitted the imperialist followers of McKinley against Bryan, the anti-imperialist Democratic candidate. The "large America" versus "small America" issue was clear cut; and the overwhelming victory of McKinley and the Republicans was interpreted as a mandate for imperialism. When McKinley was assassinated a few months after his inauguration in 1901 and Vice-President Theodore Roosevelt became President, the imperialist camp was overjoyed. That year, in the so-called Insular Cases, the Supreme Court added its sanction to that of the executive and the people. In these cases the Court held, essentially, that the Constitution did not follow the flag. In particular the Court decided that Puerto Rico was "territory appurtenant—but not a part—of the United States," and that Congress could determine afresh the "civil rights and political status" of the "native inhabitants." The Court also decided, in a case arising out of the denial of trial by jury to Hawaiian natives, that there were two kinds of rights, "fundamental" and "procedural." In its effort to "follow the election returns," the Court included trial by jury among "procedural rights," which Congress could withhold or abridge.

These cases indicated that the United States had unwittingly acquired a new class of subject people in an empire that extended halfway around the globe. In the next decade American power was to make itself felt in many independent countries whose internal policies suddenly impinged on American imperial necessities.

The principal necessities, now that America had vast interests in both oceans, were the elimination of foreign participation in any canal that might be built across Central America, and the urgent construction of such a canal by the United States. Back in 1850 the United States and Britain had agreed that neither would construct an isthmian canal independently of the other. In 1900 and 1901, in two treaties, England agreed to free the United States to build a canal alone and fortify it. Congress and President Roosevelt preferred a route across Nicaragua. The French, however, had tried for twenty years without success to build a canal across Panama in the state of Colombia and were now eager to sell their rights to the Panama route, all the more so since these rights under the French contract would soon revert to the Colombian government.

American lawyers for the French company succeeded in altering America's preference as to the route; and the United States itself, by conniving in a revolution which separated Panama from Colombia, succeeded in forestalling the latter's claims to payment for the rights it long had expected to retrieve. Colombia was outraged by American high-handedness. Roosevelt declared that nation to be "entitled to precisely the amount of sympathy we extend to other inefficient bandits." After Roosevelt's death in 1919, the United States paid an indemnity of $25,000,000 to Colombia. But long before that the Panama Canal was completed at a cost of $375,000,000. It was open to the ships of the world in August 1914.

To protect the great new waterway, United States policy was directed more than ever toward making the Caribbean an American sea. This took considerable doing since other nations had enlarged their interests in Caribbean lands. In such lands, typically, governments came and went by revolution. The victors usually ignored the debts incurred by their predecessors and thus invited the interference of the creditor nations of Europe. One such situation in Santo Domingo in 1904 prompted Roosevelt to announce a corollary to the Monroe Doctrine. Interference by other states in Latin America could not be condoned by the United States, he said, but we also would see to it that Latin American debts were paid and that interference would not become necessary. This position obliged the United States itself on a number of occasions to take over the customhouses and administer the taxes of Latin American countries.

During T. R.'s administration, American participation in affairs in Europe and the Far East also reached a peak. After her humiliation by Japan in 1895, China had embarked on a spree of westernization. In exchange for huge loans from European nations she surrendered control of her customs collections to her new creditors. China's aspirations ran so high, however, that these creditors themselves began to fear for their own spheres of interest. The best way to protect their privileges seemed to be to expand them; and by 1898 a fierce scramble was on among Britain, France, Germany, and Russia that threatened to dismember the whole vast Empire. Japan, which had just been forced by these very nations to disgorge some of her conquests in China, seethed with resentment. The United States, in turn, saw its own century-old China trade threatened. Americans also had religious and cultural ties with China, growing out of missionary and medical work there, and hoped to preserve the Empire's territorial integrity.

While Japan girded herself for future wars, the United States, in 1899, promulgated the "Open Door" policy which sought agreement among the nations involved in China to restore China's control of her customs (under which the United States had most-favored-nation treatment), and not to discriminate against the trade of outsiders (like the United States) in their own spheres of interest. Britain, fearful of the favorable position of Japan and Russia for large-scale military invasion of China, sympathized with the Open Door idea. Yet neither she nor the other powers would subscribe to the American program.

The recalcitrance of the imperialists was soon heightened by the Boxer Rebellion, which broke out in China only a few months after the Open Door failure. Many Chinese had grown restive over the headlong European invasion of their land and had organized into secret anti-foreign societies. One of these, formally named the Order of Literary Patriotic Harmonious Fists—hence the satiric western appellation "Boxers"—began in 1899 to tear up railroad lines, to destroy Christian churches, to attack foreign legations, and to murder foreigners themselves. Before they were suppressed by a combined international military force, to which the United States contributed 2,500 men, the Boxers had destroyed millions of dollars' worth of property and killed about three hundred persons.

The imperialists were now ready to tear China completely apart. The United States, on the other hand, enlarged the Open Door policy to include her interest in preserving the "territorial and administrative entity" of China, and John Hay, who had become McKinley's Secretary of State in 1898, succeeded in getting the imperialists to accept a financial indemnity from China in lieu of more territory. This served at least as a temporary check on them. The United States shared in this indemnity to the extent of $24,000,000; and the excess over the small damages we suffered in China was returned to that country. The Chinese gesture of using the money to educate Chinese students in the United States strengthened Sino-American relations.

Hay stayed on as Secretary of State during Roosevelt's first administration and he and the President continued to pursue the Open Door policy in China. At the same time, Japan's imperial interests were encouraged, with England's support, in order to counterbalance Russia's expansion across Asia. In serving as peacemaker after the Russo-Japanese War in 1905, Roosevelt had hoped to cement our good relations with the Nipponese, who, like the Americans, had just burst into global politics. Japan won much in the war; but Roosevelt forced her to forgo an immense financial indemnity from Russia to which the Japanese people had looked for tax relief, and many in Japan felt they had cause to regret American meddling.

Relations between the two countries deteriorated further when Japan learned of the action of the San Francisco Board of Education in October 1906, segregating almost a hundred Japanese children in a separate school. Roosevelt blasted this act as "worse than criminal stupidity," and forced the Board to rescind it. But he also was impelled to negotiate a "gentleman's agreement" with Japan by which, after 1908, the latter would permit no more Japanese workers to emigrate to the United States. This temporarily quieted concern over the "yellow peril" on the West Coast and elsewhere in the United States; but it only heightened the yellow peril in the international world of global politics.

Oddly enough, Japan was mollified when Roosevelt, in ordering the American fleet on a practice cruise around the world, arranged for it to visit Japanese ports. The fleet left in December 1907, ready for a "feast, a frolic, or a fight," as its commander put it. Its reception by the Nipponese was extravagant. And the good will thus restored was improved by the Root-Takahira Agreement, which both countries signed on November 30, 1908. This agreement simply stressed the virtue of maintaining the *status quo* in China and the Far Eastern islands. Since it was signed without deference to China herself, however, it left the Manchu Empire miffed.

Roosevelt's diplomacy was aggressive but often justifiable before world opinion. When he was succeeded by Taft in 1909, American policy in the Caribbean and the Orient became more meddlesome and more disliked. "Dollar diplomacy" is the name that has stuck to the efforts of this administration to force other nations to accept American investments and then to employ the navy and the marines to protect American capital. The harvest was one of immense ill will, and Wilson's administration, for all its good intentions, did little to improve matters. Wilson and his Secretary of State, Bryan, tried to impose their characteristic idealism on international relations. Efforts to cajole the nations of the world into signing arbitration treaties as an alternative to war, however, only got the Wilson administration into trouble with the United States Senate which felt that its own treaty-making powers were being nibbled away. In the Orient, Wilson and Bryan had to face up to Japan's expansive program. Almost continuous negotiations were carried on by the two countries, but their relations remained dangerously ambiguous. In effect, the United States agreed to recognize Japan's special interests and importance in the East; while Japan gave lip service to America's Open Door policy.

It was in Latin America that Wilson's and Bryan's objectives were most laudable and, in the end, most open to condemnation. Wilson's handling of the complex situation out of which grew the war between the United States and Mexico in 1916 was especially open to challenge. In 1911 the long dictatorship of Porfirio Díaz had been overthrown by the constitutionalist, Francisco Madero; but in two years Madero himself was overthrown by a new dictator,

Victoriano Huerta. Most of the nations of the world recognized Huerta's government; but Wilson preferred to support the forces of a new constitutionalist, Venustiano Carranza, who had organized a counter-revolution as soon as Huerta had grasped control.

Ultimately Carranza managed to unseat Huerta. But no sooner had he done so than his own best general, tough Francisco "Pancho" Villa, decided to seek power himself. In October 1915, after Carranza had seemingly crushed Villa's forces, the United States recognized the new government. But Villa broke loose once more, invaded American territory, and killed American citizens. On the assumption that Carranza could not control his country, Wilson sent a "punitive expedition" across the border, under General John J. Pershing. Fearful that the great power to the north was seeking to detach northern Mexico, Carranza replied by mobilizing his forces. A border clash soon broadened into larger hostilities, but peace was restored in January 1917, before a genuine war got under way. Wilson had saved Mexico from the dictatorship of Huerta and his ilk; but his method was the worst possible for the establishment of constitutional government. Carranza's rule was preserved; but Mexicans have not forgiven the United States for the invasion of their territory.

THE FIRST WORLD WAR

The Mexican affair developed so slowly and ended so promptly largely because of the World War which had begun in Europe in August 1914. Our concern over that war made us hesitate about plunging into a Mexican adventure and made us withdraw from it as quickly as possible once we were drawn in.

In his address on Flag Day, June 14, 1917, a few weeks after America's entry into the World War, President Wilson said: "This is the People's War, a war for freedom and justice and self-government amongst all the nations of the world, a war to make the world safe for the peoples who live upon it . . . the German peoples themselves included." Wilson made a convenient distinction between the "military masters of Germany" and their subjects, and explained that we entered the war against the former "not as a partisan," but as everybody's friend. Our objective was nothing less than that which by 1914 had brought about a quarter century of American expansionism and imperialism, "the redemption of the affairs of mankind."

Almost three years of doubt and indecision had preceded this brave stand. At the beginning of the war the United States became involved in difficulties only with her future allies and almost exclusively with Great Britain. These difficulties arose out of the problems of neutral shipping in wartime and America's effort to maintain the traditional freedom of the seas. Very early in the war the British declared a naval blockade of the Central Powers and mined the waters adjacent to their shores. In addition she seized all neutral ships, American included, bound for mainland neutral ports, even if such ships carried goods that were not contraband of war.

Wilson found these affronts to the American flag intolerable, but was persuaded to acquiesce in them. The result was the same as though the United States itself had deliberately boycotted Germany and her friends. In 1914 the United States had done business worth almost $170,000,000 with the Central Powers. By 1916 this business had virtually disappeared. In the same period, American trade with the Allies multiplied four times, reaching $3,250,000,000 in 1916. At the start of the war Wilson's administration banned all loans, public and private, to any belligerent. By the end of 1916, however, a softening of this policy resulted in loans to the Allies of almost $2,500,000,000, which financed the bulk of their wartime American purchases.

While the United States thus supplied the Allies with munitions and equipment, her relations with Germany and the Central Powers steadily worsened. When Germany overran neutral Belgium in 1914, many Americans had been ready to believe the worst about German aspirations to control the world. Their belief was assisted by the flow of British "atrocity" stories about the "Hun's" treatment of civilians and prisoners of war. Our willingness to yield to the British blockade even of neutral trade showed our latent hostility to the German side. When, early in 1915, the Germans announced their policy of unrestricted submarine warfare even against neutral shipping, they seemed to be offering proof of their brutality.

Like the British sea mines, the German submarines were novelties to international law. When the Germans began sinking neutral ships without warning and without providing succor for their civilian passengers, they seemed to be making a mockery even of the possibility of law among nations.

On May 7, 1915, a German submarine torpedoed the British liner, *Lusitania,* with the death of 1,200 passengers, 128 of them Americans. Any likelihood that the United States might be taunted into entering the war against the Allies now seemed to have gone aglimmering. But the likelihood that the United States would enter the war at all was still small. "There is such a thing as a man being too proud to fight," said Wilson three days after the *Lusitania* disaster, and the nation cheered him. Thereafter, relations with both belligerents declined alarmingly; but in the presidential elections of 1916 Wilson campaigned on the slogan, "He Kept Us out of War," and won. By then American physical preparedness had begun to outstrip American psychological preparedness. Despite vigorous opposition, during 1916 Congress passed legislation doubling the regular army, incorporating the local National Guards with it, providing for a big three-year naval building program, and authorizing the creation of a Shipping Board to expand, regulate, and requisition the merchant fleet. As significant as anything, as far as the future was concerned, was the decision to pay for much of the new armament by means of the graduated income tax.

By 1916 Allied and German military forces seemed to have reached a stalemate, which greatly intensified the belligerents' efforts to starve out one another. The British extended and tightened their blockade of neutral and German waters, while the Germans stepped up their submarine attacks on unprotected ocean shipping. Between them, the opposing governments made life at sea intolerable for neutrals; and Wilson soon came to the conclusion that the only way to keep the neutral United States at peace was to make a great effort to end the conflict.

Neither side, however, was prepared to accept his proposal for "peace without victory," and by February 1917, the war at sea had grown more tense and more inhuman. American losses in ships, cargoes, crews, and passengers mounted steadily, mainly victims of German submarines. Late in February, the American State Department learned of a German offer to Mexico to join the Central Powers in the event of a United States-German war, the bait being the restoration to her of "the lost territory in Texas, New Mexico and Arizona." News of this added many to the prowar camp in the United States. The Russian Revolution in March, which made many Americans surrender their distaste for an alliance with the anti-Semitic, autocratic czar, added still others to the militant opponents of Prussian militarism. On February 3, 1917, Wilson had broken off diplomatic relations with Germany. By April 2 he was ready to ask Congress for permission to lead the American people into "the most terrible and disastrous of wars." On April 4 the House, and on April 6 the Senate, adopted war resolutions.

When the United States entered the war, England and France were in much worse shape than most Americans, including the President, realized. But the United States, for all the growing spirit of "preparedness," was in even worse shape to help. On June 5, 1917, almost ten million Americans between the ages of twenty-one and thirty-one registered for the recently enacted draft; but almost a year passed before any sizable numbers of trained American troops were available to their commanding General, John J. Pershing. It took even longer for the United States to equip its forces with anything besides hand arms, and in fact most of the artillery used by them was of British and French manufacture. American tanks and planes also were late in coming and not as numerous as had been hoped. In the meantime the Germans were chewing up French and British manpower and shipping, and these nations were verging on collapse. The fiercest blow of all was the November Revolution in Russia which saw the Bolsheviks overthrow the moderate Kerensky government and make a separate peace with the Germans. This released German troops from the Eastern front and permitted the Central Powers to build up their forces for their great assault in the West in the spring of 1918.

During most of this period General Pershing had resisted Allied demands for the use of American troops to bolster French and British lines. His policy was to build up, train, and equip a huge American Army which, independently, would "draw the best German divisions to our front and . . . consume them." Before this Army was ready, thousands of American troops were made available to Marshal Foch, who was in command of all Allied military activities. The American Second Division, starting on May 31, 1918, contributed greatly to halting the Germans at Château-Thierry on the Marne, just fifty miles from Paris. This Division then helped clear the enemy out of Belleau Wood. In July 85,000 Americans helped the British and French blunt the German offensive in the Rheims-Soissons theater; and in August they took part in the Allied counteroffensive which continued right to the end of the war in November.

On August 10 the American First Army, 550,000 strong, took the offensive and wiped the Germans from St. Mihiel. In September Pershing's entire force of over a million played the major role in the Meuse-Argonne offensive which two months later crumbled the last of German resistance on land. By then the American Navy and Merchant Marine, employing the new technique of convoying, had begun to check the German U-boat offensive. Coming as it did so soon after the Russian defection, American aid to the Allied forces in the actual fighting clinched the victory over the Germans. But it is well to remember that America was a late entry and that her war dead numbered slightly more than 100,000. The allied Russians, French, and English had lost four million men.

One of Wilson's wartime innovations was the establishment in 1917 of the Committee on Public Information under the leadership of George Creel. This Committee was charged with "selling" the war to the American people, and the theme it stressed most frequently was that this war would make the world safe for democracy; that it was a war to end war. By the time the United States entered the fighting, Wilson himself had a well-developed peace plan which he hoped would implement the theme of his propaganda office.

The Allied powers, however, had long since made secret treaties looking toward the dismemberment of Germany, the exaction of heavy indemnities from her, the dismantling of her overseas empire and her navy. Russia was a party to these treaties, and after assuming power in November 1917, the Bolsheviks threatened to make a mockery of Allied claims to be fighting for "civilization" against the barbaric "Hun," and especially of American claims to be fighting for justice and humanity, by publishing the terms of the secret treaties. Wilson determined to forestall them. When England and France refused to co-operate, Wilson moved independently on January 5, 1918, to announce before a joint session of Congress the famous "Fourteen Points" in which he defined his war aims. Among these were demands for open diplomacy, freedom of the seas, the removal of trade barriers, and the adjustment of international boundaries on the principle of self-determination by the peoples involved. In point fourteen Wilson made his plea for a League of Nations "affording mutual guarantees of political independence and territorial integrity to great and small states alike."

Wilson's determination to prevent the utter destruction of Germany appealed to her war-weary people, and as their military fortunes declined in 1918, the Germans' morale fell even faster. By October 20, Germany acknowledged a readiness to accept Wilson's surrender terms; on November 8 her delegates capitulated to Marshal Foch; and three days later the war ended.

Already the discord which was to mar the peace conference had become apparent among the Allied powers. They were also aware of the likelihood of American rejection of the projected conference's work. In elections in England and France in 1918, vindictiveness against Germany paid great political dividends; hardly a word dared be spoken for a humane peace. In the American Congressional elections that year, the Republicans gained control of Congress. Wilson's partisanship during the campaign virtually insured that no "Democratic" peace could win approval in the Senate; his failure to include senators of either party among his associates at the peace conference itself only sealed the doom of that conference's work as far as American confirmation was concerned.

The peace conference at Versailles began officially on January 18, 1919. By late March little had been accomplished and on March 24 Wilson, Clemenceau of France, Lloyd George of England, and Orlando of Italy—the famous "Big Four"—took matters in hand. By the end of April they were ready to present Germany with their peace terms, and these were formally accepted by the new German

Republic—the Kaiser having abdicated the previous November—on June 23.

The Versailles Treaty did include much of Wilson's program for redrawing the map of Europe and imposing democratic forms of government on the new nations. In achieving this much Wilson made many damaging concessions as far as self-determination of nationality was concerned. His major concession, however, was most disastrous. This was his acquiescence in imposing on the new German state the crushing financial reparations demanded by the Allied European powers. If Wilson understood the hatred reparations would evoke in the German people who had known little but starvation for years, he also planned to forestall any violent expression of it by creating the League of Nations, the keystone of his entire program.

Ultimately, the Versailles Treaty did create a League of Nations, but one with no independent force of its own and dependent for effectiveness on United States participation. The rejection of the League and the entire Versailles Treaty by the vindictive United States Senate in 1920 literally killed the Messianic president and the whole justification for his adventure into the political and military maelstrom of Europe. The overwhelming victory of a nonentity like the Republican Warren G. Harding in the presidential elections of 1920 disclosed the country's fatigue with foreign involvements. Harding promised the people little but a return to "normalcy." Whatever they understood by that, the people embraced it.

Chapter Thirteen

Bolshevism, Babbitt, and the Barricades

Late one evening in Paris during the peace negotiations of 1919, Harold Nicolson of the British delegation came across Marcel Proust. How did the Conference work, the inquisitive French author wanted to know from the British diplomat. "Well," Nicolson began, "we generally meet at ten. There are secretaries behind . . ."

"Mais non, mais non," the voracious Proust interrupted. This was much too general, much too gentle. *"Précisez, mon chèr, précisez";* the melancholy anatomist of western civilization must have the unhinged, the hurting, the telltale minutiae. "So I tell him everything," Nicolson reports. "The sham cordiality of it all: the handshakes, the maps, the rustle of papers: the tea in the next room: the macaroons. He listens enthralled."

THE CRISIS IN WESTERN CULTURE

To all appearances, western society had been at its peak in 1914, though even superficial observers noted how the rise of the Kaiser's Germany in the heart of Europe and of the United States and Japan at Europe's flanks menaced the century-old balance of international power and the *pax Britannica* it had preserved. Within nations, and not least in Great Britain herself, revolutionary political movements had also been near their peak in 1914. They were nurtured by the business doldrums that had persisted inexplicably in the United States and the rest of the western world for seven lean years before the outbreak of the war.

But it was in literature and the arts that the breakdown of the

347

old order was first and most profoundly foreshadowed. Proust began making notes in 1890 for *Remembrance of Things Past,* a phenomenon of dissection that could only be performed on the cadaver of the ruling class. In 1902 the youthful German, Thomas Mann, published *Buddenbrooks,* a penetrating account of the crackup of the bourgeois family. Twelve years later the French novelist, Jules Romains, disclosed in *The Death of a Nobody* the bleak, broad gulf between the individualist tradition of western life and the everyday, aimless existence of its proletarian "replaceable parts." Years before Romains, the expatriate Irishman, James Joyce, had already embarked on his transcendent studies of the compensations—the fantasies, dreams, and nightmares—of expropriated souls. By 1914 Joyce had published *Dubliners,* completed *Portrait of the Artist as a Young Man,* and begun *Ulysses.* In the United States, meanwhile, the naturalist Theodore Dreiser had been writing for decades the anguished details of the defeated in the struggle for survival; while Edgar Lee Masters memorialized in the stony blank verse of *Spoon River Anthology* (published in 1914) the dead who hadn't even tried:

> Where are Elmer, Herman, Bert, Tom, and Charley
> The weak of will, the strong of arm, the clown, the boozer,
>   the fighter?
> All, all are sleeping on the hill.

> One passed in fever,
> One was burned in a mine,
> One was killed in a brawl,
> One died in jail,
> One fell from a bridge, toiling for children and wife—
> All, all are sleeping, sleeping on the hill.

Before the first World War, Futurism and other nonobjective vogues in painting, dissonance and jazz in music, Freudianism in psychology, the "economic interpretation" in history, all shocked the devotees of the genteel tradition in the United States. After the war, the mordant pessimism foreshadowed in the poetry of such early American expatriates as Ezra Pound (he left Crawfordsville,

Indiana, for Italy in 1908) and T. S. Eliot (he left Boston for London in 1914) became characteristic of American expression. Perhaps the foremost American writer of the 1920s was Eugene O'Neill. His characteristic milieu was the Golden Swan, known to habitués as the "Hell Hole," and described by Malcolm Cowley from personal experience in O'Neill's time as the "grubbiest drinking parlor west of the Bowery—the No Chance Saloon, Bedrock Bar, the End of the Line Café, the Bottom of the Sea Rathskeller."

In 1919, during his tour to save the League of Nations, President Wilson reminded the American people that the eagle not the ostrich was the symbol of American aspiration: "I mean," he said, "leaving the mists that lie close to the ground, getting upon strong wing into those upper spaces of the air where you can see with a clear eye the affairs of mankind, see how the affairs of America are linked with the affairs of men everywhere, see how the whole world turns with outstretched hands to this blessed country of ours and says, 'If you will lead, we will follow.'" But Wilson was born in 1856; he was older even than the skeptical generation that had matured in America and elsewhere just before the war; to the oncoming "lost generation," he and his message were veritably antique.

America refused to lead; even if she had led, Europe would not have followed. In December 1918, on the eve of the peace conference, Wilson's military adviser, General Tasker H. Bliss, remarked, "We are going to vote the proxies of millions of dead men who have died in the belief that what we do now will make it impossible for the same awful sacrifice to be demanded of their children." Six months later General Bliss wrote from France, "What a wretched mess it all is: If the rest of the world will let us alone, I think we better stay on our side of the water and keep alive the spark of civilization to relight the torch after it is extinguished over here. If I ever had any illusions, they are all dispelled."

By the end of 1922 the last thousand American troops had been called home from Europe; all but the last few American ships had been recalled from Asian waters. Seemingly snug again in their "isolated" hemisphere, Americans faced the future with growing cynicism and self-indulgence. "I think Mr. Ford is wrong," observed Will Rogers in 1922, the year of Ford's first venture into auto-biography, "when he said that 90 per cent of the people in this country are satisfied. Ninety per cent of the people in this country are not satisfied. It's just got so 90 per cent of the people in this country didn't give a damn." In Europe, meanwhile, among victors and vanquished alike, the war had demolished the swaying scaffold of life. Friendship dissolved into suspicion; universal poverty forbade Christian forbearance. Nations, like men, turned inward, the victors to lick their wounds for comfort, the vanquished to nurse their hatreds for revenge.

The Great Depression of the 1930s heightened the estrangement of the nations of the world. As they found less and less of a con-structive nature to say to one another, diplomacy itself sank into the limbo of a lost art. More than ever, indiscriminate foreign wars offered panaceas for intransigent domestic troubles. In such wars, surprise attacks and sneak invasions, covered where practi-cable by pious negotiations, became the highest order of strategy. The Japanese descent on Pearl Harbor on December 7, 1941, was but the last of a long series of such maneuvers that had already brought that people into China, the Fascists into Ethiopia, Civil War to Spain, and Nazis into eastern Europe and eventually into France.

ONLY YESTERDAY

In 1931 Frederick Lewis Allen published his first book, *Only Yesterday*. Its subtitle was "An Informal History of the Nineteen-Twenties," and from the perspective of the early years of the de-pression, with the first World War and its immediate aftermath well forgotten, it made even the most recent decade seem quaintly dis-tant, innocently iconoclastic, and rather marvelous. By the mid-1950s the focus had perhaps shifted again. Many not-so-marvelous aspects of the 'twenties, blotted from memory by the more pro-found social turmoil of the 'thirties and irrelevant to the embattled 'forties, appeared in the 'fifties to have regained a familiar ring. Not least among them were the "Red Scares," the vigilantism, and the businesslike brass-tack fundamentalism of "100 per cent Ameri-can" thinking.

The Bolshevik revolution in Russia had spawned a number of new Communist parties in many other countries of the world; one of these, the American Communist Party, was founded in 1919. Throughout the 'twenties its funds were small and its members few; but its mere existence gave a tinge of reality to the "Great Red Scare" of the immediate postwar years, and its lurid propaganda a tinge of plausibility to the indiscriminate use of the epithet, "Bolshevist," for violent and radical acts.

Of the latter there were plenty right after the armistice, when wartime unity and wartime prosperity both promptly ended. Red and anti-Red riots became common, newspaper offices were invaded, public figures and public places attacked. In 1919 and 1920 a bomb scare terrorized the country. The worst bomb disaster occurred on September 16, 1920, when a terrific explosion at the corner of Broad and Wall Streets, opposite the House of Morgan, killed thirty persons, injured hundreds, and damaged considerable property. Painstaking investigations over a period of years failed to disclose the perpetrators, though a coal operator who was in Morgan's offices at the time "promptly declared that there was no question in his mind that it was the work of the Bolshevists."

Similar inconclusiveness still characterizes the investigations into the murder of the South Braintree, Massachusetts, factory paymaster and guard for which Sacco and Vanzetti were arrested in 1920 and convicted in 1921. The flimsiness of the evidence against these Italian-born anarchists and the open bias of the judge made this case even more one of a "generation on trial" than the case of Alger Hiss in 1949. Persistent efforts to save the two men from the vindictiveness of the times could not avert their execution in 1927.

Long before World War I, American businessmen had developed the practice of associating labor unionism with "radicalism." During the war the ranks of union labor grew with unprecedented rapidity and union leaders like Samuel Gompers had been invited to sit on the war councils in Washington. Nevertheless, after the Russian Revolution of 1917, business propaganda systematically associated unionism with "Bolshevism." A large number of violent strikes right after the war thus contributed their mite to the "Red Scare."

The most famous strike was that of the Boston police in September 1919. Its suppression by Governor Calvin Coolidge of Massachusetts first brought the future president nation-wide renown. The most important strikes were those against the United States Steel Corporation that same fall, and against the coal operators (who were closely allied with the steel company) that winter. Both the Corporation and the coal operators were among the worst employers in the country; labor exploitation was made easier by their policy of hiring illiterate southern European immigrants as the bulk of their working force. These immigrants were driven by foremen who were themselves under the constant surveillance of undercover company agents.

"There is no good American reason for the strike," said the Steel Corporation. The strikers, explained its sanctimonious chairman, E. H. Gary, "sought the closed shop, Soviets, and the forcible distribution of property." None of this was true. The strike was thoroughly investigated by a Commission of Inquiry of the Interchurch World Movement under the chairmanship of Bishop Francis J. McConnell of the Methodist Episcopal Church. This Commission listed as among the leading causes for the defeat of the strike the steel company's "effective mobilization of public opinion against the strikers through the charges of radicalism, bolshevism, and the closed shop, none of which were justified by the facts." The steel and coal strikers sought only union recognition, higher wages, and a reduction in the twelve-hour day. The intervention of federal troops on behalf of the Corporation and the coal operators forced the workers back to their jobs with no gains to show for their efforts. "All the conditions that caused the steel strike," said the Commission of Inquiry, "continue to exist. . . . In the measure that workingmen become intelligent and Americanized, will they refuse to labor under such conditions."

Mobilization of public opinion against the steel and coal strikers and those in other industries was made easier by labor's support of the extension of the principle of nationalization, as applied to the railroads during the war. Late in 1917, under the authority of the Army Appropriation Act of the year before, the federal government had taken over the operation of the railroads and given railroad labor a voice in their management. In 1919, the otherwise docile railroad workers strongly advocated the Plumb Plan, by which the government would continue to run the roads and railroad unions would continue to participate in their direction. At the same time, steel workers began agitating for the nationalization of steel, and coal miners for the nationalization of the pits. The effect of this agitation was simply to frighten businessmen everywhere in the country and to speed up the return of the railroads to private control. This was done in 1920. The temper of the times is evident from Vice-President Thomas R. Marshall's denunciation of women's colleges following the determination of Radcliffe debaters to uphold the affirmative of the proposition, "Resolved, that the recognition of labor unions by employers is essential to successful collective bargaining."

It was such manifestations of "foreign ideologies" that set the "Fighting Quaker," Attorney-General A. Mitchell Palmer, on his famous "Red hunt," beginning New Year's Day, 1920. "Like a prairie fire," Palmer explained later, "the blaze of revolution was sweeping over every American institution of law and order. . . . It was eating its way into the homes of the American workman, its sharp tongues of revolutionary heat were licking the altars of the churches, leaping into the belfry of the school bell, crawling into the sacred corners of American homes, seeking to replace marriage vows with libertine laws, burning up the foundations of society." To put out the fire he had ordered simultaneous raids on every alleged Bolshevik cell in the country. In about a week, more than 6,000 men and women had been arrested, their property seized and confiscated, their friends who visited them in jail locked up on the grounds of solicitude for revolutionaries. Though supposedly armed to the teeth, the captives yielded the imposing total of three pistols and no explosives.

"The Palmer raids," as they were called, were a farce; but the nation did not view them that way. President Wilson had warned the Attorney-General, "Palmer, do not let this country see red." But Palmer, who in Josephus Daniels's words "was seeing red behind every bush and every demand for an increase of wages," failed to heed the admonition. As Wilson anticipated, vigilantism, touched off by the Attorney-General's example, spread across the land, victimizing students, professors, editors, writers, actors, and any others suspected of harboring "subversive" ideas or engaging in "un-American" activities. Wilson himself, perhaps because he was preoccupied with the League of Nations issue, did nothing to check the orgy.

The most direct attack on "foreign ideologies" took the form of excluding foreigners themselves, though opposition to the free entry of immigrants, of course, had other motivations as well. Highly focused opposition came from labor leaders who claimed that labor markets were being flooded and wages depressed by immigrants who responded poorly to union organizing campaigns. American workers themselves shared with much of the rest of the community a more generalized xenophobia which made the United States less a melting pot of racial and religious differences than a pit of racial and religious antagonisms.

On the exalted rim of the pit sat the 100 per cent Americans. Disillusioned by the "Great Red Scare" of ever making "good citizens" of foreigners, they were strengthened by the same concoction in their belief in "Anglo-Saxon" racial superiority and in their determination to restore the United States to racial—"Anglo-Saxon"—purity. As early as February, 1920, Emerson Hough, the exceedingly popular writer of cowboy lore, said in the *Saturday Evening Post,* "The whole theory of Americanization is one which J. J. Rousseau and T. Jefferson would call perfectly lovely if they were alive. It goes in well with a lot of these mentally subjective theories about altruism and democracy, which in my belief have pretty much brought America to ruin."

"Thus, while the movement for the redemption of the alien ebbed in 1920," writes John Higham, the author of *Strangers in the Land,* "the old drive for the rejection of the immigrant passed all previous bounds." In 1917, over the last of a number of Wilson vetoes, Congress imposed a literacy test on those seeking to settle in the United States. That this test was scarcely a barrier was shown in 1920 when almost a million newcomers entered the country. In May 1921, after Wilson had previously vetoed an immigration bill discriminating among persons of different national origins, President Warren G. Harding signed a measure restricting entry to the United

States on these grounds. This Act limited a country's annual quota to 3 per cent of its nationals living in the United States in 1910. But 1910 was far too late a date to satisfy the racial purists; and in 1924 quotas were lowered to 2 per cent of a country's nationals in the United States in 1890. In 1931, under a more complex system of calculation, quotas were lowered and purified even further.

These measures were so drastic that in 1932 fewer people entered the United States than departed from it. For the *entire decade* of the 1930s, net immigration was under 70,000. After the second World War the quota system was slightly relaxed; and after the Soviet suppression of the Hungarian revolt in 1956, additional exemptions were made. But rigid exclusion remained the dominant aim of American immigration policy.

While barriers against the entry of racial and religious "minorities" were being erected, the "minorities" in the United States also came under attack. In the early 1920s violence frequently flared up among mixed racial groups huddled together in seething industrial towns and metropolitan ghettos. These incidents sometimes involved "native Americans" who decried the "crime waves" brought to the United States by mysterious organizations like the Maffia and the Black Hand. But the most concerted violence was perpetrated by a domestic not a foreign band—the notorious Ku Klux Klan.

Efforts to organize the Klan had failed in 1915, but by 1920 the national climate became more favorable and by 1924 about 4,500,-000 "white male persons, native-born Gentile citizens of the United States of America," had joined the hooded group. Like most other "hate organizations" modeled on it, the Klan proved a "good thing" for its leaders. A new member was required to pay ten dollars, of which four dollars went to the Klansman who signed him up and six dollars to the Imperial Wizard in Atlanta, Georgia.

In 1924, while continuing to lynch and flog Negroes, the Klan began to terrorize other groups. In a pamphlet, *The Klan of To-morrow,* Imperial Wizard Hiram W. Evans explained: "The Negro is not a menace to Americanism in the sense that the Jew or Roman Catholic is a menace. He is not actually hostile to it. He is simply racially incapable of understanding, sharing, or contributing to

Americanism." Thereafter, Jews and Catholics bore the brunt of Klan violence, at least in the North. The strength of the Klan was shown in the Democratic National Convention of 1924 when a resolution denouncing its activities was defeated by the delegates. Thereafter, the diffuseness of the Klan's attacks and the disclosure of scandal in its own affairs greatly weakened the organization.

While the Klan would not accept as Americans any but native-born, white Protestants, and was more than willing to kill or maim those outside the pale, within Protestantism itself a still narrower fundamentalism further divided the sectarians. The focus of the fundamentalist attack was science, especially Darwinian biology, which seemed to deny divine creation of mankind as set forth in the Bible. The muscular evangelist, Billy Sunday, had begun before the war to fight "sinners, science, and liberals." After the war, under crude evangelist pressure, many states enacted laws forbidding the teaching of Darwinian theories. The fundamentalist campaign was most successful in Tennessee where, to test the state anti-evolution statute, a high school teacher named John Thomas Scopes allowed himself to be arrested in 1925. William Jennings Bryan promptly let it be known as his opinion that "this is a matter for the nation," and joined the state's prosecuting attorneys in the famous "Monkey Trial." Scopes, defended by a galaxy of lawyers led by Clarence Darrow, was found guilty by the state court; but he was only technically punished. In reality Darrow and company had won a signal victory by making fundamentalism henceforth the butt of ridicule.

It was in the business community that the "100 per cent American" spirit of the 1920s perhaps paid its greatest dividends. Most of these were earned by the so-called "American Plan," the major objective of which was to brand collective bargaining and the closed shop as "un-American." "The war taught us the power of propaganda," said Roger Babson, business's leading forecaster, in 1921. "Now when we have anything to sell to the American people, we know how to sell it. We have the school, the pulpit, and the press." As early as 1920 there were forty-six "American Plan" associations in Illinois "selling" the open shop, and there was at least one such association in every state in the Union. The National Grange, the American Bankers Association, and the National Association of

Manufacturers all contributed funds and other assistance to the campaign. Years later a Committee on Education and Labor of the United States Senate said that when the N.A.M. "achieved the retardation of labor organizations [by 1926], the hectic effort to allay what had seemed to them an impending radical revolution became unnecessary, and the association settled back to the quiet enjoyment of the fruits of their efforts during the years of prosperity."

Much the most spectacular interference with the freedom of the American people in the 1920s was Prohibition, in the enactment of which Progressivism, religious fundamentalism, and business practicality had joined hands. Drinking had been an American pastime since the beginning of settlement. By 1850 many states had prohibited the manufacture and sale of alcoholic beverages and many drinkers had "taken the pledge," but like most other social reforms, the campaign against "demon rum" foundered after the Civil War. In the same period the liquor business grew so fast as to seem to imperil both the families and the factories of the working population. To combat the evil the Women's Christian Temperance Union had been founded in 1874. Twenty years later the prohibition campaign was broadened by the formation of the Anti-Saloon League.

By 1917 three fourths of the American people lived in states which had Prohibition legislation. Wartime hostility to German brewers, and the wartime policy of conserving grain for food rather than releasing it to distillers, now played into the hands of the organized "drys." A series of local victories was capped by the national Prohibition amendment, passed by Congress in December 1917. This amendment prohibited the manufacture, sale, and transportation of alcoholic beverages in the United States. It was ratified by January 1919, and in October that year Congress passed the Volstead Act to implement it.

Though Congress had been forced by wartime public pressure to play ball with the "drys" in principle, it never voted enough money for more than token enforcement. There were rarely more than 2,000 Prohibition agents to police the entire country; while the Capone mob alone had a private army in Chicago of a thousand well-armed gangsters. Capone's and hundreds of other gangs quickly gained control of the undercover liquor business—bootlegging, rum-running, and speakeasy operation. Gangs had existed in American cities before Prohibition, and often enough they were on intimate if not controlling terms with local government. National Prohibition made liquor the main source of gang income, raised that income to sybaritic levels, and enlarged gang domination of local police and local politics. At its peak, the Capone gang took in $60,000,000 a year, of which Capone himself took $20,000,000.

For all its violence, repression, bigotry, and backsliding, the decade of the 'twenties did witness a frenetic iconoclasm. The *enfant terrible* of the decade was H. L. Mencken, sometimes known as "the Bad Boy of Baltimore." Mencken, in the opinion of Walter Lippmann in 1927, was "the most powerful personal influence on this whole generation of educated people." All the icons of the genteel tradition were ground to powder by his ridicule and the powder itself blown to the winds by the bellows of his mirthless laughter.

In the 'twenties, and especially after 1923 when he began to publish his magazine, the *American Mercury*, Mencken was the anti of antis. He was, as he said, "against all theologians, professors, editorial-writers, right thinkers, and reformers." He was against patriotism, democracy, marriage, and the family. "He pelted his enemies," writes Frederick Lewis Allen, "with words and phrases like mountebank, charlatan, swindler, numskull, swine, witch-burner, *homo boobiens,* and imbecile; he said . . . of Bryan that 'he was born with a roaring voice and it had a trick of inflaming half-wits.' " One of Mencken's favorite targets was the "American Husbandman": "No more grasping, selfish, and dishonest Mammal, indeed, is known to students of Anthropoidea." Another target was the 100 per center, the American racist, at whom he leveled broadsides such as this:

The Anglo-Saxon of the great herd is, in many important respects, the least civilized of men and the least capable of true civilization. His political ideas are crude and shallow. He is almost wholly devoid of aesthetic feeling; he does not even make folklore or walk in the

woods. The most elementary facts about the visible universe alarm
him, and incite him to put them down.

But Mencken reserved his transcending scorn for the "ordinary
Class I Babbitt," the flower—the weed, rather—of the American
"booboisie."

Yet Mencken was not all cudgel and hot air. Before the war he
had already become Dreiser's champion, Nietzsche's translator,
Shaw's apostle to the new world. Perhaps he recognized in the
'twenties how deep-seated American fundamentalism was, how
broad were the acres of American provincialism, how incessant, indeed how monotonous the blasting at localism and traditionalism
must be. Perhaps he *failed* to recognize how he himself had become trapped by his adversary, his environment.

To Mencken's own muscular esthetic (which he used like a
veritable Cotton Mather to browbeat genteel writers) all poetry
was sentiment, all sentiment "bilge." "An adult poet," Mencken
wrote in one of his own most fundamentalist moods, "is simply an
individual in a state of arrested development—in brief, a sort of
moron." Provincialism he defined as "original sin." In one of his
Prejudices, Mencken asked himself, "If you find so much that is
unworthy of reverence in the United States, then why do you live
here?" His answer was another question, "Why do men go to zoos?"
The trouble with Mencken was that to him everyone had become a
"gaping primate"; Mencken alone was the keeper. It was a trouble
that Americans on the make intellectually well understood. As
Alfred Kazin says, "By prodigious skill [Mencken] managed to
insult everyone except his readers. . . . His ferocious attacks on
Babbittry implied that his readers were all Superior Citizens. . . .
Every Babbitt read him gleefully and pronounced his neighbor a
Babbitt."

Mencken's significant virtue was that he conducted his rebellion
against the genteel tradition in the open, with bugles, trumpets, and
drums. By his very excesses he served the cause of free men in the
'twenties. If his laughter was more like a belch than a breeze, at
least it served to change the air after the dogmas of Victorianism had
grown unbearably stale. If he paraded his atheism, he also paraded

his anti-authoritarianism. If he was for free love, he was also for free speech.

Along with the hip flask and the raccoon coat, Mencken's *American Mercury* became part of the authentic paraphernalia of the "sad young men" on the country's campuses. The *Mercury* welcomed the "new" writers of the 'twenties, the Sinclair Lewises, F. Scott Fitzgeralds, Hemingways and O'Neills with hosannas, and forced reactionary critics like Stuart Sherman to acknowledge their work as the voice of America. The *Mercury* needled such old genteel journals as the *Atlantic* and *Harper's* into deepening their criticism of life in the United States. Mencken prepared the audience for the early *New Yorker,* which began publication in 1925 with the motto, "Not for the old lady in Dubuque," a motto that rather quickly had to be dusted off once a year as a reminder of the original intent. Mencken also helped sustain the atmosphere in which such journals of opinion as the *New Republic* and the *Nation* might prosper. All of these journals confronted the bigots, the racists, the super-patriots, the 100 per centers with the more humane side of the American tradition.

Yet for all the stir Mencken made among the intellectuals, the 'twenties became the golden age of hero-worship, of "ballyhoo." Many of the heroes had authentic talent; but many others were manufactured by promoters who had the advantage, in their manip-ulation of the mass mind, of nationwide communication facilities and a population generally approaching a high-school level of read-ing ability. In the 'twenties, Boosterism and Babbittry became ever more closely wedded. The main thing was to avoid rocking the boat.

Nothing showed the lasting temper of the people, the futility of the Mencken onslaught, the triumph of the old lady in Dubuque better than the elections of 1928. Harding's administration had been little more than one long betrayal of the President by the "Ohio gang" he had brought to Washington in 1921. The Veterans Bureau under Charles R. Forbes had been milked of nearly $250,000,000 for the benefit of compliant contractors and suppliers; the office of the Alien Property Custodian under Colonel Thomas W. Miller had been used to distribute for far less than their known value industrial patents captured during the war; the Department of Justice under Harry Daugherty had issued liquor permits and pardons to criminals for fancy prices; above all, the Interior Department under the notorious Albert B. Fall had secretly leased to a few oil men for their private exploitation some of the richest naval oil reserves, notably those at Teapot Dome, Wyoming, and Elk Hills, California. The dawning realization of how his friends had used him speeded Harding's death in August 1923. Vice-President "Silent Cal" Coolidge on becoming President quickly cleaned house. Forbes, Miller, and Fall went to jail; Daugherty escaped only because the suicide of his chief accomplice, Jesse Smith, deprived the courts of sufficient evidence to convict him.

Coolidge easily won the Republican nomination in 1924 and easily defeated the Democratic candidate, the Wall Street lawyer, John W. Davis. During the Coolidge Prosperity that followed the election, the business community, the main support of the Republican Party, was the party's principal beneficiary. The farm depression following the vast expansion of agricultural production during the war was permitted to continue through the 'twenties. This insured low prices for agricultural raw materials used in industry and low wages for industrial workers because of low food prices. Tariffs on foreign manufactured goods were kept at record levels; taxes were repeatedly slashed; public power development was obstructed; labor organization was impeded by the courts, while industrial organization into trusts and holding companies was encouraged.

When the time came for the selection of candidates for the 1928 election, business seemed to have merited all its political benefits. Consequently, Coolidge appeared to be the natural nominee of his party. But early in 1928 "Silent Cal" for once had let some words slip out. "I do not choose to run," he said; which certainly did not preclude his being drafted. The Republican leaders nevertheless took him at his word and turned to Herbert Hoover, the famed "great humanitarian" of the immediate postwar years and Coolidge's Secretary of Commerce.

The Democrats nominated Governor Al Smith, the "Happy

Warrior" of New York. Smith was not only wet; he was liberal in labor matters, believed in public ownership of hydro-electric power, state and federal regulation of business enterprise, the expansion of state welfare activities, and the protection and enlargement of civil liberties. Moreover, he was an Irishman, a Catholic, a New Yorker —in short, the incarnation of everything hated by the 100 per cent Americans. Their fight against his nomination in 1928 widened the split in the already divided Democratic Party; their fight against his election broke the "solid South" for the first time since the end of Reconstruction.

Prohibition became the popular issue in the campaign. The drys gave Hoover their enthusiastic support. But largely as a result of the whispering campaign against Smith, the Republican candidate polled 58.2 per cent of the popular vote, a proportion higher than Eisenhower's in 1956 and exceeded in history only by Harding in 1920 and Roosevelt in 1936. Rarely had third parties done so poorly, moreover.

During the campaign Hoover had promised to look into the "noble experiment," and in 1929 named a Commission under former Attorney-General George W. Wickersham to investigate enforcement of the Volstead Act. The Commission's report in 1931 fully disclosed the connection between gangsterism and Prohibition; yet a majority of the Commission voted for continuing the "experiment." Repeal of the Eighteenth Amendment had to wait for the return of the Democrats to power in 1933.

BOOM AND BUST

The business boom that began about the time Coolidge became president in 1924 and continued with only slight interruptions to the fall of 1929, made it easy for Americans to ignore the straitening of opinion, the social conflicts, and the political corruption following the war. This boom was one of the longest in American history; and it fed a fond belief that the United States had found a perpetual-motion prosperity machine. The fact that the stock market magnified even the real progress of the American economy, especially during the later phases of the boom, (and precipitated it to unplumbed depths once the bubble burst) has caused the emphasis to be placed on the speculative side of business during the 'twenties. This is as it should be; though no longer unchallenged as the ruler of the economy, Wall Street remained more closely related to its functioning in the 1920s than since. Yet this emphasis tends to obscure some of the genuine economic gains of the decade and how they were made.

As late as 1927 an unhappy director of General Motors complained that "bankers regard research as most dangerous and a thing that makes banking hazardous, due to the rapid changes it brings about in industry." The craft unions that made up the American Federation of Labor subscribed enthusiastically to the bankers' sentiments. By 1927, however, considerable scientific progress had been made in American industry, to which the war itself had contributed much.

For one thing, the war had loosened the bankers' grip on the economy. Wartime profits were so high in key industries that they were less dependent upon the open money market for financing. Even when such corporations needed money, they found they could borrow outside of Wall Street channels or sell stock without knuckling under to the financial oligarchs of the Morgan era. One reason for this was the way the vast Liberty and Victory Bond campaigns had accustomed millions of Americans to invest in securities for the first time. These campaigns so widened financial channels that a few investment bankers no longer could dominate the security market.

Wartime tax policies added their influence to that of the wartime financial policies in furthering the application of science to industry. In particular, wartime excess-profits taxes encouraged corporations to plow back their heavy earnings into modernized, electrified, low-production-cost plants and equipment. Wartime labor shortages, in turn, often made such technological advances mandatory.

Many new industries created by the war or matured by its demands also were based on scientific concepts and methods. The boom period, for example, saw the coming of age of commercial aviation, the possibilities of which first were underscored by the successful use of airplanes in the recent hostilities. After Congress voted mail subsidies and other assistance to the airlines in 1926, commercial flying became big business almost overnight. Further stimulation came the next year from Charles A. Lindbergh's magnificent nonstop solo flight from New York to Paris. By 1930, one hundred and twenty-two American airlines employing about ten thousand pilots carried almost half a million passengers over fifty thousand miles of air routes.

The war gave the American chemical industry an even greater boost than it gave flying. Before the war American chemical companies had concentrated on the production of relatively simple heavy acids and alkalies used in basic industrial processes. During the war large numbers of explosives plants were built and their use after the war was encouraged by two government measures. The first was the confiscation of German coal-tar patents and their assignment to American chemical companies. The second (furthered by demands for chemical self-sufficiency in case of a new war) was the placing of prohibitively high tariffs on European chemical products. By 1929 the beneficiaries of these measures, such as DuPont, Allied Chemicals, and Union Carbide, had grown far bigger than any similar firms or groups of firms in Europe.

In combination with electricity, chemicals also continued to revolutionize other industries. Signal improvements in the production of electricity itself furthered this development. Between 1920 and 1929 technological advances in the production of electricity were such that a 25 per cent increase in the coal used resulted in a 100 per cent increase in the kilowatt hours generated. These advances so cheapened electric power that by 1929, 70 per cent of American factory machinery was electrified. The most spectacular gains from electrochemical processes were made in the petroleum industry. Between 1913 and 1928, for example, electrochemical processes had tripled the amount of gasoline obtainable from a gallon of crude oil. Such processes also forwarded improvements in the manufacture of electrical appliances, like floor and table lamps, phonographs, radios, refrigerators, washing machines, and vacuum cleaners, all of which grew in importance in the American economy and the American home.

Wartime experiences in Europe made many thousands of Americans aware for the first time of the poverty of the outside world, but this only fostered their appreciation of their own good fortune. "If you wish to make a democracy conservative," Lord Randolph Churchill had said in the 1880s, "you must give it something to conserve." By 1927 the Frenchman, André Siegfried noted that "what Americans have to conserve is their standard of living, and a sacred acquisition it is in which they will allow no reduction, and which they will defend to the uttermost against the competition and surreptitious invasion of other continents." During the boom of the 1920s, "keeping up with the Joneses," once the motivation for conspicious consumption only among the leisure class, became the great American aspiration.

The growth of the movie industry and of national distribution of family-type magazines filled with advertising heightened the standardization of American taste. During the decade, radio broadcasting also became a billion-dollar entertainment and advertising medium. Above all, the advance of the automobile industry broke down American localism and in many other ways revolutionized American life.

In the first decade of the twentieth century the automobile had remained the rich man's plaything. "Nothing," said Woodrow Wilson in 1906, "has spread socialistic thinking in this country more than the automobile . . . a picture of arrogance and wealth." By the 1920s, however, it became possible to say that nothing had allayed the spread of "socialistic thinking" as much as the spread of the automobile. In 1920 about nine million automobiles were registered in the United States. By 1930 registrations had risen to nearly thirty million. "We'd rather do without clothes than give up the car," said a "Middletown" housewife in the mid1920s "I'll go without food before I'll see us give up the car," said another.

In our own day of "drive-in" movies, roadside shopping centers with acres of parking space, grandiose motels, the movement of factories and families to the suburbs, weekend traffic problems, choking congestion in every great city, and six- and eight-lane freeways, thruways, and parkways, it hardly seems necessary to elaborate the continuing social effects of the automobile. Certainly one of its most significant attributes is the power it places at the command of the individual at the wheel. From the start, the exercise of this power became a kind of freedom to kill. In 1930, 32,000 Americans died in auto accidents. Since then, although automobile registrations have more than doubled and mileage driven has grown proportionately even greater, this figure, miraculously, has been held steady. This achievement is one to arouse the feeling of pride until the size of the figure itself is recalled.

The automobile has been "murder" in another way. "Our highway engineers," Lewis Mumford wrote in 1957, "are butchering good urban land as recklessly as the railroad builders did in laying out their terminals and . . . yards." Nevertheless highway construction quite early became an important factor in sustaining the vigor of the economy. As late as 1921 not a highway in America was numbered. "Chains on all four wheels," and "a shovel with a collapsible handle," were recommended equipment for automobile tours. In the next ten years, government expenditures for new street and highway construction exceeded the capital outlay of any single line of private enterprise. This was a hidden subsidy to the automobile industry, and indeed to the entire economy. Viewed in this way it also disclosed the hidden weakness in the business boom. Just as in the war boom preceding the 1920s and in the war and postwar booms of the 1940s and 1950s, government outlays shored up private enterprises. When private investment in most industries slowed down in the late 'twenties, and government outlays even for highways failed to compensate for the decline, the crash and the depression loomed.

The application of chemistry and electricity in industry in the 1920s greatly increased the productivity of the labor force. "Real" wages rose markedly for those employed in modern industries; but there was also a steady if slow growth of technological unemployment. Older industries such as coal mining and textile manufacturing remained depressed during most of the decade, while farm income never approached the historic highs of the war period nor even the average levels of the decade before the war.

The business community tried to compensate for these soft spots in the economy in various ways. Advertising became a favorite panacea. But its benefits, after all, were limited by the purchasing power of the public. Purchasing power was stretched by the extraordinary development of installment buying and "personal credit" institutions. But these also had their limits, which were reached when it was found that people were paying more for interest than for goods.

In the 'twenties certain American businessmen again turned their eyes abroad for opportunities that seemed to be disappearing at home. Yet isolationism within the business community was at least as marked after 1920 as it had been before. Total American direct investment abroad between 1912 and 1929 rose from one and three quarters to nearly seven and a half billion dollars. But even the seemingly astronomical 1929 total was surpassed by the net profits of American corporations in that one year.

These profits themselves had risen spectacularly, even embarrassingly. Yet efforts to spread corporate income by other means than large wage increases failed to sustain the economy. "Welfare capitalism," including employee stock-ownership and profit-sharing, though much publicized and much enlarged during the decade, was really operated as a union-busting rather than a wealth-spreading technique. Efforts to expand business research and experimentation and business support of science and education never amounted to much financially, and only helped raise efficiency and profits. As a result business companies came to use their accumulating funds in stock-market speculation, and to draw the public's savings, piled up in banks and insurance companies, into securities manufactured by mergers and reorganizations.

Never before in history were corporate structures "pyramided" to such heights. Ingenious manipulators like the Van Sweringen brothers and Sidney Z. Mitchell used every known Wall Street device to manufacture securities for the hungry speculators and yet to retain control of their empires. The key to their paper edifices was the holding company, a corporation which usually owned nothing but the securities of other corporations, some of which were also holding companies. The most fantastic pyramid of all was Samuel Insull's public utilities empire which was so complex that even Owen D. Young, the expert corporation lawyer and board chairman of General Electric, despaired of understanding its ramifications. "It is impossible," Young said, "for any man to grasp the situation of that vast structure . . . it was so set up that you could not possibly get an accounting system which would not mislead even the officers themselves."

Accompanying and often intensifying the stock-market boom was a real-estate boom. In the past land speculation had been a standard feature of American boom periods. In the 1920s real-estate speculation was centered very largely in the cities. Here many great banks erected skyscrapers at fabulous land and construction costs. These skyscrapers they hoped to fill with brokers' offices where the stock-market boom would be kept humming. Paper profits from the soaring stock market, in turn, were hypothecated for new real-estate plunges.

When the stock market collapsed in October 1929, the whole paper structure came tumbling down. President Hoover warned the country not to panic. Business, he advised, was "fundamentally sound," and prosperity was "just around the corner." The inability of the United States to sell goods abroad was pounced upon by Hoover as an appropriate "foreign" scapegoat for the American catastrophe. But the fundamental shortcomings of the home economy soon became apparent. By 1933 the economic outlook in America was darker than at any time in history. In that year Franklin D. Roosevelt took office after defeating Hoover in the presidential elections of 1932. Roosevelt had promised to chase the money changers from the temple. Actually, as early as November 1931, according to the disgusted testimony of Hoover himself, they had already fled. "After a few weeks of enterprising courage," the President had said that month, "the bankers' National Credit Association became ultraconservative, then fearful, and finally died. It had not exerted anything like its full possible strength. Its members —and the business world—threw up their hands and asked for governmental action."

A "NEW DEAL"

"October 1939, tenth anniversary of the Wall Street crash," wrote *Fortune Magazine* in the brilliant issue of February 1940, celebrating its own first decade, "marked the end of a ten-year industrial depression in the U.S." There remained, however, "some nine mil-

lion American citizens who were, as the term is, 'unemployed.' And
there may be more today." With their dependents these "members
of the dispossessed . . . total about thirty millions."

"There are two main reasons," the magazine went on, "why employment has failed to keep pace with production. One is the technological reason"; new machines had greatly increased the productivity of those actually at work. "The other reason is anything but
technological, and is much more important. At least six million of
the nine million 'unemployed' were neither tractored off the farm
nor rationalized out of the roundhouse nor spray-gunned off the
scaffold nor mechanized out of the mine nor even eroded onto the
highways. Six million, as a strictly statistical matter, have never had
jobs at all. They are the net increase in the working population. By
simply growing up during the last ten years the members of this idle
horde silently inform the nation that to achieve in 1939 the production levels of 1929 is no achievement at all. Such, in simplified
form," *Fortune* concluded, "is the problem that like the ghost of
his guilt freezes the tongue of any honest American who is otherwise
proud of his economic system. . . . For nearly one-fourth of the
population there is no economic system—and from the rest there
is no answer."

When, toward the end of his campaign in 1932, President Hoover
told the country, "had it not been for the immediate and unprecedented actions of our government things would be infinitely worse
today," the "men on the sidewalks" just pressed their lips a little
tighter and went on "clapping their hands in a queer way," as an
observer noted, "obviously just to be doing something." Had it
occurred to F.D.R. to take such a negative stance toward the end of
1939, he would, in fact, have had a good deal more to point to. "A
meager and infrequent market," *Fortune* said of the dispossessed,
"they would be no market at all were it not for public largesse,
which since the beginning of the New Deal totalled no less than
$19,000,000,000 in Federal, state and local expenditure to keep
them alive. . . . As animals they are sick twice as often as their
neighbors. As souls they seem considerably more hopeful than they
have reason to be."

The farther the critics of the New Deal and its "chief architect" get from 1932, the more comprehensive they become. One of the latest of these critics, the historian Edgar Eugene Robinson, wrote in 1955 in his book, *The Roosevelt Leadership,* "when [Roosevelt] ceased to lead, the effect of his years in power was manifested in a weakened constitutional system, in imperiled national security, in diminished national morale, in deteriorated political morality, and in an overburdened economy." This typical neo-Hooverite goes on: "The deepest wound that had been given the American practice of self-government had been given by its friends. Every argument, every program, every success on behalf of the American people made them less able to perform the function of a self-supporting people."

None of this is true. The idea of a "self-supporting people," whatever meaning may be read into that epithet, had itself become increasingly anachronistic in the United States once the eastern railroads had been joined into great trunk lines and the western transcontinentals had been built. Following the industrial consolidations of the Civil War period and the depression of the 1870s, self-reliant agriculture and self-reliant small business had become increasingly characteristic only of the byways of American life, the founts neither of its modern corporate character nor its modern corporate wealth. What the railroads and the trusts left unfinished, the automobile and the highways completed.

In politics, moreover, no one did more than Hoover himself, with his promotion of the idea of "co-operative competition" while Secretary of Commerce under Harding and Coolidge, to subvert the notion of a "self-supporting people." "One may say," Mark Sullivan writes, "that Hoover regarded our entire business structure as a single factory, conceiving himself, as it were, consulting engineer for the whole enterprise." And as for the morality of it, before his political ambitions made him circumspect in his avowals, the "Great Engineer" once waved aside the misappropriation of investors' funds by corporate officials, averring in an English mining journal that capital is "often invested" by insiders "to more reproductive purpose than if it had remained in the hands of the idiots who parted with it."

Traditions often are the hardiest of social phenomena, outlasting buildings, bridges, monuments, laws. Americans either as individuals or as a nation have not been a "self-supporting people" for generations. Fortunately, in politics in the 'thirties they continued to act as if they were. In an unprecedented crisis in which their self-appointed leaders had thrown up their hands in fear and panic, it is to be wondered what the neo-Hooverites might deem the "function of a self-supporting people" if not to vote in, by orderly and constitutional means, new leaders of their own choosing. In four New York City hospitals in 1931 ninety-five persons died of starvation. In Akron in the year 1929, the Family Service Society dealt with 257 needy cases; in the next two years it collapsed under a load of 5,000 cases a *month*. "If the time should ever come that the voluntary agencies of this country are unable to find resources with which to prevent hunger and suffering," President Hoover said in 1931, "I will ask the aid of every resource of the federal government." The time had come; but the Great Humanitarian turned away in horror.

"The government should assist and encourage . . . movements of collective self-help by itself co-operating with them"; anything more, Hoover held in 1917, in 1926, and in 1931, would find the people "Prussianized." "A whole generation has gone mad on that word co-operation," Roosevelt exclaimed. If any President had a mandate from a politically "self-supporting people" to confront, as he said in his first inaugural, "the dark realities of the moment" with measures appropriate to them it was Franklin D. Roosevelt in 1932 and 1936. The "self-supporting people" had elected for deeds in place of threadbare dogma; they had saved, not weakened, their "constitutional system"; they had restored their rotting "national morale"; they had strengthened their "political morality" by confronting it at long last with the facts of life; and they had not in fact "burdened" their economy enough.

As for "national security," at a minimum Roosevelt may be said to have kept faith with the electorate while at the same time yearning to take the lead in defense of values which alone made "national security" worth defending. Those who claim that Roosevelt "imperiled" national security have even shorter memories of the Nazis astride Europe and the North Atlantic in 1941 than of the famine, fear, and futility astride the prostrate United States in 1931.

F.D.R. was the spoiled only child of a doting mother and a rich aristocrat old enough to be his grandfather. It is fashionable for historians to laugh at Roosevelt's business career in the 'twenties, which included an unsuccessful flier in a company organized to sell commodities by automatic vending machines. But this experiment appears much less farfetched in the 1950s, and only shows how far ahead of his times Roosevelt was likely to be. In politics, in his first electoral campaign for the state legislature in 1910, Roosevelt canvassed votes, unprecedentedly, by automobile. Ten years later, as Democratic candidate for vice-president, he said of the League of Nations, "it may not end wars, but the nations demand the experiment." As Governor of New York early in the depression he had become one of the sponsors of business plans for "stabilization of employment," which became famous in the 1950s as the "guaranteed annual wage." On his nomination for the presidency in 1932, he broke all precedents by flying to the convention, and by accepting the nomination in person. As early as May 1932, Roosevelt had called for "bold, persistent experimentation. If it fails," he said, "admit it frankly and try" something else. "But above all try something. The millions who are in want will not stand by silently forever while the things to satisfy their needs are within easy reach."

"I happen to know," Roosevelt said in a radio talk soon after his inauguration in March 1933, "that professional economists have changed their definition of economic laws every five or ten years for a long time." That perhaps was the extent of Roosevelt's knowledge of economics; but given the economists' knowledge of society, it is hardly a fault not to have studied them more carefully. Professor Irving Fisher of Yale, the dean of the economics guild, had declared late in 1928 that the stock market had reached "what looks like a permanently high plateau." The day after the great crash of October 29, 1929, Fisher remarked, "Yesterday's break was a shaking out of the lunatic fringe that attempts to speculate on margin." The following summer distracted Americans, writes Quincy Howe, "spent a million dollars a day playing miniature golf on thirty-five thousand courses that represented an investment of one hundred and thirty-five million dollars. Still crazier than the addicts . . . or the proprietors of the courses were the economists who seriously hailed it as the remedy for the depression. The fad collapsed in 1931 . . . having provided a brief and inexpensive diversion for the new poor who soon found other uses for their vanishing reserves of hard cash."

Not until 1936 did John Maynard Keynes publish his epochal *General Theory of Employment, Interest, and Money,* which is sometimes said to have become the bible of the New Deal. In December 1933, Keynes had written in an open letter to Roosevelt: "You have made yourself the trustee for those in every country who seek to mend the evils of our conditions by reasoned experiment within the framework of the existing social system. If you fail, rational change will be gravely prejudiced throughout the world, leaving orthodoxy and revolution to fight it out."

Actually, Roosevelt's first steps as President did not go far beyond belated ones taken by Hoover himself, though F.D.R.'s were accompanied by braver words. When Hoover saw the bankers abandon their role as bellwethers of the economy, he got Congress to create the Reconstruction Finance Corporation in January 1932. In the next twelve months this agency loaned a billion and a half dollars to five thousand banks, insurance companies, other credit agencies, and railroads. In July 1932, Congress passed the Federal Home Loan Act which enabled financial institutions holding home mortgages to obtain cash for current needs without foreclosing private dwellings. Later that month Hoover signed a bill permitting the RFC to lend nearly two billion dollars to state and local governments to strengthen their finances and to undertake self-liquidating public works. But Hoover had already estranged millions by vetoing bills for *federal* relief of the unemployed and indigent, and a measure providing for the immediate payment of the deferred bonus promised to veterans of the first World War. Hoover's other measures failed to restore either the economy itself or confidence in the future.

When Roosevelt took office on March 4, 1933, thousands of American banks verged on insolvency. Runs on them by frightened depositors had drained them of their reserves. To protect the banks most of the states had already declared "bank holidays"; and on

March 6, Roosevelt made the "holiday" countrywide for four days. Emergency legislation then empowered both the Federal Reserve System and the RFC to assist essentially sound banks with new currency. When Roosevelt reported these acts to the country on March 12, confidence was restored sufficiently for people to redeposit their money. Additional legislation in the next few months further stabilized the financial life of the country and set the pattern for reform legislation later. Still more or less in the Hoover pattern was an Act of June 1933, setting up the Home Owners Loan Corporation. This agency eventually was empowered to borrow as much as $4,750,000,000 and to make this money available to home owners for refinancing their mortgages. A year later Congress created the Federal Housing Administration which insured mortgages extended by banks to home owners for home construction or repair.

The stock market crash and the collapse of the commercial banking system had disclosed glaring abuses in the practices of the country's financial institutions. The first reform measures of the New Deal were directed toward improving the country's financial structure. The Glass-Steagall Act of 1933 required the complete separation of commercial banks from their investment-banking affiliates with the objective of protecting the deposits of the former from speculative uses by the latter—a practice which had helped precipitate the 1929 crash. A new Banking Act in 1935 revised the Federal Reserve System and gave its board of governors broad control over the activities of commercial banks.

By then the Truth-in-Securities Act of 1933, supplemented the next year by the Securities Exchange Act, had established the Securities and Exchange Commission. Henceforth most large corporate security issues had to be sanctioned by the SEC, and the marketing practices of security brokers and the stock exchanges themselves came under the Commission's jurisdiction. One of the worst offenders in issuing tricky securities and otherwise manipulating the investment market was the electric power industry. In 1935 Congress passed the Public Utility Holding Company Act forbidding the pyramiding of utility holding companies and placing the activities of legal holding companies under the scrutiny and control of the SEC.

Perhaps the greatest bugaboo of the power industry in the 1920s was the growth of public power, and the industry had successfully obstructed its development. One of the New Deal's first acts was the establishment in April 1933, of the Tennessee Valley Authority, "a corporation clothed with the power of Government but possessed of the flexibility and initiative of a private enterprise." Ostensibly a national flood control project, TVA was given control of the power resources of a vast multi-state area covering 40,000 square miles. The Tennessee Valley at this time was one of the most impoverished and backward areas of the nation. Under TVA the valley blossomed into a rich farming and industrial region. TVA itself became a yardstick for the performance of the private power industry.

The power companies have never ceased fighting both the principle and the practices of TVA. Their long campaign seemed near success when President Eisenhower himself in 1954 and 1955 sanctioned the so-called Dixon-Yates private power project to dismantle TVA. But the industry's methods in promoting the Dixon-Yates scheme became so unsavory that the President was forced to withdraw his support, and TVA survived. The power industry also fought the Rural Electrification Administration, set up by the New Deal in May 1935, and extended two years later. The REA was designed to provide electric power in areas too thinly populated to attract private investment. It did its job so well that it has withstood constant private sniping.

From reform of institutions and practices that appeared to have deepened the depression, the New Deal turned early to measures of relief for the depression's victims and the economy as a whole. The first relief act was passed in April 1933. It set up the Civilian Conservation Corps under the supervision of the War Department. By 1940 CCC had given employment to 2,250,000 youths who worked on valuable reforestation, soil conservation, and flood control projects. In May 1933, Congress appropriated an initial $500,000,000 to help the states give direct relief to the 15,000,000 unemployed. The cost of this program eventually ran into billions. The most dramatic relief measures were those providing a Public Works Administration with $3,300,000,000 for a vast public building program. PWA was established under one provision of the National Industrial Recovery Act of 1933 which represented the New Deal's first major effort to reinvigorate American industry. Designed as a massive pump-priming measure, PWA was administered so cautiously that its impact on the economy was scarcely felt.

The National Recovery Administration as a whole also failed. Back in the 1920s Secretary of Commerce Hoover had begun to encourage business to organize trade associations for the better planning of industrial production and distribution, and he developed this program further as President. Under NRA the New Deal proposed to use these trade associations to administer the codes by which business henceforth would be conducted. Written by committees representing industry, labor, and the government, NRA codes set up minimum wage and hour standards for hundreds of different industries. They also recognized labor's right to organize, in exchange for which business itself got the right to stabilize prices and production without fear of anti-trust suits. As long as the NRA codes were administered by business groups, business was happy under them. By late 1934, however, two things had happened. "Little business" found that the codes were rigged to benefit the great firms in their industries, and the great firms found that government bureaucrats were gradually encroaching on their administrative prerogatives. NRA was beset with conflicts when, in May 1935, the Supreme Court declared the Recovery Act unconstitutional.

NRA reflected the New Deal's acceptance of the "mature economy" theory which held that the country had passed its greatest period of growth and that henceforth business must not be permitted to overexpand. Thus the controls on hours of work and free competition. The same theory was reflected in the Agricultural Adjustment Act, passed in May 1933. The major objective of AAA was to raise prices of farm staples to the point where the farmer's purchasing power would equal that of the favorable period, 1900-14. These "parity prices" were to be achieved by reducing the acreage sown, and this reduction was to be won by compensating farmers in various ways for acreage left fallow. When the crops of 1933 threatened to overwhelm the market the AAA took the drastic step of plowing under a large portion of them. That fall it also established the Commodity Credit Corporation to lend money to farmers who held their crops off the market in anticipation of higher prices later. These measures greatly improved farming conditions between 1933 and 1935. But AAA suffered the same fate as NRA before the Supreme Court in January 1936.

Though the AAA had noticeably aided staple farmers, neither it nor the NRA succeeded in shaking the economy loose from the depression. By the time of the Congressional elections of 1934 five dreary years had passed since the crash. The coalition of industry, labor, farmers, and government which had marked the critical first New Deal months was breaking under the strain. In August 1934, business leaders in revolt against the NRA had organized the American Liberty League to combat further New Deal encroachments on business freedom, especially in the field of labor relations. The unemployed, on the other hand, had responded by the millions to the share-the-wealth campaigns of such demagogues as the radio priest, Father Coughlin; the author, Upton Sinclair; Dr. Francis E. Townsend; and Louisiana's Senator Huey Long. Tenant and subsistence farmers for whom the AAA had done nothing joined the urban unemployed in backing these panacea-mongers. The Liberty League gave the Republican Party's campaign a new focus, but the Democrats swept the election. The social worker, Harry Hopkins, had been influential in designing the Democratic campaign strategy and tireless in working for the ticket. He now rose near the top of the inner circle of Roosevelt's advisers.

The "Brains Trust" that Raymond Moley had organized for Roosevelt even before the 1932 presidential election had been a conservative group with limited objectives. Most of the members had had training in economics. NRA was essentially their idea and business was their instrument for reviving the economy. Hopkins, on the contrary, was interested in the salvation of the unemployed, the indigent, the sick, the aged. He was accustomed as a social worker to direct action, not to theories of distribution of wealth through market mechanisms. Under the whip of this new and more imaginative leadership, the new Congress proceeded to enact what came to be considered characteristic New Deal measures.

Since business apparently could not employ the millions still abortively seeking work, Congress in 1935 set up a five-billion-dollar Works Progress Administration. With WPA the government instituted a remarkably comprehensive program of work relief. At the same time the President himself established the National Youth Administration which gave work to school-age people while they continued to attend classes and thereby kept them off the regular labor market. The President also set up in the Agricultural Department, a Resettlement Administration to rehabilitate half a million tenant farmers and others on the stricken soil.

In August 1935, Congress passed the first Social Security Act which in two years covered 28,000,000 workers and has since been extended to the point where virtually the entire working population is protected by old-age insurance.

At about the same time Congress enacted the National Labor Relations Act, a Magna Carta for the beleaguered unions. This Act provided for a National Labor Relations Board with power to issue cease-and-desist orders to corporations engaged in unfair labor practices, and to conduct elections by which workers could vote freely and securely for their own bargaining agents in the making of labor contracts.

The cost of these measures Congress proceeded to place upon those best able to pay. This was accomplished by the Revenue Act of August 1935, which significantly raised surtax levies on large personal and corporate incomes. Congress also enacted measures extending federal control over the coal industry, retailing, railroads, busses and trucks, the merchant marine and the airlines.

On this record, which earned the solid support of labor in particular, the Democrats and Roosevelt swept to an overwhelming victory in the presidential elections of 1936. Alfred M. Landon, of Kansas, the Republican candidate, carried the electoral votes only of Vermont and Maine.

Often in the past the Supreme Court had proved the supreme defender of the *status quo*. During 1934 and 1935, after business had broken with the administration, it seemed that the history of the Court would repeat itself. Invalidation of NRA and AAA were but two instances of the Supreme Court's attack on the New Deal. In other cases the Court rejected a Railroad Retirement Act which had required contributions by the railroads themselves, and a Farm Mortgage Act which forestalled normal foreclosure proceedings. Both measures, the Court argued, deprived persons of property without due process of law. In its railroad retirement decision the Court added that federal control over interstate commerce did not extend beyond control of goods in transit. By this reasoning both the Social Security Act and the National Labor Relations Act were also vulnerable, and indeed in lower federal courts hundreds of injunctions against the enforcement of the labor act had been granted by the end of 1936. After his smashing victory in the elections that year, the President decided the time had come to end the Court's vendetta against the entire New Deal and the concept of national welfare that underlay it.

To curb or correct the Court, Roosevelt submitted to Congress on February 3, 1937, a Judiciary Reorganization bill which would permit the President when any federal judge failed to retire at the age of seventy, to appoint a new judge to assist him. Since six of the Supreme Court justices were over seventy, this would have given Roosevelt the power to expand the Court to fifteen judges, six of whom he would have power to appoint immediately.

If this proposal came as a surprise to the country and even to the leading politicians, the anger it aroused in both parties came as a shock to the President. The Reorganization bill was defeated. But Roosevelt had his victory none the less, for the proposal startled the middle-of-the-roaders on the Court into a realization that more radical reforms would be in the offing if the justices failed promptly to give deeper consideration to the needs and the will of the country. Their new attitude was confirmed in May 1937, when the Court upheld the Social Security Act. The previous month, in an epochal decision, it had upheld the National Labor Relations Act.

By the time the Court had made its labor decision a virtual revolution had taken place in union organization. For a long time a group within the American Federation of Labor, led by John L. Lewis of the United Mine Workers, had been trying to force the Federation to organize the mass of industrial workers outside the specific crafts. Of particular concern were the Negro workers who had flocked to Detroit and other northern industrial cities since the first World War but had gained no recognition by the union bosses. In November 1935, Lewis led a rump group of A. F. of L. leaders in the formation of a Committee for Industrial Organization to bring the masses of labor into the union scheme. Ordered to disband by the official A. F. of L. leadership, the Committee refused. When ten of the co-operating unions were expelled from the A. F. of L. in March 1937, they formed the independent C.I.O., known after October of that year as the Congress of Industrial Organizations.

By then the Steel Workers under Philip Murray had already won their historic victory in gaining recognition of their C.I.O. union by the United States Steel Corporation. "Little Steel" proved much tougher to organize, and here the C.I.O. campaign was met with traditional gunfire and bloodshed. Only the intervention of the newly validated National Labor Relations Board forced "Little Steel" to concede recognition in 1941. In the meantime the C.I.O. had organized large numbers of rubber, textile, clothing, and electrical workers and others in smaller industries.

C.I.O. efforts to organize the automobile industry in 1936 and 1937 were marked by the revolutionary tactic of the "sit-down strike," during which workers simply occupied the plants in an effort to win recognition. The corporations naturally tried to dislodge them by cajolery, law, and force. When Frank Murphy, the Democratic Governor of Michigan, refused to use the National Guard against the General Motors strikers, the corporation grudgingly yielded to the C.I.O. faction of the A. F. of L. This was in February 1937. Chrysler capitulated in September. At Ford the union organizing campaign was inept. At the same time, Ford's anti-union espionage and intimidation were the most highly perfected in the industry and his "goons" the most numerous and best trained. The C.I.O. had to fight until 1941 to bring Ford workers into the fold.

In 1932, after a century or more of organization work, fewer than 3,000,000 Americans were members of labor unions. By 1941 the C.I.O. had grown into a massive organization of 5,000,-000 while the A. F. of L., forced to bestir itself, had also mushroomed to 4,500,000 members. A million other workers were enrolled in independent unions. When the C.I.O. and A. F. of L. reunited in 1955, their joint membership had risen to 15,000,000 and the total unionized labor force to over 16,000,000. The impetus the New Deal gave to this development was one of its most significant achievements.

DOMESTIC AND FOREIGN CRISES

Between 1933 and 1937 the combined efforts of government, labor, and industry had reduced the number of unemployed from about fifteen million to less than eight million. The rise in jobs and the improvement in farm income helped revive the market for goods. Indeed, between 1933 and 1937 business enjoyed a continuous if mild upswing. Soon after Roosevelt's second inauguration, however, business again went into a tailspin and 4,000,000 returned to the unemployment rolls. As usual the President was ready with appropriate phrases. Lashing out at "economic royalists" who were choking opportunity, he got Congress to establish a Temporary National Economic Committee to disclose the monopolistic structure of American business and to propose new legislation to combat it. At the same time the Department of Justice initiated a new series of antitrust suits. The TNEC published an enormous amount of information about the business community but neither it nor the activities of the Justice Department significantly affected the business structure. The President also decried the fact that while private enterprise nodded, one third of the population remained ill-fed, ill-clothed, and ill-housed.

In 1937 and 1938 Congress passed new legislation to help the farmers, to provide funds for cheap public housing, and to continue WPA. But such measures no longer evoked confidence as in the early New Deal days. On the contrary, they smacked of the "recipe as before," and as *Fortune* suggested early in 1940, they depressed rather than raised the country's spirit.

In the Congressional elections of 1938, for the first time in nearly a decade, the Republicans made notable gains. But intraparty strife over foreign policy, and especially over the war once again brewing in Europe, cost them any chance of victory in the presidential elections of 1940.

As long as no great crisis threatened world peace American

policy even under Republican administrations after the first World War had not been strictly isolationist. In the 1920s the United States took the lead in trying to control naval building among the nations of the world and to allay unrest in such trouble zones as China. The United States had also sought agreements, like the Kellogg-Briand pact of 1928, to outlaw war as an instrument of settling international disputes and had co-operated with the League of Nations toward this end.

Under the New Deal, United States policy toward Latin America showed that our peaceful spirit was not simply verbal. There we reversed the "big stick" policy of the past, withdrew from the management of the internal affairs of some Latin American countries, and invited them to join with us as equals in defense of the hemisphere against European encroachments. Firmly convinced that trade barriers were the basic cause of war, Roosevelt's Secretary of State, Cordell Hull, also tried continuously to work out agreements with many nations for the mutual lowering of tariffs and the removal of other impediments to the free flow of goods and the easy exchange of currencies. American recognition of the Soviet Union in 1933 was motivated in large part by the desire to restore trade between the two countries.

None of these activities, however, seriously engaged the attention or sympathy of the American people. But when Hitler's advent early in the 1930s revived the menace of a new world war, American isolationism flowered. Popular enthusiasm greeted the "merchants of death" investigation of 1934, in which a Senate committee placed the onus for war on munitions makers. In 1935 Mussolini invaded Ethiopia while the United States and the members of the League of Nations stood by. In 1936 Mussolini and Hitler helped General Franco to establish his tyranny in Spain. Later that year Germany and Japan completed the Berlin-Tokyo axis to which Italy was admitted in 1937. The American response to this lengthening chain of aggression was a series of Neutrality Acts based on the Senate committee's findings. The culminating measure was the Neutrality Act of May 1937, which forbade the lending of money and the sale of munitions to belligerent nations and permitted them to buy other commodities in the United States only for cash and only if they carried them off in their own ships.

In the summer of 1937 Japan resumed the attacks on China which she had begun in 1931. Japan's aggression prompted President Roosevelt, in October 1937, to make an electrifying speech in which he urged that aggressor nations be "quarantined." But neither the American people nor our allies in Europe responded favorably to the idea.

Confident that the American neutrality statutes would deter England and France from offering resistance, Hitler early in 1938 seized Austria. Later that year he occupied most of Czechoslovakia. But the western world's response was simply Neville Chamberlain's "appeasement" visit to Munich in September 1938, when Hitler cynically stated that he would remain satisfied with his gains so far. In the spring of 1939, however, Hitler grabbed Prague and the rest of free Czechoslovakia, and on August 23 he made the notorious nonaggression pact with Stalin which freed him to attack Poland without fear of Russian reprisals. The German invasion of Poland began September 1, 1939. Their guarantees to Poland at last forced England and France to declare war on Germany. World War II had begun.

"When peace has been broken anywhere," Roosevelt told the American people over the radio on September 1, "peace of all countries everywhere is in danger." On September 21 he called Congress into special session; after six weeks of stern debate Congress revised the neutrality laws to the extent of permitting belligerents to purchase munitions for cash provided they carried their purchases in their own vessels. This was on November 4, 1939. By then Poland had succumbed to German arms, and, in accordance with the "secret additional protocol" of their nonaggression pact, Hitler and Stalin proceeded to carve her up. Characteristically, Stalin enlarged his claims under the protocol to include Lithuania as well as Estonia, Latvia, and Finland as Russian spoils, claiming later that the Baltic states were to provide a buffer between the Soviets and the West. Hitler acquiesced in order to direct his attentions westward. All but Finland had already been conquered and late in November 1939, Stalin attacked her. The Finns resisted magnificently, but on March 12, 1940, were forced to surrender to overwhelmingly superior forces.

While Stalin was occupied with Finland, Hitler was conducting the "phony war" in the West. During the winter of 1939, he let Chamberlain's Britain bathe in a welcomed sense of security and encouraged the French to complain bitterly over the costs of mobilization for hostilities that never seemed to materialize. Morale fell to new lows in both countries. The phony war came to a spectacular end on April 9, 1940, when in a single day Hitler's blitzkrieg overran Denmark and all the major North Sea and Atlantic ports of Norway. Sweden, at the same time, was immobilized, her iron ore and air bases Hitler's to command. The shock of this triumph blew Chamberlain out of office on May 10, when he yielded the premiership to Winston Churchill. On the same day, Hitler's forces tore into the Netherlands and reduced them in ninety-six hours. Belgium surrendered before the end of May; France before the end of June.

One of Churchill's first tasks was to supervise the evacuation of 340,000 beleaguered British troops from Dunkirk on the French Channel coast. On June 4, the day this incredible operation was completed, Churchill addressed his people with words that kindled the spirit of the free world:

> We shall defend our Island, whatever the cost may be, we shall fight on the beaches, we shall fight on the landing grounds, we shall fight in the fields and in the streets, we shall fight in the hills; we shall never surrender, and even if, which I do not for a moment believe, this Island or a large part of it were subjugated and starving, then our Empire beyond the seas, armed and guarded by the British Fleet, would carry on the struggle, until, in God's good time, the New World, with all its power and might, steps forth to the rescue and the liberation of the old.

The next day Hitler attacked France in earnest and on June 17 France fell. On July 10 the Battle of Britain began.

Hitler's smashing conquest of France convinced most of the American people of their own imminent danger. During the summer of 1940 Congress appropriated nearly sixteen billion dollars for "defense," and a huge air force and a two-ocean navy were in the making. In August the government initiated joint defense planning with Canada, already a belligerent. In September Con-

gress also ordered the first peacetime draft in history. At the same
time Congress acquiesced in Roosevelt's bold offer of fifty over-age
destroyers to Britain in exchange for the right for a period of
ninety-nine years to set up naval, air, and military bases in British possessions forming a protective screen from Newfoundland
to British Guiana. Churchill thought that "according to all the
standards of history," Roosevelt's daring move would "have justified the German Government in declaring war." But Hitler had no
desire to incite the United States while Britain remained uncon-
quered. This gave credence to the American isolationists' claim
that Hitler had no designs on the United States at all.

If Roosevelt wanted an excuse to run for an unprecedented
third term, the need for an experienced hand during the mounting
global crisis supplied it. Many Democratic politicians had tired of
F.D.R., but when he made himself available they could not oppose
him. The Republicans were even less united. Republicans had led
in forming the isolationist America First Committee and many similar organizations which appeared during the summer and fall of
1940. All were solidly opposed to American involvement in foreign wars. They seemed to prefer, as Roosevelt himself pointed
out, to fight only on our own territory where our cities and homes
would be destroyed, and only after all our potential allies had been
wiped out. They described their own position somewhat differently.
They conceded Europe (including Britain) to Hitler and proposed
to do business with him. Many other Republicans, especially among
the younger party members, were more realistic. In the end they
carried the Republican convention and nominated Wendell Willkie,
a confirmed internationalist, for the presidency. Willkie put up a
real fight and while he failed to win, he cut F.D.R.'s 1936 margin
considerably. Strengthened by his victory, the President promptly
promised Britain all aid short of joining the shooting.

In a broadcast on December 29, 1940, Roosevelt proposed to
make the United States the "arsenal of democracy." A few days
later he enunciated as the goal of this policy the establishment of
the Four Freedoms throughout the world: freedom of speech and
of worship; freedom from want and from fear. By March Roosevelt's program had materialized in the act of Congress establishing

"lend-lease." By this act the President was empowered to make available to "the government of any country whose defense the President deems vital to the defense of the United States" not money in the form of repayable loans, but any service, any "defense article," and any "defense information."

By the time the Lend-Lease Act was passed, American and British naval officers had already spent months in secret sessions working toward agreement that, even if Japan entered the war, Germany would remain the number one object of attack, and preparing joint attack plans. Soon after, two momentous military events occurred. First in June 1941, British airplane production had caught up with the Germans' and victory in the air Battle of Britain seemed imminent. Second, Hitler seemed to sense defeat in the air battle when, on June 22, he broke his nonaggression pact with Stalin and turned the blitzkrieg on the Russians.

For all his misgivings about international Communism, Churchill joyfully accepted the Russians as comrades-in-arms. In August 1941, he held his first wartime conference with Roosevelt in the hope of further speeding the Nazis' end by enlarging American contributions to the fighting. Simply by participating as a non-belligerent in a conference with belligerent Britain, Roosevelt showed how glad he was to do what he could.

The most striking result of this conference, which was held at Argentia Bay, Newfoundland, was the promulgation of the Atlantic Charter. Victory was far off, but Roosevelt strove to define the glorious purposes for which Americans might join the "war for survival." Churchill was willing to go along to help Roosevelt carry the American people. The Charter reiterated many of Wilson's Fourteen Points covering the right of peoples everywhere to "choose the form of government under which they will live"; to trade freely on free seas and have "access, on equal terms," to the world's raw materials; and "pending the establishment of a wider and permanent system of general security," to live at peace in a disarmed world.

Among the more immediate objectives of the Argentia conference, as Churchill put it, were to "proclaim the ever closer association of the British and the United States," to "cause our enemies concern," to "make Japan ponder," and to "cheer our friends." If Japan pondered, she was not deterred. The Japanese assault on Pearl Harbor on December 7, 1941, only hastened the United States' total involvement in what would become the deadliest war in history.

Chapter Fourteen

The One World of the Twentieth Century

In September 1957, the U.S.S.R. claimed to have achieved the world's first successful flight of an intercontinental ballistic missile capable of reaching American cities from Soviet launching bases. At almost the same moment, the Ford Motor Company announced for 1958 what it called the first entirely new full line of automobiles in the United States since 1939. The most revolutionary feature of the new car, a secret that was as well protected as the first atomic bomb, proved to be the vertical arrangement of the chrome on its front grille. The Russians have the ICBM, grumbled global-minded American commentators, and we have the Edsel.

This remark was reminiscent of Hermann Goering's observation on the eve of our entrance into the second World War: "The Americans can't build planes, only electric ice boxes and razor blades." Many Americans themselves had then shared this defeatist view; and some would not shed it for years to come. When President Roosevelt mentioned 8,000 planes a year as a possible goal in 1938, almost everyone thought he was having dreams of grandeur. When he called for 50,000 planes a year in June 1940, his explanation of our and the free world's pressing need was denounced by Charles A. Lindbergh and other isolationist experts as "hysterical chatter." "Our dangers are internal," said Lindbergh. "Nobody wishes to attack us, and nobody is in a position to do so." Even in January 1942, when Roosevelt demanded 60,000 planes that year, as well as 45,000 tanks and eight million tons of ocean shipping,

388

Donald Nelson, the head of the new War Production Board, said, "We thought these goals were out of the question."

In 1940 and 1942 (as in 1950 and 1957) the American people were confronted with the choice, as the phrase goes, of guns or butter. As often in the more distant past, they voted for butter—until the need for guns became unbearable. "We almost lost the war before we got into it," a sobered Nelson wrote later. "At best it was a hair-line verdict. Just a few more mistakes would have turned the trick—a little more unwillingness to look into the face of reality, a little more shrinking from hard facts and figures . . . a little more tremulous indecision."

Unfortunately, fantastic conceptions of national defense and of national productive capacity in emergencies have frequently prompted some of America's most influential leaders to advocate limitations or delays in arming, and the dissipation, or destruction of allies, almost to the point of national suicide. Until he was educated by General George C. Marshall, who became wartime Army Chief of Staff, and by Roosevelt himself, Harry Hopkins, the President's closest wartime associate, believed (as Robert Sherwood reports it) that "if an enemy fleet approached our shores, we would merely line up our own Navy (which was always 'second to none') like a football team defending its goal line in the days before the invention of the forward pass; any hostile ships that might break through the Navy would be handled by our coast defenses." Roosevelt demolished this conception (which Hopkins shared with Nelson and others high in authority) once and for all in August 1940, by taking Hopkins to a map and explaining that our Navy and our coastal installations together "could defend less than one and one-half per cent of our coastline." An enemy could land unmolested in innumerable places; it was far better, said Roosevelt, if we or our friends landed on him first, preferably with air power.

An even more dangerous conception was that advanced just before the fall of France by Senator Robert A. Taft, certainly the most influential political spokesman for the American industrial community. "I do not know what the Germans may do," Taft said:

. . . until they are freed from the present war and have an opportunity to show. When they do, we can adopt the same methods. We can take the same steps that may be necessary to meet the particular kind of German "blitzkrieg," if there is such a blitzkrieg, at the time we find out what it is.

Nothing attests more strongly to the peaceful intentions of the American people than their preference for butter over guns, for Edsels over ICBMs. Yet for all the vast dangers to our security in overburdening our economy with hasty and excessive investments in armaments and allies, nothing could be more risky than the dissipation of both. Weakness has always invited aggression. In modern wars involving complex machines, the aggressor has had tremendous and ever-increasing initial advantages. It takes years to move the latest military equipment from designing board to mass production; it takes almost as long to train military personnel in the operation and maintenance of new equipment and tactics and strategy relevant to it. To wait until an enemy's blitzkrieg is mounted and rolling, as Chamberlain's government did in Britain and as Taft and his followers advocated that we do here, was simply to invite annihilation. In atomic war, the aggressor's initial advantages, once the deterrents of might and spirit falter, are likely to be unanswerable.

In World War II, only Churchill's heroic rallying of his people rescued Britain at the zero hour from a disaster more complete than that of France. Only Roosevelt's urgent rallying of our productive talents ("against the advice of some of this country's best minds," as Donald Nelson acknowledged) preserved the United States and the free world.

PRODIGIES OF PRODUCTION

Of all the prodigies of production in World War II the most momentous was the development of an atomic bomb that could be manufactured in quantity by assembly line techniques. This development, though among the last to attain success, was one of the first to be undertaken. The Anglo-American decision in the spring of 1941 to consider Germany target number one even if Japan should enter the war on the side of her Axis partner was prompted to a considerable extent by the agreed-upon need to destroy Hitler before the Germans manufactured an atomic bomb themselves. To accomplish his destruction such a bomb of our own would be useful.

Even before Munich, Nazi scientists, following an old Einstein lead, had been the first in the world to release energy by splitting the uranium atom. Thereafter, a way to employ this incredible energy in a deliverable weapon was feverishly sought. Lindbergh, who had recently returned to the United States after several years' residence in Europe where he was attracted to Nazism, "scared the living daylights" (the words are Robert Sherwood's) out of influential listeners at private meetings with stories of the incomparability of Nazi science and the imminence of our atomic destruction.* But certain Americans did not easily "scare"; among them was the knowledgeable Dr. Vannevar Bush, formerly Dean of Engineering at M.I.T. and then President of the Carnegie Institution in Washington. Forewarned, for once, was to be forearmed. Dr. Bush responded to Lindbergh's importing of Hitler's "strategy of terror" not with paralysis of nerve, but with immediate action to parry and improve on the threat.

As early as January 1939, certain American scientists had learned from the eminent Danish physicist, Niels Bohr, the nature of the German atomic experiments. Later that year Einstein, who had fled Germany when Hitler took power, and two other foreign-born scientists, Leo Szilard and Eugene Wigner, had managed to convey to F.D.R. the full meaning of the approaching mastery of atomic science by the "master race." Roosevelt promptly established an advisory committee on uranium; but the "crash" program on the production of an atomic bomb was not decided upon until the spring of 1941, when the British, whose atomic research was considerably ahead of our own, agreed to share their knowledge. The whole program was placed under the supervision of the Office of Scientific Research and Development (OSRD) which Dr. Bush had earlier organized (under another title) to mobilize American scientists and engineers for work on all scientific phases of the defense effort.

The most fruitful subsequent work on the atom was done at the

* After the United States did go to war, Lindbergh put his knowledge of German airplanes at the service of this government and contributed significantly to the progress of our air arm.

universities of California and Chicago and at Columbia. This work demonstrated that a practical bomb could be made by using plutonium as the "fissionable element." Plutonium was a new element made by splitting the uranium atom in a cyclotron or atom smasher. On May 1, 1943, the job of producing plutonium in large quantities was given to the sacredly secret Manhattan District Project established under General Leslie R. Groves at Oak Ridge, Tennessee, where the immense water and electric power resources of TVA were available. At approximately the same time, the responsibility for building a practical bomb was placed upon Dr. J. Robert Oppenheimer and the brilliant team of British, American, and European scientists he gathered at Los Alamos, New Mexico. On July 12, 1945, final assembly of the first atomic bomb began. At five-thirty in the morning four days later, at Alamogordo air base in New Mexico, the terrible weapon was detonated.

By then V-E day was more than two months past. Hitler's "thousand-year Reich" had come crashing down in flames and suicides amid the woeful stench of concentration camps and gas chambers on May 7, 1945. As early as 1942 Nazi scientists had decided that an atomic bomb was not feasible. Their alternative weapons failed to offset even the nonatomic achievements of the scientists of the free world.

Next to the bomb, perhaps the most important of these achievements was "microwave-search radar." Radar-equipped patrol planes and ships could determine the exact location of enemy submarines (and other water and air craft) far beyond the range of sight and "coach in" friendly craft "for the kill." Essentially a British invention, radar was largely responsible for victory in the air Battle of Britain and almost wholly responsible for ridding the sea lanes of U-boats in the Battle of the Atlantic. A third crucial weapon, developed exclusively under the auspices of the OSRD in 1942, was the proximity fuse. This fuse was in effect "a radio set in the head of the shell that detonated it by proximity to the target." Allied generals, fearful that an unexploded shell equipped with the fuse might fall into enemy hands, forbade its use by ground troops until December 1944, when it was employed with devastating effect in beating back the German counteroffensive in Belgium. For years previously, the proximity fuse had done yeoman work against enemy aircraft over Pacific and European waters.

During World War I the United States ferried two million men across the Atlantic. Those who actually engaged in fighting used English and French equipment—from rifles and machine guns to airplanes—almost exclusively. In World War II the United States sent four million fully equipped men virtually to every outpost of the known world and outfitted more than that many in allied forces. "American factories," write the historians Samuel Eliot Morison and Henry Steele Commager:

> equipped French and Chinese armies; built harbor works in the Persian Gulf, India, and New Caledonia; provided millions of feet of steel landing mats for hundreds of air fields scattered around the earth; supplied locomotives to Iran, trucks to Russia, jeeps to Britain, aircraft to China; built the Burma Road; completed the Alaska Highway; constructed aluminum plants in Canada; laid oil pipe lines in France, and performed a thousand similar tasks. To hard-pressed Russia went almost 400,000 trucks, 52,000 jeeps, 7,000 tanks, 130,000 field telephones, 420,000 tons of aluminum, and enough planes to equip two air forces the size of the United States Ninth Tactical Air Force, which was the world's largest. Britain received enough planes for four such air forces, over 100,000 trucks and jeeps, six million tons of steel, one billion dollars worth of ordnance, thousands of radar sets, and millions of feet of radar-interception foil. One year after Pearl Harbor the United States was producing more war material than all the Axis nations combined.

By the end of 1942 Roosevelt's demand for 60,000 planes had been missed by only 12,000; the next year American factories produced 85,930 planes; by the end of the war nearly 300,000— most of them larger and faster and with greater fire power than any dreamed of when the war began. By the end of 1942 Roosevelt's demand for eight million tons of merchant shipping had been met on the nose; the next year American yards produced 19,296,000 tons; by the end of the war more than 55,000,000 tons. This represented 5,425 ships, including mass-assembled Liberty ships and Victory ships, and tankers with record capacity, speed, and cruising range. We also produced 71,000 naval vessels from the minutest auxiliaries to gigantic aircraft carriers like *Essex, Bunker Hill,* and *Independence.* Many of the new vessels were ingeniously designed for amphibian landings and innumerable other special purposes.

Armament and equipment were only a few of the end products (others included hospitals, camps, roads, machinery, and medicines) of vast expansion in basic industries. For some of the most strategic materials we had been entirely dependent upon imports which were cut off by the war. The most critical of these was raw rubber. One of the outstanding stories of the "battle of production" was the creation from scratch of the synthetic rubber industry.

The United States is far better equipped for war today than at the time of Pearl Harbor. But it was far better equipped then than for World War I. This was partly due, of course, to Roosevelt's foresight in beginning to make American industry the "arsenal of democracy" in 1940 and to the expansion of arms production to implement lend-lease after March 1941. Yet even more of the credit goes to New Deal agencies like TVA, the source of power for the Manhattan District Project. The much maligned WPA and PWA, moreover, contributed immensely in such intangible ways as maintaining the morale and loyalty of our citizenry during a depression that might easily have alienated class from class as it did in France and (fortunately to a lesser extent) in Britain.

But WPA and PWA also made important tangible contributions. Most noteworthy, perhaps, was their role in developing public power projects on the West Coast. Without depression-built Grand Coulee and Bonneville Dams our wartime aluminum—and hence our wartime aircraft—production would have fallen disastrously short of requirements. WPA and PWA funds had also given construction employment and experience to army engineers at a time when isolationist Congresses were starving the armed forces and military career men were too frightened to fight for funds. Warily, but wisely, F.D.R. had used PWA funds to build aircraft carriers *Enterprise* and *Yorktown* and to lay the keels of other naval vessels before Hitler's invasion of Poland. He had also used WPA workers, as the *Army and Navy Register* said in May 1942, "who saved many Army posts and Naval stations from literal obsolescence . . . in the years 1935 to 1939."

There were less salutary carry-overs from New Deal days. The "hate Roosevelt" attitude of big business was not an inconsiderable element in the steel industry's delay in expanding capacity before Pearl Harbor. Nor was this attitude absent from the automobile industry's "business as usual" policy, reflected in its reluctance to convert to armaments just when the boom created by our "arsenal of democracy" and lend-lease programs was reviving the market for cars. Fairly complete conversion ultimately was achieved; but industry's old fear of excess plant capacity forced the government, through the Defense Plants Corporation, to build virtually all the new wartime factories and such transportation facilities as the cross-country "Big Inch" and "Little Big Inch" pipe lines. Farmers, in turn, played "politics as usual." They had enjoyed large subsidies and other protection under the New Deal, and now they used their political power to drive a hard bargain—in the form of a guarantee of high prices for the duration and high parity support for at least two years after the war—before yielding to the government's demand for vast increases in production to meet wartime needs.

Organized labor, another element that owed its strength to New Deal policies and politics, was not so fortunate. In exchange for a government promise to keep wartime prices down, the A. F. of L. and the C.I.O. had made no-strike pledges after Pearl Harbor. The Office of Price Administration, under Leon Henderson, did a historic job of containing inflation throughout the war period. Yet price rises did occur, sometimes steep ones. There were many "wildcat strikes" for higher wages in 1943, after the most critical days of the "battle for production" were past. The worst labor troubles occurred in the coal mines where John L. Lewis kept up his "war as usual" with the recalcitrant coal operators. The President's seizure of the mines in May 1943, deterred neither Lewis nor his men from striking on June 11. Later that month an embattled Congress replied with the harsh Smith-Connally Act authorizing the government to operate struck plants and making strikes against federally run plants a criminal offense. "There are no strikes in foxholes," was the type of slogan that slapped at rebellious workers. But their response, "There are no profits either," seemed to meet the polemic requirements.

American resistance to total mobilization was perhaps heartening evidence of the persistence of freedom even under war conditions. Freedom was manifested in other ways, not least by the constant clamoring for priorities and other privileges as the web of Washington red tape reached out to every factory, farm, and home in the land. Roosevelt himself added to the occasions for confusion and complaint by his practice, carried over intact from "politicking" New Deal days, of piling agency upon agency. New "alphabet" administrations were given responsibilities and functions of which old ones were not specifically relieved. This helped make the central government a jungle where professional "influence peddlers" thrived; while in many far corners of the land a sense of unfairness and frustration curdled the cream if not the milk of patriotism.

Yet no one forgot the "date which will live in infamy." Pearl Harbor united the nation more firmly than any single event in history. Naturally, in a country given to extremes, the single major blot on wartime tolerance was one of the blackest ever. At the outbreak of the war, 126,000 persons of Japanese origin lived in the United States; two thirds of them were Nisei, or American-born citizens. Right after Pearl Harbor, 112,000 of these persons were herded from their homes by the War Department, shorn of their property, and barricaded for the duration in prison camps. This invasion of the rights of citizens of the United States by their own government was an act of sheer hysteria for which no evidence of disloyalty had been provided previously nor discovered since.

This inexcusable occurrence aside, no earlier war period enjoyed such freedom of expression, thought, and assembly as World War II. Few earlier periods of war or peace, moreover, enjoyed such prosperity and freedom of opportunity. All told, the war cost the United States $350,000,000,000 (of which $50,000,000,000 went for lend-lease. Against this we received nearly $8,000,000,000 in "reverse lend-lease" from the British and others). Taxes covered an unprecedented 40 per cent of American wartime expenditures. Federal corporation and graduated personal income taxes reached record highs, which brought a good deal of grumbling but few criminal attempts at evasion. Yet corporation profits *after* taxes, swollen by the standard "cost-plus" contracts, rose from $5,000,-

000,000 in 1939 to nearly $10,000,000,000 five years later. Personal income rose even faster, and while new fortunes were made, income also was more fairly distributed.

Before Pearl Harbor more than six million unemployed persons had been restored to payrolls in defense industries and other industries prospering from the defense boom. In the following war years, when fifteen million men and women were mobilized in the armed services, three million women joined the labor force. Hundreds of thousands of Negro men and women, heretofore largely excluded from industrial employment by segregation practices of business and unions as well as by the depression, also helped run the machines of war production.

Early in the war factories began to operate three shifts. Between 1939 and 1944 the average industrial work week rose from thirty-eight to forty-five hours; the average industrial weekly paycheck, including premiums for overtime, rose from $23.86 to $46.08. Often there were two or three weekly paychecks in one working family. Farm income also soared. Many farmers enjoyed special exemption from the draft; but many also enlisted in the armed forces or sought the livelier life of the new industrial boom towns. Mechanization more than made up for these defections. By 1945 each farm worker was producing, on the average, twice as much as his prototype of the golden age of 1910-14, and his income reflected it. By the end of the war, the American people, deprived of many familiar consumer goods, had amassed $140,000,000,000 in savings and were aching to spend it.

Wartime prosperity sparked a social revolution in the United States which continued with increasing momentum in the postwar years. The New Deal promises of full employment and social security at last were realized by those who survived the holocaust. Racial, religious, and national minorities, obviously bearing the costs of war as heroically and with as great good will as the white Protestant population, and making at least equally significant contributions to victory, took giant strides in and out of the armed forces toward social equality. The poor, long impoverished for no fault of their own, also felt a new surge of participation and confidence.

One of the striking features of the war boom was the baby boom. Young men and women were marrying earlier than during the depression and having the children wartime incomes made possible. Housing shortages became excruciating; after V-J day the biggest housing boom in our history failed to keep up with the mushrooming demand that came chiefly from newly created families and from those able at last to abandon the doubling up in city apartments for split-levels in suburbia.

The first quest of those enjoying an improved way of life was broader educational opportunities. The wartime population burst created a postwar schoolroom crisis even more acute than that in housing. For the first time, this crisis was extended to the colleges. In June 1944, a grateful Congress enacted the measure since known as the "G.I. Bill of Rights." Besides providing billions of dollars for veterans' medical care and for the support of the housing boom through federally guaranteed veterans' mortgages, this Act made a college education and professional training available to qualified veterans almost wholly at government expense. More than a million World War II veterans returned home to go to college, some of them before the end of the war. During the war the government had also cushioned the fall in college income and enrollment by expenditures for scientific research and the training of service personnel. Thousands of young officers enjoyed their first taste of campus life, most of them for short periods, many for full courses in engineering and medicine. Like the other G.I.s, they were determined that their children have the advantages of higher education.

At no time did American mobilization become as "total" as that of Germany, Britain, or Russia, nor were our ultimate losses in men and fortune as great as those of our allies or enemies. World War II was the harshest war in American experience, but, as one commentator put it, "it was not all 'blood, sweat, and tears' by any means." The recrudescence of American society, the rediscovery of national purpose during the war indeed underlay the awesome performance of our production machine. For all the publicity given to strikes, scarcely more than one tenth of one per cent of industrial man-hours were lost because of work stoppages, and they were more than compensated for by innumerable feats of endurance. For all the publicity about the farmers' "grab," their bumper crops kept industry supplied with agricultural raw materials and fed allied forces and peoples around the globe. For all their complaints of bureaucracy, businessmen often worked themselves to exhaustion supplying the executive and technical leadership required by our suddenly vastly expanded industrial plant. The originality of their mass-production methods, the application of such methods for the first time to former crafts like shipbuilding and airport construction, the ingenuity of design in special-purpose automatic factory equipment, the launching of entire new industries of vast scope—all were essential to victory and evidence of the vigor of free men and free minds in pursuit of it.

THE WAR AT SEA

"Nothing succeeds like excess," Churchill once remarked in admiration of American wartime productivity. But this glittering performance need not blind us to the fact that during the first act of the drama we were in the shadow of the arm that held the Nazi gun. Until very near the end, moreover, much of our production became disheartening waste. In 1940 and 1941, British, Allied, and friendly neutral merchant marines lost eight and a half million tons of shipping to marauding U-boats—more than our entire output of merchant vessels in 1942. Yet the war at sea in 1942 was far more costly than in any earlier year; and not until July 1943, did the Allies manage to turn the tide of U-boat "wolf-pack" attacks. These attacks occurred within sight of vacationists at Virginia Beach, off the mouth of the Mississippi and the entrance to the Panama Canal. The glare of Broadway made sitting ducks of merchant ships approaching the Ambrose Channel entrance to New York Harbor; while "Miami and its luxurious suburbs," in the words of Samuel Eliot Morison, "threw up six miles of neon-light glow, against which the southbound shipping that hugged the reefs to avoid the Gulf Stream were silhouetted. Ships were sunk and seamen drowned in order that the citizenry might enjoy business and pleasure as usual."

Of course, not only men and ships were lost. "The massacre enjoyed by the U-boats along our Atlantic Coast in 1942," said a wartime *Navy Training Manual,* "was as much a national disaster as if saboteurs had destroyed half a dozen of our biggest war plants. . . . If a submarine sinks two 6000-ton ships and one 3000-ton tanker . . . in order to knock out the same amount of equipment [as that carried in three such small ships] by air bombing, the enemy would have to make three thousand successful bombing sorties."

North Atlantic sea lanes were essential for supplying Britain; Arctic sea lanes from Iceland rendezvous to frigid Murmansk were the main channels for lend-lease bound for Russia; Caribbean sea lanes were the life lines by which South American oil was carried to fuel our Pacific fleet. U-boats swarmed in these major waters and elsewhere at sea throughout the war. British air attacks pummeled the yards where the raiders were built and mined the waters of their home bases. But U-boat launchings reached a peak of more than one a day in 1944, and most of the boats managed to get out to fight. That year the Germans had ready for production the electric-driven "Schnorkel" that was faster and could stay submerged longer than any other sub. But by then Germany was too beset with other problems to proceed with it, and radar and allied antisubmarine tactics had much reduced the conventional U-boat menace.

The United States had entered the Battle of the Atlantic at least three months before Pearl Harbor. On September 4, 1941, the U.S.S. *Greer,* unofficially part of an American convoy, was attacked by a U-boat it was trailing south of Iceland. This incident gave Roosevelt the opportunity to order the Navy to "shoot on sight" any German vessel in western waters. In December 1943, Germany acknowledged Allied victory in the war at sea. "For some months past," Admiral Karl Doenitz, Hitler's commander in the Atlantic advised the Fuehrer at that time, "the enemy has rendered the U-boat ineffective. He has achieved this object through his superiority in the field of science; this finds its expression in the modern battle weapon, detection. By this means he has torn our sole offensive weapon from our hands."

The "Battle for Production" was the first Allied offensive victory of the war. Victory in the Battle of the Atlantic alone made the battle for production worth while. Both victories underlay all later successes and the ultimate Allied triumph.

THE DEFEAT OF GERMANY AND JAPAN

Until December 1941, World War II had been confined to Europe and North Africa, the Atlantic Ocean and the Mediterranean Sea. Thereafter, as Japan surged through southeast Asia and the islands of the Pacific, and Latin America mobilized on the Allied side, the entire globe became embattled. In Europe only Portugal, Spain, Eire, Switzerland, Sweden, and Turkey officially remained neutral, and they were deviously used by opposing camps whose levies they dared not refuse. All told about eighty million persons served in the armed forces of their respective lands. Approximately fourteen million of them were killed. Millions of civilians also perished in air raids, in concentration camps, from famine and disease. Millions more, whose homes and families were destroyed or who fled before opposing armies, became "displaced persons" of a desperately permanent sort.

Yet once the Allies gained the offensive, two points in all the world loomed as their objectives—Berlin and Tokyo. Berlin was the heart of Hitler's *Festung Europa,* the vaunted "Fortress Europe," whence the entire continent from Stalingrad to the Pyrenees was sucked into his service. Tokyo was 5,437 discouraging sea miles from San Francisco, 3,350 sea miles from Pearl Harbor. "The way to victory is long," Admiral Ernest J. King, Chief of Naval Operations, told Americans on Christmas Eve 1941. "The going will be hard." Many important decisions were made during the war on the supposition that success against the Axis powers, if achieved at all, would be delayed seven to fifteen years.

The decision to "beat Hitler first" did not mean that the fine Japanese Navy would have the run of the Pacific unmolested. The United States Navy never got over the idea that the Pacific theater, the scene of its nadir at Hawaii, had become the supreme sector of the entire war. On April 18, 1942, Japan received a startling foretaste of the future when American Army B-25s led by Colonel James H. Doolittle took off from "Shangri La" and dropped a load of bombs on Tokyo. "Shangri La," the name F.D.R. jokingly gave to the B-25s' base, turned out to be a group of American airplane carriers commanded by Vice-Admiral William F. Halsey. All of the bombers were lost in China where their crews had to bail out; and the sortie did little damage to the Japanese capital. Nevertheless it had momentous consequences.

Doolittle's raid is credited with infecting the Japanese with what one of their admirals called "victory disease." To regain face, the Japanese war lords mounted a sudden new offensive even before they had begun to digest the immense fruits of their initial thrust. This offensive was aimed at nailing down a naval and air line of defense from Attu, the westernmost of the Arctic Aleutians, to Port Moresby, the best harbor in New Guinea on the far side of the Equator. Anchor points were to be at Japanese-held Wake and American-held Midway. Inside this line Japan expected to chew up China at her pleasure and perhaps India as well. In May 1942, a fresh Japanese fleet sailed for Port Moresby but was met in the Coral Sea by a group of American and Australian fighting ships dispatched by the American naval commander in the Pacific, Admiral Chester W. Nimitz. The Japanese soon broke off the engagement and returned home. Coral Sea, in the words of Admiral King, was "the first naval engagement in . . . history in which surface ships did not engage a single shot." Indeed, they never saw one another. The entire battle (which set a pattern for most other Pacific engagements) was fought by carrier-based planes beyond their respective ships' horizons. One month after the check in Coral Sea, a much larger Japanese fleet was caught off Midway and devastated. The Battle of Midway, June 4-5, 1942, was Japan's first major naval defeat. But Allied forces were not yet sufficiently formidable to follow up their victory with a broad offensive.

One of the theories of modern warfare disproved by the atomic bombing of Hiroshima and Nagasaki held that an enemy could not be knocked out by air attack. This theory had gained much credence from London's survival in the Battle of Britain. It gained further credence from Germany's withstanding severe British and American bombing after the summer of 1942. The AAF, shielded by fighter planes, flew at high altitudes during broad daylight for pinpoint bombing on selected targets. The RAF buzzed in low under cover of night for saturation raids on general areas. Together they dropped more than two and a half million bombs, not always on their objectives. German civilian morale was shaken but not broken. German transportation was disrupted but not destroyed. The bombs significantly diminished German refinery deliveries of aviation fuel. Perhaps most important, they set back schedules for critical Nazi items like the "Schnorkel" sub and the V-1 and V-2 missiles.

These eerie monsters, with which the Germans resumed the air Battle of Britain in June 1944, almost beat the A-bombs in disproving the theory that air attack alone could not win a war. The V-1 was a pilotless airplane, loaded with explosives, whose mechanism enabled it to hold a predetermined course until it blew up with terrible force on contact with its target. The V-2 was a rocket which descended from the immense height of its arc with such speed that "the first warning of its coming was the explosion. During flight it could not be heard, seen, or intercepted." The first V-1 struck London on June 12, 1944, six days *after* D-Day. The first V-2 arrived early in August.

"The effect of the new German weapons," General Eisenhower writes in *Crusade in Europe:*

was very noticeable upon morale. Great Britain had withstood terrific bombing experiences. But when in June the Allies landed successfully on the Normandy coast the citizens unquestionably experienced a great sense of relief. . . . When the new weapons began to come over London in considerable numbers their hopes were dashed. Indeed, the depressing effect of the bombs was not confined to the civilian population; soldiers at the front began again to worry about friends and loved ones at home.

General Eisenhower continues:

It seemed likely that, if the German had succeeded in perfecting and using these new weapons six months earlier than he did, our invasion of Europe would have proved exceedingly difficult, perhaps impossible. I feel sure that if he had succeeded in using these weapons over a six-month period . . . Overlord might have been written off.

The preliminaries to OVERLORD, the code name for the invasion of western Europe, were exceedingly complex and opened disputes which are still being carried on in the immense literature of World War II. No conflict in history was so remorselessly recorded in official documents, so eagerly refought in the analyses of national protagonists, so avidly recounted by participants and their champions. The disputes took place not only among the Allied countries but among the different services—air, ground, and sea—of each.

Yet it is foolhardy to forget that acrimony arose only against a background of unprecedented unity of purpose and performance. This was especially true in the United States where the conduct of the war was placed largely in the hands of the Joint Chiefs of Staff—King for the Navy, Marshall for the Army, and General Henry H. Arnold for the Air Force. Their major decision (one not taken by the British to their misfortune) made for unity of command in each theater—that is, the commander designated by the JCS, whatever his particular service, had supreme jurisdiction over all American forces engaged and could co-ordinate their roles in any campaign and in the general strategy.

This kind of "combined operation" was carried over to relations between the forces of the United States and the United Kingdom, and its success was abetted by the extraordinary conference-diplomacy of Churchill and Roosevelt. At the first of their many meetings after Pearl Harbor—that at Washington in December 1941 and January 1942—the Prime Minister and the President cemented the "Grand Alliance" which henceforth fought the war under the direction of the "Combined Chiefs of Staff" of their two countries. Economic as well as military efforts were co-ordinated by groups of experts whose work was done mainly in Washington. Pooled with British and American resources were those available to the Free French (later, the Jugoslav Partisans as well) and the many governments-in-exile which had fled Hitler's fortress and set up shop in London.

Relations between the western powers and the U.S.S.R. never grew this close. Since the American engagement in the European theater had to be in the West for obvious geographical reasons, close co-operation with Soviet military plans was relatively insignificant for the conduct of the war. In so far as co-operation was required, as in the case of the Allied air strikes against eastern German cities which required the bombers to land on Soviet bases, the necessary arrangements were worked out. By far the most important reason for the lack of liaison which did occasionally plague the Allied cause was the distrust Soviet leaders and those of the West, especially Churchill, felt for one another. Little of this doubt and fear was ever dispelled. Yet when the momentous merging of effort among the western Allies was made known to the world on New Year's Day 1942, by the "Declaration of the United Nations," Maxim Litvinov, Stalin's Foreign Minister, did subscribe on behalf of the Soviet. The United States, Great Britain, and China also subscribed that day, and the following day twenty-two more nations signed.

The United Nations *Organization* was still some years in the future. But the Declaration, by reiterating the aspirations of the Atlantic Charter, at least gave the signatories more positive goals than Churchill's "needless war" and Roosevelt's "war for survival" suggested. Still, the "common struggle against the savage and brutal forces seeking to subjugate the world" (as the Declaration stated it) had first to be resolved.

Somehow, *Festung Europa* had to be leveled faster than bombs gave hope of doing; somehow the Axis armies had to be pulverized, Berlin itself occupied. From the moment Hitler's blitz had turned eastward in June 1941, Stalin (and Communists in the United States and elsewhere, who until then had been in league with Lindbergh, Taft, and company in obstructing preparation and intervention) began calling for a second front in the West. Allied leaders faced up early to the likelihood that this second front had to be established in France itself. But they dared not contemplate a cross-Channel assault (such as Hitler had funked against England at the outset of the war) without absolute assurance of success.

Such assurance could only come from a massive buildup of ships, planes, arms, and men in England herself; and indeed before D-day the British Isles were transformed into one vast air and military base. But on New Year's day 1942, even this preliminary accomplishment lay two and a half years ahead (U-boat activity at the time made it seem far more distant still); and there was scant expectation, even in Russia, that the U.S.S.R. could hold out that long—or at all—against Hitler's hammering.

A plethora of reasons—or excuses—were advanced for the Allied "'second front" in North Africa as an alternative to a premature frontal assault on France. But the galvanizing impulse came from the Nazis themselves. By April 1941, Hitler's armies had conquered Bulgaria, Jugoslavia, Greece, and Cyprus and had driven the British from their Mediterranean island fortress of Crete westward to tiny Malta. This left the defense of the Suez Canal, the rich oil fields of Arab lands, and India almost entirely in the hands of the British Army in Egypt. Since September 1940, Egypt had been under constant harassment from numerous but inefficient Italian forces which the British, led by General A. P. Wavell, had handled well—so well, that by May 1941, they had divested Mussolini of his entire *East* African Empire. To keep pressure on Egypt, Hitler, early in 1941, dispatched General Erwin Rommel and a formidable tank corps to Tripoli in Italian North Africa and greatly strengthened Axis air power in Sicily across the way. Rommel promptly set about making his reputation as the "Desert Fox," and only extraordinary generalship by Wavell and his successor, General Sir C. J. Auchinleck, preserved Egypt.

But in June 1942, just when Russian cries for a second front had become most importunate, Churchill and Roosevelt, again meeting in Washington, learned that Rommel was to be reinforced. Disaster faced the thin line of defenders of the Middle East, and this predicament quickly settled all arguments over Churchill's eagerness to strike *Festung Europa* first in the presumed "soft under-belly" of the Balkans (chiefly to keep the Russians out), and Eisenhower's and Marshall's enthusiasm for a limited assault in France in anticipation of the big attack to come. Plans were immediately laid for Allied reinforcement of Egypt where Field Marshal Sir H. Alexander was put in command of the British forces and the masterful Montgomery was placed at the head of the key Eighth Army. The over-all operation was under General Eisenhower whom the Combined Chiefs of Staff had just named Supreme Allied Commander in the Mediterranean theater.

Rommel had dug in at El Alamein, virtually on the Nile in Egypt, and there, on October 23, 1942, the first great Allied land offensive of the war began. In twelve days Montgomery's forces sent Rommel's famed *Africa Korps* and its Italian contingents streaming back toward Libya and Tripoli. "Up to Alamein," crowed Churchill, "we survived. After Alamein we conquered."

Quickly broadening the conquest were the 185,000 Allied troops under Eisenhower which had been landed at Algiers, Oran, and Casablanca in French North Africa during the three weeks following November 8. These landings had been as tricky politically as tactically. The politics of Torch, the North African invasion's code name, revolved around the touchy relations of the Allies with leaders both of the collaborators and the devoted undergrounds (often dominated by trained and disciplined Communists) in Hitler's Europe.

The Allied aim in French North Africa was to land the troops as expeditiously and safely as possible. But it was difficult to keep Torch secret from the Germans and thereby gain all the advantages of surprise while at the same time informing the French that friendly forces were approaching. Moreover, most of the French administrators and the French Navy in North Africa (largely out of hatred for the British) had remained loyal to Vichy, so the invaders were not necessarily friends. The landings at Algiers met little resistance; those at Casablanca and Oran encountered heavy fire and heavy fighting from the French fleet, parts of which were sunk. French land forces, in turn, would have nothing to do with General Henri Giraud, a hero of the fall of France who had escaped from prison in Germany and was brought to North Africa by Eisenhower. The troops proved more responsive to Admiral Jean Darlan, chief of all Vichy forces, who was visiting a sick son in Algiers (perhaps this was a pretext) and became impressed with Eisenhower's strength. Darlan imposed a cease-fire on Vichy-oriented French troops in North Africa on November 11.

Conveniently for the Allies, this political chameleon was assassinated on Christmas Eve, 1942. A tussle for French African leadership followed between Giraud and General Charles de Gaulle, the uncompromising foe of Vichy. De Gaulle won; and while he personally became a thorn to the mutually congenial Churchill and Roosevelt, his work and that of his Free French forces contributed to victory and to the eventual resuscitation of France herself.

North Africa was completely liberated when Rommel surrendered his army of 350,000 men in Tunisia on May 13, 1943. Nazi North African sub and air bases were wiped out. The threat of Franco Spain's intervention on Hitler's behalf was dissipated. The southern waters of the Mediterranean became available once again at only normal wartime risk. Pressure on the Middle East was eased.

The momentum of El Alamein had given hope and flair to Allied planning as well as performance. Never in history had an American President left the country in wartime. But, as Roger Butterfield writes, "global strategy called for a globe-trotting Commander in Chief." In January 1943, following a flight of 4,000 miles, Roosevelt met Churchill at Casablanca to project strategy in all theaters for the rest of the war. Their most controversial decision was to demand "unconditional surrender" of the Axis countries when the time came.* More important was their determination, at last, to divert sufficient strength to the Far East to take the offensive there and to establish a combined planning staff in London to prepare for a real second front in France. In May 1943, in Washington, Roosevelt and Churchill set the date for OVERLORD exactly one

---

* After the war, when he was looking helplessly for strong European allies with whom to rebuild the balance of power on the continent, Churchill added to the controversy over "unconditional surrender" by asserting that it had made enemy resistance desperate and prolonged the slaughter of men and property. But that is not what he thought at Casablanca where he reached for credit for the idea.

Even more serious were Churchill's postwar strictures on the decision to make "war criminals" of all Nazis who had "taken a consenting part in the . . . atrocities, massacres, and executions" of the regime. Such a policy, he writes in the last volume of his history of the war, must "certainly stir" war leaders to "fight to the bitter end . . . no matter how many lives are needlessly sacrificed." Yet it was Churchill who first promulgated this policy, promising at the time of the Foreign Ministers conference in Moscow in October 1943, that "the recoiling Hitlerites and Huns . . . will be brought back, regardless of expense, to the scene of their crimes and judged on the spot by the peoples whom they have outraged."

year ahead. In August, at Quebec, the two "naval persons" made this decision "firm" and elaborated the plan. In November, at Cairo, they named Eisenhower OVERLORD's supreme commander. In December, at Teheran, they met with Stalin for the first time and apprised him of OVERLORD's details as of that date. In January 1944, Eisenhower flew to London and got down to the deadly work.

Unfortunately, OVERLORD was not the only project on the Allied leaders' minds. The capture of Sicily had quickly followed the North African triumph, and in September 1943, the Italian mainland itself was invaded. Advance notice had been sent on July 25 by way of a 560-plane raid on Rome that had more explosive consequences than expected. The bombing of Rome blew Mussolini out of office and into jail and in his place King Victor Emmanuel named old Marshal Badoglio with instructions to probe for peace. On September 3, Badoglio capitulated unconditionally, surrendered Italy's fleet, and agreed to demobilize her army. The momentous collapse of his Axis partner was kept secret from Hitler until September 8, when Eisenhower, accompanying the Allied liberators to Italy, broadcast the news of the Fascist fall to the world. Churchill's cherished freeing of the Balkans would come next, and perhaps even an assault on southern France!

Allied disillusionment was prompt and bitter. While Badoglio bargained, Hitler had barricaded the peninsula. The Italian campaign, in the words of British General Maitland Wilson, became a "slow, painful advance through difficult terrain against a determined and resourceful enemy." The Allies had taken Naples on September 28, 1943. Rome lay but a hundred miles north, but could not be captured until June 5, 1944, the day before D-day in France. On April 28, 1945, Italian partisans captured Mussolini, murdered him, and mutilated his body. But the Nazis fought on in Italy until May 2, only five days before the Reich itself collapsed.

Everything abetted OVERLORD except the weather. Victory in the Battle of Britain had won the Allies command in the air. Victory in the Battle of the Atlantic and in North Africa had secured command of the seas. The amphibious landings and the establishment of beachheads at Casablanca, Oran, Sicily, and Salerno had yielded invaluable experience. Even the awful, disappointing stalemate in Italy which engaged needed Allied manpower, tied down enemy troops and equipment that Hitler needed much more desperately in France. Above all else, victory depended on success in the Battle of Production, and in the very first weeks following D-day American productivity met the severest test.

For four years Hitler had concentrated on making northern France the most impregnable wall of his fortress. For six weeks Allied air attacks pulverized this wall and the communication lines leading to it. Then, on June 4, 1944, 2,876,000 men—supported by 2,500,000 tons of supplies, 11,000 airplanes, and a vast fleet of ships—stood straining in England for the takeoff. Tension mounted unbearably when a storm over the Channel forced Eisenhower to withhold the signal twenty-four hours. The next night's weather was scarcely better, but OVERLORD was on. The first troop carriers with 176,000 men anchored off the Normandy beaches at 3 a.m., June 6. Two weeks later almost half a million Allied soldiers were fighting in Normandy when a mighty hurricane ripped up the shore. The havoc it left was terrifying, and only the prior success of the air arm in sealing aff the ravaged zone from enemy reinforcements averted a dreaded German counterattack. The ultimate effect, however, was heartening:

> There was no sight in the war [writes General Eisenhower] that so impressed me with the industrial might of America as the wreckage on the landing beaches. To any other nation the disaster would have been almost decisive; but so great was America's productive capacity that the great storm occasioned little more than a ripple in the development of our build-up.

There were other checks in Normandy. The landings there—as against obviously more suitable places—had caught the Nazis completely by surprise; but so intensive had been their preparation, they were able to mobilize strong resistance quickly. Then came the worrisome V-1s and V-2s, whose rain of terror on London was not stemmed until their very launching sites were captured. Nevertheless the build-up continued and OVERLORD progressed. By July 24, more than a million Allied troops had subdued 1,500 square miles of Normandy and Brittainy. The next day, General George S. Patton, Jr.'s magnificent Third Army swept after the Germans and turned their retreat into a rout. On August 25, assisted by a Free French division under General Leclerc, Patton liberated Paris, where, two days later, de Gaulle installed himself as President of a provisional government. Patton himself kept going, with Omar Bradley's First Army moving more slowly on his left. Farther north Montgomery, with Canadian and British forces, was hurtling through Belgium, where they liberated the key port of Antwerp on September 4.

The Germans, having lost half a million men and virtually all of France, had decided to take refuge behind their long neglected West Wall in the homeland across the Rhine. Patton hungered to burst after them. At the same time, Montgomery was straining for permission to make "one powerful and full-blooded thrust towards Berlin." But the speedy Allied offensives had so stretched supply lines that only one of the two could safely be turned loose. In one of his most difficult decisions, Eisenhower leaned toward Montgomery in whose path lay the Nazi access roads to Antwerp and the bases of the V-weapons. Patton judged this "the most momentous error of the war," and with Bradley's backing acted as though it were not final. Eisenhower, whose over-all strategy had favored blunting both Patton's and Montgomery's epic thrusts in order to gain "the whole length of the Rhine before launching a final assault on interior Germany," failed to resolve the conflict over priorities of supply. Montgomery's momentum was dissipated; Patton's progress slowed.

Hitler used the lucky respite to rally his forces. On December 16, 1944, he startled the Allies with his breakout in the thinly defended Ardennes forest in southern Belgium. In ten days his armies advanced fifty miles until checked by the heroic American stand at the cross roads towns of Bastogne. By mid-January 1945, in the famous "Battle of the Bulge," the Germans had been pushed back to their old line with the satisfaction, such as it was, of having delayed Eisenhower's final grand push another month.

In the meantime, the Russians had taken every advantage of Hitler's occupation with the second front. The apex of the Nazi invasion of the Soviet had been reached in the Crimea in the summer of 1942 at the approaches to the industrial city of Stalingrad on the River Volga. The battle for Stalingrad opened in July. In November Marshal Zhukov grasped the initiative, and on January 31, 1943, after one of the "dourest, bloodiest, and most prolonged" battles of the war, the German armies capitulated.

Soviet reclamation of the Crimea began that spring and was completed when the signal for OVERLORD was given. Elimination of Nazi forces in the Balkans started in the summer of 1944. Only in Greece, where Churchill in October at last got in his Balkan licks by dispatching troops to bend the civil war there to the conservative side, were the Communists thwarted in establishing subservient regimes. By February 1945, Finland also had yielded again to Russian arms, Poland had been organized as a Communist state, Hungary had fallen, Czechoslovakia had been penetrated, and Vienna's collapse was imminent. At the time of the Yalta Conference, February 4-11, 1945, Soviet armies stood only fifty miles from Berlin. No people besides the Jews had suffered more from Nazi atrocities; none of the Western Allies had sacrificed as much as the Russians in the fighting itself. Soviet claims on the sympathy and support of the free world were immense. Few foresaw, scarcely any of them Americans, the use she would make of them.

Russia had begun compensating herself long before Yalta. Here she made verbal concessions—to the establishment of the United Nations Organization in April 1945, and to "holding free and unfettered elections as soon as possible" in Poland and elsewhere—in exchange for promises of even greater territorial gains. Most of these were to be at the expense of Japan, with whom Russia was still at peace, so the promises were kept secret. The Soviet was also given, along with reparations in goods, the privilege of the "use of German labor" in her own reconstruction. Tentative decisions were also made at Yalta (and more or less confirmed at the Potsdam Conference, July 17 to August 2, 1945) for the multiple administration of Berlin and the partitioning of Germany, for the trial of "war criminals," and the planning of a general peace conference that (we know now) will never be held.

To Churchill the vagueness of the Yalta understandings was

ominous. By the time of the meeting he had learned—to his fright —of America's determination to withdraw her entire force from Europe within two years of V-E day. To offset the resulting preponderance of Soviet strength on the continent he insisted that France be included among the "Great Powers" who would share control of Germany and the emergent world organization. In Roosevelt's eyes, Russian concessions on the prompt establishment of the world organization, and Russian agreement to participate in "liberating China from the Japanese yoke" in "two or three months" after the European war ended, justified everything.

The European war ended soon, but not without more tough and costly fighting. On March 7, 1945, the Allies at last plunged across the Rhine over the railroad bridge at Remagen, the only bridge still standing. On April 25 American and Russian troops made contact at the Elbe. On May 1 Hitler committed suicide in Berlin. On May 2 the flaming capital capitulated. On May 7 General Jodl, Hitler's heir in authority, signed the unconditional surrender at Eisenhower's general headquarters.

Two of the Axis partners had succumbed. Within a week half the American air force in Europe was bound for the Pacific and the demobilization of the massive American Army had begun. "Meanwhile," Churchill asked in anguish on May 12, "what is to happen about Russia? . . . An iron curtain is drawn down upon their front. We do not know what is going on behind."

Exactly one month earlier, on April 12, 1945, Roosevelt had died suddenly of a cerebral hemorrhage in Warm Springs, Georgia. At Teheran, at the end of 1943, he had presumably suffered a slight stroke, but this became the second best kept secret of the war. In his campaign against Thomas E. Dewey, the Republican candidate in the elections of 1944, F.D.R. appeared to most people as the "Old Champ." "Dr. New Deal" had retired, but "Dr. Win the War" had taken over the familiar office. Few knew how badly he needed a doctor himself or how little one could do for him. Not since the assassination of Lincoln did the removal of a president so move the American people. To many in both political parties and all classes it was as though a pillar had fallen from the earth's foundations. Men and women wept openly in the streets. Most appalled of all, perhaps, was F.D.R.'s modest successor, Harry S. Truman, who even as Vice-President had been kept in ignorance of the war's best kept secret, the imminent perfection of the atomic bomb. Postwar Russia became his problem. But the problem of wartime Japan required attention first.

Following their failure at Midway in June 1942, the Japanese had consoled themselves by grasping the Aleutian islands of Attu and Kiska from the United States. For the moment Alaska seemed on the verge of doom and Seattle itself threatened by attack from the North. Men and materials needed elsewhere were rushed to the Territory; the "Alcan Highway" across Canada was begun; and operations were planned which retrieved Attu in May and Kiska in August 1943.

The Japanese had been even less successful in a second attack (this one by land) on Port Moresby in southern New Guinea, the proposed equatorial base of their defense perimeter across the Pacific. To protect this attack, they had begun to clear an air strip on Guadalcanal, one of the near-by (as South Pacific distances go) Solomon Islands. The United States at the same time was eyeing Guadalcanal for the starting point of its own first offensive on Japan's more exposed bastions, especially the island fortress of Rabaul off New Britain.

On August 7, 1942, the first combined American and Australian landings on Guadalcanal were begun against sharp resistance. Two days later a Japanese cruiser force swooped down on the half-unloaded Allied transports in the Solomons' Savo Sea and in "the worst defeat ever suffered by the United States navy" (the words are Admiral Morison's) sank virtually all the protective fighting ships. The transports ran, and the Japanese force, its mission accomplished, moved off. For six months ill-equipped, half-starved Marines clung to Guadalcanal's air strip at Henderson Field while huge naval actions covering reinforcement attempts by both sides raged in the surrounding waters. The turning point came in mid-November, and in January the Japanese were ordered by Tokyo to evacuate the island, which they did successfully on February 9, 1943.

Before the end of the year the Japanese had also been cleared out of most of New Guinea. In addition, they had been forced to yield enough of Bougainville, the northernmost of the Solomons, for the Allies to maintain air operations on the island. Bougainville lay only 235 miles from Rabaul—near enough for Allied bombers to neutralize that fortress's arms.

Guadalcanal was the Pacific theater's El Alamein. The Japanese never succeeded in establishing the line behind which they could exploit their "co-prosperity" sphere on the Asian mainland. After Guadalcanal they became fully occupied with defending the Pacific and mainland redoubts they did hold as a screen for their home islands. This defense was fanatical. The Japanese Navy continued strong and ably led. The Japanese Army and air force, much under-rated by prewar commentators, was recruited from the impoverished peasantry and treated by the war lords like fatted calves. The soldiers' devotion to their leaders and their cause was beyond reason. Allied leaders like Douglas MacArthur, chief of Southwest Pacific operations, learned this lesson early and built their strategy upon it. The Joint Chiefs of Staff in Washington became so impressed with Japanese fortitude that even at the time of the Yalta Conference, when the brilliance of Allied strategy had been well demonstrated, they advised Roosevelt that the Pacific War had at least two years to run with full Russian assistance and considerably longer without.

Allied success in the South Pacific—their establishment in the Solomons, the neutralizing of Rabaul, the clearing of New Guinea —greatly augmented the security of Australia where MacArthur was preparing for his dramatic return to the Philippines as the last step but one to the taking of Tokyo. The prospect was tempting, but the way bristled with snares. North and east of the Solomons lay the Gilbert Islands; north of them, the Marshalls, and farther north still, Wake. Together they marked the easternmost advance of Japanese power; and even the barren atolls of each configuration had been armed with air strip, artillery, and adamant men. To the west of this arc, ranging once more from south to north, lay the Palau Islands, the Carolines, Guam, and the Marianas, all, as befit their greater proximity to Japan, even more intensely armed than the outermost line. Farther north and west lay formidable Iwo Jima; and in the shadow of Honshu itself, Okinawa. This defense in depth extending more than 3,000 miles, shielded Tokyo and exposed invasion from the Philippines to murderous flanking fire.

To roll back this defense island by island, atoll by atoll, fanatic by fanatic, would occupy a generation. MacArthur's command devised the bold alternative of "island hopping," a strategy designed to open quickly a path to the heart of Japan while leaving to mobile air power the task of neutralizing the uncleared rear. Even so, hundreds of unsung battles were waged by armies as large as those that once decided the fate of nations for atolls where there "had probably never been twenty white men assembled together at any one time." The burden of this offensive was placed in the hands of Admiral Nimitz and his Central Pacific fleet. But every assault involved unprecedented co-ordination of the forces of sea, land, and air. None was easy. Tarawa established the Allied hold on the Gilberts in November 1943, Kwajalein control of the Marshalls in February 1944. In May, Wake was taken. On June 19-20, in the immense naval Battle of the Philippine Sea, Admiral Raymond Spruance thwarted a Japanese effort to reinforce the Marianas, and by August 1 Saipan and Tinian there, as well as adjacent Guam, all had succumbed. In September, after some of the most costly hand-to-hand fighting for armed caves, Peleliu in the Palaus was cleaned out.

Three heartening results were earned by this savage surge. First, Truk in the Carolines, Japan's main Central Pacific naval station, was made innocuous without costly frontal assault by the control established over the surrounding island groups. Second, from Saipan and the other Marianas giant Superfortresses could reach Tokyo, and the capital and other home island cities henceforth were systematically assaulted with fire bombs that consumed their wooden buildings and decimated the civilian population. Third, the path from New Guinea to the Philippines was opened. On October 19, 1944, a grand armada carrying MacArthur and 250,-000 men set out for the Philippine island of Leyte. Four days later virtually the entire Japanese Navy converged on Allied transports in Leyte Gulf, and from October 23 to 25 the greatest sea battle in history was fought. At its end the United States emerged in complete command of the Pacific. Manila fell to MacArthur's forces on February 23, 1945, but not until July 5 were the remnants of Japanese resistance rooted out.

By then, Iwo Jima and Okinawa had been taken at a sickening cost of 70,000 men. *Kamikaze* attacks by Japanese suicide fliers who plunged their bomb-laden planes into American fighting ships accounted for many of the American casualties at Okinawa. Both campaigns—Iwo had been gained by March 16, 1945, and Okinawa by June 21—wiped out any lingering doubt that the Japanese would resist invaders to the last knife or bullet or breath.

Their power to resist by means of instruments of modern warfare had by then been sorely depleted. The island-hopping campaign had done for all but the remnants of their navy and their air force. American submarines, the silent service, had sunk more than half of their once proud merchant marine which kept them supplied with the oil, rubber, tin, and grain of their mainland conquests. These conquests themselves, moreover, had been under strong attack since the winter of 1943-44 by British and American forces. The Allies struggled to get Chiang Kai-shek to fight harder for China—the British for the protection of India, the Americans for the eviction of Japan—but Chiang was nursing his arms for a future showdown with the Communists who were gathering their forces in the Chinese North. Most progress was made against the Japanese in Burma where Rangoon, the principal port, was retaken in May 1945. But Japan did not yield her other mainland territories until her total collapse at home had been brought about by extraordinary means.

On July 26, 1945, three weeks after the reconquest of the Philippines, ten days after the first successful detonation of the A-bomb, Allied leaders assembled at Potsdam sent an ultimatum to the enemy: "The alternative to surrender is prompt and utter destruction." No surrender came. On August 6 the first atomic bomb to be used in warfare was dropped on Hiroshima. Still no word from Japan, but Russia, intent on being in on the imminent kill, declared war on August 8, the very deadline for her "two to three months after V-E day" promise at Yalta, and overran the

Japanese forces in Manchuria. On August 9 a second bomb was dropped on Nagasaki. At last, on August 10, Toyko sued for peace—but made a condition: that the Emperor Hirohito be permitted to retain his throne. This condition was accepted by the Allies and on September 2, 1945, formal surrender ceremonies were conducted in Tokyo Bay on the battleship *Missouri,* with General MacArthur accepting for the United States.

The most terrible war in history had ended in the most terrible display of force. After the bombing of Nagasaki, President Truman said, "We have spent two billion dollars on the greatest scientific gamble in history—and won." A few days later he added, "The atomic bomb is too dangerous to be let loose in a lawless world. That is why Great Britain, Canada, and the United States, who have the secret of its production, do not intend to reveal that secret until means have been found to control the bomb." While Russia had retired behind the "iron curtain," the West had retired behind a kind of scientific Maginot Line.

THE UNITED NATIONS AND A WORLD AT BAY

Only a common fright had brought the western Allies to the point of waging a common war on Germany after September 1939; and only a common enemy had united them with the Communists against the Axis two years later. Once the fright was dissipated and the enemy reeling, the members of the "Grand Alliance" quickly fell out. The U.S.S.R., of course, was the touchstone of trouble. Communism divided Russia from the free nations of the west; and these nations themselves split early and often on their attitudes toward the Soviet.

All the grandeur of Churchill's style in his magnificent six-volume history of *The Second World War* fails to hide the fact that he had no prescription for the peace to come except a return to balance of power diplomacy. Churchill was at least as aware as anyone and infinitely more aware than most of the menace of a victorious Stalin. What he consistently shut his eyes to was the fact that with Germany prostrate, France embittered and unreliable, and Britain bled white, Stalin and the U.S.S.R. must become the mainstays and manipulators of any "balance of power in Europe" (the phrase really had become an empty box) that Churchill could construct.

Roosevelt did not fall prey to Churchill's nostalgia. On March 1, 1945, on returning from Yalta, he said the conference there "spells the end of the system of unilateral action and exclusive alliances and spheres of influence and balances of power and all the other expedients which had been tried for centuries—and have failed." His own vision—nostalgic too—was more Messianic. "We propose to substitute for all these," he said, "a universal organization in which all peace-loving nations will finally have a chance to join"—including the U.S.S.R.!

Churchill's anguish over Roosevelt's concessions to Stalin at Yalta in order to win grudging acquiescence in the establishment of the world organization was hardly assuaged by the ascent of Truman. "We can see now," Churchill writes in volume six of his *History,* "the deadly hiatus which existed between the fading of President Roosevelt's strength and the growth of President Truman's grip on the vast world problem."

During this alleged "hiatus" at the very climax of the war, American armed service chiefs in the field were left with the major responsibility for American policy. Their training had stressed the traditional American distinction between "military" and "political" objectives, unfortunately to the detriment of the latter. As the fighting drew toward a close they became obsessed with the idea simply of "getting the boys back home." The State Department, almost too clever in its suspicion of Churchill and his imperial chestnuts and too engrossed in the coming world organization to be sufficiently suspicious of Russia, ratified the generals' on-the-spot program. Congress, bombarded by "Bring-Daddy-Back-Home" clubs in the United States and "I wanna go home" troop demonstrations in theaters overseas, backed the generals and the diplomats.

By October 1945, Secretary of the Navy Forrestal was writing that the country is "going to bed at a frightening rate, which is the best way I know to be sure of the coming of World War III." Churchill may have believed that Roosevelt could have stemmed such action. But there is little evidence that this is not more wishful thinking. Indeed, F.D.R.'s single-minded concentration on the U.N. was itself a hedge against American anti-militarism, not to say American isolationism. Truman simply followed where Roosevelt had led. Truman writes in his *Memoirs:* "General Marshall and I, in discussing each military phase, agreed that if we were to win the peace after winning the war, we had to have Russian help. I was trying to get Churchill in a frame of mind to forget the old power politics and get a United Nations organization to work."

Lest their world scheme get bruised like Wilson's by all the bargaining in postwar settlements, Roosevelt and Secretary of State Hull, the architects of the United Nations, sought, as we have seen, to win the adherence of their future allies as early as 1941, when the United States still held most of the bargaining cards. In the fall of 1943 the two world planners got overwhelming Congressional support for the principle of a *permanent* world organization. This support was dramatically strengthened in January 1945, when the leading Republican member of the Senate Foreign Relations Committee and a leading isolationist, Arthur H. Vandenberg, announced his endorsement of the proposal that the President be granted power to use American troops on a world organization's behalf without first seeking Senate consent.

While progressing in the realm of principle, Roosevelt and Hull had also moved forward in the realm of practicality. Well before the United Nations Organization itself was formally created, many ancillary bodies were set up and put to work. Among the most important of these was the United Nations Relief and Rehabilitation Administration (UNRRA), which was formed in November 1943. In July 1944, two more major agencies were created. One, the International Bank for Reconstruction and Development, was to lend money for the purposes indicated by its name; the second, the International Monetary Fund, would aim to stabilize national currencies, thereby combating inflation and furthering the revival of international commerce.

The establishment of such bodies showed that the nations involved were willing to sacrifice national sovereignty in significant areas. Work on the more crucial U.N. agencies found the participants more sticky. After preliminary discussions at the wartime conferences of the heads of state and elsewhere, secondary officials of the United States, Great Britain, the U.S.S.R., and China convened at Dumbarton Oaks in the District of Columbia in August 1944, to write a preliminary draft of the U.N. charter. Many difficulties arose between the Americans and the Russians (foreshadowing the mood and method of all subsequent negotiations) which the British, at odds with the United States over the future of Italy and Greece, did nothing to meliorate. On most of these issues Stalin verbally yielded at Yalta in February 1945.

The final details of the United Nations Charter were arranged at a general meeting in San Francisco in the spring of 1945. Fortysix nations sent delegates. Absent, however, were Roosevelt, who had recently died, Hull, who had retired because of ill health, and Churchill who, though he scarcely credited the possibility, was on the verge of being thrown out of power by a war-weary British electorate. Stalin, in turn, had become suspicious of western military maneuvering which looked to him like an effort, a few weeks before V-E day, to make a separate peace with the Germans (something forbidden by the original U.N. Declaration of 1942). Only at the last moment would he consent to Foreign Minister Molotov's attendance.

The new Charter incorporated in the U.N. the going economic and social agencies. It also established an International Court of Justice but left its powers vague. The two most important bodies were the Assembly and the Security Council. The entire structure was to be administered by a Secretariat headed by a permanent Secretary-General. The first meetings of the U.N. took place in London in 1946, but soon the world organization was established in its shimmering glass house in New York City.

The U.N. Assembly became a useful debating society in which the voices of small nations could be heard around the world. The Assembly's principal power lay in its right to place international disputes on the Security Council's agenda. The Security Council itself was the U.N.'s pre-eminent agency. Composed of five permanent members—the United States, Great Britain, the U.S.S.R., "Free" China, and France—and six others chosen for two-year terms by the Assembly, the Council was empowered to investigate international disputes and take steps to settle them. Its Achilles' heel lay in the principle of unanimity requiring the consent of *all* the permanent members for Council action; by a simple veto, any permanent member could forestall distasteful moves. No nation was to avail itself of this privilege more cynically than the constantly outvoted Russians. Yet it was the Americans, still fearful of isolationist opinion, who proposed it. Article 51 of the Charter, moreover, specifically sanctioned the "inherent right" of any nation or group of nations to "individual or collective self-defense." This again was an American qualification.

The Charter optimistically provided for U.N. armed forces, with the expectation that these would be supplied largely by the five "Great Powers" of the Security Council. Four of these powers agreed that their contributions be "comparable," with the ability of each to supply men and materiel taken into account. The U.S.S.R., openly scornful of the "Great Power" status of some of her colleagues on the Council, demanded that contributions be "equal" or nothing. "Equal" contributions would have resulted in merely token forces; and the Russian proposal, as planned, drew the teeth from the U.N. at its inception.

The U.N.'s subsequent failure to control atomic weapons underscored its fatal weakness. In 1946 the Assembly had created an International Atomic Energy Commission whose American member was Bernard Baruch. That year Baruch offered his plan for an International Atomic Development Authority which would control atomic energy in its military and peaceful applications. Violators of the Authority's regulations were to be punished by it, and could not escape by resort to the veto which this plan would abolish in atomic matters. To this body the United States proposed gradually to yield its atomic secrets and ultimately, when control proved effective, it promised to destroy its stockpile of atomic bombs.

Quick to see how this would check their own atomic development while leaving the United States atomically armed for an indefinite period, the Communists countered with a different plan. They would have the entire stockpile of bombs destroyed *before* agreeing to international control and would retain such control in the hands of the Security Council where the veto against punishment of violators would remain effective. This proposal was as unrealistic to the Americans as their own was to the Russians, and the hideous race for atomic armed supremacy began.

The U.N. quickly showed that its good intentions in other areas were also supported by inadequate machinery. In three years from 1944 to 1947 UNRRA disbursed nearly four billion dollars to the neediest countries of Europe, most of them on the edge of the iron curtain. Virtually all of this money was sucked into the piteous channels of "relief" for the naked, starving, and homeless. The little that could be spared for "rehabilitation" of productive resources and economic life had largely been dissipated by the "business as usual" contingents in stricken lands. At the same time other U.N. agencies, such as the International Bank and the International Monetary Fund, though costly enough in their operations, proved far too slow in getting going, far too conventional in their approaches, far too cautious in their ultimate programs.

By 1947 the free European economy thus faced a crisis in which local Communist parties, effectively directed from Moscow or by Moscow-trained provocateurs, were the only gainers. Their propaganda was all the more effective since the crisis seemed to have begun with the abrupt termination of American lend-lease in August 1945, and to have grown with the development of the so-called "dollar gap" between Western Europe's requirements and her ability to finance them in the United States. Especially in France and Italy, where social reforms were a century overdue, the Communists threatened to throw their country's lot in with the Russians; but even in Britain the left wing of the Labor Party which had unseated Churchill grew more bitter in its attacks and more poisonous in its suspicions of "Uncle Shylock."

At best the Communists have considered the United Nations a western invention which they might join in self-defense, and as a listening post for western intentions and a sounding board for projects of their own. At worst they have used it as an instrument for aggravating discord among western nations. The U.N.'s weakness as an international agency and western Europe's economic tribulations made the United States look all the more anxiously to the atomic bomb as the "great deterrent" to world war and the bulwark of its own defenses.

Yet this policy proved as much a curse as a cure-all. The tactical inflexibility of the bomb tied our hands and terrified our allies. Dependence on the secret of the bomb's manufacture, moreover, raised our concern over atomic espionage to a veritable mania for "loyalty" which soon poisoned the very freedom of the free world.

Beginning in 1947, all employees of the Federal Government (and following this example, of most state and local governments as well and of private companies engaged in "sensitive" work) were required to take oaths of loyalty. Government loyalty procedures were made much more stringent in 1950, after the conviction of Alger Hiss, a high official of the State Department with an impeccably American background, for perjury arising out of alleged espionage activities in the 1930s. At the same time the Communist Party and Communist-front organizations were required to register their members with the Attorney-General; and foreigners who had been Communists were denied admission to the country. Once again the bandwagon virulence of the 1920s was repeated; and teachers, actors, radio and television celebrities, writers, and others likely to be influential in the making of opinion were attacked for nonconformist views. Worse, leading scientists and civil servants with foreign-sounding names were made the victims of baseless suspicions and their services lost to the country.

The peak of the "loyalty" surge came after the Republican victory of 1952 placed Senator Joseph McCarthy of Wisconsin in a powerful committee post. Earlier, following the Communist conquest of China and the "hot war" in Korea (see pp. 434-35), McCarthy had used the Senate floor to smear with impunity the reputations of hand-picked victims who were innocent almost without exception, among them no less a figure than General Marshall. Even worse were the "treason" label McCarthy pinned on the Democratic Party for involving the country in World War II and his almost total stultification of the State Department for its "disloyal" postwar diplomacy. Until McCarthy was censured by his Senate colleagues in 1954, he made the Eisenhower administration as well as the Truman administration the victims of right-wing Republican "patriotism." That this was no attack by the lunatic fringe Senator Taft's consistent endorsement of McCarthy's technique made clear. "McCarthy should keep talking," Taft said in 1950, "and if one case doesn't work out he should proceed with another." Mc-Carthyism made it easier for the enemies of the United States to equate American "totalitarianism" with the Soviet's, made it harder for America's friends to raise the voice of liberty without hypocrisy.

Our vaunted bomb, moreover, while lulling Americans into false confidence, only spurred the Russians to produce bombs of their own. In 1946, writes *The New York Times*, "Maj. Gen. Leslie Groves, who had directed the American atomic bomb project, said it would be five to twenty years before even 'the most powerful of nations' could 'catch up' with the U.S. in atomic bomb development. Russia exploded her first atomic bomb on September 22, 1949.

"The United States," the *Times* continues, "exploded its first thermonuclear device in November, 1952. Some U.S. experts thought it would be a long time before the Soviet Union reached that stage of atomic development. But the Russians exploded their first thermonuclear device in August, 1953. Later that year Secretary of Defense Charles E. Wilson said he thought the Russians were 'three or four years behind where we are' in developing an H-bomb which could be dropped from a plane. The Russians dropped their first H-bomb in November, 1955; the U.S. dropped its first in May, 1956.

"On Aug. 26 [1957] Russia reported her 'successful tests of an inter-continental ballistic missile.' And then [on October 4] she used I.C.B.M. rocket engines to launch the first earth satellite." By then Americans were calculating that it would take five years for *them* to catch up with the Russians. But as *Time* suggested on October 14, even to catch up Americans would have to lift not only their performance but their sights. The Russians, Dr. Edward Teller told a Senate committee on November 25, have been willing "to take greater gambles in their development program." The United States, Dr. Vannevar Bush told the same committee, must arouse itself from "complacency and egotism. . . . We have continually been telling ourselves how good we are. We have been taking the easy way."

Truman's scientific Maginot Line of 1945 had proved as futile as France's military Maginot Line of 1940. All the while the "cold war" between capitalism and Communism continued within and outside the United Nations.

"CHALLENGE AND RESPONSE IN UNITED STATES POLICY"

Communist theory has long held World War III to be unavoidable. Stalin, for example, was fond of the following quotation from Lenin, to which in his notes he appended, "Clear, one would think":

> The existence of the Soviet Republic side by side with the imperialist states for a long time is unthinkable. In the end either one or the other will conquer. And until that time comes, a series of the most terrible collisions between the Soviet Republic and the bourgeois states is inevitable.

In February 1946, Stalin himself said, "Under the present capitalist development of world economy," there could be no peace; and he urged his people to prepare for "any eventuality." Soon after, George F. Kennan, then Counselor of the American Embassy in Moscow, analyzed Soviet-American relations for the State Department. "We have here," he said, "a political force committed fanatically to the belief that with the U.S. there can be no permanent *modus vivendi,* that it is desirable and necessary that the internal harmony of our society be disrupted, our traditional way of life be destroyed, the international authority of our state be broken, if Soviet power is to be secure."

"The stress laid by Stalin on the importance of theory," Kennan wrote in *Foreign Affairs,* January 1949, "is so foreign to American habits of mind that we are prone to underestimate the influence which theory plays in determining his action. Any such tendency would lead us into especially grave error when we come to estimating the importance of his theoretical conception of the nature of revolution; for on this he has been amazingly consistent." Kennan continues:

For the period of world revolution, Stalin's grand strategy is to use the Soviet Union as a base linking the proletariat of the west with the movements for national liberation from imperialism in the east into "a single world front against the world front of imperialism." In this way he harnesses two of the major contradictions of capitalism to his chariot—contradictions between proletariat and bourgeoisie, and contradictions between capitalist and colonial countries. The front thus formed is to be used to exploit the third contradiction of capitalism—that between capitalist countries, whose rivalries for spheres of influence must lead periodically to war, the event most propitious for revolution.

As late as October 1957, Nikita Khrushchev, most recent of Stalin's successors as leader of the Russian state, made clear in a series of interviews with James Reston of *The New York Times* that neither he nor Communists generally have deviated from Stalinist theory. "Competitive co-existence" was how Khrushchev innocently described the process by which the United States and the non-Communist world were called upon "to recognize what has historically taken place" in one Communist conquest after another, until the whole world is swallowed up by Stalin's "single world front." In November 1957, buttressed by the success of the Soviet ICBM and the launching of the first space satellite, Khrushchev warned that "the next war will be fought on the American continent, which can be reached by our rockets." Political and social unrest then current in Soviet-dominated lands made the threat of Soviet foreign adventures all the more ominous.

Leninist-Stalinist theory, of course, did not develop in Russia in a vacuum. For almost a hundred years before World War II Germany had been the strongest nation on the continent of Europe, impelled by a fierce *Drang nach Osten,* "Urge to the East"; and for almost fifty years Japan had eyed all of Asia. Between the two stretched the vast and beckoning empire of the czars. To this empire and to the traditional danger of attack from the militaristic powers at its flanks, the U.S.S.R. had fallen heir. The utter collapse of Japan in World War II left Asia, as one commentator put it, "out of control." No one had a greater incentive or a greater opportunity to reduce it to "order" than the Communists. The virtual annihilation of Germany, moreover, left western Europe, in Churchill's darkly imaginative words, with a vision "of Soviet and Russian imperialism rolling over helpless lands." Communist revolutionary theory gave scope, resilience, drive, and continuity to Russia's traditional policy of security by expansion.

At the same time, the situation, needs, and (in John Foster Dulles's phrase) the "enduring national principles" of the United States played into Russia's hands. For half a century before World War I American borders were free of foreign menace, American ships enjoyed freedom of the seas, the American continental expanse provided all the food and almost all the industrial raw materials Americans required. United States "foreign policy" in that century* consisted of little more than high tariffs to keep out foreign manufactures, and wide open gates welcoming foreign capital and labor. America offered unlimited opportunity to all, or so it seemed, for enterprise, ambition, ascent—and safety, within secure national borders.

Such political and geographical good fortune bred a profound national pride which nourished the belief that America's peaceful, industrious, and democratic "conduct and example" (Hamilton's phrase from *Federalist* Number One) would, in Dulles's words, "influence events throughout the world and promote the spread of free institutions." Yet this pride itself bred a profound insularity which Americans, despite their engagement in two world wars, have been slow in shedding. "Americans have traditionally felt," Dulles wrote in *Foreign Affairs,* October 1957, in an article entitled "Challenge and Response in United States Policy," "that it would be better for their Government to avoid involvement in international issues." By the end of World War II, Dulles said, "it had become obvious that the conduct and example of our people no longer, alone, sufficed to prevent recurrent challenges to our security and our way of life." Yet, "there still remains a nostalgia for the 'good old days.' " **

This nostalgia stems in part from the record postwar prosperity

* With exceptions toward the century's end, of course. See Chapter Twelve above.

** There is no evidence that "conduct and example . . . *alone*" ever did offer Americans security. Dulles's statement reveals the lingering "nostalgia" even of our most active international traveler.

of the United States, during which American economic requirements from the "outside world" actually became smaller, proportionately, than ever. Between 1945 and 1957 the goods and services available to the American people doubled. Yet near the peak of the boom American foreign trade was scarcely seven per cent, annual American foreign investment outside the Western Hemisphere scarcely one-fourth of one per cent of gross national product. Since World War I, moreover, there has been little foreign capital seeking investment in the United States; and we have shut our gates to foreign labor and kept them shut to foreign goods.

The postwar prosperity, Dulles boasted in 1954, offered Americans "a Paradise compared to most of the world." To be sure, a persistent inflation which saw the value of the dollar slide dangerously fast, brought hardship to millions living on fixed incomes and to such white-collar groups as teachers whose salaries lagged behind the general rise in wages and profits. There were also occasional legislative setbacks. The so-called Taft-Hartley Act of June 1947, for example, deprived organized labor of many privileges won during New Deal days.* Other New Deal legislation, on the other hand, such as measures for social security, minimum wages, support of farm prices, and government participation in slum clearance and housing finance, survived even the Republican victories of 1952 and 1956 and helped immensely to underpin the business surge. Most significant among postwar legislation was the Maximum Employment Act of 1946, which committed the Federal Government to the "Welfare State." This Act established the Council of Economic Advisers to keep the President informed on business trends and on federal measures required to avert depressions and otherwise implement federal responsibility for "maximum employment."

* The Taft-Hartley Act outlawed the closed shop, gave employers the privilege of suing unions for broken contracts and for damages brought about by strikes, forbade unions to donate money to political campaigns. Union leaders, moreover, were required to swear they were not Communists before their organizations could make use of the services of the National Labor Relations Board. Organized labor branded this measure a "slave bill," but union membership nevertheless rose from about 14.5 mllion in 1947 to some 17 million in 1952, when it leveled off.

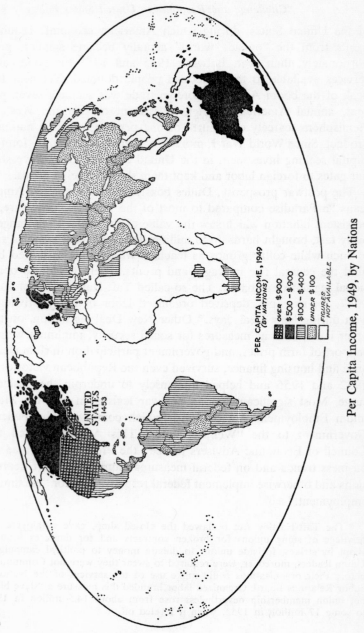

Per Capita Income, 1949, by Nations

Yet it was the business system itself (abetted, to be sure, by renewed expenditures for armaments and war after 1949) that was principally responsible for bringing the level of employment at the peak of the boom nearer seventy million than the sixty million that had been considered illusory during the war; for lifting Negroes and other minorities out of the slough of poverty to which segregation in industry had earlier consigned them even in the North; and for introducing the liberalizing forces of modern industrialism to many parts of the rural, racist South.

The Supreme Court decision of May 1954, declaring that "separate but equal" schools for Negroes were unconstitutional under the Fourteenth Amendment, that segregation in education was itself deprivation of equality under the law, was but the culmination of many forward strides in income and status made since the war by the seventeen million colored Americans whose services the country sorely needed. The Civil Rights Act of 1957, which aimed to insure Negroes the vote in segregated states, was a further step toward their full participation in American life.

Such social and economic gains were made at the cost of immense social friction; but that prosperity, which brought a steady rise in the standard of living of most Americans, also brought net social progress in other ways cannot be doubted. A rising standard of living, like property in Locke's conception, is one of the founts of the dignity of man, one of the props of his individuality.

"The American economy," wrote *Life,* in January 1954, "yields the American a standard of living roughly three times as high as the Englishman's, six times as high as the Italian's, 11 times as high as the Turk's, 18 times as high as the Peruvian's, 40 times as high as the Indonesian's. Most of the world's 2.5 billion people," *Life* adds, "are crowded between the Peruvian and Indonesian points on the scale." Why shouldn't Americans, then, whose standard of living is so much the highest in the world, continue to enjoy their pride in their "conduct and example," their insularity of mind?

One answer, of course, is the Communist challenge. Before the ICBM touched the nerve of danger, Americans persistently sought to evade this challenge by passing responsibility to a weak United

Nations, by brandishing the almighty bomb and by diplomatic bluffing.

There have, of course, been many decisive, generous, heroic American actions in the cold war. When straitened circumstances in 1947 forced Britain to terminate her support of Greece and Turkey, which lay under the Soviet gun, the United States responded with the Truman Doctrine in which the President let it be known to the world "that it must be the policy of the United States to support free people who are resisting subjugation by armed minorities or outside pressure." Between 1947 and 1950 the United States appropriated about $660,000,000 for Greece and Turkey and thereby helped to preserve their freedom and that of the adjacent oil-rich Middle East. When the British terminated their mandate over Palestine in 1948 and the Jews set up their independent state of Israel in May that year, President Truman immediately recognized the new nation, and thereby strengthened another Middle Eastern outpost.

In June 1947, meanwhile, Truman's Secretary of State, General George C. Marshall, facing up to the economic chaos in Europe, had declared that: "Our policy is directed [toward] the revival of a working economy in the world so as to permit the emergence of political and social conditions in which free institutions can exist." Appropriations for carrying out the "Marshall Plan" were delayed by resurgent isolationists in Congress until the whip of a Soviet coup in Czechoslovakia where a Communist government was installed by force in February 1948, stung them into silence. Starting that April, Congress during the next three years appropriated $12,000,000,000 for European recovery. Communist countries were declared eligible for Marshall Plan aid; but the Soviet Union forbade their participation and also set up the Cominform to enlarge Communist propaganda and subversion in the West.

Marshall Plan administrators recognized that Germany was the hub of the western European economy and early in 1948 proceeded with the full rehabilitation of the free zone. The Soviet replied instantly with a blockade of all land approaches to Berlin, with the object of forcing western officials from the capital and undermining their prestige with the German people. The United

States and Britain met this challenge with "Operation Vittles." From June 1948 until the Soviet raised the blockade in May 1949, they kept Berlin supplied by air. In September 1949, the Bonn Republic was recognized as a sovereign nation (subject to American, British, and French surveillance in certain matters) and later became a major base for the "containment" of Communist expansion.

After March 1947, in recognition of the toothlessness of the United Nations in a tense world, western European countries had signed numerous mutual defense treaties. In June 1948, a Senate resolution authorized the United States to participate in regional military alliances, and in July 1949, the Senate approved the agreements by which we joined eleven other nations in the North Atlantic Treaty Organization. NATO members agreed that an attack on one would be considered an attack on all; and to repel such an attack NATO forces were created under the initial direction of General Eisenhower and supplied with arms, largely from the United States.

In the meantime, Douglas MacArthur was pressing forward with the reconstruction of the religion, society, and economy of Japan; and that nation on Russia's Asiatic flank was restored to "full sovereignty" in 1951, without Soviet assistance. By then a number of newly independent countries in Asia and Africa, with an aggregate population of nearly half a billion, had dramatically joined the concert of nations after centuries of subjugation to European rulers. Promptly they became battlefields for the contending forces of Communism and capitalism. Most important among these countries were India and Indonesia. Others included Pakistan, Burma, Ceylon, and Jordan. Korea was freed from Japanese rule after the war; but, failing Soviet-Western agreement on her future, was divided in 1948 into a Communist state north of the 38th parallel, and a democratic state south of that line.

Most "colored" peoples of the world had experienced capitalism in the form of repressive imperialism or corrupt upper-class self-interest. Communism was something new. Its methods cost lives, but no more, perhaps, than capitalist exploitation and capitalist wars. They knew that Communist methods had liberated Russia from medieval poverty and in a single generation raised her to world power. To offset Soviet "conduct and example" among such peoples, President Truman announced his "Point Four" program in his inaugural address in January 1949, after his surprising defeat of Thomas E. Dewey in the 1948 elections. By 1954 nearly $400,-000,000 had been expended under this program in an effort to bring modern medicine and technology to underdeveloped areas, frequently over opposition from stay-at-home elements in the United States and elements in the recipient countries who feared a new incursion of western imperialism.

Outside of Germany the stakes in the cold war were greatest in China; and here the United States had lavished about $2,000,000,-000 in civilian and military assistance on Chiang Kai-shek before he was chased from the Chinese mainland to Formosa by Chinese Communist forces in 1949. Few events in the "outside world" shocked Americans more than the fall of the 450 million Chinese to the Communist camp. Though the United States in 1946 had made peace treaties with Bulgaria, Rumania, and Hungary, thereby recognizing the Communist governments of those Soviet-dominated countries, we persistently refused recognition to the Mao government and permission for Chinese Communists to sit in the United Nations. The involvement of Chinese Communist "volunteers" in the Korean War, which started when North Korean forces invaded South Korea on June 25, 1950, hardened the policy of non-recognition. As it happened, the Soviet Union at the time had boycotted the U.N. for its failure to seat Mao's men. With Russia's veto power absent, the United States succeeded in rallying the United Nations to support the militant American stand against Communism's spread.

"The attack upon Korea," President Truman said on June 27, 1950, "makes it plain beyond all doubt that Communism has passed beyond the use of subversion to conquer independent nations and will now use armed invasion and war." The President was more than eager to meet fire with fire and so were the American people until things went sour in Korea. After vigorous fighting back and forth across the 38th parallel, which cost American forces under General MacArthur more casualties than any war other than the Civil War and World War II, the opposing armies settled down to a miserable stalemate. Eager to enlarge the war into a full-scale offensive against Communist China itself, MacArthur was rebuffed by the Joint Chiefs of Staff and recalled from his post by the President in April 1951. After July 1951, the military stalemate was prolonged by a deadlock between Communist and western negotiators for an armistice.

"I believe other nations think we are crazy," observed the wife of an American army officer in Korea in a book she wrote even before the fight there had begun. As the military and diplomatic stalemate dragged on, millions in the United States had come to share her view. "Had enough?" was the Republicans' electioneering question in the presidential campaign of 1952 in which General Eisenhower won a landslide victory over Adlai Stevenson, the Democrats' "egghead" candidate. This question referred to other features of what the Republicans called "the mess in Washington" as well as to "Truman's War," but the war was its principal target and the leading issue in the election. During the campaign, Eisenhower dramatically announced that if elected he would fly to Korea personally to see about a "cease-fire." He fulfilled the promise to fly in December 1952; but the cease-fire was delayed another seven months. The fighting ended at last in July 1953, when the *status quo ante bellum* was resumed in the battle-scarred land.

The United States and the United Nations had made a determined and successful stand against the enlargement of Communist domains. But as other distant and to Americans often unpronounceable and previously unheard-of places came under Communist attack, or Communist pressure, American indecisiveness grew. "No one nation," Truman had told the country in January 1951, "can find protection in a selfish search for a safe haven from the storm." But as prosperity waxed at home, American concern with free-world problems and American alertness to Communist adventures and Communist growth dissipated themselves. In 1956, Eisenhower was again nominated by the Republicans, and though he had suffered a "moderate" heart attack the year before and a subsequent digestive failure which required surgery, the voters carried him to another convincing victory over Stevenson. Great faith had been placed in the "great General," as though the symbol of military might in the White House would charm away the unceasing Communist challenge in the real world.

"It has now been twelve years since World War II ended," wrote Senator Paul H. Douglas in August 1957, in an article in *The New York Times Magazine* called "A New Isolationism—Ripple or Tide?" "One emergency has followed another and the American public has risen to each . . . We have been forced to spend no less than $60,000,000,000 on overseas aid of one form or another and increase our own national budget to $70,000,000,000 a year. . . . Probably no other nation in human history has ever exerted itself so intelligently to preserve its own safety or to be helpful to others.

"But it is natural," Senator Douglas went on, "for even the most tireless and far-sighted advocates of international cooperation to grow weary as year follows year and no respite appears. . . . The resistance to isolationism is therefore being greatly weakened by this emotional and intellectual fatigue." At the same time, "opposition to further foreign aid, . . . a return to protection, and support [of] a less co-operative attitude on foreign affairs" are spreading. "Unless a countervailing movement sets in," the Senator warned six weeks before the launching of Sputnik I, "the foreign policy of this country may therefore grow increasingly in the direction of isolation."

The United States responded to the Russian space satellites with revelations of its own military might, which was terrible enough although increasingly obsolescent, and with promises of enlarged expenditures and a deeper urgency to catch up and keep abreast on missiles. At the same time—that is the weakness of a "challenge and response" policy as against policy based on initiative and leadership—the continuing challenge of Communism and Communist theory in other areas was neglected. After the sputniks, the strains in the alliances and friendships of the western nations deepened, as Russians since Lenin had hoped they would. These strains were aggravated by the "crisis of confidence" among NATO countries following the Soviet's demonstration of its ICBM; but more divisive were the old colonial or excolonial problems—in Egypt, Algeria, Pakistan, and other "colored" lands—where nationalism was embraced as the only honorable escape from the degrading past.

Worst of all, the peoples of former colonial countries, though participating in the world-wide "revolution of rising expectations," were growing poorer all the time. "Poor people," wrote Kingsley Davis, United States representative on the United Nations Population Commission, in September 1957, "are more numerous today than ever before, because population is skyrocketing in the poorer countries. . . . If the young cannot find employment," Professor Davis continued, "they naturally seek remedies for their plight. They are ready to follow any revolutionary leader who promises a quick and preferably violent way out."

The knowledge of American "conduct and example" offered no solace to such distressed people in their frustrating slide to "proletarianization." Nor would American sputniks give them hope. "What the vast majority of the world's people need and want," warned *The New York Times* in an editorial in November 1957, "are not sputniks and rockets, but adequate food, clothing, housing and the other elements that make a decent standard of living." They wanted more; they wanted respect, consideration, guidance, leadership. This was much the greatest challenge to the United States.

THE AMERICAN MISSION

"Since the founding of this nation," Dulles has written, "the American people have believed that it had a mission in the world." Perhaps it was the atrophying of this sense of mission, even more than the Communist challenge, that made Americans in the mid-1950's dissatisfied even with their rising standard of living and salutary social changes. "What is wrong with us?" queried Louis B. Seltzer, editor of the *Cleveland Press,* in an editorial that was copied by scores of other papers across the country and made Seltzer's life "a madhouse" for days afterwards keeping up with the congratulatory messages and sympathetic queries:

"What is wrong with us? . . .
"It is in the air we breathe. The things we do. The things we say. . . .
"We have everything. We abound with all the things that make us

comfortable. We are, on the average, rich beyond the dreams of the kings of old. . . . Yet . . . something is not there that should be— something we once had.

"Are we our own worst enemies? Should we fear what is happening among us more than what is happening elsewhere? . . .

"No one seems to know what to do to meet it. But everybody worries. . . ."

A hundred years ago, Ralph Waldo Emerson observed that "Every nation believes that the Divine Providence has a sneaking kindness for it." In the century that followed Americans had every reason to wear this belief on their sleeves, indeed, on their countenances. In Emerson's time, democracy was a bright new idea in the world, industrial capitalism the admiration of transcendentalist philosophers seeking perfection on earth. Emerson also said, "We think our civilization is near its meridian, but we are yet only at the cockcrowing and the morning star." Historians of American civilization still borrow this optimism from the simple past; like American writers, who, it is said, never seem to grow up, the country itself often finds it hard to escape its pleasant childhood and youth.

Yet there have been momentous signs of change. Americans have no assurance today that democracy is any more stable than monarchy was in the era of the American Revolution, that capitalism can survive an era of expanding socialism and Communism, that individualism can flower in an age of bureaucracy, technology, and science. Nevertheless we and our allies have met many of the challenges of a new barbarism almost despite ourselves. Our values remain humane; we cherish the preservation of the single life, the individual spirit, voluntary unity. The preservation and extension of American ideals is the task of our maturity.

Books for Further Reading

Titles marked by an asterisk* are available in paperbacks.

I. GENERAL WORKS

A. BASIC REFERENCE AND SOURCE BOOKS. *The Harvard Guide to American History* (1954), edited by Oscar Handlin and others, is a comprehensive index of the literature of American history and of bibliographies on many special subjects. R. B. Morris and H. S. Commager, eds., *The Encyclopedia of American History* (1955), supplies concise and scholarly summaries of major events and lives of major personalities. More elaborate are *Dictionary of American Biography* (21 vols., 1928-44), edited by Allen Johnson and Dumas Malone; and *Dictionary of American History* (6 vols., 1940), edited by J. T. Adams and R. V. Coleman. H. S. Commager, ed., *Documents of American History* (1949), is an excellent collection of official materials since 1492. Of the many volumes of less formal contemporary materials, the following two are among the more interesting: R. W. Leopold and A. S. Link, eds., *Problems in American History* (1957); and W. Thorp, M. Curti, and C. Baker, eds., *American Issues: The Social Record* (1955). Excellent for contemporary foreign comment on the United States is Oscar Handlin, ed., *This Was America* (1949). *Historical Statistics of the United States, 1789-1945* (1949), issued by the U. S. Department of Commerce, is an invaluable storehouse of quantitative information in tabular form. C. O. Paullin, *Atlas of the Historical Geography of the United States* (1932), is the best collection of maps.

B. GENERAL HISTORIES. R. R. Palmer and J. Colton, *A History of the Modern World* (1956), is a perceptive work which supplies the European background of American history and places events in the United States in a world setting. Two large collaborative series offer interesting books on most phases of American history: Allen Johnson, ed., *Chronicles of America* (50 vols., 1918-21; plus six supplementary volumes edited by Allan Nevins in 1950-51); and A. M. Schlesinger and D. R. Fox, eds., *A History of American Life* (13 vols., 1927-48). R. Hofstadter, W. Miller, and D. Aaron, *The United States: The History of a*

Republic (1957), is the most up-to-date comprehensive one-volume work. C. A. and M. Beard, *The Rise of American Civilization* (2 vols., 1933), is a rightfully famous general study. Roger Butterfield, *The American Past* (1957), is the best history of the United States in pictures, and contains illuminating writing as well. Max Lerner, *America as a Civilization* (1957), is an intensive report on "Life and thought in the United States today," with a sure grasp of historical perspective. Two studies of the United States by foreign visitors are literary classics: Alexis de Tocqueville, *Democracy in America* (2 vols., 1835); James Bryce, *The American Commonwealth* (2 vols., 1888). An interesting recent interpretation of American history by an English scholar is Frank Thistlethwaite, *The Great Experiment* (1955).

C. COMPREHENSIVE WORKS ON SPECIAL FIELDS. W. E. Binkley, *American Political Parties* (1945), and C. R. Fish, *The Civil Service and the Patronage* (1905), are standard on machine politics. More penetrating is M. Ostrogorski, *Democracy and the Party System in the United States* (1910). R. Hofstadter, *The American Political Tradition* (1948), provides stimulating reading on the relations of political thought and action. A. H. Kelly and W. A. Harbison, *The American Constitution* (1948); and Charles Warren, *The Supreme Court in United States History* (2 vols., 1937), are scholarly accounts of constitutional and judicial history. American foreign affairs are studied with stress on the role of public opinion in T. A. Bailey, *A Diplomatic History of the American People* (1955); and with stress on the functioning of diplomacy in J. W. Pratt, *A History of United States Foreign Policy* (1955).

E. C. Kirkland, *A History of American Economic Life* (1951), is a full-scale, readable account. T. C. Cochran and W. Miller, *The Age of Enterprise* (1942), is a more opinionated study of the period since 1800. R. A. Billington, *Westward Expansion* (1949), is an admirably organized work on all aspects of the history of the frontier. Useful on American land policy is R. M. Robbins, *Our Landed Heritage* (1942). Roger Burlingame, *March of the Iron Men* (1938), and *Engines of Democracy* (1940), are brilliant social histories of technological development, the first, to 1865; the second, since 1865. W. Miller, ed., *Men in Business* (1952), contains scholarly essays on the whole range of American business history. Joseph Dorfman, *The Economic Mind in American Civilization* (3 vols., 1946-1949), is discursive yet penetrating. J. R. Commons and others, *History of Labor in the United States* (4 vols., 1918-35), is detailed on working conditions, unionism, and labor legislation.

A satisfactory general account of immigration is Carl Wittke, *We Who Built America* (1940). Excellent on the "old" immigration is M. L. Hansen, *The Atlantic Migration 1607-1860* (1940). *The Uprooted* (1951) by Oscar Handlin is a sympathetic study of the "new" immigrants. Intensive studies of anti-immigration feeling are R. A. Billington, *The Protestant Crusade 1800-1860* (1938), and John Higham, *Strangers in the Land 1860-1925* (1955). A popular account of the fight for women's rights is I. H. Irwin, *Angels and Amazons* (1933). John Hope Franklin, *From Slavery to Freedom* (1956), is a first-rate history of the American Negro from earliest African days to date. Two complementary books on the American Indian are J. C. Collier, *Indians of the Americas* (1947), and Paul Radin, *The Story of the American Indian* (1927). The only book on its subject, fortunately a satisfactory one, is A. W. Calhoun, *A Social History of the American Family* (3 vols., 1917-19). A colorful yet scholarly record of American high society is Dixon Wecter, *The Saga of American Society* (1937).

V. L. Parrington, *Main Currents in American Thought* (3 vols., 1927-30), remains the most stimulating general study of the American intellect. M. E. Curti, *The Growth of American Thought* (1951), is a scholarly work of great scope. R. E. Spiller and others, *Literary History of the United States* (3 vols., 1948), is more descriptive than critical. Better reading is Van Wyck Brooks, *Makers and Finders* (5 vols., 1936-52). An excellent short history is Marcus Cunliffe, *The Literature of the United States* (1954). Constance Rourke, *American Humor* (1931), is a brilliant study of national character. A lavishly illustrated introduction to American art is O. W. Larkin, *Art and Life in America* (1949). W. W. Sweet, *The Story of Religion in America* (1950), is a standard work. A brilliant study in religious history is H. R. Niebuhr, *The Social Sources of Denominationalism* (1929). Excellent on American higher education and far less limited than its title suggests, is R. Hofstadter and W. Metzger, *The Development of Academic Freedom in the United States* (1955). A first-rate text is E. P. Cubberley, *Public Education in the United States* (1934). The history of American newspapers is adequately told in F. L. Mott, *American Journalism* (1950). The same author's *History of American Magazines* (4 vols., 1930-57), is the only scholarly work in its field.

II. SELECTED WORKS ON SPECIAL TOPICS

A. DISCOVERY, EXPLORATION, SETTLEMENT. The most useful single volume on early American history is C. P. Nettels, *The Roots of American Civilization* (1938). Henri Pirenne, *A History of Europe, from the Invasions to the XVI Century* (1955), is unsurpassed on the "European Crisis 1300-1450." A masterly work on the same subject is J. Huizinga, **The Waning of the Middle Ages* (1924). Two books by E. P. Cheyney are excellent on the age of discovery: *The European Background of American History 1300-1600* (1904), and *The Dawn of a New Era 1250-1453* (1936). E. Sanceau, *The Land of Prester John* (1944), is an intriguing work by a Portuguese historian. S. E. Morison, *Admiral of the Ocean Sea* (2 vols., 1942), is superb on Columbus and his times. J. B. Brebner, **The Explorers of North America 1492-1806* (1933), discusses all the great adventurers. L. D. Baldwin, *The Story of the Americas* (1943), is a racy work with emphasis on Spanish settlement and Latin American history. The brilliant studies of the French in the New World in the many books by Francis Parkman have been reduced to one tasteful volume, *The Parkman Reader* (1955), by S. E. Morison. W. Notestein, *The English People on the Eve of Colonization 1603-1630* (1954), is an illuminating study by an expert. J. R. Seeley, *The Expansion of England* (1883), is a classic on the first and second British Empires. Indispensable on New England's early history are two books by Perry Miller, *The New England Mind: The Seventeenth Century* (1939), and *From Colony to Province* (1953). Indispensable on the South is Carl Bridenbaugh, *Myths and Realities* (1952). On the "carnall" side an excellent work is Bernard Bailyn, *New England Merchants in the Seventeenth Century* (1955). Extraordinarily illuminating too is, C. S. Sydnor, *Gentlemen Freeholders, Political Practices in Washington's Virginia* (1952). Excellent on Pennsylvania, the leading "middle colony," are F. B. Tolles, *Meeting House and Counting House* (1948); and C. Van Doren, *Benjamin Franklin* (1938).

B. TOWARD INDEPENDENCE. A standard work on the commercial relations of the colonies and the mother country is Volume IV of C. M. Andrews, *The Colonial Period of American History* (4 vols., 1934-38). A galaxy of scholarly articles on this subject and many related ones will be found in R. B. Morris, ed., *The Era of the American Revolution* (1939). The English political background is intensely studied in L. B.

Namier, *England in the Age of the American Revolution* (1930). The role of George III, as it appears to modern scholars, is analyzed by Namier in three brilliant essays in his collection, *Personalities and Powers* (1955). Carl Becker, *The Declaration of Independence* (1922), is much the best study of that document. Excellent short accounts of the surge toward independence are: L. H. Gipson, *The Coming of the Revolution* (1954), and E. S. Morgan, **The Birth of the Republic* (1956). Outstanding biographies include those on Washington by D. S. Freeman (6 vols., 1948-54; a seventh volume by J. A. Carroll and M. W. Ashworth, published in 1957 after Freeman's death, completes the "Life"); on Jefferson, by D. Malone (2 vols., 1948-51), and by G. Chinard (1929); on Hamilton, by B. Mitchell (1957); on Sam Adams, by J. C. Miller (1936); on John Adams, by G. Chinard (1933). A popular account of the difficulties of the Continental Congress is L. Montross, *The Reluctant Rebels* (1950).

C. THE YOUNG REPUBLIC. Historians still argue over how bad conditions were under the Articles of Confederation. The classic account of the "bad" side is John Fiske, *The Critical Period of American History* (1888); of the "good" side, C. A. Beard, *An Economic Interpretation of the Constitution of the United States* (1913). Beard's penetrating analysis is elaborated in Merrill Jensen, *The New Nation* (1950) and overzealously attacked by R. E. Brown, *Charles Beard and the Constitution* (1956). A straightforward work on the making of the Constitution is C. Van Doren, *The Great Rehearsal* (1948). Perhaps the deepest insight into the times will be found in Hamilton's, Madison's, and Jay's **The Federalist*, collected in innumerable editions from the newspapers of 1787 and 1788 in which these essays first appeared. Colorful accounts of Washington's administrations are C. G. Bowers, *Jefferson and Hamilton* (1925), whose strong anti-federalist bias is more than corrected in the highly federalist *Life of John Marshall* (4 vols., 1916-19) by A. J. Beveridge. On the subsequent period, George Dangerfield, *The Era of Good Feelings* (1952), is excellent. Allan Nevins, ed., *The Diary of John Quincy Adams* (1951), is replete with the acute insights of the sixth president.

F. J. Turner, *The Frontier in American History* (1920), established the West as a field of study. An excellent work is B. W. Bond, Jr., *The Civilization of the Old Northwest 1788-1812* (1934). Interesting biographies of early western speculators include C. S. Driver, *John Sevier* (1932); and W. H. Masterson, *William Blount* (1954). The role of the

West in fomenting the War of 1812 is analyzed in J. W. Pratt, *Expansionists of 1812* (1925); but Pratt's argument is subjected to searching analysis in A. L. Burt, *The United States, Great Britain, and British North America* (1940). Marquis James, *The Life of Andrew Jackson* (1938), is a stirring and scholarly biography. More contentious (and contended against) is A. M. Schlesinger, Jr., *The Age of Jackson* (1945). A first-rate study of the entire Jacksonian epoch is Bray Hammond, *Banks and Politics in America from the Revolution to the Civil War* (1957).

D. CIVIL WAR AND ITS LEGACY. The period from the middle 1840s to 1860 is analyzed at length but always with insight and readability in Allan Nevins, *Ordeal of the Union* (2 vols., 1947), and *The Emergence of Lincoln* (2 vols., 1951). Two excellent works on the expansionist drive in ante-bellum America are N. A. Graebner, *Empire on the Pacific* (1955), and A. K. Weinberg, *Manifest Destiny* (1935). On the commercial and rising industrial spirit of the North the following are selected from a rich literature: J. Mirsky and A. Nevins, *The World of Eli Whitney* (1952); G. R. Taylor, *The Transportation Revolution* (1951); Volume I of V. S. Clark, *History of Manufactures in the United States* (3 vols., 1928); L. C. Hunter, *Steamboats on the Western Rivers* (1949); R. G. Albion, *The Rise of New York Port* (1939); W. J. Lane, *Commodore Vanderbilt* (1942); F. A. Cleveland and F. W. Powell, *Railroad Promotion and Capitalization* (1909).

Clement Eaton, *A History of the Old South* (1949), is probably the best general history of the slave states. More penetrating and brilliantly written is W. J. Cash, *The Mind of the South* (1941). An illuminating contemporary account is F. L. Olmsted, *The Cotton Kingdom,* issued in an excellent modern edition in 1953. On slavery itself, U. B. Phillips, *American Negro Slavery* (1918), should be contrasted with K. M. Stampp, *The Peculiar Institution* (1956). Two challenging theses on the coming of the Civil War are presented in D. L. Dumond, *Anti-Slavery Origins of the Civil War* (1939), and R. F. Nichols, *The Disruption of American Democracy* (1948). A readable, recent one-volume biography is B. P. Thomas, *Abraham Lincoln* (1952); but it does not supplant C. Sandburg, *Abraham Lincoln, The Prairie Years* (2 vols., 1929), and *The War Years* (4 vols., 1939); or A. J. Beveridge, *Abraham Lincoln 1809-1858* (2 vols., 1928).

The standard work on the Civil War is J. G. Randall, *The Civil War and Reconstruction* (1937). A good concise account is F. Pratt, *A

Short History of the Civil War (1952). The military history of the Union side is described in B. Catton, *This Hallowed Ground* (1956). The "rebel" side is told in C. Eaton, *A History of the Southern Confederacy* (1954); and in the excellent biography by D. S. Freeman, *R. E. Lee* (4 vols., 1934-35). The works of Cash and Randall noted above discuss Reconstruction in detail. Excellent also are two books by C. V. Woodward, *Tom Watson: Agrarian Rebel* (1938); and *Origins of the New South 1877-1913* (1951). P. Buck, *Road to Reunion* (1937), stresses the factors reuniting the sections. The best study of Grant's administrations is in A. Nevins, *Hamilton Fish* (1936). A sound general history of the South from settlement to date is F. B. Simkins, *A History of the South* (1953).

E. THE INDUSTRIAL NATION. A. Nevins, *The Emergence of Modern American 1865-1878* (1927), supplies an excellent survey of the postwar North and West. A. M. Schlesinger, *The Rise of the City 1878-1898* (1933), and I. M. Tarbell, *The Nationalizing of Business 1878-1898* (1944), continue the story in interesting fashion. Matthew Josephson, *The Politicos 1865-1896* (1938), is a detailed and penetrating study. E. F. Goldman, **Rendezvous with Destiny* (1951), presents the story of the "reform" attack on the practices Josephson analyzes. The politics of the farm "revolt" against "big business" has an extensive literature. A leading older work is J. D. Hicks, *The Populist Revolt* (1931). A newer and more penetrating book is R. Hofstadter, *The Age of Reform* (1955).

Much the best account of the Wild West before its absorption in the industrial nexus is W. P. Webb, *The Great Plains* (1931). Much insight into the problems of the prairies and the plains is to be gained from J. C. Malin, *The Grassland of North America* (1948). Mark Twain, *Roughing It* (2 vols., 1872), is excellent on Nevada prospecting. E. S. Osgood, **The Day of the Cattleman* (1929), covers the history of the range. F. A. Shannon, *The Farmer's Last Frontier* (1945), is a tough-minded analysis of the problems of the western farmer in the industrial age. The novels of O. E. Rölvaag, especially *Giants in the Earth* (1929), and of Willa Cather, especially *O Pioneers!* (1913), and *My Antonia* (1918), dramatically recreate early plains farm life.

I. M. Tarbell, *The History of the Standard Oil Company* (2 vols., 1904), is excellent on the spirit of the early oil men and the impact of Rockefeller's drive toward monopoly. More sympathetic to Rockefeller and to the institutional drives of modern capitalism is A. Nevins, *John*

D. Rockefeller (2 vols., 1940; rev. ed., 1954). J. H. Bridge, *The Inside History of the Carnegie Steel Company* (1903), contains much information that will not be found in the authorized biography by B. J. Hendrick, *The Life of Andrew Carnegie* (2 vols., 1932), nor in Carnegie's *Autobiography* (1920). Two books by W. Z. Ripley offer the best general accounts of railroad history: *Railroads: Rates and Regulation* (1912), and *Railroads: Finance and Organization* (1915). T. C. Cochran, *Railroad Leaders, 1845-1890* (1953), is a pioneering study of the thinking of American business executives. A colorful account of the transcontinentals is Oscar Lewis, *The Big Four* (1938). Especially good on the tooth-and-claw competition in nineteenth-century business is D. A. Wells, *Recent Economic Changes* (1890). The literature on the trust movement and attempts to control it by legislation is immense. The most recent and comprehensive study is H. B. Thorelli, *The Federal Antitrust Policy* (1955); an illuminating and unusually well-written critique is T. Arnold, *The Folklore of Capitalism* (1937). Samuel Yellen, *American Labor Struggles* (1936), provides dramatic accounts of the great strikes of the late nineteenth and early twentieth centuries. Enlightening books by participants in the labor movement include T. V. Powderly, *Thirty Years of Labor* (1889), and *The Path I Trod* (1940); and Samuel Gompers, *Seventy Years of Life and Labor* (2 vols., 1925).

F. THE TWENTIETH CENTURY. A thorough history of the United States since the 1890's is A. S. Link, *American Epoch* (1955). The period around the turn of the century was one of soul-searching in the United States and contemporary books as well as later studies reflect the prevailing mood. A good introduction to the questioning of the times is D. Aaron, *Men of Good Hope* (1951). Robert Hunter, *Poverty* (1904), and R. H. Bremner, *From the Depths, The Discovery of Poverty in the United States* (1956), are revealing studies. Jacob Riis, *How the Other Half Lives* (1890), and *The Battle with the Slums* (1902) are moving accounts of conditions in New York's ghetto. *The Pittsburgh Survey* (6 vols., 1910-14) reports a thorough investigation of life in the leading steel city by the Russell Sage Foundation. A good summary of the social needs of the period is R. C. Dorr, *What Eight Million Women Want* (1910). The whole issue of urbanism is discussed in numerous books by Lewis Mumford, of which perhaps the most relevant is *The Culture of Cities* (1938). A classic account of the changing spirit of architecture is Louis Sullivan, *The Autobiography of an Idea* (1922).

W. A. Starrett, *Skyscrapers* (1928), is a useful study of the creation of tall beehives to house the "interchangeable parts" of the modern business office. An excellent account of urban transportation before the automobile age (among other subjects) is H. C. Passer, *The Electrical Manufacturers 1875-1900* (1953).

The unconventional economic thinking of the age is reflected in Thorstein Veblen, *The Theory of the Leisure Class* (1899), and *The Theory of Business Enterprise* (1904); unconventional political thinking in H. Croly, *The Promise of American Life* (1909); W. Weyl, *The New Democracy* (1912); and *The Autobiography of Lincoln Steffens* (2 vols., 1931). Ray Ginger, *The Bending Cross* (1949), is a useful biography of Eugene V. Debs. Max Lerner, ed., *The Mind and Faith of Justice Holmes* (1943), and A. T. Mason, *Brandeis, A Free Man's Life* (1946), disclose the challenging judicial thinking of the two great dissenters. R. Hofstadter, *Social Darwinism in American Thought* (rev. ed., 1955), is the leading study of the vogue of the Spencerian philosophy against most aspects of which the "Progressive Era" rebelled. L. D. Brandeis, *Other People's Money* (1914); and F. L. Allen, *The Lords of Creation* (1935), are good introductions to the Morgan era. On the politics of Progressivism, one may read with profit H. F. Pringle, *Theodore Roosevelt* (1931); M. Josephson, *The President Makers 1896-1919* (1940); A. S. Link, *Woodrow Wilson and the Progressive Era, 1910-1917* (1954); and J. Blum, *Woodrow Wilson and the Politics of Morality* (1956). On Progressive militarism and imperialism, in addition to Hofstadter on Social Darwinism (above), illuminating works are W. Millis, *The Martial Spirit* (1931); J. W. Pratt, *Expansionists of 1898* (1936); D. Perkins, *The United States and the Caribbean* (1947); A. W. Griswold, *The Far Eastern Policy of the United States* (1938). A suggestive introduction to twentieth-century foreign policy is G. F. Kennan, *American Diplomacy 1900-1950* (1951). American participation in World War I is discussed from the isolationist attitude of the 'thirties in W. Millis, *The Road to War* (1935); and C. C. Tansill, *America Goes to War* (1938). More generous to Wilson is C. Seymour, *American Diplomacy During the World War* (1934). A general account of the war and postwar periods will be found in P. W. Slosson, *The Great Crusade and After 1914-1928* (1930).

A lively introduction to the spirit of the 'twenties is F. L. Allen, *Only Yesterday* (1931). On the literature of the period, see Alfred Kazin, *On Native Grounds* (1942); on the politics, S. H. Adams, *Incredible Era* (1939), and W. A. White, *A Puritan in Babylon* (1938);

on the economics, W. E. Leuchtenburg, *Perils of Prosperity 1914-1932* (1958), G. Soule, *Prosperity Decade 1917-1929* (1947), and J. K. Galbraith, *The Big Crash* (1955). Herbert Asbury, *The Great Illusion* (1950), tells the tale of Prohibition.

T. C. Cochran, *The American Business System, 1900-1955* (1957) is an excellent introduction to the century's business life. Dixon Wecter, *The Age of the Great Depression* (1948), and B. Mitchell, *Depression Decade 1929-1941* (1947), reveal the depths of the business collapse. The failure of the Hoover administration is discussed in detail in A. M. Schlesinger, Jr., *The Crisis of the Old Order* (1957). Frank Freidel's definitive biography, *Franklin D. Roosevelt* (3 vols., 1952-56) has carried F.D.R. only through the election of 1932. More complete is J. M. Burns, *Roosevelt, The Lion and the Fox* (1956). Perhaps most interesting, since it is the product of one of the leading participants in the New Deal, is R. G. Tugwell, *The Democratic Roosevelt: A Biography of Franklin D. Roosevelt* (1957). A penetrating account of early New Deal thinking and early disillusionment with F.D.R. is R. Moley, *After Seven Years* (1939).

The most thorough studies of American diplomacy on the eve of World War II are those by W. L. Langer and S. E. Gleason, *The Challenge to Isolation 1937-1940* (1952), and *The Undeclared War 1940-1941* (1953). The attack on Roosevelt's policies can be read in C. A. Beard, *President Roosevelt and the Coming of the War* (1941), and C. C. Tansill, *Backdoor to War: The Roosevelt Foreign Policy, 1933-1941* (1952). A spirited and sympathetic account of the Roosevelt epoch in peace and war is R. E. Sherwood, **Roosevelt and Hopkins* (1948). The best short accounts of the fighting in World War II are C. Falls, *The Second World War* (1948), and F. Pratt, *War for the World* (1951). But these, of course, cannot compare with Winston Churchill's magnificent work, *The Second World War* (6 vols., 1948-53). D. D. Eisenhower, *Crusade in Europe* (1948), is authoritative on the European theater. On the Pacific theater, S. E. Morison, *History of Naval Operations in World War II* (9 vols., 1947-54), overshadows all others. Morison also covers the naval side of the war in the West. An excellent study of the wartime conferences of the Allied leaders, much illuminated by hindsight, is H. Feis, *Churchill, Roosevelt, Stalin* (1957).

For Truman's administrations, see *Memoirs,* by Harry S. Truman (2 vols., 1955-56). Nowhere does Truman mention the Hiss case, an oversight which the reader can correct with A. Cooke, *A Generation on Trial: USA v. Alger Hiss* (1951); W. Chambers, *Witness* (1952);

and A. Hiss, *In the Court of Public Opinion* (1957). For Eisenhower's administrations, see R. Rovere, *Affairs of State, The Eisenhower Years* (1956), and R. J. Donovan, *The Inside Story* (1956). An interesting account of the postwar boom is F. L. Allen, *The Big Change* (1952). The boom's impact on economic thinking is well illustrated in J. K. Galbraith's brilliantly written, *The Affluent Society* (1958). Outstanding on a major domestic issue, segregation, is H. S. Ashmore, *An Epitaph for Dixie* (1958). Two well-written narratives are concerned with details of the decade, 1945-55: E. F. Goldman, *The Crucial Decade* (1956); and H. Agar, *The Unquiet Years* (1957). Never in history, it seems, has a people so self-consciously investigated itself (spurred on by the use of polls for almost anything) as the American people have in the postwar years. Innumerable books have resulted, of which five of the more penetrating are: S. Lubell, *The Future of American Politics* (1951); C. Wright Mills, *White Collar* (1951), and *The Power Elite* (1956); D. Riesman and others, *The Lonely Crowd* (1950); and W. H. Whyte, Jr., *The Organization Man* (1956).

Index

Frelinghuysen, Theodore: 74
French East India Company: 42
French Indo-China: 322
French North Africa: 407-409
French Revolution: 68, 136-7
Freneau, Philip: 135
Freud, Sigmund: 13, 348
Friends, *see* Quakers
Froude, James Anthony; 96
Fry, Roger: 301
Fugger, Jacob: 31
Fugitive slave law: 194-195
Fulton, Robert: 165, 171
"Fulton's Folly": 171
"Fundamental Orders of Connecticut": 55
Fur trade: 36-39, 48-50, 63, 66, 78, 83, 89, 117, 133, 241, 249

G. I. Bill of Rights: 398
Gadsden, Christopher: 76, 101
Gadsden, James: 195
Gage, General Thomas: 104
Galena, Illinois: 175
Gallátin, Albert: 140, 149; Secretary of the Treasury, 142, 145
Gama, Vasco da: 15, 18, 24
Garfield, James A.: 220
Garrett, John W.: 265
Garrison, William Lloyd: 186
Gary, E. H.: 352
Gates, John W. ("Bet-a-million"): 286-287
Gaulle, General Charles de: 407-408, 411
General Electric Company: 367-368
General Federation of Women's Clubs: 288, 308
General Motors Corp.: 293-294, 304, 363, 380
General Theory of Employment, Interest, and Money (Keynes): 373
Genêt, "Citizen" Edmond: 136
George I, King of England: 68, 94
George II, King of England: 63, 68, 94, 98
George III, King of England: 68, 92, 95, ftn 95, 96, 98, 103, 105-106, 108, 115, 136
Georgia: 71, 76, 85, 88, 99, 109, 125, 132, 158, 163, 190, 194, 210-212, 215, 219, 222, 224, 228, 233, 238, 355, 413; founded, 63; Yazoo River region held by, 143; secession, 206
Germany: 32-33, 84, 89-90, 113, 161, 303-304, 321-322, 330, 337,

382-383, 386, 389-391, 398, 427, 432-434; Samoa, 324-325; World War I, 340-347; World War II, 383-385, 400-412, 418
Gettysburg, Pa.: 209-210
Ghengis Khan: 4, 8, 10, 12, 15, 16, 20
Ghent, Treaty of: 150-152
Gibbons v. Ogden: 165
Gilbert, Humphrey: 41
Gilbert Islands: 415-416
Gilpin, William: 239
Girard, Stephen: 112
Giraud, General Henri: 407
Gladden, Washington: 307
Glass-Steagall Act (1933): 374
Glidden, Joseph: 257
"Glorious Revolution": 93
Goering, Hermann: 388
Gold: 5, 11, 14-16, 22, 24-30, 35, 41, 46, 68, 79, 113, 194-195, 241, 245-247, 258
Golden Hind, 41
Gómes, Estevan: 19, 20
Gompers, Samuel: 279-280, 351
Gorges, Fernando: 51
Gould, Jay: 259, 265, 272, 279
Grady, Henry: 211-213, 234-235, 238
"Grand Alliance": 404, 418
Grand Army of the Republic: 220
Grand Coulee Dam: 394
Granger movement, *see* National Grange
Grant, Ulysses Simpson: 134, 184; President, 209-210, 221-222, 225, 227, 312, 323-324; re-elected President, 226
Gray, Elisha: 276
Gray, Horace: 262
Great Britain, *see* England
"Great Compromise": 121
"Great Migration": 158
Great Northern Railroad: 267
Greeley, Horace: 174-175, 197, 226
Green, Norvin: 275-276
Green Mountain Boys: 104
Greene, General Nathanael: 107
Greenland: 18
Greer, (U.S.S.): 400
Grenville, George: 100
Gresham, Walter Q.: 325
Grimes, Senator James W.: 198
Groves, General Leslie R.: 392, 425
Grundy, Felix: 147
Guadalcanal: 414-415
Guadalupe Hidalgo, Treaty of: 194